Complete
Guide to
Vegetables,
Fruits & Herbs

Meredith® Books
Des Moines, Iowa

Complete
Guide to
Vegetables,
Fruits & Herbs

Keys to Successful Gardening   **6**

Make a Plan   **7**
Strategies for Top-Notch Crops   **8**
Water Wisely   **10**
Guarding the Harvest   **11**

Making a Garden   **12**

Selecting a Site   **14**
Start with Soil   **17**
Using Fertilizers   **20**

Getting in Tune with the Seasons   **22**

Preparing for Spring   **23**
Season-Stretching Devices   **24**
Spring Planting   **25**
Summertime   **26**
Fall Gardens   **27**

Gallery of Vegetables   **28**

Living with Herbs   **70**

Plant Types   **72**
Plant Parts   **73**
Growing and Caring for Herbs   **74**
Pruning   **76**
Propagation   **77**

Gallery of Herbs   **78**

Fruits, Berries & Nuts 114

Fruits in the Landscape **115**
Climate and Microclimate **116**
A Sample Garden **117**
Dwarf Trees **118**
Planting and Caring for an Orchard **120**
Soil **122**
Planting **124**
Fertilizing and Watering **126**
Fruits in Containers **128**
Pests and Diseases of Fruits **130**
Pruning and Training Fruits **140**
Pruning Specific Fruits **146**

Gallery of Temperate Fruit 154

Gallery of Temperate Fruit **154**
Berries **171**
Nuts **182**

Growing and Caring for Subtropical Fruits 186

Gallery of Subtropical Fruits 192

USDA Plant Hardiness Zone Map **211**
Frost Maps **212**
Resources **213**
Index **217**
Metric Conversions **223**
Credits **224**

KEYS TO SUCCESSFUL
Gardening

IN THIS CHAPTER

Make a Plan **7**

Strategies for
Top-Notch Crops **8**

Water Wisely **10**

Guarding the
Harvest **11**

Vegetable gardens yield heaping helpings of tastebud-tempting goodies without a lot of investment.

Growing a garden should be an enjoyable hobby, not an endless stream of chores. Nothing compares to garden-fresh flavor, and while every harvest hinges upon hard work, your garden doesn't have to own you.

You'll learn cost- and time-cutting strategies by trial and error and personal experience, but you can also glean ideas and discover inspiration by reading about the kind of garden you'll be cultivating—before you break ground. Try a few of the following tips to make your garden more rewarding—and fun—from the start.

Blend herbs and vegetables to create a living work of art that's as easy on the eyes as it is pleasing to the palate.

Make a Plan

Spontaneity is a wonderful aspect of gardening, but a certain degree of organization in your gardening life proves helpful, if not indispensable. By developing a good garden design, you create a framework for a successful, fulfilling experience.

Before you tuck that first seed into the ground, establish a plan. It can be as specific or as general as you wish, though the more details you include, the more useful it will be. You can record it on anything from index cards to a computer, but the best tools for a workable garden plan are simple ones—a notebook and a calendar. The calendar helps you organize your schedule and keep track of daily tasks. The notebook lets you map out your gardening dreams and chart your progress.

A spiral-bound or loose-leaf notebook that is divided into several sections and has pockets is ideal. In one section, sketch a garden diagram with measurements, the desired layout, and a list of crops that you intend to grow. This arrangement may change year to year, so set aside some blank pages for future gardens. Use another section to record planting schedules, and a third for a crop diary. Track planting dates, yields, crop rotations, pest problems, and weather conditions.

Devote additional sections to data such as soil-test results, fertilizer and pesticide applications, and important phone numbers (your county agricultural agent, for example). Stuff the pockets with seed catalogs and other reference materials, receipts, and photographs.

Remember, a garden plan should guide you, not constrain you. Stay flexible and make any adjustments as necessary to suit your changing needs, goals, or growing conditions.

Good gardeners consider a garden plan as essential to success as compost.

Strategies for Top-Notch Crops

Tidy rows of vegetables make a beautifully symmetrical scene and prove easy to tend.

PLANT FAMILIES

APIACEAE (CARROT FAMILY): carrot, celery, parsley

ASTERACEAE (SUNFLOWER FAMILY): chicory, endive, lettuce

BRASSICACEAE (MUSTARD FAMILY): broccoli, Brussels sprouts, cabbage, cauliflower, Chinese cabbage, collard, kale, kohlrabi, mustard, radish, rutabaga, turnip

CHENOPODIACEAE (GOOSEFOOT FAMILY): beet, chard, spinach

CUCURBITACEAE (GOURD FAMILY): cantaloupe, cucumber, pumpkin, squash, watermelon

FABACAE (PEA OR PULSE FAMILY): bean, pea, peanut

LILIACEAE (LILY FAMILY): asparagus, chive, garlic, leek, onion, shallot

POACEAE (GRASS FAMILY): corn

SOLANACEAE (NIGHTSHADE FAMILY): eggplant, pepper, potato, tomato

If you choose and plan well, you can grow vegetables throughout the year by selecting crops that are adapted to each season and by planting over a longer period.

Study seed catalogs, books, and cooperative extension bulletins to determine which crops are most suitable for your region. Focus first on those you can plant in late winter or early spring, such as carrots and radishes. Then consider what you'll plant in their places in summer.

For crops, such as snap beans and tomatoes, spread sowing dates over two to three weeks so the crops mature and bear fruit in succession rather than all at once. If your climate offers only a limited planting window, select several varieties with different maturity dates. These all can be planted at the same time, but they will mature at different intervals.

Sizable options

Bigger is not necessarily better in vegetable gardening. Large gardens increase your workload, quickly become unkempt if you can't keep up with them, and may yield more produce than you can use. Small, well-kept gardens can be more enjoyable and often yield better-quality produce. With good planting and design, a 10×15-foot site is ample space for a high-yielding vegetable garden.

Estimate how many people you hope to feed from your garden plot. A 50-square-foot area easily can feed one person. Consider how much time you want to devote to working the garden and processing and storing your produce.

Think small when planting, choosing several plantings of a few different varieties within the same crop. You can test new, unfamiliar varieties this way without investing lots of time and money.

Interplanting wisdom

Interplanting crops saves space, looks good, and sometimes aids growth. To interplant, imagine what will be going out of season when something else is coming in and consider which plants use different zones of a space. For example, plant late-season leeks alongside beans. The beans will stop producing before the leeks are ready, and the leeks hold their own while the beans are growing. Quick-germinating radishes mark rows of slower-germinating carrots and are long gone when the carrots are ready. Plant lettuce

Interplant vegetables for maximum use of space.

between tomato seedlings. You'll harvest lettuce long before the first tomato is ready, but while it grows, the lettuce thrives in the shade cast by the tomato foliage and controls weeds under the taller plants. Plant garlic with eggplants, marigolds with melons, and cilantro with tomatillos. These strategies are kitchen gardening at its best!

Crop rotation

Vegetable crops are classified according to their botanical families (see PLANT FAMILIES, *opposite*). Because closely related vegetables tend to attract the same pests and diseases and consume the same nutrients from soil, too much family togetherness can cause problems.

To avoid these difficulties, don't plant related crops in the same spot season after season. For example, if tomatoes were in one row this year, move them to another location next year. Plant something unrelated, such as beans or melons. Wait three to four years before returning vegetable relatives to the original row.

The same principle applies when practicing succession planting during a growing season: Don't plant related vegetables in the same spot in both spring and fall.

The virtues of mulch

Mulch is an invaluable tool for gardeners. It takes little initial effort to apply, but the benefits are very worthwhile.

Mulch can decrease your workload throughout the growing season and can increase yields by as much as 50 percent. Mulch helps control weeds, reduces erosion, retains moisture in the soil, moderates soil temperature, and by reducing watering, reduces the loss of soil nutrients. Some mulches add organic matter and nutrients to your soil.

A mulch is any material applied around your crop on top of the soil. Organic mulches, such as sawdust, leaves, bark chips, partially rotted hay or straw, or grass clippings, will break down during the growing season. They can then be tilled into the soil at the end of the year. (Never apply fresh manure as a mulch because of disease contamination concerns.)

Organic mulch layers should be about 3 to 6 inches deep, depending on the bulk of the mulch. Because they settle and decompose as the season progresses, put down a larger amount initially. As the mulches degrade, add more material to maintain the ideal 3- to 6-inch depth.

Inorganic mulches, such as plastic sheeting (1.5 to 2 mils thick) or fabric weed barrier, cannot be incorporated into the soil at the end of the season. However, many inorganic materials can be reused for several years.

Light-colored plastic and aluminum-coated mulches control weeds and help keep soil cool in the heat of the summer because they reflect sunlight. Clear plastic will not control weeds because the sun can shine through it, but it helps retain moisture and nutrients in the soil. Black plastic mulches both control weeds and accelerate your planting season by absorbing sunlight and heating the soil, which may allow you to plant earlier in the spring. However, as summer progresses these mulches can overheat the soil. Remedy this problem as temperatures rise by placing a light colored organic mulch on top of the plastic or by removing it altogether.

Far left: A sawdust mulched pathway keeps weeds from sprouting and mud off shoes.

Left: Grass clippings form a beneficial mulch, unless they contain pesticide residues. In that case, dispose of them.

Water Wisely

Backflow preventer

Hose connector

Drip tubing

Punch

Emitters

Spaghetti tubing

Drip watering systems deliver water slowly and only to desirable plants, saving water and reducing weeds.

Water is a necessity for a productive garden. For best yields, vegetables need enough water to keep the soil around their roots moist, not drenched. Most vegetable plants require roughly 1 inch of water per week (in arid regions, 2 inches). Larger plants, such as corn and squash, typically need more water than smaller ones, such as salad greens.

Most gardens require supplemental water, especially during hot, dry weather. Soil type partially determines how much additional water is needed. Sandy soils or soils low in organic matter require more frequent irrigation than

soils high in clay or organic matter. Heavy clay soils, on the other hand, can retain too much water. Mulch decreases irrigation needs by reducing evaporation from the soil surface.

When watering, saturate soil to a depth of about 6 inches, then allow it to dry out partially before irrigating again. A thorough weekly watering encourages plants to sink roots deeply into soil, while frequent superficial watering keeps roots close to the soil surface. Shallow-rooted plants succumb to heat and drought more easily than plants with deep roots.

If possible, irrigate early in the morning. Applying water to your garden in the late afternoon or early evening

may leave excess moisture on and around your plants, which can promote disease and pest problems.

Garden sprinklers supply water at highly variable rates. You may have to run the sprinkler for several hours to soak soil to 6 inches deep, or cycle-water to avoid runoff.

Drip irrigation consists of perforated hoses capped at one end. Place these hoses directly on the ground beside plants to provide a slow (you have to run them for hours), steady supply of water directly to soil around roots. Drip irrigation systems cost more than hose-end sprinklers but save as much as 60 percent of the water that would be used by a sprinkler.

In mild winter regions, Bermudagrass is a common weed pest, spreading quickly into vegetable beds during summer.

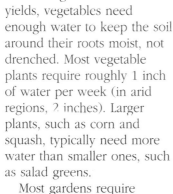

Soaker hoses deliver water directly to soil around roots, watering this garlic crop evenly.

Water crops deeply, soaking soil to a depth of 6 inches to encourage roots to grow. Drip irrigation saturates soil in such a way that roots dive deep underground.

Guarding the Harvest

In a wide-row planting system, vegetables are bunched together to form blocks. The result is higher yields in less garden space.

Weeds compete with vegetables for water, sun, and soil nutrients. If you ignore the weeds, they will reduce your harvest.

Attack weeds before they grow large. Don't let them establish a foothold or give them a chance to form seed heads. Use one or, better still, a combination of these methods to defeat weeds in your garden.

MULCH: For most weeds, mulching provides easy, long-term control. Mulch smothers weed seeds, and makes them easier to pull if they do germinate and grow.

TILLING: Rototill to control weeds along garden rows and walkways, but don't till close to vegetables.

MOWERS: Mow around the garden before weeds form seed heads to help keep weeds in check.

HOEING: In unmulched soil, hoeing kills weeds and loosens any crust that forms on soil. Crust can prevent water from entering soil. Work only the top inch of soil, hoeing lightly every few days.

HAND WEEDING: You can remove weeds with a dandelion fork or trowel. Insert the tool under the roots of the plant and lift up.

Weeds are easier to remove from moist earth, so hand weed after rain or watering. Pull the weed out by the roots; breaking it off at the soil surface is ineffective.

After hoeing or pulling, leave annual weeds to wither and die and serve as a mulch for the garden. Or till them into soil for organic matter, letting them dry out on the ground for a day beforehand. Do not till or mulch with weeds that are setting seed.

You can compost weeds if your pile is heating sufficiently to kill seeds and roots (140° F). When in doubt, toss weeds in the trash.

SOLARIZATION: For new planting areas, solarize, or cook, weed seeds, roots, and pests, such as nematodes. Lay clear plastic on freshly tilled soil. Shovel soil over plastic edges to anchor and seal it; leave it for six weeks. The temperature of soil 10 inches deep should rise at least 10° F, so solarization is effective only in sunny areas.

HERBICIDES: Most herbicides are formulated to kill specific types of plants. Apply them with care to avoid damaging your crop or the environment. Always follow label directions.

Row covers

Many insect pests can be kept in check simply by placing a lightweight floating row cover over crops at planting time. Row covers allow light and water to penetrate but not insects. Remove the cover when flowers of insect-pollinated vegetables such as melons appear, when you weed (weeds proliferate under row covers), and when you harvest.

Vegetables in nontraditional colors make dinnertime deliciously colorful.

CHOICE TOOLS FOR WEEDING

Weeding is easier when you invest in quality tools. Start with a pair of rubber or washable leather gloves to protect your hands.

Fishtail weeders, also called dandelion forks, dig weeds easily. Slip the tool tip under the crown of the weed, then lift up.

Use a hand cultivator to pry up clumps of grass. Slip the prongs under the clump and pull back on the handle like a lever.

Before buying a hoe, try out different models to see which feels most comfortable. Hoes come in various weights and handle lengths, so pick one to match your size and strength.

To keep tools in shape, pour about a quart of used motor oil into a bucket of sand. After removing soil from tools, shove them deeply into the bucket several times, then store. The oil coating prevents rust.

MAKING A GARDEN

IN THIS CHAPTER

Selecting a Site **14**
Start with Soil **17**
Using Fertilizers **20**

Gardens are far more than food-production sites. They also reflect personal style and taste, forming a living expression of who you are and what's important to you.

If you're an art lover, you can capture and communicate your passion for color in the vegetable garden by choosing varieties that yield fruits, roots, and leaves in a palette of hues. You can also weave threads of color into your veggie patch by blending petal-pushing bloomers into the planting mix. Cheery annuals feel right at home among food crops and beckon pollinators by the dozens, which will enhance food yields.

It may be that artistic efforts provide no appeal to you but you enjoy working with your hands to create textural, functional elements in your home and garden. Vegetable endeavors require supports of all sorts, and you can showcase your handiwork by erecting, constructing, and inventing the necessary vegetable-growing gear yourself.

Some vegetable gardeners prefer to cultivate a traditional scene of tastebud-titillating goodies, laying out orderly rows of plants. With French-style vegetable gardens, called *potagers,* you can take tradition and give it a twist by sowing seeds and positioning vegetables, herbs, and flowers to form intricate geometric designs that also maximize space.

Focus on the harvest and you may discover mathematical instincts brewing inside of you that you did not know you had. Wide-row plantings, intercropping, square-foot gardening—each method focuses on ways to increase vegetable yields in small spaces—and to exercise some brain power!

The way you choose to design your produce patch is limited only by your creativity and resources. You need to conquer the basics of sowing, tending, and reaping, but beyond that, you can unleash your imagination and plan a garden that's purely you. Search for inspiration on garden tours, in magazines, on television, and by visiting local botanical gardens.

Conquer the basics

To fulfill your gardening desires with any level of success, your proposed excursion into the world of harvest baskets and homegrown goodness will need to meet a few fundamental requirements, including finding an appropriate site with good soil, sunshine, water, and air. This chapter will reveal the basic needs of every vegetable garden and then assist you to determine what must be done to ensure top productivity in your specific climate.

Productive vegetable gardens don't need to occupy acres of real estate to fill dinner plates at your house. A tidy raised-bed garden that blends the beauty of blossoms and produce into a tongue-tickling, eye-catching garden fits well in any landscape. These raised beds are built with arsenic-free treated lumber to last a long time and to safely produce food.

Selecting a Site

Raised beds prove easy to tend and maintain. Soil warms faster in raised plantings, speeding harvest.

Among the many factors to consider when choosing a garden site, put beauty and access at the top of your list. What place in your yard lends itself to the charms of a vegetable garden? Where will a vegetable garden look best in your current and future landscaping plans? Is that place easy to reach from your house, especially from your kitchen and the water spigot? Will you need fences or motion sensors and lighting to discourage vandals or neighborhood dogs?

Next consider what's already present in and around the area you select. Digging into buried septic fields, utility wires or pipes can be a significant hazard, especially when starting a new garden. Rupturing or cutting one of these lines can cause utility losses and be dangerous. If you're planning to dig (or drive stakes) in your yard, call your utility companies first. They will send personnel out to mark the lines for you at no charge.

Keep in mind that most gardens need irrigation. Choose a spot that's close to an accessible water source or plan to install a handier water line to make irrigation easier on you.

Growing conditions

Of course, the most important consideration when selecting a site for your vegetable garden is ensuring that it meets requirements for plants to thrive and yield a harvest.

SUNLIGHT: Look for a spot away from shrubs and trees. Their root systems will compete with crops for moisture and nutrients, and they may shade your plants. Most vegetables need eight hours or more of direct sunlight for best growth. The surest way to select an adequate site is to observe the sun and shade patterns in your yard throughout a summer day. A little shade cast by buildings or trees will not hurt your crop, and intermittent, late-afternoon shade may be helpful. But if shade is cast on your site for more than three hours a day, pick another spot or plan to grow mostly shade-tolerant crops, such as salad greens.

AIR CIRCULATION: Moderate air circulation reduces the possibility and severity of disease because breezes help dry foliage. Damp, still environments promote the spread of fungal and bacterial diseases. Pick a site where air can flow. If you live where strong prevailing winds are common, windbreaks may protect your crops from severe gusts.

LOW SPOTS: Low-lying areas or areas shielded by shrubs, trees, or fences may thwart good air circulation and can also become frost pockets. Cold air naturally drains into low areas, so frost can settle on your crop even when surrounding areas are frost-free. If you plant in a frost pocket, your growing season is likely to be shorter and the risk of freeze damage to crops higher.

WATER DRAINAGE: Few crops thrive if their "feet" are always wet. In poorly drained soil plants cannot absorb nutrients easily and roots also may rot. So it's best to select a garden site that isn't prone to floods or standing water. If your only choice tends to be wet, you can overcome some problems by cultivation, raised beds, or drainage systems.

Drainage may be a problem because soil has become compacted and formed a hardpan, an impermeable layer of soil. Compaction occurs if you work the soil when it's wet, frequently walk or play on it, or rototill it repeatedly. Compaction shows up as puddles on the soil surface and poor plant growth. In most residential areas, the compacted layer is thin, and tilling deeply before planting can shatter the pan and improve drainage.

If your site demands a complex drainage system, consult a specialist, such as a soil engineer or landscape architect. For small problems, consider a simple drainage system such as installing trenches and perforated plastic pipes. The trenches should be 18 inches deep and about 4 feet apart. Lay the pipes in these trenches and cover them with 1 inch of gravel, then fill the rest of the trench to ground level with topsoil. Arrange trenches so they direct water away from the garden.

Raised beds provide another option in poorly drained areas. Mound topsoil to form a seedbed at least 4 inches higher than ground level. If you're building beds to manage drainage problems, leave trenches between them so water can easily drain.

Rows

Emulating farmers, gardeners have planted vegetables in rows because rows are easy to cultivate, manage, and harvest. But that shouldn't keep you from creating a unique garden design. Follow a few simple guidelines, and your garden will be productive, whatever its pattern.

Plant tall crops, such as corn and okra, on the north side of your garden to keep them from shading smaller crops. If you want to cast intermittent shade on smaller, heat-sensitive plants such as lettuce or peas, position towering vegetables on the south side of your patch.

Spacing varies greatly depending on what you plant. Follow recommended spacing for best productivity. Seed packets usually provide specific spacing information. In general, rambling crops such as squash, cucumbers, and watermelon need 4- to 6-foot-wide rows with plants spaced 2 to 3 feet apart in the row. Large plants such as okra and eggplant need rows at least 3 feet wide and should be spaced 30 inches apart in the row. Smaller plants such as onions and radishes can tolerate rows 8 to 9 inches wide and can be planted 2 to 4 inches apart.

In gardens that you intend to hand cultivate, you can sow seed closer than these guidelines because you won't be taking equipment into the plot. Plant crops close enough together for them to develop a solid canopy of leaves over the soil as they mature. The canopy keeps soil under plants moist and cool and shades out weeds.

Raised beds

Raised beds provide several advantages. They reduce drainage problems and demand less bending and stooping. Often, yields are higher because you have more control over soil quality. Design a raised bed to suit your needs. Some people simply contour their soil into high rows, while others construct a frame to create more formal beds.

To build frames, employ materials such as wood, brick, concrete blocks, or plastic boards. Use cedar, redwood, or landscape timbers for wooden frames. Avoid creosote treated lumber; the timbers may leach toxins and contaminate both the soil and your food.

Raised beds brimming with salad crops makes harvest easy and successive sowing simple to track.

Selecting a Site
(continued)

SHADE-TOLERANT PLANTS

No vegetable plants will thrive in heavy shade, but many leafy greens can get by with only four to six hours of direct sunlight. If they have adequate spacing, the following vegetables are good choices for growing in partial shade: arugula, chard, collards, leaf lettuce, and spinach.

An ideal size for a raised bed is 4 feet wide. At this width, you can easily reach into the center of the bed from either side. Length will depend on available space and personal preference.

If practical, orient raised beds on a north-south basis if you're planting low-growing crops, and on an east-west axis for taller plants. This will minimize shading and maximize sun exposure.

Before building a raised bed, till or loosen the base soil. Then add good-quality topsoil and additional organic matter, such as composted leaves or composted manure. Test the soil, then fertilize it based on the results. In a raised bed, you literally create your own soil, so make the best soil possible.

Raised beds with a wide frame provide a natural place to sit or kneel while tending and harvesting your crops.

Containers

Window-box and container gardens are quite popular among people who live in cities or who have limited access to land. They do constrain the crops you can grow. Smaller vegetables, such as lettuces, patio tomatoes, and peppers, work beautifully. To gain more space, train vines such as cucumbers or squash on trellises and put pole beans on tepees.

VEGETABLES IN CONTAINERS

Most vegetables grow quite well in containers such as pots, boxes, tubs, or gallon buckets. Large, broad containers are ideal because they retain more moisture than small, narrow ones. Pots 6 to 10 inches in diameter are fine for small crops, such as green onions and many herbs. For larger vegetables, such as tomatoes, peppers, eggplant, or squash, 5-gallon containers prove a better choice.

Container-grown vegetables require more frequent watering and fertilizing than in-ground plants because they're limited to what is available in the pot. Make sure your containers have holes in the bottom for drainage, and use high-quality potting soil. Do not use garden soil, which may harbor disease organisms.

Crops suited for container growing include cherry and patio tomatoes, small-fruited peppers, bush beans, small carrots, salad greens, and dwarf cucumbers and squash.

Room to move

As you lay out your garden, remember to leave a little elbow room for weeding and harvesting.

If the garden is small enough to reach all parts from the side, you won't need access to move within the garden. But if your garden is large enough that you have to get into it to weed or harvest, add walkways. A foot or two between rows is plenty of room to bend and squat. Add more space if you plan to use a garden cart between rows: Measure your vehicle and add 2 inches to each side. If you plan to mow between rows to control grass and weeds, measure the mower and add 4 inches. For long rows, you may need wider middles to turn your equipment.

Start with the Soil

Vegetables thrive and taste better if they grow in good soil. A high-quality soil is fertile and has a physical structure that provides the proper balance of air and water around plant roots. Soil itself is composed of a mixture of mineral particles, organic matter, air, and water.

Two layers of soil are important to a home garden—topsoil, which is the layer of soil closest to the surface, and subsoil, the layer immediately below the topsoil.

Topsoil is where most plant roots reside, and it's the place plants need the most organic matter and fertility. Ideally topsoil should be at least 18 inches deep and porous enough for air and water to move through. A soil test can provide you with information on the composition and quality of your topsoil and advise you on any amendments that would improve its condition.

In many sites, erosion has diminished the amount of available topsoil. If your topsoil is shallow, consider buying a load and spreading it on your garden. Purchase enough to create a layer at least 4 to 6 inches deep. Before buying, inspect the soil to ensure that it's of high quality—loose, crumbly, and dark—and free of weed seeds and pesticide residue.

Subsoil tends to be more compact and denser than topsoil. If it's too compacted, it restricts water flow and root growth. In many places, especially in new housing developments in which the land has been recently farmed, the subsoil may have become so compacted it has formed a hardpan. If you encounter a hardpan within 18 inches of the soil surface, break it up by double-digging (removing the topsoil, tilling the subsoil, mixing in organic matter, and replacing the topsoil).

Clay, sand, and loam

Soil texture is determined by the type and size of mineral particles it contains. These are divided into three categories: sand, silt, and clay. Clay has the smallest particles; sand, the largest.

The most desirable soil—loam—has a mixture of all three particle types. An ideal loamy soil is soft textured and rich in organic matter. It's easy to work yet holds moisture well. Loamy soil, when squeezed, forms a loose clump that's easily rubbed apart with your fingers.

Most soils have an excess of one particle type. Too much clay makes soil clump together and difficult to cultivate. Clay soils aren't porous, so little air and water moves through them. Too much sand creates a loose texture that won't retain water or nutrients.

Stock your garden shed with the most useful digging tools: trowel, spade, digging fork, and round-nose shovel.

Roots and tubers develop best in high quality topsoil that is fertile and that has good structure.

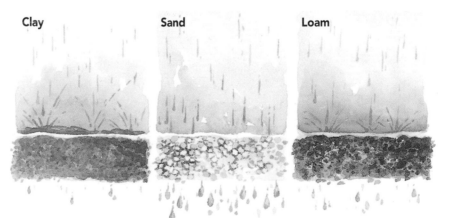

Clay   **Sand**   **Loam**

Water enters clay soils slowly, but is then held a relatively long time and air is excluded. Sandy soils are the opposite. Loam holds moisture yet leaves room for air.

Start with Soil
(continued)

A cover crop of buckwheat in summer crowds out weeds and adds organic matter to the soil. Work it into soil just before plants flower and set seed.

Soil amendments

If you aren't blessed with perfect soil, don't worry. You can improve soil quality by adding organic matter, such as compost and manure. In fact most soil will benefit from added organic matter.

Organic matter comes in many forms, from free waste products to commercially produced materials. It is rich in nutrients, helps promote good soil texture, and provides a favorable environment for microorganisms, which help decompose new additions of organic material and release nutrients. Soils rich in organic matter tend to be dark brown or black.

Sources of organic matter include decayed leaves, sawdust, grass (including lawn clippings, straw, and hay), peat moss, wood chips, compost, and animal manure.

Avoid sources of organic matter that may have been contaminated with weed seeds or herbicide or pesticide residue.

Work organic matter into the upper 3 to 6 inches of soil. You may not have to add significant amounts every year, but it won't hurt to add a little every time you dig in the garden.

COMPOST: Compost is decomposed organic matter. You can make your own from the steady supply of organic material found in your home and yard. Appropriate items for composting include vegetable and fruit scraps, garden and yard waste, lawn clippings, sawdust, and manure. Avoid meats or heavily oiled items; these draw unwelcome animals into your yard and can actually slow down the composting process. Larger items, such as tree branches, should be chopped or shredded first so they take up less room and break down more rapidly. Unless you know that your compost heats to 140° F, don't throw weeds or diseased plants onto the pile, or you risk spreading these problems.

A compost pile can be merely a heap in the back corner of your yard or a more formal structure, such as a wood or wire-mesh container, or a commercially made bin. An ideal size for a compost pile is 64 cubic feet (4 feet tall, wide, and long).

Put the pile in a shady, well-drained area. If starting it on open ground, till or dig the soil underneath before you begin to fill the area.

Compost heats up as the organic material biodegrades. This heat kills pathogens and speeds decomposition of the raw materials. While you can throw items into the compost all year, the air temperature must be above 50° F for any real activity to occur. The internal heat of your compost should reach 140° to 150° F. Monitor the temperature in the pile with a large compost thermometer, available at garden centers.

To accelerate the composting process, keep your pile moist, but not wet— a handful should feel like a squeezed-out sponge. Turn the pile with a shovel when it reaches 140° F to encourage the breakdown of organic matter. Adding fresh topsoil or manure also speeds up the process. A mix of half "brown" ingredients (such as straw, sawdust or dry leaves) and half "green" ingredients (such as grass clippings) fosters faster composting.

How much compost should you apply to the garden? To reach the desired level of 5 percent organic matter in your soil, incorporate about 200 pounds of compost per 50 square feet of garden space each year. Till it into the soil about a foot deep.

MANURE: Animal manure is a great source of nutrients, especially nitrogen, for your plants. Composted or rotted manure is best because fresh manure can be "hot," meaning it contains such a rich supply of nitrogen that it can burn your plants and injure or kill them. If you use fresh, uncomposted manure and you are applying it just before spring planting, till it into the soil as early as possible before planting the crop.

You can apply fresh manure to the top of the soil in the winter because it will break down before you are ready to till and plant in spring.

Manure is often available free from farms. However, because it hasn't been aged, most manure that comes straight from the farm is more likely to harbor weed seeds than the commercially bagged manure available at most garden centers.

OTHER ORGANIC MATTER: Leaves and grass clippings, old hay and straw, rotted sawdust, and other forms of decaying plant material can be used for organic matter. You may also be able to get waste material such as peanut or cottonseed hulls in your area.

COVER CROPS: Even when your garden is lying idle for the winter, you can improve its quality by planting a cover crop. Cover crops not only add nutrients and organic matter to soil, they also help reduce erosion.

A cover crop is typically created by planting nutrient-rich plants, such as ryegrass,

Sow a cover crop of hardy grass in the fall, then work it into the soil the following spring.

clover, and vetch, in your garden during the fall or winter, or off-season. Some grow (or survive under snow) throughout the winter, and many are legumes, which trap atmospheric nitrogen and add it to the soil as they grow. In most cases, you simply broadcast the seed over areas that have quit producing for the season.

Till cover crops into the soil in spring at least three

weeks before you plant the garden. This allows the plants to decompose in the soil. Some cover crops are left until they die, then tilled in. Or till them into the soil while they are still lush to provide a "green manure" for your garden.

There is an appropriate cover crop for every region and season. Check with your local extension agent to learn which is the best where you live and how to grow it.

TEST YOUR SOIL!

To truly know your soil, test it. The results will provide guidelines on how much lime, if any, and fertilizer to add to your garden.

You should test soil every 3 to 5 years because it changes as you plant, add organic matter, and fertilize the garden. In many states, soil test kits are available from local cooperative extension offices and private labs. Fees are affordable and the results are well worth the expense. Do-it-yourself kits are available at nurseries and garden centers, though they will not supply you with detailed information.

If possible, sample the soil in late fall or early winter to allow time to add needed amendments, and for the adjustments to take effect well in advance of next year's planting season. You will also get your analysis back more quickly than if you wait until spring.

Checking whether your soil is sand, clay, or loam is simple. Place a quarter cup of soil into a pint jar. Fill the jar with water, put the lid on, then shake it up. Set the jar aside for a few days and wait for the various components of the soil to form layers.

Sand settles to the bottom of the jar first; it's the heaviest particle in soil. The next layer will be silt. Over that, you'll find organic matter. The top layer is clay, the finest component of soil. Clay is so lightweight, it may take weeks to settle and you'll recognize it only by the cloudy water.

The thickness of each layer provides a clue as to the soil type. For example, the thicker the sand layer, the sandier your soil is. Ideally, you'll want the sand, organic matter, and clay layers to be nearly equal, indicating a loamy soil.

Using Fertilizers

Design your vegetable garden to fit your outdoor living space, and you'll find tending crops is a snap.

Plants need certain nutrients to grow and thrive. They absorb most of them from the soil through their roots, but they also take up nutrients through leaves and stems.

Plant nutrients

The three primary nutrients plants require are nitrogen, phosphorus, and potassium.
NITROGEN: Plants use nitrogen to develop stocky stems and lush leaves. It keeps plants green and flourishing. Leafy vegetables, such as cabbage and spinach, are called heavy feeders and need lots of nitrogen. Tomatoes, peppers, and other plants that produce flowers and fruit, if given too much nitrogen, yield huge plants with few flowers and fruit.
PHOSPHORUS: Root development, overall plant growth, and fruiting hinge upon phosphorus.
POTASSIUM: Plants require potassium for vigor and strength. It encourages early root development, increases

resistance to certain diseases, and helps plants tolerate heat and drought.
MICRONUTRIENTS: Plants also need some nutrients, such as sulfur and iron, in tiny amounts. But micronutrient deficiencies are rare in vegetable gardens because most soils contain sufficient amounts in available forms.

Types of fertilizers

While some soils naturally contain enough nutrients to grow healthy vegetables, you should assume you'll need to fertilize your garden.

Fertilizers come in many forms—synthetic and organic, fast-release and slow-release, granular and liquid. They contain nutrients in various ratios. The three hyphenated numbers on a fertilizer label indicate the ratio of nitrogen, phosphorus, and potassium. A balanced fertilizer, such as 10-10-10, contains equal amounts of each nutrient. Choose a fertilizer with the ratio recommended by your soil test results.
SYNTHETICS: Synthetic fertilizers are manufactured

nutrients. These include fast- and slow-release types that come as granules or in liquid and water-soluble forms.

Fast-release synthetics, such as ammonium nitrate, supply nutrients to plants quickly, but they do have drawbacks. Because they're more potent than organic fertilizers, they can burn roots and leaves. They're highly soluble and may leach into groundwater. Improper or excessive use can inhibit activity of soil microbes vital to healthy soil and plants.
ORGANIC FERTILIZERS: Commercial organic or natural fertilizers are made from pelletized fish meal, composted manure, or mixtures of pulverized seed meal. Liquid forms, such as fish emulsion, are mixed with water and poured onto soil.

Because nutrients are less concentrated they are less likely to burn plants. Still, don't overapply them, and follow the directions on the product label.

Over the long term, organic fertilizers help build soil and provide a splendid source of nutrients for vegetables. But if

UNDERSTANDING pH

One aspect of fertility is pH, which refers to a soil's acidity or alkalinity. A neutral pH is 7. Below 7, soil is acidic; above 7, it's alkaline. Most vegetables grow best with a pH of 6 to 7. In that range, the most nutrients are available to plants in the highest amounts. A pH imbalance causes certain nutrients to become unavailable, leaving the plants to grow poorly and perhaps die. Imbalances also promote some diseases. But many plants are adaptable. Asparagus and onions can grow in soils with a pH as high as 8, while potatoes and radishes grow in soils where the pH is as low as 4.5. To determine pH, test your soil. The results will tell you how much lime or sulfur to apply. Lime reduces acidity (raises pH), while sulfur increases it (lowers pH).

SYMPTOMS OF NUTRITIONAL DEFICIENCY

When diagnosing a deficiency, keep these points in mind:
- Not all plants exhibit the same typical symptoms.
- Not all typical symptoms are due to a deficiency but may be caused by diseases, insects, and environmental stresses.
- If you see symptoms, damage has already occurred.

TYPICAL SYMPTOMS
- **Nitrogen:** Plants stunted, grow slowly. Lower leaves are pale green or yellow, later dropping off the plant.
- **Phosphorus:** Plant grows slowly and may be stunted. Leaves become unusually dark green. Lower leaves later turn reddish purple. Common in acidic, or cold and wet soils.
- **Potassium:** Plants become spindly. Lower leaf edges turn gray or tan, then dry up. Tiny yellow spots may appear on leaves.
- **Iron:** Upper leaves turn yellow, with veins remaining green. Iron deficiency is common where soil pH is higher than 6.8.

To sidedress fertilizer, sprinkle it alongside growing plants, scratching it into the soil with a hand cultivator. Water thoroughly afterward.

a crop shows signs of nutrient deficiency, few organic fertilizers provide a quick fix.

Applying fertilizer

Base the initial fertilizer dose for your vegetable garden on soil test results, adding it to soil before planting. Never exceed recommended rates on the package. Overapplying fertilizer wastes time and money and may harm crops (by burning leaves and roots) and the environment (by polluting the water supply).

Spread dry fertilizers over the garden and till them into the top 6 inches of soil, or irrigate.

Depending on the kind of fertilizer you use, the type of soil, and the crops you grow, you may need to fertilize several times a season. Most fast-release fertilizers are available to plants for only two to six weeks. Sandy soil requires frequent fertilizing. And some crops are heavy feeders, while others need a

boost during certain stages of growth, such as when sweet corn forms ears. Slow-release fertilizers vary, but they may provide nutrients from eight weeks to nine months.

Sidedress plants with a midseason application of fast-release fertilizer. Scratch the material into soil around plants, then water it.

You can also foliar fertilize by spraying plant leaves with liquid and water-soluble fertilizers, or pour the solutions over the roots. Make foliar applications in early morning, early evening, or on a cloudy day. Water evaporates more slowly at these times, so the crop absorbs more nutrients.

Another quick boost for plants is to brew a nutrient "tea." Combine one part manure or compost with three parts water. Place the manure in a cloth bag in the bottom of a 30-gallon garbage can. Add water, let steep for 24 hours, then pour tea around the base of plants.

Till compost into planting beds to improve the soil's structure and its water-holding capacity.

Manure tea provides plants with the nutritional equivalent of a booster shot. Apply manure tea in conjunction with other long-term feeding strategies.

GETTING IN TUNE WITH THE SEASONS

IN THIS CHAPTER

Preparing for
Spring **23**
Season-Stretching
Devices **24**
Spring Planting **25**
Summertime **26**
Fall Gardens **27**

Cool-season crops like cabbage, onions, carrots, and parsley thrive in spring and fall.

Garden planning, cultivating, planting, and harvesting can occupy you all year. Using each season efficiently will improve the quality of your vegetables, extend your growing season, and sustain your gardening passion.

Matching crops to the appropriate season or using season-stretching techniques can supply you with produce for many months. Even in winter, you can be busy gardening—starting transplants and ordering seeds. This chapter will help you make the most of the entire gardening year.

Match crops to seasons

Vegetables usually are divided into two categories—cool- and warm-season crops. No matter where you live, you should be able to grow both kinds. The trick is timely planting and succession gardening, both of which allow you to plant cool-season crops early in the year, follow them with warm-season crops during the summer growing season, and then replant cool-season crops for fall and winter harvest.

Cool-season vegetables

Many plants of European origin, such as lettuce and cabbage, thrive in cool weather, when temperatures range between 40° and 75° F. In most areas, cool-season crops can be planted two to four weeks before the last spring frost. They will stop producing in early summer.

In regions where nights remain cool, you can make small, successive sowings throughout summer. In hotter regions, plant cool-season vegetables as early as possible in spring and then replant them for a fall harvest.

Some cold-hardy vegetables can survive throughout the winter in some regions. These include kale and Brussels sprouts.

Warm-season vegetables

Warm-season vegetables, such as tomatoes, peppers, corn, and okra, originated in subtropical climates. They are killed by frost, and they don't germinate or perform well when temperatures fall below 50° F.

You can sustain many warm-season crops into fall— well past frost—if you protect them from frosts and freezes with cold frames, row covers, or other season-extending devices. But in most regions they perform best during the height of summer, when days and nights are warm.

Preparing for Spring

Sow seeds indoors in late winter to get an early start on the garden by growing your own transplants.

CONTAINERS: Peat pots, compressed peat pellets, plastic pots, fiber blocks, and egg cartons all make good containers for sowing seed. All need drainage.

SOIL: Seed-starting soil mix is lightweight but moisture-retentive. Create a mix by blending organic matter, sterilized topsoil, or buy a commercial seedling mix.

SOWING: Fill your container with soil mix, water well, and let it drain. Plant seeds about 1 inch apart. If you're using an undivided seedling flat, make rows by pressing a narrow board into the medium to form a trench. Planting depth varies among vegetables; follow seed-package recommendations.

WATERING: Place a watertight tray beneath your container. Water plants from the bottom, adding ¼ to ½ inch of water to the tray to water.

LIGHT AND HEAT: Place seedlings near a south- or southwest-facing window in a room with a nighttime temperature of no more than 60° F. Cool nights make seedlings stocky and robust.

Most vegetable seeds sprout at room temperature, but some, such as peppers and tomatoes, germinate faster in warmer soil. Raise soil temperature by placing containers on a root zone heating mat. Shut off the heat at night.

Natural late-winter light is usually insufficient to grow good quality seedlings, so use fluorescent grow lights. Place lights 2 inches above plants, raising them as plants grow. Plants that must stretch toward light form long, flimsy stems—easily damaged and too weak to yield a harvest. Provide 12 to 14 hours of light per day.

In warmer regions, grow seedlings outside in protected areas or cold frames.

THINNING: Seedlings typically first unfold two small, delicate leaves. A third leaf, the first "true" leaf, emerges as they mature. This leaf is usually larger and has a different shape. When plants are about 1 inch tall and before the first true leaves develop, thin them to no more than three strong seedlings per 2-inch pot. Pinch or clip stems at soil level; don't pull seedlings up.

FERTILIZING: You'll need to feed seedlings when the first true leaves have formed. Use a water-soluble fertilizer diluted with twice the amount of water recommended. Fertilize seedlings every seven to 10 days.

DAMPING OFF: This root disease, caused by soilborne fungi, makes seedlings fall over and die. To prevent this, use a sterile, peatmoss-based seed starting mix, maintain optimum soil temperature, and provide air circulation.

INSECTS: Keep growing areas pest-free. Follow pesticide label directions for treating insects on seedlings.

HARDENING OFF: Prepare seedlings for the outdoors by hardening off. Reduce the growing temperature, withhold water, and increase light intensity. An easy way to harden off seedlings is to set them outside in mild weather during the last two to three weeks before planting in the garden. Bring them indoors if frost is expected.

Sow just a few seeds per container. Plant seeds about an inch apart.

You can plant peat pots directly into the garden. Just be sure to bury the pot completely.

To thin seedlings, clip stems at soil level. If you pull seedlings, you risk damaging roots.

Expose seedlings to outdoor growing conditions (hardening off) to reduce transplant shock.

VEGETABLES FOR SPRING GARDENS

SOW AND GROW IN COOL SPRING SOIL:
Arugula
Beet
Broccoli
Cabbage
Carrot
Chard
Kohlrabi
Lettuce
Mesclun
Mustard
Onion
Parsley
Parsnip
Peas
Potato
Radish
Spinach

START INDOORS AND TRANSPLANT IN MID- TO LATE SPRING:
Artichoke
Celery
Eggplant
Pepper
Tomato

PERENNIALS TO HARVEST IN SPRING:
Asparagus
Rhubarb

Season-Stretching Devices

Many gardeners use special devices to grow plants outside before the weather warms up, including cloches, cold frames, and plastic tunnels. All of these devices protect crops from cold weather and cold soils early in the season.

Cloches

Cloches fit over the top of plants to form mini-greenhouses. Gallon-size plastic milk jugs work as well as commercial glass or plastic cloches.

To make a milk-carton cloche, remove the jug's bottom and cut a V-shaped slit in the top of the handle. Place this modified jug over each plant and push a stick through the handle and into the ground deep enough to anchor the jug in the soil. Leave caps off the jugs unless frost is expected. Remove the jugs on warm, sunny days (50° to 60° F) to prevent excessive heat buildup in the jugs, but replace them at night if a cold snap is expected.

Plastic milk-jug cloches protect plants from frostbite during spring's lingering chilly nights.

A cold frame acts like a mini-greenhouse, keeping seedlings warm on otherwise cold nights.

Cold frames

Cold frames are boxes with translucent tops that you place over a garden area to let the sun in and keep the wind out. They allow you to control temperatures to an extent, by ventilating them during warm, sunny days, and closing them at night to protect from frost. Cold frames are also useful for raising transplants with better light intensity than is available indoors, as well as for hardening off transplants.

Cold frames are available commercially, or you can build one using lumber for the sides and corrugated fiberglass for the top. Recycled building materials such as cement blocks and old windows also make fine, low-cost cold frames. Simply place blocks (or straw bales) around your crop and set windows on top.

Tunnels

Plastic tunnels work much like cold frames. Cut support hoops of 10-gauge wire or ½-inch bendable pipe into pieces long enough to arch 14 to 18 inches over your beds or rows. Six-foot-long supports fit perfectly over 3-foot-wide beds. Push the hoops 2 inches into the ground on each side of the row. Space them 2 feet apart.

Cover supports with clear plastic sheeting (at least 2 mils) and secure the edges to the ground with bricks, cement blocks, or landscape timbers. Remove the tunnels when daytime temperatures consistently reach 60° to 70° F.

Remember to water plants growing under cold frames and tunnels regularly so they don't dry out.

Row covers

Although not as warm as greenhouses, row covers do protect vegetables in cool weather, keeping them 2° to 3° F warmer than the surrounding air. It's a small difference, but often enough to save crops from a late-spring frost.

Spring Planting

You can plant many cool-season seeds and transplants directly into the ground once soil reaches about 40° F and is fairly dry. It's dry enough to plant if you can press a handful of soil in your fist and it crumbles.

Before planting, loosen the soil by tilling or turning it with a long-handled garden fork. Topsoil should be finely textured and free of large clods. This allows sprouts to push through the soil surface and water and fertilizer to seep into the root zone. After tilling, shape the soil into rows or beds.

Sowing seeds directly

When direct-seeding, dig a shallow furrow in the middle of the row with a hoe or trowel. For straight rows, run a plumb line from two stakes located at the end of each row as a guide. Cover small seeds such as lettuce and carrots with a scant ¼ inch of soil; cover larger seeds such as corn and beans with an inch or more. Check the seed-packet recommendation for planting depth.

Water your garden gently as soon as seeds are planted; soil should be moist but not wet. Watch the garden daily to make sure soil stays moist until seedlings have emerged and look vigorous. Apply a thin layer of light mulch such as straw over seeded beds to retain moisture. Remove the mulch gently as soon as seedlings begin to emerge so they can get full sun.

Some seeds simply will not germinate, so you should initially plant them close together. Thin them to their proper spacing when they are 1 to 2 inches tall. Grab seedlings by the stem close to the soil surface, or cut them with scissors.

If nothing emerges from a planting, you may have planted seeds too deeply or a crust may have formed over a slow-to-germinate vegetable. It's also possible you have a batch of nonviable seed. Some vegetable seeds, such as okra and beans, remain viable for years if stored correctly, but others, such as onion and lettuce, have a shelf life of three years or less. Always store seeds according to package directions.

Transplanting

Prepare the soil for transplants by cultivating so that the top 4 inches or more is finely textured and free of clods. Spread fertilizer over the soil, and water well after transplanting to prevent wilting and to keep the fertilizer from burning young tender roots.

If using purchased transplants, buy young seedlings. Pick up the flat and examine the base for roots growing out the drainage holes. Excessive root growth indicates older plants. Set transplants in the garden as soon as you buy them or move them to larger containers if you can't plant within a few days.

Gently loosen pot-bound roots so they don't continue to grow around themselves, and then plant at the same depth as they grew in the pot. Plant lanky tomato or broccoli seedlings deeper so they don't flop over. They'll actually grow roots on the buried stem, which further helps stabilize them.

Soak corn seeds in warm water before sowing to hasten germination.

Bury tomato seedlings deeply so the plant is upright and stable. New roots will form along the buried stem.

Summertime

Tomato flowers are self-pollinated, the reason saved seeds are true-to-type.

Pair lettuce and leeks to make rows pull double-duty.

A floating row cover guards crops from pests and nibbling rabbits, but remove it for pollinators, weeding, and harvest.

VEGETABLES FOR SUMMER GARDENS

SOW AND GROW IN WARM SUMMER SOIL:
Basil
Beans
Cantaloupe
Corn
Cucumber
Okra
Peanut
Pumpkin
Squash
Watermelon

TRANSPLANT TO GARDEN IN LATE SPRING:
Eggplant
Globe artichoke
Pepper
Tomato

Life becomes hectic in the garden during summer. Crops mature, weeds take off, and insects become more prevalent. Good planning minimizes the chaos.

Direct-seeded summer crops grow faster than their spring cousins, so monitor them carefully for thinning, spacing, and watering.

Summer transplants may need help adjusting to the heat. If temperatures exceed 80° F, shade plants under a row cover for the first few days after transplanting.

Summer watering should provide the soil with a deep soaking—it's a good time to switch to drip irrigation.

After planting, apply mulch to keep soil cool, retain water, and control weeds. Spread it 3 to 6 inches deep.

Managing pests

Home-garden pest control begins with basic gardening common sense, such as choosing resistant varieties, good soil preparation, regular watering, and monitoring for signs of trouble. Maintaining a diversity of plants and habitats also helps. Water and an abundance of flowering, nectar-bearing plants will encourage and sustain beneficial insects, such as ladybugs, spiders, and other predatory creatures. Marigolds planted in large numbers repel a variety of insect pests.

Discover the most notorious garden insect pests in the Gallery of Vegetables (page 28), paired with the plants they're most likely to attack.

The least-toxic pest control strategy uses barriers, such as row covers, to exclude pests from crops altogether. Using a pesticide should be your last resort and only when the pest is clearly out of control and an important crop is at risk.

When a pest arrives, integrated pest management (IPM) is the preferred approach. IPM is a problem-solving process that considers pesticide resistance, biological controls, and environmental pollution, as well as problems caused by the pest. IPM integrates many pest-control methods and minimizes insecticide use, particularly of the more toxic, broad-spectrum kinds. It uses simple, noninvasive remedies first. Often, doing nothing at all—letting nature take its course—is the best approach.

Pollination

Most vegetables, except leafy greens and root crops, form fruit from flowers, which means they must be pollinated to produce a crop. Usually, nature takes care of everything. Although some are self or wind-pollinated, most will require insects such as bees to transfer the pollen. Don't spray insecticides when crops are flowering, because they may also kill pollinating insects. If using a row cover to keep bugs at bay, lift it occasionally to give pollinating insects access to your crop. Help wind-pollinated corn by shaking the stems while tassels are shedding pollen.

Choose insecticides with care and always follow instructions.

Fall Gardens

Remember to remove row covers when crops are flowering so insects can pollinate blooms.

Shade lettuces in summer to lengthen your harvest window.

In some areas of the country, fall is another growing season. Many cool-season crops thrive in autumn, and some even taste better. Some, such as chard and spinach, can take a light frost. Others, such as leeks, carrots, and parsnips, can be harvested until the ground freezes.

The biggest challenge is getting crops into the ground early enough to produce before a freeze. Fall crops may take longer to reach maturity than those planted in spring, so timing is critical. Use the date of your area's first predicted frost to estimate planting schedules. Add 14 days to the estimated time to maturity on the seed package, then count back from the frost date to set a planting date. Add another two weeks to this figure for fall plantings of warm-season vegetables, such as bush beans, cucumbers, and squash.

Some cool-season vegetable seeds won't sprout in the heat of summer, sow these seeds indoors. Move seedlings to the garden when they are about a month old.

Gardening with frost

Many warm-season crops are damaged by light frost, but you can cover them with blankets for protection during early mild frosts. Remove blankets the next morning. These crops hardly grow once night temperatures reach 55° F or less. Cool-season crops often taste better after a light frost, and early frosts help prepare them for the harder freezes to come.

If frigid temperatures arrive suddenly, cover all crops with light-weight sheets or boxes. Also, water plants thoroughly on the eve of a hard freeze because saturated soil freezes more slowly than dry soil.

Don't assume that cold-hardy vegetables are dead just because they've been frozen. All the cold-hardy plants listed (*right*) can recover from a hard freeze, although they fare better and are less susceptible to rot if you grow them in cold frames or under tunnels during winter.

Cleaning up

As crop production wanes, consider removing the waning crops and replacing them with new cool-season ones.

Carrots sweeten after a hard frost. Dig them when soil is moist.

When plants die, remove them from the garden. Dead plants provide a home where pests and diseases overwinter. Pull plants up by the roots and throw them into the compost heap. If plants were diseased or insect infested, throw them into the trash to avoid harboring problems.

In late fall, turn under any old mulch and dig out weeds. Spread fresh mulch or plant winter cover crops. If soil is dry enough for tilling, add organic matter.

In cold climates, mulch around cold-hardy vegetables, such as carrots, beets, and parsnips for added protection.

VEGETABLES FOR FALL GARDENS

	TRANSPLANT IN LATE SUMMER:
Arugula	
Carrot	
Chard	
Fennel	Broccoli
Kale	Brussels
Kohlrabi	sprouts
Lettuce	Cabbage
Mesclun	Cauliflower
Mustard	Chinese
Radish	cabbage
Spinach	Parsley
Turnip	Scallion

COLD-HARDY VEGETABLES

Brussels sprout
Cabbage
Garlic
Kale
Lettuce (some varieties)
Mâche
Parsley
Spinach

Vegetables

When a seed such as corn germinates, moisture causes the seed coat to crack open and roots to emerge.

Additional roots continue to form as seed leaves stretch skyward. Sunlight tints seed leaves bright green.

By the time the first true leaves unfurl, roots are actively growing, absorbing moisture and nutrients from the soil.

The following guidelines apply to all vegetables in this encyclopedia, unless otherwise noted:
■ Vegetables prefer a soil pH of 6.2 to 6.8.
■ If a spacing range is provided, plant bush or smaller varieties at the closer spacing and larger varieties at the wider spacing.
■ You don't have to plant in straight rows; many crops thrive in wide rows or beds.
■ Use lightweight floating row covers at planting to exclude insect pests and keep young seedlings warm.

■ When possible, prevent pests before they're a problem. When that's not effective, respond with the simplest, least-disruptive remedies first.
■ Before using any pesticide, always read the label and follow directions carefully.
■ At the end of the season, remove spent plants to eliminate overwintering sites for pests. Throw nondiseased and non-insect-ridden plants on the compost pile.
■ Rotate crops to aid disease prevention. Keep a record—written, photographic, or video—of each year's planting arrangement.

The varieties listed for each vegetable in this encyclopedia are widely adapted and easy to grow. But the world is full of wonderful varieties whose flavors, colors, and tolerance to growing conditions vary widely. Experiment to find the vegetables best suited to your taste and garden.

When corn tassels release pollen, wind carries it to fertilize the silks on ears.

Brown silks on ripe ears of corn are dry at the tips but pliantly green near the ear.

Cynara scolymus
SIN-a-ra SKOLL-i-mus

- Site: Full sun, well-drained rich soil. Small amounts of fertilizer mixed into soil before planting.
- Planting: Plant root divisions after last frost.
- Spacing: 6 feet apart in rows 8 feet apart.
- Harvest: Late summer. Leave an inch of stem.
- Storage: Refrigerate for up to two weeks. Days to harvest: 90–100 from transplanting.

Artichokes are thistles without the sting. Both the tender hearts of their large flower buds and the bases of their thick scales are edible.

Where winters are mild and summers cool and foggy, artichokes are short-lived perennials that bear well for three or four years. In northern areas, grow as annuals.

HOW TO GROW: Six weeks before your last frost, plant three seeds in

ARTICHOKE

4-inch pots. Keep soil moist and warm until sprouts appear, then move seedlings to strong light. Two weeks after germination, thin to one seedling per pot. In northern areas, induce earlier flower budding by moving transplants outdoors so they receive 10 to 12 days between 32° and 50° F.

After all danger of frost is past, transplant seedlings into the garden. Keep soil constantly moist for two weeks or until plants are established.

Flower buds develop atop stems in late summer. Cut them when they are at least 3 inches in diameter, taking a 1-inch stub of stem with each bud.

In Zones 7 and 8, artichokes overwinter in the ground if protected. In spring, fertilize crowns with a 1-inch mulch of rotted manure and a balanced fertilizer.

One-, two-, and three-year-old plants produce a good crop of buds

in early summer. After harvesting, prune plants back by a third to get a fall crop.

SELECTED VARIETIES: For perennial artichokes, try 'Violetto' and 'Green Globe Improved'. For an annual, the top choice is 'Imperial Star'.

Site thistlelike artichokes where their spiny foliage won't poke you. Inset: Layers of scales enfold the tasty heart.

Asparagus officinalis
uh-SPARE-a-gus o-FISH-i-nal-is

- Site: Full sun to part shade. Well-drained, highly organic soil.
- Planting: As crowns, 4–6 weeks before last frost. Spacing: 5–6 inches deep, 14–18 inches apart.
- Care: Water during dry spells. Mulch annually.
- Harvest: Snap off young shoots at base. Do not harvest the first year after planting; second year, harvest for 2–4 weeks. Subsequent years, harvest for 5–6 weeks. For highest yields, plant only all male cultivars.
- Storage: Spears will last in the refrigerator for several days with stems in water.
- Pests: Asparagus beetle, asparagus rust

Long-lived asparagus can flourish for 10 to 30 years. Dense crowns of long, fleshy roots send up so many spears that you can harvest them for

ASPARAGUS

up to six weeks each spring. From early summer to fall, allow plants to grow freely; they'll die back completely in winter, having stored up strength for the following year. Weed, clean, and fertilize beds with compost every winter while the plants are dormant.

Asparagus grows in Zones 4–8, and thrives in California's Zone 9 where much of commercial crop is produced.

HOW TO GROW: Gain one to two years of harvesting time by starting with dormant roots or crowns. Plant crowns in late winter or early spring, 14 to 18 inches apart in a well-cultivated trench 6 inches deep and 16 inches wide. Cover crowns with 2 inches of soil. After the first sprouts grow a few inches tall, fill in the trench with soil. Asparagus are heavy feeders, so add generous amounts of composted manure mixed with the soil as you backfill.

SELECTED VARIETIES: For maximum yields, choose all-male disease-resistant varieties. The "Jersey" series offers 'Jersey King', which is widely adapted to various climates and soil conditions. Choose 'Jersey Knight' for heavy clay soils. In mild winter regions grow 'UC 157'.

Harvest asparagus spears by cutting them off just below ground level. Leave roots behind to resprout.

Phaseolus vulgaris
fa-ZEE-o-lus vul-GARE-is

Indulge your sense of adventure by growing different types of beans in your garden. Some varieties have colorful flowers before producing seed-bearing pods. They need full sun and well-drained soil and, except for favas, are warm-weather

'Fin de Bagnols' bean is a French filet or string bean grown since the 1800s.

Heirloom shell beans yield a rainbow harvest that's beautiful and delicious.

Eat young scarlet runner bean pods. Pick mature pods for fresh shell beans.

BEANS

crops, easily damaged by frost. Bean seeds germinate best in soil temperatures above 60° F.

With the help of soil-borne rhizobia bacteria, beans are able to take nitrogen from the air and store it in nodules on their roots until it's needed for growth, a process called nitrogen fixation. To encourage fixation on poor soils or in a new garden, dampen the seeds and dust them with inoculant powder before planting. Most fertile, established gardens will already have this bacteria in the soil.

Bush beans

- Site: Full sun; part shade reduces yields. Well-drained soil of average fertility, consistent moisture.
- Planting: By seed, after danger of frost has passed.
- Spacing: 1 inch deep, 2–3 inches apart in rows 18–24 inches apart. Thin to 4–6-inch spacing.
- Care: Don't leave over-mature pods on the vine.
- Harvest: Daily for maximum tenderness; see text below for information on different types. Days to harvest: Varies from 40–100.
- Pests and problems: Mexican bean beetles, bean leaf beetle, aphids, mildew, bean mosaic virus, anthracnose, and rust. Very frost-sensitive. To stop disease spread, do not work among wet plants.

These grow knee high and produce edible pods about 60 days after sowing. After the last frost, plant seeds 2 inches apart and 1 inch deep. Thin seedlings to 4 to 6 inches apart when they have at least three large leaves. Make several small sowings three weeks apart for a long harvest. Better yet, fill your garden with an assortment of different types of bush beans.

Snap beans have round or flat pods that vary in color from green to yellow to purple. 'Venture', 'Derby', and 'Provider' are some of the many dependable varieties. 'Roc d'Or' is a good bush wax (yellow) bean, while 'Royal Burgundy' is a purple-podded bush bean variety.

French filet beans, such as 'Maxibel', produce a light crop and are ideal for growing in small spaces. Pick them daily when a quarter inch in diameter to ensure tender pods and good flavor.

Shell beans can be harvested as green snap beans when pods are young and tender, or you can let them ripen until seeds become plump and pods feel leathery. They reach peak flavor before they actually dry. To store shell beans, cook and then freeze them.

Dry shell beans are similar but have tough, bitter-tasting pods; red kidney, pinto, and black beans are examples. Allow dry beans to ripen on the plants until the pods turn brown and the plants begin to die. To harvest, pull up plants and dry them for a week in a hot place before cracking open the pods. Spread beans in a single layer on cookie sheets and warm them for 20 minutes in a 175° F oven to kill any pests. Store in an airtight container.

All bush beans exhaust themselves after producing two or three heavy pickings and are best pulled up and composted when flowering and pod-setting subside.

Pole beans

- Site: Same as bush beans.
- Planting: At base of sturdy 5–8-foot poles.
- Spacing: 2–3 inches apart or place several seeds at each pole.
- Harvest: Same as bush beans.
- Pests and problems: Same as bush beans.

Large pods, full-bodied flavor, and a long season of production are hallmarks of pole beans. Pods come in many shapes and colors. The plants grow as vines, that should be trained on a trellis made from string, wire, thin wooden stakes, or slats.

Most pole beans produce about 60 days after sowing and bear until frost. To keep plants productive for a long time, promptly pick young pods before they develop large seeds. If some pods do overripen, harvest them as fresh shell beans, discarding the shells.

For pole beans with deep green pods and a long harvest, consider 'Kentucky Blue', 'Kentucky Wonder', 'Romano', or 'Blue Lake'.

Scarlet runner beans are easily confused with pole beans, but they are actually a different species, *Phaseolus coccineus*. They produce a profusion of beautiful red blossoms, but the pods are edible only when young. The mature pods can be harvested for their tasty, colorful, fresh shell beans.

Lima, fava, and asparagus beans

- **Site:** Asparagus beans, same as bush beans. Limas need warmer weather; favas require a long, cool season.
- **Planting:** By seed, after danger of frost.
- **Spacing:** Limas: same as bush beans; asparagus beans: 1–2 inches deep, 1 inch apart in rows 4 feet apart, thin to 6–12 inches; favas: 1–2 inches deep, 1 inch apart in rows 2–3 feet apart. Thin to 6–12 inches.
- **Harvest:** Same as bush beans.
- **Pests and problems:** Limas and asparagus beans have same pests as bush beans; aphids, thrips, and mites favor favas.

Lima beans *(Phaseolus lunatus)* tolerate heat, humidity, and pest and disease challenges well.

Fast-maturing bush limas such as 'Fordhook 242' will grow in northern gardens, but other limas are most productive in areas with long, hot summers. Plant them in early summer, when soil temperature is above 75° F.

Sow seeds of bush varieties 3 inches apart. Pole varieties, such as 'King of the Garden', require 6-inch spacing and a sturdy trellis.

For buttery flavor, harvest limas when the beans are plump but still glossy. At this stage the pods change from dark to pale green and the beans become easier to remove. Limas can be eaten fresh, frozen, or preserved as dry beans.

Fava beans

Fava beans *(Vicia faba)* have a high protein content. They require cool weather and can survive temperatures as low as 10° to 20° F. Plants are large and upright, growing to 5 feet tall.

Plant fava beans in fall in climates with mild winters or in spring where summers are cool. They are tremendous nitrogen fixers and may be used as a cover crop.

Large-seeded strains such as 'Broad Windsor' usually have the best flavor. To cook as a fresh shell bean, harvest the pods while they are still green. You also can let pods dry and use favas as dry beans.

Asparagus beans

Also known as yard-long beans, asparagus beans *(Vigna unguiculata)* feature vigorous vines with glossy leaves and purple flowers. They grow best in warm climates.

The twining stems may grow up to 10 feet long, and the pencil-thin pods often reach 30 inches. Plant

Pick lima beans after pods turn bright green. Eat, freeze, or dry the beans.

seeds in late spring, 8 inches apart. Train them up a tepee-type trellis at least 6 feet tall or a high chain-link fence.

Harvest asparagus beans while they are young and green; they cook and eat like snap beans.

PEST WATCH: MEXICAN BEAN BEETLE: The leading pest of garden beans is a mustard-brown beetle with black spots.

Starting in early summer, the adults lay clusters of 40 to 60 bright yellow eggs on the undersides of bean leaves. The eggs hatch into yellow larvae, which rasp away leaf tissue, leaving numerous pale patches.

The best natural approach is to handpick the eggs and larvae; use a neem-based insecticide for heavy infestations. Other garden pesticides labeled for use on beans will also kill the beetles if applied to both sides of the leaves.

Yard-long beans yield pods as thin as a pencil and up to 30 inches long.

Beta vulgaris
BAY-ta vul-GARE-is

BEETS

- **Site:** Full sun to part shade. Light, organic soil free of stones. Consistent moisture. Low to average fertility, pH near 7 or higher.
- **Planting:** Seed, 2–3 weeks before last frost. Succession crop every 3 weeks.
- **Spacing:** ½-inch deep, 1 inch apart in rows 15 inches apart. Thin to 4 inches.
- **Care:** Sidedress with compost and mulch.
- **Harvest:** Baby beets when roots are just rounding out. Days to harvest: 45–60.

Valued for both their sweet roots and earthy-tasting greens, beets also bring interesting colors to the vegetable garden. Many varieties have bright red leaf stems and veins, and roots come in colors such as red, yellow, white, and striped.

Beets are a cool-season crop best grown in spring and fall. Let them mature in cool soil for best color and flavor.

HOW TO GROW: Plant beets in fertile, light-textured soil with a neutral or slightly alkaline pH. If your soil is acidic, work in a cup of lime per 10 square feet of planting space. Keeping pH near 7 will help prevent scab disease. Enrich the soil with a 2-inch layer of well-rotted compost before seeding.

Beet seeds often germinate sporadically. You'll get a better stand by sowing seeds in shallow trenches filled with a mixture of compost and vermiculite. Plant seeds ½ inch deep and 1 inch apart. Begin planting two to three weeks before the last spring frost. Keep the soil constantly moist until seedlings appear.

In areas with cool summers, make additional sowings of beets at three-week intervals into the summer. In hotter climates, sow most of your beets in late summer and early fall. Light frosts do not damage fall-grown beets.

Beet seeds are actually a fruit containing several seeds, so one sowing produces a thick stand. Gradually thin seedlings to 4 inches apart. The leaves of young plants are edible. Carefully remove weeds by hand and mulch around plants with a 1-inch-deep layer of organic matter, such as hay or straw.

Keeping the soil moist and cool is key to growing sweet, uniform roots. If hot weather arrives before beets begin to swell, cool the roots by adding more mulch or hilling up loose soil around the plants. Beets

The bright dyes of beets will permanently stain plastic and wooden serving items.

are heavy feeders prone to nutrient deficiencies, so it's helpful to amend the soil well with compost before planting. Add supplemental fertilizer based on a soil test.

Begin harvesting beets when roots are golf-ball size. Baby beets fully mature to 1-inch-diameter roots in 50 to 55 days, while most table beets grow to 2 inches in diameter in 60 to 70 days. Fall crops will hold in the garden until soil begins to freeze. Where winters are mild, some hardy varieties can be left in the garden.

SELECTED VARIETIES: Fast-maturing hybrid varieties, such as 'Red Ace', show extra vigor from germination to maturity in hot climates and in soils with less-than-ideal fertility and texture. 'Early Wonder' and 'Detroit Dark Red' are popular for their fine flavor in greens and roots. 'Golden' produces yellow-fleshed roots with a smooth, tender texture. 'Blankoma' yields white roots. 'Chioggia' is an unusual heirloom variety with pinkish-red and white rings.

In deep, loamy soils, grow cylindrical beets, such as 'Cylindra' and 'Formanova'. For winter beets in Zones 7 and 8, grow extra-hardy varieties such as 'Lutz Green' or 'Lutz Winterkeeper'.

Cultivate a crop of colorful beets and you'll be serving multihued meals to your family and friends. The bright roots entice even picky eaters to eat the tasty crop.

Brassica
BRASS-i-ka

BROCCOLI AND OTHER COLE CROPS

Broccoli, cabbage, Brussels sprouts, cauliflower, collards, kale, and kohlrabi are closely related. Each is unique in flavor and hardiness. All grow best in cool weather and taste sweeter after exposure to cool fall temperatures.

Most cole crops grow into large plants that demand excellent soil fertility and wide spacing. They do best with a soil pH around 6.5.

Broccoli

- Spacing: 12–20 inches apart and between rows.
- Care: Use low-nitrogen fertilizer; excess nitrogen may cause hollow stems.
- Harvest: Cut off heads when they are full but flowers not yet open. Days to harvest: 40–120.

Where summers are cool, make two plantings of broccoli one month apart in spring. In warm climates, plant in spring and late summer for harvest in fall and winter. Mature plants usually survive temperatures into the low 20s. Under plastic tunnels, you can grow broccoli well into winter in Zones 6 and 7. Farther south, it requires no winter protection.

HOW TO GROW: For spring crops, start seeds indoors 6 weeks before your last frost date. It helps to cover them with a cloche or grow them in cold frames for two weeks after transplanting. In fall, start seeds indoors 10 to 12 weeks before the first frost. Set them out when a month old. Or, direct-seed 10 to 12 weeks before the first frost date.

Enrich planting holes with compost, and mix in a handful of fertilizer. Space plants 12 to 22 inches apart. Close spacing encourages side shoots, while wide spacing promotes larger main heads.

Six weeks after planting, sidedress with water-soluble fertilizer and add a ½-inch layer of compost. Then mulch with a 2-inch layer of organic mulch, such as chopped leaves or straw.

Cut the primary head while buds are tight but fully expanded. Most varieties produce numerous smaller side shoots, which are also edible. The side shoots get smaller as the plant gets older. Use side shoots in stirfry or salads.

SELECTED VARIETIES: Hybrids such as 'Green Comet' and 'Packman' are dependable producers spring or fall. An open-pollinated strain called 'DeCicco' excels at forming tender side shoots over an extended period. 'Purple Sprouting' is a late-fall to winter type with small purple heads. 'Premium Crop' is an early variety with large blue-green heads.

Broccoli raab is in the broccoli family, but you harvest and eat the stem, leaves, and buds before the flower opens. Its flavor is unique and it is a favorite in Italian cooking.

Brussels sprouts

- Spacing: 15–20 inches apart in rows 24 inches apart.
- Care: Pinch off top 4–6 inches of plant when lower sprouts are ½ inch wide.
- Harvest: Harvest after frost for best flavor. Sprouts should be firm, round, ½ to 2 inches in diameter. Begin harvest at bottom of stalk. Days to harvest: 80–130.

This is one vegetable that is always best when it matures in cold weather. In the north, start seeds indoors for transplanting in midsummer; in the south, transplant in late summer.

HOW TO GROW: Set out plants in early spring (or when cool-weather is anticipated) in well-fertilized soil, 18 inches apart. Water regularly. Plants often reach 30 inches in

Harvest broccoli when the head is 3 inches across and before flowers open. Use a knife to cut the stems.

height by the time the first sprouts appear on the main stem close to the soil, in early fall.

Mature plants withstand hard freezes. Twist off sprouts between freezes, when plants have thawed. Where plants are likely to remain frozen for more than a week, pull them up before the ground freezes. Store in a cool root cellar for up to a month. In other areas, harvest sprouts as you wish through winter and pull plants in early spring.

SELECTED VARIETIES: 'Prince Marvel' and 'Jade Cross' are available as seed and transplants. Some newer hybrids, such as 'Bubbles', are more productive and worth trying. 'Rubine Red' has unique dark red sprouts.

Don't wash Brussels sprouts until you're ready to use them. Nutmeg and grated cheeses blend flavorfully with sprouts.

BROCCOLI AND OTHER COLE CROPS *(continued)*

Cabbage

- Spacing: 18–24 inches apart in rows 32 inches apart.
- Harvest: Prevent splitting by harvesting as soon as heads are mature or giving heads a quarter-turn twist while still in the ground. Cut across base with a knife. Leave remaining stem in the ground, and tiny heads may form later. Days to harvest: 65–100.

'Stonehead' cabbage forms tidy, tight heads ideal for single servings.

In cooler climates cabbage planted in spring will produce huge heads by late fall. In warmer areas it's better to plant a fast-maturing spring crop and a longer-growing midseason crop for fall harvest.

HOW TO GROW: Start seeds indoors five to seven weeks before the last frost. Set out the seedlings at four to six weeks old, spaced 12 to 18 inches apart. Mulch with a 1- to 2-inch-thick layer of organic matter. In early summer, cut heads as they become firm. Either leave summer-harvested plants to develop small side heads or pull up the plants.

The hardiest varieties can grow through the winter in regions where temperatures rarely drop below 10° F. The root stub left behind in fall after cutting the main head often produces tufts of tender leaves or small, secondary heads that are delicious cooked.

SELECTED VARIETIES: Choose cabbage varieties well adapted to your climate and the proper season. Try varieties with wrinkled, curled leaves, such as 'Savoy Express', or red varieties, such as 'Ruby Perfection'. Fall varieties known for flavor and hardiness include 'Late Flat Dutch'. 'Dynamo', and 'Stonehead' form smaller heads and are ideal for individual servings.

Cauliflower

- Site: Avoid hot or dry.
- Spacing: 18 inches apart in rows 32 inches apart.
- Care: Protect from heavy frosts. Fertilize monthly with balanced liquid fertilizer. Grow self-blanching varieties or blanch head by pulling outer leaves over it and holding in place with twist tie.
- Harvest: When head is full and firm. Cut with knife at base. Days to harvest: 55–90.

You can grow beautiful cauliflower both in spring and early fall.

HOW TO GROW: Start seeds indoors 4 weeks before the last spring frost or 10 to 12 weeks before the first fall frost. Grow seedlings under lights for three weeks and harden off plants for a week before transplanting them to the garden.

When plants develop their first true leaves, fertilize with a half-strength solution of a balanced fertilizer. Space plants 18 inches apart, and mulch lightly.

Most varieties need blanching to form white heads. When small heads form in the centers of the plants, blanch the heads by pulling several leaves up and over the head, securing them with a soft cloth strip. Seven to 10 days later, the heads should be ready to harvest. Cauliflower bears only one head per plant.

SELECTED VARIETIES: Fast-maturing hybrids such as 'Snow Crown' and 'Fremont' are the best choice for a spring crop; they also perform well in fall. Except in the far north, any variety that requires more than 80 days to mature should be grown in the fall. Colorful varieties such as lime-green 'Panther' or purple 'Violet Queen' are most dependable when grown from late summer to fall. 'Snowball' is a self-blanching variety with small heads.

Cauliflower (above) and mustard greens (right) thrive in cool weather.

A frost sweetens kale leaves. Always harvest leaves from the bottom first.

Collards

- **Site: Tolerates drought, but quality is best in moist soil.**
- **Spacing: 12 inches apart in rows 20 inches apart.**
- **Care: Mulch to overwinter. Stake tall varieties.**
- **Harvest: Pick individual leaves as needed. Days to harvest: 70–85.**

Fast-growing collards are nonheading cabbages that can tolerate a slightly acidic pH and drought conditions. Plants are hardy to between 10° and 15° F.

HOW TO GROW: Sow seeds in late summer so the plants reach picking size just after the first frost. Plant seeds 1 inch apart and ½ inch deep. When seedlings reach 3 to 4 inches, thin to at least 8 inches apart.

After a frost, harvest hand-sized leaves from the top third of the plants. Leave the large basal leaves intact. Continue to pick this way through winter. In early spring, gather the small green flower buds before they turn yellow. Although not well known in this country, the succulent buds are a delicacy.

SELECTED VARIETIES: For fast growth and winter hardiness, 'Champion' and 'Flash' are the best bets. The heirloom variety 'Green Glaze' deters cabbage worms and other pests.

'Georgia' is a good variety for areas with mild winters.

Kale

- **Spacing: 12 inches apart in rows 18 to 24 inches apart. Or direct-seed ½ inch deep, 3 inches apart. Thin to 12 inches.**
- **Harvest: Pick individual leaves as needed.**

This highly nutritious green comes in many colors and all (including the ornamental kales) are edible.

The young, tender leaves of spring-planted kale are excellent in salads. Leaves harvested in warm weather, however, lack the sweet, nutty taste of winter-picked leaves. Kale can be grown through winter in almost any region.

HOW TO GROW: Sow seeds 1 inch apart and ½ inch deep in late summer 8 weeks before your first frost. Thin seedlings to 8 inches apart when they are 4 inches tall. Around the time of your first frost, sidedress plants with an inch of compost.

Cold weather makes kale extra sweet and crisp. Harvest leaves as you need them throughout winter, taking only three or four from each plant at a time.

SELECTED VARIETIES: Varieties with curly leaves, such as 'Winterbor' and 'Red Bor', become frillier in cold weather. 'Lacinata' (or dinosaur kale) features heavily blistered, dark green leaves. Among smooth-leafed varieties, 'Red Russian' is popular for its red-veined leaves that turn green after cooking.

Kohlrabi

- **Site: Best with 60°–70° F temperatures.**
- **Planting: Transplants.**
- **Harvest: When stems are 2–3 inches in diameter. Slice off at base. Days to harvest: 40–60.**

Kohlrabi is a fast-growing plant whose stem swells into a round ball just above the soil line. Peeled and eaten either raw or cooked, it has a flavor like a watery, crunchy, mild turnip. You can grow them in spring and fall.

HOW TO GROW: Sow seed indoors and transplant seedlings when they have five leaves, or plant seeds in the garden 2 inches apart in fertile soil with a near-neutral pH. Thin plants to 4 to 6 inches apart, and water regularly. Fertilize with a balanced liquid fertilizer.

Harvest spring kohlrabi when the stems swell to the size of a tennis ball. Flavor and texture are best if plants mature in cool weather. Fall crops will hold in the garden for several weeks; in Zones 7–9, they can last all winter.

SELECTED VARIETIES: In the spring, grow fast-maturing hybrids such as 'Grand Duke' and 'Winner'. For fall and winter harvest, plant 'Early White Vienna' or 'Early Purple Vienna'. 'Kolibri' has purplish skin and stems.

Kohlrabi need consistent moisture to yield stems that aren't tough or woody.

Daucus carota sativus
DAW-kus ka-RO-ta sa-TY-vus

- **Site:** Full sun. Deep, loose soil free of stones, high in organic matter. Plentiful moisture.
- **Planting:** By seed. In north, sow in spring 2–3 weeks before last frost. In south, sow seed midwinter through spring and midsummer into fall.
- **Spacing:** ½ inch deep, ½ inch apart in rows 12 inches apart. Thin to 3 inches.
- **Care:** Maintain a consistent supply of moisture.
- **Harvest:** Harvest when carrots are fully colored yet tender. Days to harvest: 50–75.
- **Pests and problems:** Carrot rust flies, maggots, and blight. Exposed "shoulders" can turn green and bitter; mulching keeps shoulders covered. Roots can become twisted and forked in heavy, stony soil.

CARROTS

Fresh garden-grown carrots are remarkably crisp and juicy. They come in different shapes, sizes, and colors. Carrots grow best in cool weather. In many areas, crops sown in fall can be harvested through winter.

HOW TO GROW: To develop long, straight roots, carrots require deep, loamy soil free of stones. If your soil is clay, plant short, stubby varieties.

A slightly acidic soil of moderate fertility is best. Dig an inch of compost into the soil before planting, but don't add other fertilizer. The texture of heavy clay soil can be amended with compost.

Grow carrots in rows or broadcast the seeds in a raised bed. Plant seeds thickly, three or four per inch of row because some will not germinate. Mulch lightly with potting soil, sand, or grass clippings to help keep the soil moist until seedlings appear. After a month, thin the seedlings to 3 inches apart.

Carrots pull easiest from moist soil. Harvest after rain or water the bed first.

Harvest carrots at full size because flavor improves with maturity, but take care to dig up the roots before they turn woody. Fresh carrots often do not require peeling; simply scrub them with a soft brush.

Carrots can develop forked roots as a result of excess nitrogen fertilizer or heavy soil. In some areas the larvae of carrot rust flies make numerous reddish holes in roots. Where this pest is common, add beneficial nematodes to the soil in late spring, or grow carrots under row covers. You can prevent this pest and other problems by rotating carrots to different spots in the garden each year.

SELECTED VARIETIES: Experiment to find the best varieties for your soil. Nantes and Imperator hybrids usually produce well in sandy loam. Danvers hybrids tolerate both heavy and sandy soils. 'Mokum' and 'Nelson' are sweet Nantes carrots. 'Tendersweet' is a good Imperator type. 'Healthmaster' is a sweet, crisp carrot that juices well.

In clay soils or containers, plant miniature carrots that form round or short cylindrical roots. Good miniature varieties include 'Minicor', 'Thumbelina' and 'Little Finger'. 'Fly Away' is a Nantes type that is carrot rust fly resistant.

Grow colorful varieties such as 'Purple Dragon', 'White Belgium', 'Sweet Sunshine', and 'Nutri-red' to daub tasty hues into dishes.

After pulling carrots, cut off their tops; the tops will only steal moisture from your crop of ruddy-skinned roots.

CELERY

Apium graveolens
APE-ee-um gra-VEE-o-lenz

- **Site:** Full sun to part shade. Rich soil, high in organic matter. Consistent, plentiful moisture. Long, cool growing season.
- **Planting:** Sow seeds indoors 10–12 weeks before last frost. Set out transplants 2 weeks before last frost.
- **Spacing:** 12 inches apart in rows 18 inches apart.
- **Care:** Fertilize monthly.
- **Harvest:** Cut off entire head at the base. In mild climates, allow some inner stems to remain to lengthen harvest. Days to harvest: 80–125.
- **Pests and problems:** Rarely troubled by insects but occasionally by diseases, including black heart and several blights. Keep plants well fertilized and watered and rotate crops to control.

Harvest celeriac for storing by digging up the roots. Store plants as close to 32° F as possible, keeping them upright in buckets with moist sand or soil around their roots.

Homegrown celery is more flavorful and much darker than what you buy at the store. Commercial producers grow celery under conditions that are almost impossible to duplicate in most gardens. So why try? For one, think of your celery as a unique vegetable that can only be gathered from a home garden.

HOW TO GROW: Cool weather is best for growing celery, but young seedlings must not be exposed to temperatures below 55° F for more than a week. If they are, plants will bolt (flower and set seed prematurely).

Start seeds indoors 10 to 12 weeks before your last spring frost. Sow about 20 seeds in a 6-inch pot, cover the pot with plastic, and keep it moist and warm until the seeds germinate 2 weeks later. Thin to four plants per pot when the seedlings show their first true leaves.

Before transplanting seedlings to the garden, enrich the soil with as much compost as possible. Harden off the seedlings for a few days, and move them into the garden before the last frost. Leave at least 8 to 12 inches between plants.

Water plants as often as needed to keep the soil moist. Apply a balanced liquid fertilizer. Begin harvesting individual stalks when they are about 10 inches tall.

To blanch almost-mature plants, wrap the stems with folded newspaper secured with string or large rubber bands. Then hill up 6 inches of soil around the plants. Harvest the entire plant three weeks after wrapping the stems.

SELECTED VARIETIES: Tall Utah types, such as 'Ventura', grow steadily and mature about 100 days after transplanting. 'Ventura' is crisp, widely adaptable, and has some disease resistance.

An heirloom variety, 'Giant Red', has strongly flavored stalks blushed with red. It is best used as a "cutting celery" to flavor cooked dishes.

CONSIDER CELERIAC: Also known as celery root, celeriac is an easy crop to grow as long as you give it plenty of water. Grow seedlings just as you would celery and harvest the roots when they are at least 2 inches across. In fall, you can hill up a few inches of soil over the roots to store them in the ground through early winter. Try varieties such as 'Brilliant' or 'Monarch'.

Blanching yields white and tender stalks. Wrap a brown bag, drainage tile or newspaper around stalks and mound soil at its base to hold it in place.

Beta vulgaris cicla
BAY-ta vul-GARE-is SI-cla

- Site: Full sun to part shade. Loose, fertile soil high in organic matter. Consistent moisture.
- Planting: Sow seeds in spring 2–3 weeks before the last frost.
- Spacing: ½ inch deep, 5–6 inches apart in rows 18 inches apart. Thin to 9 inches.
- Care: As plants age, cut back

'Rainbow' Swiss chard unfurls leaf stalks in many hues, brightening both the garden and the dinner table.

CHARD

to about 3–5 inches and they'll send up new shoots.
- Harvest: As needed. Cut stalks at soil level, removing only a stalk or two from each plant.
- Days to harvest: 50–55.
- Pests: Aphids and leaf miners.

Beautiful and productive, Swiss chard is related to spinach and beets. Eat young leaves raw in salads. Cook mature leaves like spinach or lightly steam the thick leaf ribs. Chard tolerates hot weather better than other greens. Plants are moderately winter hardy.

HOW TO GROW: Chard needs rich soil (add 3 to 4 inches of compost) and constant moisture. Add lime if soil is acidic. Sow seeds in spring for summer harvest. In areas with mild winters, plant again in late summer.

Soak seeds overnight before planting them ½ inch deep and 1 inch apart. Like beets, the seeds

are actually a fruit containing several seeds, so seedlings appear in clusters. Thin seedlings to 2 inches apart (they are edible) until your best plants stand 9 inches apart.

Mulch with organic material to keep soil from splashing into the leaf crevices. Watch for aphids and leafminers.

Harvest chard by breaking off two or three outer leaves from each plant. Young leaves less than 10 inches long usually taste best. To obtain many young leaves in fall, cut back plants to 3 inches tall in late summer. Delicately flavored new leaves will grow from the centers of the plants.

SELECTED VARIETIES: 'Lucullus' and 'Fordhook Giant' have white ribs; 'Rhubarb', bright red. 'Bright Yellow' has all yellow ribs. 'Bright Lights' variety includes a mixture of plants with ribs in electric shades.

Brassica rapa
BRASS-i-ka RAY-pa

- Site: Full sun to part shade. Fertile, well-drained soil high in organic matter. Consistent moisture. Cool.

'Joi Choi' is a dependable pac choi variety that grows quickly (left). Chinese cabbage 'Kajumi' forms a tight head (right).

CHINESE CABBAGE

- Planting: For a spring crop, transplant seedlings 4–5 weeks before average last frost (use bolt-resistant varieties). Direct-seed in midsummer in northern regions, early fall in southern areas. Or start indoors 2–3 weeks before setting out.
- Spacing: ½ inch deep, 1 inch apart, in rows 18 inches apart. Thin to 12–18 inches. Space fall crops 3 inches apart.
- Harvest: In fall before a hard freeze. Cut off heads; remove outer leaves. Days to harvest: 45–90.
- Pests: Flea beetles, aphids, cabbage worms, cabbage maggots, and slugs.

Combine the flavor of cabbage with the crispness of lettuce and you have Chinese cabbage. Heading types, such as Napa Chinese cabbage, grow into tightly wrapped, barrel-shaped

cylinders. Nonheading types, such as pac choi, have loose dark green leaves with white veins that form a cluster.

HOW TO GROW: You can grow Chinese cabbage in both spring and fall, but warm weather causes flowering stalks, and bitter leaves.

Water regularly and feed plants with a water-soluble fertilizer monthly. Keep soil moist. Begin to harvest as soon as heads form.

Mature Chinese cabbage tolerates light frosts and continues to grow after weather cools. If hard freezes threaten, cover plants or harvest and store in the refrigerator.

SELECTED VARIETIES: For a spring crop of Napa-type Chinese cabbage, plant bolt-resistant varieties: 'Two Seasons', 'Blues', 'China Express', and 'Michihli'. Napa types do well in fall. Among pac choi, 'Joi Choi' grows fast. Dwarf 'Mei Ching Choi' is suited to small gardens and pots.

CORN

Zea mays
ZEE-a MAYS

- **Site:** Full sun. Well-drained, fertile soil. Consistent, plentiful moisture. Long, warm season.
- **Planting:** Sow seeds about a week after average last frost. Plant in blocks for best pollination.
- **Spacing:** 1 inch deep, 3–4 inches apart in rows 2–3 feet apart. Thin plants to 1–2 feet apart.
- **Care:** Apply a granular fertilizer at planting, when plants are a foot tall, and again when silks appear. Keep soil moist.
- **Harvest:** after silks turn brown. Check for ripeness by occasionally sampling an ear until kernels are filled out, tender, and sweet. Days to harvest: 60–95.
- **Storage:** For maximum flavor, consume as soon as possible.
- **Pests:** Cutworms, corn borers, corn earworms, leaf blights, and smut.

Sweet corn fresh from the garden is so delicious you may find yourself devouring it like a raccoon or deer.

Old-fashioned varieties contain less sugar than the newer hybrids. Whatever the variety or color, the sugar content of modern sweet corn—supersweet and sugar-enhanced types—is higher than in some fruit.

Corn requires warm weather and more space than most vegetables, but today's hybrids can be grown close together if they are well fertilized. Still, the minimum requirement for a successful planting of sweet corn is a sunny spot at least 6 feet long and 5 feet wide.

HOW TO GROW: Sweet corn requires warm, fertile soil with a slightly acid pH between 5.8 and 7. It is a notoriously heavy feeder, so enrich the soil with rotted manure or compost along with a balanced fertilizer before planting. Organic fertilizers rich in alfalfa or blood meal are suitable for corn, or you can mix a 10-10-10 fertilizer into the site at the rate of 4 cups per 100 feet of planting row.

Corn is usually planted in rows spaced 28 to 36 inches apart. For good pollination, plant in blocks of at least three or four rows. Sow seeds about 1 inch deep, 4 inches apart in the row.

Corn will not germinate well until the soil temperature has risen to 65° F. For a small early planting, start seeds indoors in individual 2-inch peat pots. Set the seedlings out without disturbing their roots after the last frost. Wait until a week after the last frost date to direct-seed in the garden. To extend your harvest season, sow a midseason variety when the early corn reaches 2 inches tall.

When plants are 6 inches high, thin to 12 inches apart (2 feet apart for very tall varieties). This is also a good time to remove weeds.

After thinning and weeding, fertilize corn with a light sprinkling of a high-nitrogen fertilizer. If using 10-10-10, apply at a rate of ½ cup per 10 feet of row.

In the period from pollination to harvest, corn needs 1 inch of water each week. Drip irrigation is best to avoid interference with pollination. Soaker hoses laid between rows work well to supply water right to the roots. A light mulch of hay or straw helps retain soil moisture and suppress weeds.

POLLINATION: Wind effectively distributes corn pollen in large plantings more than four rows deep. In small plantings, it is helpful to hand-pollinate sweet corn. As soon as the tassels and silks appear, gather pollen from the tassels into an envelope and sprinkle it onto the silks of neighboring plants. This helps ensure ears will be well filled with uniform kernels.

'Sugardots' bicolor sweet corn forms ears with a blend of corn-flavored yellow kernels and sweet white ones.

Prevent cross-pollination with starchy field corn. Plant the two types at least 400 feet apart. Supersweet varieties must be isolated from all other types of corn by at least 400 feet—or by timing, so that when the supersweet variety is tasseling, the others aren't. To isolate varieties using timing, stagger plantings so they mature at two-week intervals or grow varieties that mature at different times.

CORN (continued)

HARVEST: Sweet corn is usually ready about 24 days after the silks appear. Most plants produce one or two ears. Begin checking ears when the silks appear dry and brown. Mature ears usually have silks that are dry and brown on the ends but still greenish toward the ear.

Corn is ripe when the kernels look firm and glossy and milky juice bursts out when you puncture a kernel with your fingernail. Sweet corn has the highest sugar content when harvested in the morning. In hot weather the sugar will quickly begin to convert to starch. However, many modern supersweet hybrids hold their sugar for up to a week when stored in the refrigerator and for several months when frozen.

After picking corn in the morning, store it in the husks in the refrigerator until you're ready to cook it. If you can't use the corn for a day or two, when you pick it, cut it so each ear has a few inches of stem with it. Store the stems in a bucket of water in a root cellar or in the refrigerator until cooking time.

Most folks enjoy boiled ears of corn, but roasted corn has a fabulous flavor. Roast it on the grill or in the oven. Pull out the silk with a firm tug, then roast in the oven at 325° F or over low heat on the grill for about 50 minutes. Remove husks with care; they'll be very hot.

SELECTED VARIETIES: In short-summer climates, stick with early-maturing varieties such as 'Sugar Buns' (yellow) or 'Earlivee' (yellow). Early varieties produce in 60 to 70 days.

The larger ears of midseason varieties are well worth an extra two-week wait. Standard late-season sugary hybrids such as 'Silver Queen' (white) and 'Honey N Cream' (bi-color) are good choices.

"Sugar enhanced (se)" varieties have a unique combination of sweetness, creamy texture, and rich corn flavor. Varieties include 'Bodacious' (yellow), 'Kandy Korn' (yellow), and 'Quickie' (bicolor). There's even a red-kerneled sweet corn called 'Ruby Queen'. Some people find supersweet varieties too sweet for fresh eating, but 'How Sweet It Is' (white), 'Honey 'n Pearl' (bicolor), and 'Early Xtra Sweet' (yellow) are excellent choices.

PEST WATCH: CORN EARWORM: Hidden beneath a flawless husk, usually near the tip of the ear, you may encounter one or more pasty, beige caterpillars munching away on sweet corn. These are corn earworms, the larvae of a moth that lays eggs on corn silks.

Upon hatching, corn earworms crawl inside the ear and begin to feed. A few drops of mineral oil or granules of *Bacillus thuringiensis* (Bt) placed in the tips of the green ears as the silks wilt and begin to turn brown can reduce infestations. Early crops tend to have fewer earworms. Ears damaged by earworms are still fine for eating. Just cut out the worm.

In small plantings, hand-pollinate ears. Gather pollen from tassels in an envelope and then pour it on the silks of nearby plants.

Cucumis sativus
kew-KEW-mis sa-TY-vus

CUCUMBERS

- Site: Full sun. Warm, well-drained soil. Plentiful moisture. Long growing season.
- Planting: Sow seeds in hills or rows after last frost. In southern areas, plant in midspring and midsummer for two harvests.
- Spacing: 1½ inches deep, 4–6 seeds per hill, or 3–4 feet apart in and between rows. Thin to three plants per hill.
- Harvest: As soon as fruits reach full size. Do not allow to become large. Days to harvest: 55–70.
- Pests and problems: Cucumber beetles, bacterial wilt, anthracnose, mildew, mosaic virus, scab, and leaf spot. Grow resistant varieties to prevent diseases. May develop bitter taste in dry sites.

Fast, productive, and easy to grow, cucumbers come in bush and vine varieties. They tend to produce more fruit than most gardeners can use, so limit the size of plantings unless you plan to make lots of pickles. Six plants of any type provide plenty of fruit to eat and share.

With planning and season-stretching techniques, you can grow two or three crops each year. Make plantings in spring, early summer, and, in the south, about 10 weeks before the first fall frost date. Even a light frost will kill cucumbers.

HOW TO GROW: Cucumbers require warm weather and well-drained soil to grow well. Before planting, add generous amounts of organic matter—compost, sawdust, or peat moss—to the soil. Direct-sow seeds when soil temperature is 70° F. When seedlings develop their first true leaves, thin to 6 inches apart.

For transplanting in areas with short growing seasons, start seeds indoors a month before the last frost. Harden off seedlings before planting and warm the soil with black plastic.

Grow cucumbers in rows, beds, containers, or hills. Tunnels with row covers protect plants from pests and cold. When vines bloom, remove covers to let pollinating insects in.

Plant spacing and trellising needs vary. Compact, short-vined types need no support. Cucumbers with long fruit need a sturdy trellis of string or wire to keep fruit straight. Train vines up a trellis by tying them with strips of soft cloth.

Pick cucumbers young, before seeds harden. Push on the stem with your thumb until the fruit breaks free. Refrigerate to keep fruit firm.

Cucumbers are prone to several diseases, many of which are spread by insects. Control diseases by planting resistant varieties, destroying infected plants, and growing plants under row covers.

SELECTED VARIETIES: The 8-inch-long, dark green cucumbers sold at grocery stores are American hybrids. Garden varieties include the productive and disease-resistant 'Fanfare' and 'Diva'.

Oriental varieties like 'Suyo Long' and 'Orient Express', bear burpless, mild fruit that need a trellis to keep from developing kinks. The burpless

Grow cucumbers on a trellis to keep vines from gobbling garden real estate.

'Sweet Success' is self-fertile, doesn't require pollination, and can grow under row covers until fruit ripens.

Bush cucumbers include disease-resistant 'Spacemaster' and 'Salad Bush'. Small-fruited pickling cucumbers produce heavily all at once. Use them fresh and for pickling. Compact pickling varieties include 'Bush Baby' and 'Bush Pickle'. 'H-19 Little Leaf' is self-fertile and disease-resistant; 'County Fair' is bacterial wilt-resistant.

Heirloom varieties, including 'Lemon', 'Apple', and others with light skin, are easy to grow but not as productive as pickling types.

PEST WATCH: Cucumber beetles (striped or spotted) are ¼-inch-long winged beetles with black stripes or spots on their back. Adults feed on cucumber flowers, leaves, and fruit, and larvae eat the roots.

As adults feed, they may transmit an incurable disease called bacterial wilt from one plant to another. This disease causes vines to wilt and die within a week.

Protect young plants from striped and spotted cucumber beetles with row covers; then use yellow sticky traps to catch adult beetles.

Solanum melongena
so-LAY-num mel-on-GEE-na

Long and slender Oriental varieties are a good choice where the growing season is short.

EGGPLANT

- **Site:** Full sun. Well-drained, fertile soil high in compost. Moderate moisture.
- **Planting:** Start seeds 7–8 weeks before last frost. Transplant 2 weeks after frost.
- **Spacing:** 18–24 inches apart in rows 30 inches apart.
- **Care:** Stake plants with heavy fruit set. Mulch with black plastic. Needs two or more months with temperatures of 70°–80° F.
- **Harvest:** Cut fruit when full, firm, tender, and glossy. Days to harvest: 65–80 from transplanting.
- **Pests:** Colorado potato beetles, cutworms, and flea beetles.

Eggplant tolerates high heat and humidity well but will barely grow in cool climates. Where nights are consistently cooler than 65° F, plants may fail to set fruit altogether.

HOW TO GROW: Buy seedlings in late spring or start seeds early. Transplant seedlings after last frost date. The best soil is slightly acid (pH 5.6 to 6.8) and rich in organic matter. Set plants 20 inches apart. Mix well-rotted compost or manure in each hole. Cover plants with cloches or tunnels for two weeks to protect from late cold spells. Where summers are cool, grow eggplant under tunnels covered with perforated plastic or beneath a row cover. Eggplants are easy to grow in containers as well.

SELECTED VARIETIES: In northern areas, plant fast-maturing hybrids that produce small- to medium-sized fruit: 'Neon', 'Asian Bride', 'Ping Tung Long', and 'Orient Express'. For large fruit, plant 'Black Beauty'. In warm climates grow 'Black Bell'. Novelty types, including striped 'Purple Rain', 'Rosa Bianca', and 'Bambino', are perfect for pots.

Foeniculum vulgare dulce
fe-NICK-yu-lum VUL-gar-ee DULL-see

- **Site:** Full sun. Well-drained soil high in organic matter. Adaptable to broad range of soil and climatic conditions.
- **Planting:** Direct sow 2–3 weeks before average last frost. Can

Fennel often requires staking. Plant it along a fence or add supports after thinning seedlings.

FLORENCE FENNEL

continue sowing seeds through summer. Generally planted in late summer in southern regions.
- **Spacing:** ¼ inch deep, 1 inch apart in rows 2 feet apart.
- **Harvest:** Leafy stalks for flavoring soups and salads. Cut at soil level, when base of plant is about 3–4 inches in diameter.
- **Days to harvest:** 65–90.
- **Problems:** May require staking.

Also known as finocchio, this unfamiliar vegetable's main attraction is its crisp aboveground bulb (technically a swollen leaf base, which has a nutty, slightly anise-like flavor.

HOW TO GROW: Florence fennel is a cool-season vegetable that tends to bolt prematurely if planted in spring. It's best to sow in summer for harvest in mid- to late fall. In much of the southern United States, August is the best month for planting.

The garden site should have full sun and well-drained soil. Fennel tolerates dry soil if it contains plenty of organic matter and the pH is near neutral. Sow seeds 1 inch apart and ¼ inch deep. You can start plants indoors, setting them out when they develop a tuft of ferny leaves.

Thin or transplant seedlings to 8 inches apart, then mulch lightly. Hand weed—fennel doesn't shade out nearby weeds. Supplement with a liquid fertilizer after transplanting. Add more mulch to blanch bulbs, which keeps them tender.

Harvest plants as you need them by pulling them up, roots and all. Keep only the tender bulb, removing the outermost two or three stalks, which are tough and stringy.

SELECTED VARIETIES: 'Zefa Fino' bulbs are white, firm, and highly aromatic. 'Zefa Tardo' prefers cooler temperatures so is recommended for fall plantings.

Lactuca sativa
lak-TOO-ka sa-TY-va

LETTUCE

- **Site:** Full sun to part shade. Well-drained, cool, loose soil. Plentiful moisture. Adaptable to many growing conditions, but 60°–70° F temperatures are best.
- **Planting:** By seed in spring as soon as the soil can be worked. Broadcast in a patch or sow in a row. Plant every 3 weeks for succession crops.
- **Spacing:** ⅛ inch deep, 1 inch apart in rows 12 inches apart.
- **Care:** Keep soil moist and plants growing fast. Mulch. Spray every 2 or 3 weeks with a dilute liquid fertilizer.
- **Harvest:** For heading types, remove entire head at the base with a knife. For other types, remove outer leaves and let inner ones grow for continual harvest. Days to harvest: 45–85.
- **Pests and problems:** Slugs, and tips burn in hot weather.

Lettuce is a cool-season crop, but by choosing cold-hardy and heat-tolerant varieties and using special techniques, you can grow it almost year-round. Several types are available, each with different shapes and textures, including romaine (same as cos) Boston or butterhead, and loose-leaf or head lettuces.

'Buttercrunch' bibb lettuce is heat tolerant with full-flavored leaves.

A salad garden unfurls a textural and colorful masterpiece in the garden.

HOW TO GROW: Lettuce has shallow roots, so it needs soil that holds moisture. Enrich all soil types with a balanced, slow-release fertilizer and compost before planting. Lettuce grows fast, so make a succession of small plantings instead of one large sowing. Plant only 1 or 2 square feet of garden space at a time.

Start seeds indoors four weeks before last frost. Place seedlings under lights for stocky growth. After four weeks, move them to a cold frame or transplant in the garden with protection. Before the last frost date, transplant seedlings into the garden 6 inches apart. At the same time, make a small sowing of seeds spaced 1 inch apart. Lightly cover seeds with compost or other material that won't form a crust. Provide constant moisture. In two weeks, thin seedlings to 2 inches; two weeks later, thin to 4 to 6 inches.

Harvest tightly spaced young lettuce plants by cutting handfuls of leaves just above the crown. For large heads, thin plants to 8 to 12 inches apart. Pull up plants as soon

'Sangria' butterhead lettuce forms loose heads brushed with red.

as the main stem begins to lengthen and form flowers. Spring lettuce usually bolts in early summer.

In late summer, start a fall crop indoors. Begin direct-sowing cold-tolerant lettuce varieties at the same time you set out fall seedlings. Hardiest varieties will grow under plastic tunnels through winter. When days lengthen in early spring, plants will explode with new growth.

SELECTED VARIETIES: Leaf lettuce varieties include light green and crispy 'Green Ice', crinkly-leaved 'Red Sails', and early 'Black-Seeded Simpson'. For summer, plant heat-tolerant 'Salad Bowl' or 'Oakleaf' in filtered shade beneath tomatoes or corn.

Butterhead lettuces such as 'Buttercrunch', 'Bibb', and 'Four Seasons', boast crisp, buttery leaves. Hardy varieties for overwintering include 'Arctic King', 'North Pole', and 'Winter Marvel'.

Iceberg lettuce needs more cool weather than most climates offer and bolts easily. Good alternatives are Batavian- or French-crisp varieties, such as 'Sierra' or 'Nevada'.

Plant romaine, or cos, lettuce in fall: It tastes best when it matures in cool weather. Varieties such as green 'Winter Density' and bronze 'Rouge d'Hiver' are cold-hardy. Sow in early fall and grow under plastic tunnels well into winter. Other good varieties: 'Paris Island Cos', 'Little Gem', 'Rosalita', and 'Freckles'.

Cucumis melo
kew-KEW-mis MEE-lo

- Site: Full sun. Warm, well-drained soil high in organic matter. Consistent, plentiful moisture. Long growing season.
- Planting: Direct-seed 1–2 weeks after average last frost. Or start transplants in peat pots 3 weeks before you set them out.
- Spacing: 6 seeds per hill, hills 4–6 feet apart; or seeds 1 foot apart in rows 3 feet apart. Thin plants to 2–3 per hill. Closer spacings are possible if plants are trellised.
- Care: Melons grow well with plastic mulch. In hot summer areas, use organic mulch. To prevent insect damage, set developing fruits on pots or pieces of wood. Support trellised melons with a sling made from netting or fabric.
- Harvest: Generally fruit is ripe when the stem separates from fruit with only slight pressure; color may deepen and yellow; blossom end may soften; noticeable sweet aroma.
- Days to harvest: 70 to100 days after transplanting.
- Pests: Cucumber beetles, mildew, and wilt.

Honeydew melons boast Mediterranean roots. The yellow-green fruits require a long season to ripen.

MELONS

Many types of melons are well suited to home gardens.

- **True cantaloupes** (French or Charentais melons) have a warty, ribbed rind and sweet, orange flesh. The cantaloupe you buy at the store is actually a muskmelon.
- **Muskmelons** have netted, yellowish rinds and orange flesh.
- **Mediterranean melons** come in a variety of forms and flavors. Casaba melons have a wrinkled, golden rind and white flesh. Honeydews have a smooth rind and green flesh. Crenshaws have a yellow rind and green to pink flesh. Galias have skin like a muskmelon and green, banana-scented flesh.
- **Spanish melons** have sweet, white flesh, a yellow rind, and can be kept for one month in the refrigerator without spoiling.

Whatever melon you grow, they all have the same needs. They are warm-season plants closely related to cucumbers. Their vines run along the ground, and flowers must be pollinated by insects to form fruit.

Depending on the variety of the melon and the health of the plant, you can expect to harvest from three to five melons from each plant.

HOW TO GROW: Because melons produce male and female flowers that require cross-pollination, grow at least five plants of any variety to be sure that there is enough pollen for bees and other insects to spread among the blossoms.

The plants require a site with full sun and well-drained soil that is high in organic matter. They grow best in hot weather and need plenty of water while vines are running.

Vines usually grow at least 10 feet long, and every leaf needs full exposure to sunshine. In rows, space plants 3 feet apart. You also can grow melons in hills spaced 5 feet apart, two to three plants in each hill. Either way, you will need a space 15 feet wide and 20 feet long for six plants.

Muskmelons are what most folks know as orange-fleshed canteloupes, courtesy of the grocery store.

Sow seeds directly when the soil temperature is at least 70° F. Or start seeds indoors in 3- or 4-inch peat pots and set out seedlings one week after the average date of your area's last frost.

Weeds can be a problem because you can't always get to them among the vines. Covering the soil between rows with black plastic or newer IRT (infrared transmitting) dark green plastic at planting time is an excellent weed-prevention strategy. Plastic mulch also heats up the soil and retains soil moisture.

Several insects, including spotted and striped cucumber beetles, can cripple unprotected melon plants. The simplest way to prevent insect injury is to cover seedlings with a floating row cover as soon as they are planted. Make sure the cover fits loosely and leave some fabric to accommodate growing vines. Instead of burying all the edges, keep one side secured with boards so you can easily lift the cover to check on plants and let in pollinators.

If plants grow slowly or their leaves turn yellow, fertilize them with a balanced fertilizer soon after the vines begin to run.

The first flowers that appear will probably be males, which cannot set fruit. A mix of male and female flowers usually opens about one week later. When this occurs, remove the row covers for two or three days to allow pollinating insects access to the flowers. Before putting the row cover back on, thoroughly spray the plants with water to get any insects moving. As insects scramble to escape the shower, handpick squash bugs and cucumber beetles that crawl to the top of the leaves. As further insurance against insect damage, treat plants with an appropriate insecticide before putting the row covers back in place.

Melons especially need water (1 inch per week) while they are vining, yet the flavor of the fruit is best when you let the soil become somewhat dry as the melons reach full size and ripen. Slight wilting of the leaves is normal in the middle of a hot summer day, but don't let the soil become so dry that the leaves remain wilted into evening.

HARVEST: Use your senses to tell when melons are fully ripe. First examine them with your eyes. Many muskmelons develop a textured surface on the outside of the melon, called netting, which turns buff brown as the fruit ripens. Honeydews with smooth rinds change colors too, from creamy green to ivory-yellow.

Next, touch the point where the stem joins the fruit. Many melons begin to separate from the stem as they ripen, evidenced by small cracks at the stem end of the fruit. Gently pushing on the stem will cause the fruit to "slip," or break, free. Sometimes the leaf closest to the melon also turns yellow as the fruit fully ripens.

Then smell your muskmelons; you can usually detect a distinct fruity aroma at the blossom end of a ripe fruit.

Stored at room temperature, melons will keep up to two weeks after harvest.

SELECTED VARIETIES: Among muskmelons, both the 'Earligold', 'Sweet & Early', and the 'Earliqueen' varieties mature quickly and produce 3- to 4-pound fruit on disease-resistant vines. 'Ambrosia' and 'Pulsar' mature two weeks later and bear large melons.

Charentais melons produce small, 2-pound fruit with spicy yet sweet orange flesh. Two excellent varieties that mature in about 80 days are 'Alienor' and 'Savor'. They do not slip from the vine when ripe, so check the leaves closest to the melon instead. 'French Orange' is a cross between a Charentais and a muskmelon. Plants have good disease resistance and fruits possess a wonderfully rich fragrance.

A good Galia variety is 'Passport' with its large tropical-looking fruit and mint green flesh. 'Earlidew' and 'Honey Orange' are good honeydew hybrids that form 2- to 3-pound melons. 'Sweet Barcelona' is an excellent Spanish melon.

PEST WATCH: Cucumber beetles (see page 41) feed on melon leaves, blossoms, and fruit. However, they do the worst damage by infecting plants with a disease called bacterial wilt. Infected plants gradually wilt and die over a period of one to two weeks, and there is no way to restore their health. Protect plants under floating row covers. Alternatively, place yellow sticky traps among your vines to snare the beetles. Once you start finding beetles in the traps, treat plants weekly with an insecticide labeled for use on cucumber-family crops.

Crenshaw melons, such as 'Burpee's Early Hybrid', are medium to large fruit with green to orange flesh.

Place ripening melons on reflectors to concentrate heat and to hasten fruit maturation.

Abelmoschus esculentus
a-bel-MOS-kus es-kew-LEN-tus

Okra flowers are showy, and the dried pods are prized by crafters. Pods of 'Burgundy' (above) are dark purple.

OKRA

- **Site:** Full sun. Well-drained, dry, slightly alkaline, warm soil.
- **Planting:** Direct-seed after danger of frost has passed. In southern regions, make successive sowings late April through mid-August.
- **Spacing:** ½ inch deep, 3 inches apart in rows 24 inches apart. Thin to 15–18 inches.
- **Harvest:** Pick pods when 4 inches long. Days to harvest: 50–60.

Okra thrives in warm weather. A single early-summer sowing yields tender pods nonstop until frost. **HOW TO GROW:** Soak seeds in warm water overnight before planting. In late spring, start indoors in 2-inch pots. Keep containers warm. Thin to one seedling per pot.

Plants do best in a somewhat dry soil. Before planting, raise soil temperature by mulching it with black plastic. After the last frost, transplant seedlings into holes cut in the plastic, 12 inches apart. Don't disturb plant roots.

In warm climates, direct-sow okra in early summer, 3 inches apart and ½ inch deep. When seedlings are 6 inches tall, thin to 15 to 18 inches apart. Okra's large leaves shade soil and discourage weeds, so mulching is unnecessary. Overfertilization yields huge leaves and few pods.

Harvest tender pods before they reach 5 inches long. Many people develop a contact dermatitis from touching the prickly hairs on plants and pods, so wear gloves and a long-sleeved shirt as a precaution. **SELECTED VARIETIES:** For small spaces and cool summers, grow early dwarf varieties such as 'Annie Oakley II' or 'Baby Bubba'. 'Cajun Delight' is a widely adapted, productive variety. Red-podded 'Burgundy' is an edible ornamental. If your skin is sensitive to the hairs, plant hairless 'Clemson Spineless'.

Allium species
AL-lee-um

Onions

- **Site:** Full sun. Well-drained soil high in organic matter, neutral pH. Consistent moisture.
- **Planting:** By seed, transplants, or sets. Sow seed indoors 6–8 weeks before setting out. Transplant seedlings, plant sets,

ONIONS, LEEKS, AND GARLIC

or direct-sow seed 3–4 weeks before average last frost in north or in the fall in south.
- **Spacing:** Transplants: 1 inch deep, 3 inches apart; sets: 2½ inches deep, 1 inch apart; direct-sown seed: ¼ inch deep, ½ inch apart. Thin to 4 inches, 15 inches between rows.
- **Care:** Control weeds.

- **Harvest:** Scallions: about 8 weeks after planting or when 12 inches tall; bulbs: when tops begin to fall over. Cure by drying in a warm, dry area.
- **Storage:** Trim leaves so that 1 inch remains above bulb when outer skins feel papery and dry. Store at around 40° F. Days to harvest varies.
- **Pests:** Thrips, onion maggots, and soil-borne diseases. Move all onions to a new site each year to avoid problems.

Most members of the onion family grow in any garden. Perpetual onions—chives, shallots, and bunching onions (also called green onions or scallions)—can be grown from year to year by planting divisions in fall or spring. **BULB ONIONS:** Onions are heavy feeders requiring well-fertilized and well-drained soil. Raise from seeds, plants, or small bulbs (sets). Seeds

An easy way to cure onion and garlic bulbs is to place the crop on chicken wire tacked to a wooden frame.

ONIONS, LEEKS, AND GARLIC (continued)

Leeks are ready to harvest when the stem base, called a shank, is an inch around.

need 6 to 8 weeks to reach transplant size. A month after planting, harvest every other plant for eating.

Weed often and use a light mulch. Feed monthly with a balanced water-soluble fertilizer. Clip flower stalks to preserve bulb size and quality.

When bulbs swell, tops of plants begin to yellow, and 80 percent naturally fall over, harvest them. Cure bulbs in a warm, dry place for one week before moving them to cooler storage.

SELECTED VARIETIES: In the south, choose short day varieties, such as 'Yellow Granex', 'Vidalia', and 'Texas Grano'. Northern gardeners grow long-day varieties. 'Walla Walla' and other sweet Spanish types have mild flavor. Stronger-tasting 'Copra' and 'Buffalo' store well. Day-neutral types ('Candy' and 'Super Star') grow in the north or south. 'Stockton Red' and 'Red Burgermaster' are widely adapted red onions.

SHALLOTS: Shallots split into a cluster of 3 to 10 tiny, teardrop-shape-onions. Save the largest ones for replanting. In the south, plant in fall; in the north, in early spring. Harvest when tops die back. Store in a cool, dry place until replanting.

BUNCHING ONIONS AND CHIVES: Set out seeds or plants in spring in any sunny, well-drained spot. Clip leaves from chives as needed, but don't harvest bunching onions until

fall. Both types often go dormant in summer, then new tops grow as weather cools. When properly handled, bunching scallions such as 'Red Baron', 'Evergreen Long White' or 'Evergreen Hardy White', produce almost all year.

Propagate chives and scallions in fall by digging and replanting sections in new sites. Both can grow indoors in pots through the winter.

Leeks

- **Site:** Same as for onions.
- **Planting:** Sow seed indoors 8 weeks before average last frost date. Transplant around the last frost date. Or direct-seed 4 weeks before last frost.
- **Spacing:** 4 inches deep, 6 inches apart in rows 20 inches apart. Direct-seed ½ inch deep, 1 inch apart, rows 20 inches apart. Thin to 6 inches.
- **Care:** To blanch, mound soil around stems as leeks grow. Plants respond well to mulching.
- **Harvest:** Pull when stem base is about an inch in diameter.
- **Days to harvest:** 70–120.

Leeks thrive in cool weather; grow from fall through spring in mild-winter areas. Mulch leeks with organic material to keep roots cool and constantly moist. Apply a balanced fertilizer monthly. Begin harvesting leeks when shanks grow more than an inch thick. Plant the fast-growing 'King Richard' and the cold-tolerant 'Laura' and 'Blue Solaise'.

Garlic

- **Site:** Full sun. Well-drained, fertile soil. Slightly dry.
- **Planting:** By individual cloves split from a bulb. Leave papery husk on and set cloves with tips up. Plant from October to early November in the north, November to January in the

south. Northerners may succeed with an early-spring planting.
- **Spacing:** 2 inches deep, 6 inches apart; elephant garlic requires slightly wider spacing.
- **Care:** Mulch. Remove woody flower stalks as they appear.
- **Harvest:** In summer when at least half of the leaves have begun to yellow and the "necks" are still soft. Cure bulbs by drying in a warm, well-ventilated spot for several days.
- **Storage:** Cut off tops after curing. Store in a cool, dry place. Softneck types keep for 6–8 months.
- **Problems:** Bulbs may rot in heavy, wet soils.

There are three types of garlic: hardneck, softneck, and elephant. Hardnecks are the most cold hardy (dependable in Zones 3 and 4). Garlic sold in stores is usually softneck, which keeps the longest and is hardy to Zone 4 (but some survive only to Zone 7). Elephant garlic is the least cold hardy; plant it first thing in spring in cold areas.

HOW TO GROW: The best time to plant garlic is in fall. In cold areas, mulch heavily after the ground freezes to limit soil heaving. When top growth appears in spring, plants need at least an inch of water per week.

SELECTED VARIETIES: For softnecks, consider 'California Early' and 'Silverskin'. 'Russian Red', 'Persian Star', and 'German Red' are good hardneck varieties.

Store softneck garlic in braids.

Petroselinum crispum
pet-ro-se-LY-num KRISS-pum

Use curly-leaf parsley to add a pretty textural and tasty element to the late-summer vegetable garden.

PARSLEY

- **Site:** Full sun to part shade. Well-drained, highly organic soil. Plentiful moisture. Cool weather.
- **Planting:** Sow seed indoors 10 weeks before average last frost. Transplant about the average last frost date. Direct-seed in fall. Parsley is a biennial. If allowed to flower, it may reseed.
- **Spacing:** 6 inches apart.
- **Harvest:** Leaves as needed.
- **Pests and problems:** Attracts parsley worm, the larvae of the swallowtail butterfly. Seed germinates slowly; soak for several hours before planting.

Parsley is hardy, flavorful, and makes a great ornamental plant.

HOW TO GROW: For a steady supply of leaves, sow seeds in spring and fall. Seed often takes three weeks to sprout, germinating best in soil that's 50° to 70° F. Sow seed ½ inch deep and ½ inch apart. When seedlings develop their first true leaves, thin to 10 inches apart. Set out container-grown seedlings without disturbing roots. When plants grow to 2 inches, mulch to keep soil cool and moist.

Pinch parsley stems as you need them. Healthy plants survive winter in mild winter climates, even though the tops die to the ground. In spring, the year-old plants produce a fresh crop of leaves, then send up a yellow flower cluster, signaling the end of the planting. Swallowtail butterflies often lay eggs on parsley, so it's favored for butterfly gardens.

SELECTED VARIETIES: Curly parsley grows less than 12 inches tall, has a mild flavor, and must be mulched to keep soil from gathering in leaf crevices. Flat-leaf or Italian parsley has a stronger flavor and grows to 18 inches. Hamburg or parsnip-rooted parsley bears flat-leaf flavored leaves and long, white edible roots. Sow in spring and harvest roots in fall.

Arachis hypogaea
A-ra-kis hy-po-JEE-a

When mature, peanuts have stiff shells and reddish-brown seed coats. Always buy named varieties from a nursery.

PEANUTS

- **Site:** Full sun. Deep, well-drained, light-textured soil, high in organic matter. Long, warm growing season. Consistent moisture until seed set.
- **Planting:** Direct-sow raw, shelled seed; in the north, start transplants indoors 4 weeks before average last frost. Set out plants 1 week after last frost.
- **Spacing:** 1 inch deep, 6 inches apart in rows 24 inches apart.
- **Care:** Mulch lightly. Do not use high-nitrogen fertilizers.
- **Harvest:** Harvest plants in fall. Dry pods in warm, ventilated place for several days; remove seeds and store. Lightly roast in a 325° F oven. Days to harvest: 110–150.
- **Storage:** Throw out moldy seeds.
- **Pests and problems:** Bothered by animals; may rot or become hollow in heavy, wet soils.

Tropical in temperament, peanuts crave warmth. Given 120 toasty days, a single plant can yield more than 50 peanuts.

HOW TO GROW: Lightly mix a balanced fertilizer into soil before planting. Peanuts are legumes, so are able to utilize atmospheric nitrogen. When planting, keep the reddish seed coat intact as a disease barrier.

Space plants in single rows at least 24 inches wide. Thin to 15 inches a month after planting. Hoe to keep soil hilled up in an 18-inch-wide circle around each plant.

In summer, short stems emerge from the plants' centers, each topped with a yellow flower. These stems form pegs that gradually bend and "plant" themselves to form a peanut.

SELECTED VARIETIES: Spanish-type 'Valencia' bears slender pods of small nuts. 'Virginia Jumbo' yields one or two large nuts per pod.

Pisum sativum, Vigna unguiculata
PY-sum sa-TY-vum,
VIG-na un-gwi-kew-LA-ta

Spring peas

- Site: Full sun to part shade. Well-drained soil of average fertility. Cool, damp.
- Planting: North: Sow seed in spring as soon as soil can be worked. Plant for a second crop in early fall. South: Plant in fall and late winter.
- Spacing: 2 inches deep, 2 inches apart in rows 10 inches apart.
- Care: Avoid high-nitrogen fertilizers. Trellis tall, vining types. Keep soil moist.
- Harvest: English peas: when pods fill out; snap and snow peas: when peas are full, yet tender; dry peas: let them dry on the plant. Harvest the whole plant, allow to dry, then remove peas from pods.
- Days to harvest: 55–75.
- Pests and problems: Heavy watering or rain during flowering can interfere with pollination. Bothered by rabbits and aphids.

Treasures of the spring garden, shell (English), snow, and snap peas collectively make up the group known as garden peas. These are cool-season crops.

HOW TO GROW SPRING PEAS:

Young garden peas are cold-hardy and not damaged by heavy frost. Sow them as soon as the soil can be worked—up to a month before your area's last frost date. An early start is important because peas must flower and set fruit before temperatures reach 80° F.

To stretch the harvest season, plant on the same day two or three varieties that mature at different times. Where night temperatures cool to 50° to 60° F in August, you can plant peas in July for fall harvest. Increase your success in fall by growing dwarf types that mature

SPRING AND FIELD PEAS

quickly or snow pea varieties that don't need to fill out to be edible.

Grow peas in rich, moist, well-drained soil where they have not been planted for at least two years. Pea roots host a persistent soil-borne fungus that builds up quickly and causes root rot.

Before planting, lightly fertilize and install a trellis down the middle of the row to help support the vines. Tall varieties grow best on a 5-foot trellis made of chicken wire, string, or polyester netting. You can support compact varieties by pushing twiggy branches into the soil down the center of the row.

To save space, plant peas in double rows 10 inches apart. Sow seeds 2 inches apart. Thin seedlings to 4 inches apart when they are 2 inches tall.

When planting peas in new garden soil or in poor soil, treat the seeds with an inoculant powder (purchase at garden centers) that places the rhizobia bacteria that help peas fix nitrogen right next to their roots. Put a tablespoon of inoculant in a jar with soaked or dampened pea seeds. Shake the jar gently to coat seeds with the powder.

Harvest shell peas when pods are still glossy and the peas inside taste sweet and tender. Pick snow peas when the peas just begin to swell into small lumps. Snap peas taste best when pods are plump and the peas inside are young and tender.

SELECTED VARIETIES: Modern
varieties of English peas, such as 'Maestro', are resistant to enation pea virus and powdery mildew, serious problems in the northwest and areas of the upper midwest. Where the virus is not a threat, try older varieties famous for their rich flavor, including 'Green Arrow' and 'Alderman'. The lastest English pea varieties with unique traits include the 2-foot-tall 'Little Marvel', the leafless 'Novella', and the baby pea 'Petit Pois'.

When planting peas in a new garden, coat seeds with rhizobium bacteria.

Traditional English peas thrive in cool weather, yielding plentiful harvests.

You can eat the pods and the seeds of snow peas and snap peas. Among snow peas, 'Oregon Giant' and 'Oregon Sugar Pod II' are disease-resistant with large pods that are sweet and crisp. Snap peas are tremendously productive. 'Super Sugar Snap' grows to 5 feet tall. Dwarf varieties such as 'Sugar Ann', 'Sugarsprint', and 'Sugar Star' need only a short trellis. 'Alaska' and other starchy peas are best for drying.

'Super Sugar Mel' snap pea bears pods that are deliciously sweet.

Field peas

- Site: Same as asparagus bean on page 31. Preferred in the south over lima and snap beans because of their resistance to heat and insects.
- Spacing: Sow seeds 1–2 inches deep, 1 inch apart, 2–3 feet between rows. Thin plants to 6–12 inches within a row.
- Harvest: Pick pods as you would green shell beans, or leave them on the plant as dry peas. Days to harvest: 55–75.
- Problems: Susceptible to cold weather; typically grown in the southern states.

Where the growing season offers at least three months of warm 80° F days, semitropical field peas thrive.

HOW TO GROW FIELD PEAS: They go by many names, including black- or pink-eyed peas, crowders, and cream peas. Names refer to a specific type of pea, but collectively, the group is also known as field peas, cowpeas, or southern peas.

Field peas are hot-weather crops so need plenty of heat and humidity. Plant seeds from early to midsummer 4 inches apart. Thin seedlings to 10 inches apart when they are 3 inches tall. Field peas benefit from regular watering during hot, dry weather. For fresh eating, harvest when the texture of the pods changes from firm to slightly leathery.

SELECTED VARIETIES: Shop at local feed-and-seed stores. In most areas, pink-eyed varieties such as 'Pinkeye Purplehull' are most productive. Crowder peas are strong nitrogen fixers, ideal for poor soil. Some varieties, such as 'Dixielee', develop small peas—called lady peas or cream peas. These are good to eat but tedious to shell.

Spring peas require a trellis to support vines, which climb by way of tendrils.

Grow snow peas that are resistant to enation and mildew, such as 'Oregon Giant', which yields large pods.

Cowpeas or field peas, thrive in the sultry growing conditions of the south.

Let field pea pods ripen on the plant to harvest peas for shelling.

Capsicum annuum
KAP-si-kum AN-u-um

- **Site:** Full sun. Well-drained, light, fertile soil high in organic matter. Warm.
- **Planting:** By transplants. Sow seed indoors, ¼ inch deep, 7–8 weeks before setting out. Keep flats or peat pots indoors in a warm, sunny location. Transplant after average last frost.
- **Spacing:** 18–24 inches apart in rows 24 inches apart.
- **Care:** Mulch with plastic. Two to three light sprays of seaweed or fish emulsion can be beneficial when plants are young. High-nitrogen fertilizers promote vegetative growth instead of fruit production.
- **Harvest:** Remove fruit by cutting when full-sized and either fully colored or still green. Green peppers will turn red (or other colors) as they mature. Use rubber gloves when preparing hot varieties. Days to harvest: 60–75 from transplanting.
- **Pests and problems:** Temperamental fruit set if temperatures are too hot or cold. Pests include tarnished plant bug, aphids, and pepper maggots. Blossom end rot is partly caused by uneven moisture supply, so mulching helps alleviate the problem.

Growing peppers can be a hobby in itself. Given exacting care, the plants produce generously. Peppers are tropical perennials that grow best when temperatures range between 60° and 80° F. Where summers are short, set out transplants as soon as possible in early spring and cover them with plastic cloches or tunnels.

Where summers are hot, peppers often remain barren through summer, then produce dozens of fruit when nights cool in early fall. These won't fully ripen but provide plenty of sweet green peppers.

PEPPERS

HOW TO GROW: To start seedlings, sow seed 7 to 8 weeks before the last frost. Seeds germinate best at 80° to 85° F. Pepper seedlings need intense light, continuous warmth, and room to grow unrestricted roots. Transplant seedlings to 4-inch pots when they have four leaves. Keep plants under lights or in a warm cold frame until days hit 70° F and nights stay above 55° F. Harden off seedlings for a week before transplanting.

SITE: Any sunny, well-drained spot rich with organic matter. Peppers benefit from two or three hours of afternoon shade in hot climates. Dig planting holes 12 inches deep and wide, enriching each with compost.

TRANSPLANTING: Set out seedlings on a warm, cloudy day, 18 inches apart. Protect transplants with a plastic cloche or row cover. In cool climates, use plastic tunnels and/or black plastic mulch to help soil stay warm. Keep soil moist at all times.

FRUIT SET: Peppers develop fruit best when nighttime temperatures are between 60° and 75° F and daytime temperatures are below 80° F. In hot climates, large bell peppers set fruit better if temporarily shaded in midsummer. The simplest method is to cover plants with a shade cloth attached to stakes. Make sure air circulates under the cloth.

HARVEST: You can harvest peppers when they're green, but they become much sweeter when fully matured to their ripe color, which may be red, yellow, or orange. Brittle stems break easily, so cut off fruit with a sharp knife or pruning shears.

The pungency of hot peppers correlates strongly with variety, and warm weather maximizes their sting. The same hot pepper that matures in cool conditions won't sizzle as much as one that ripens in hot weather. For best flavor, harvest hot peppers when they change color or when seeds inside are fully formed.

The mature color of peppers proffers the sweetest flavor. For 'Gypsy', that means leaving yellow fruit on plants until they blush fiery red.

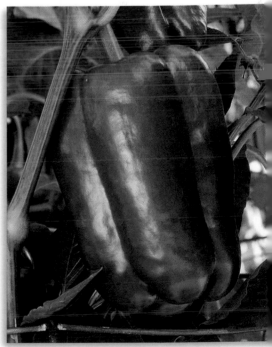

The secret to lush pepper crops is hidden below ground: Give plants ample moisture and rich soil.

PEPPERS *(continued)*

SELECTED VARIETIES: Sweet peppers include the typical blocky bell peppers and numerous varieties with fruits shaped like spinning tops, cones, and bananas. 'Ace' and 'Northstar' have earned a reputation for producing their ripe red fruit in cool northern climates.

Large bell peppers such as 'Big Bertha' grow best in areas where late summers are warm. Small-fruited banana peppers such as 'Sweet Banana' and hybrid Caribbean types such as 'Gypsy' bear reliably in a wide range of climates.

The pungency of hot peppers is rated in terms of Scoville Units (S.U.'s). Mild varieties with S.U. ratings of less than 3,000 include 'Garden Salsa' and 'Salsa Delight'.

For roasting and stuffing, grow large poblanos, anaheims, or 'NuMex' chiles, such as 'Big Chili' and 'NuMex Joe E. Parker', with modest ratings of 1,000 to 1,500 S.U. These peppers usually mature in less than 80 days from transplanting, but they don't produce well where nights are too cool or too warm.

Pick a peck of hot peppers, and you'll discover that the multihued skins bear sizzle that can leave you speechless.

Jalapeños are easy to grow in many climates and are available in both hot and mild forms. 'Senorita' has a low heat rating, while other varieties range to 10,000 S.U. Slightly hotter serrano peppers have a unique flavor that many associate with spicy Mexican food. Cayennes, habañeros, and most Thai peppers are extremely hot and should be handled with care. Some varieties, such as 'Caribbean Red', 'Super Cayenne II', and 'Thai Dragon', should be used sparingly in cooking unless you like ultra-hot foods. Their S.U. ratings start at 50,000 and can exceed 100,000. When cutting hot peppers, wear rubber gloves and keep your hands away from your face and eyes.

Peppers can be used as ornamental edibles as well. Many varieties, such as 'Pretty in Purple' and 'Riot', not only feature delicious hot fruits but also have colorful foliage and fruits. Plant these peppers in the flower, herb, or vegetable garden or in containers.

One of the best ways to sample hot peppers is to purchase a mix of varieties at a farmer's market. Next year grow the ones that suit your fancy.

'Banana Supreme' sweet peppers ripen from yellow to red in September. Fruits picked earlier offer a sharper flavor.

Solanum tuberosum
so-LAY-num too-ber-ROW-sum

POTATOES

Mulch helps keep soil consistently moist, which produces larger potatoes.

- **Site:** Full sun. Well-drained soil high in organic matter with pH 4.8–5.8. Plentiful moisture. Cool climates best (65°–70° F), but adaptable to heat.
- **Planting:** Cut seed potatoes into pieces, each containing two eyes. Dry pieces for up to 2 weeks. Plant in shallow, 4-inch-deep trenches with eyes facing up. Plant in fall or winter in southern regions, as soon as soil can be worked in cool climates, and late April to mid-May in northern areas.
- **Spacing:** 10–12 inches apart in rows 2 feet apart.
- **Care:** As stems grow, mound soil loosely around their bases. Repeat several times throughout the growing season. Mulch with straw or hay.
- **Harvest:** About 6–8 weeks after planting for new potatoes. Do not disturb plants, dig gently along the sides, then replace soil. To harvest mature potatoes, wait until tops die down. Gently remove soil, harvesting tubers by hand. Dry, then brush off soil.
- **Storage:** In a cool place. Do not expose tubers to sunlight. Discard any green potatoes; cut out green patches before eating.
- **Pests:** Colorado potato beetle and late blight.

Freshly harvested potatoes have a unique texture found only in the homegrown version. They are easy to grow, and each plant should produce at least five spuds. If your garden space is limited, you can grow potatoes aboveground in large boxes or bins.

HOW TO GROW: Potatoes are a cool-season crop best planted in early spring, about three weeks before the last frost. In the south, you can also plant them in fall or winter.

Seed potatoes are available at local nurseries, but mail-order companies provide a wider selection. These have been inspected and certified to be free of pests and diseases. Don't try growing grocery store potatoes because these have been treated with a sprouting inhibitor that slows growth.

Before planting seed potatoes, place them in a sunny spot for one to three days. Warmth makes them break dormancy and start sprouting, and light causes solanine, a chemical compound with a green pigment, to develop just under the skin. While poisonous to humans, solanine protects the plants from insects.

Cultivate a 30-inch-wide double row of light-textured, well drained soil for planting. Potatoes are more productive when grown in double rows because neighboring plants shade and cool the soil. Planting corn or another tall crop to provide afternoon shade may improve yields in warm climates.

Plant seed potatoes whole if they are less than 2 inches in diameter. Cut larger ones into chunks so that each piece has at least two sprouting eyes. Plant the pieces 4 inches deep and 10 to 12 inches apart. Potatoes can tolerate a mild frost, but if an unseasonably hard frost threatens young plants, cover them at night with a blanket or row cover.

Potatoes do not need rich fertilizer. Keep the pH acidic and never add fresh manure to the bed, because these two things can contribute to problems with potato scab. Keeping pH between 4.8 and 5.8 helps prevent scab disease.

Mound soil around the newly emerging plants and again two to three weeks later. Mulch plants with organic material such as hay or straw. Add more mulch as needed to maintain a depth of at least 3 inches. Hilling and mulching keeps the soil moist, allowing for more and bigger potatoes to be produced.

Dust cut sections of seed potatoes with sulfur to reduce scab disease.

POTATOES *(continued)*

HARVEST: To harvest, loosen soil with a digging fork, then pull up the plants once they have died back. It's easiest to dig potatoes in dry soil. Always harvest potatoes on a cloudy day and protect tubers from exposure to light to prevent solanine production. You can leave potatoes in the ground for a few weeks after tops die, but if weather is wet the tubers may rot.

STORAGE: Don't wash potatoes after picking. Brush soil from tubers and cure by placing in a humid 65° to 70° F spot for about 2 weeks. Then store potatoes in a cool, dry place. An unheated cellar is ideal, or you can keep them in a cooler sunk into the ground. Pile mulch on top for insulation. To preserve potatoes that have begun to sprout, blanch and freeze them.

SELECTED VARIETIES: Where the summer is short, grow fast-maturing varieties that mature in 60 to 70 days, such as 'Red Norland' (red skin, white flesh), 'Caribe' (purple skin, white flesh), 'Superior' (tan skin, white flesh, and scab resistant), and 'Yukon Gold' (tan skin, yellow flesh).

In warmer areas, plant both early and midseason potatoes. The midseason group includes a wide selection of colors and types, such as oblong 'Desiree' (red skin, yellow flesh), round 'Red Gold' (red skin, yellow flesh), 'Norgold Russett' (brown skin, white flesh), and 'All Red' (red skin and flesh).

Late-maturing types, such as 'Kennebec' (brown skin, white flesh), 'Butte' (brown skin, white flesh, high in vitamins), and 'All Blue' (blue skin and flesh), develop best in northern gardens, where 50° to 60° F nights prevail all summer.

Small fingerling potatoes are worth a try in any climate. Most are late-maturing, but they produce so many small tubers that you will get a good crop even where the season is short. 'Rose Finn Apple' is a disease-resistant fingerling that stores well.

PEST WATCH: COLORADO POTATO BEETLE: Mustard-yellow with black stripes, adult Colorado potato beetles are ½ inch long. They lay clusters of bright orange eggs on the undersides of potato leaves. From these eggs hatch brick-red, soft-bodied larvae, sometimes called potato bugs, which have an insatiable appetite for potato and eggplant leaves.

Handpick larvae and adults if there are only a few; check plants—especially the undersides of leaves—every few days for new infestations. If the problem is severe, treat with the 'San Diego' strain of *Bacillus thuringiensis* (Bt), or use a neem-based insecticide. Floating row covers also protect plants from the beetle.

A homegrown potato harvest can boast a palette of tubers that paint flavorful, colorful mealtimes. Tubers shown in box are (clockwise from lower left): yellow 'Katahdin', red 'Huckleberry', purple 'Caribe', and dark 'All Blue'.

RADISHES

Raphanus sativus
RAF-an-us sa-TY-vus

- **Site: Full sun to part shade. Well-drained, loose soil high in organic matter. Plentiful, steady moisture. Cool weather.**
- **Planting: Direct-sow seed 3 weeks before average last frost. Plant every 2 weeks until summer for continuous harvest.**
- **Spacing: ½ inch deep, 1 inch apart in rows 12 inches apart. Thin to 2 inches apart.**
- **Harvest: Pull root once size is appropriate for the variety. Heat intensifies pungency.**
- **Pests and problems: Cabbage root maggots and flea beetles.**

The fastest growing of all vegetables, radishes are often ready to harvest a month after sowing.
HOW TO GROW: Radishes require cool weather and constant moisture. Hot weather increases their peppery flavor and makes them woody.

To plant, use one of these three strategies. Make a series of 1-square-foot plantings every 2 weeks, beginning before the last frost and continuing until days reach 80° F. Or use radishes to mark rows between lettuce, onions, and other spring vegetables. As the larger plants gain size, harvest the radishes. Or blend radish seeds with carrots or beets in a wide row. The radishes' speedy germination loosens soil for the slow-growing carrots and beets. As radishes mature, pull them to give root crops room to grow. In most regions, you can sow radishes six weeks before the first fall frost.

Keep soil moist while radishes are growing. Radishes stay in perfect condition only a few days, then turn woody.
SELECTED VARIETIES: Red, round salad radishes include 'Cherry Belle', 'Cherry Bomb II', and 'Cherriette'.

French radishes, such as 'French Breakfast' and 'D'Avignon', form 4-inch-long cylinders with white tips and red shoulders.

Oriental Daikon radishes form carrot-shape roots that can weigh several pounds. Grow in fall; they bolt when spring-grown.

Raise traditional round radishes (above) or carrotlike Daikon types (top).

RHUBARB

Rheum ×cultorum
REE-um kul-TOR-um

- **Site: Full sun to part shade. Well-drained, fertile soil with high organic matter. Consistent moisture. This is a long-lived perennial crop; give thought to its location.**
- **Planting: By dormant crowns in spring.**
- **Spacing: 2 inches deep, 3 feet apart.**
- **Care: Mulch. Remove flower stalks as they appear.**
- **Harvest: Don't harvest the year after planting. Harvest only several stalks the second year after planting.**
- **Storage: Refrigerate stalks for up to 2 weeks.**
- **Pests: Rhubarb curculios.**

Rhubarb is a perennial that grows best where the ground freezes in winter. The thick stalk is edible, but leaves are not.

HOW TO GROW: Dig holes 15 inches deep and 24 inches wide; add 2 gallons of compost per hole. In porous sandy soil, add a balanced organic or slow-release fertilizer.

Set roots so the central bud is a scant 2 inches below the soil surface. Cover and water well. In early summer, mulch with organic material. Where summers are hot, add mulch as needed to keep it at least 2 inches deep.

Harvest for two weeks the second year, but for 8 to 10 weeks in subsequent years. Never remove more than ⅓ to ½ of the stalks at any time so that the plant can rebuild food reserves. Cut off flower stalks to help the plant form stems. Fertilize plants every spring with compost. Rhubarb plants may become crowded. If stems become thin, dig and divide plants in spring or fall. Cut the roots into pieces at least 2 inches across; don't injure buds on the tops of the pieces. Immediately replant the best chunks.
SELECTED VARIETIES: The best strains are propagated by division rather than from seed. For red stems, try 'Valentine' and 'Crimson Red'.

Don't harvest leaf stalks from young rhubarb the first year after planting.

Root crops are the convenience food of the garden because they can be left in the ground for several weeks—or even months—until needed. Where the ground freezes hard in winter, dig most roots in late fall and store them in a cool cellar or unheated basement.

Jerusalem artichoke

- **Site:** Full sun. Well-drained soil. Tolerates a wide range of sites and soils.
- **Planting:** Cut large tubers into pieces, or plant individual tubers in spring 2 weeks before average last frost.
- **Spacing:** 3 inches deep, 18 inches apart.
- **Care:** Remove yellow flowers the first year to give strength to plant. Keep moist in dry periods.
- **Harvest:** Dig tubers after leaves die back in the fall, leaving some for the next season.
- **Pests:** Unless all tubers are harvested, the plant can become a pest itself, spreading invasively. Just mow over any shoots that pop up.

Native Americans prized Jerusalem artichokes for their tuberous, nutty-flavored roots.

ROOT CROPS

Also known as sunchoke, Jerusalem artichoke (*Helianthus tuberosus*) is a perennial sunflower with sweet, nutty tubers. The tubers look like knobby potatoes and can be eaten raw or cooked.

This indigenous vegetable thrives in any type of soil. Plant it in spring in a corner of the garden where the 6- to 8-foot-tall plants will not shade other crops.

Small yellow sunflowers appear in late summer. You can harvest roots anytime after the soil cools, but a few hard freezes improves the flavor.

Store a few starter roots for the next season in a 12-inch-deep hole dug in the ground and harvest the rest as needed all winter. In midspring, check the area where you grew this crop the year before and dig out unwanted plants. If allowed to naturalize, Jerusalem artichokes may become invasive.

Parsnip

- **Site:** Full sun to part shade. Moist, well-drained, fertile soil.
- **Planting:** Direct-seed 2–3 weeks before average last frost.
- **Spacing:** ½ inch deep, 1 inch apart in rows 18 inches apart. Thin to 6 to 8 inches apart.
- **Care:** Cut thinnings so as not to disturb nearby roots. Mulch.
- **Harvest:** After frost, dig roots all at once or mulch plants and pull as needed through winter.
- **Days to harvest:** 90–120.
- **Storage:** For 2 weeks in plastic bag in refrigerator or for several months in cool, moist root cellar.
- **Pests:** Root maggots.

Parsnips (*Pastinaca sativa*) have a crisp texture and distinctive nutty flavor that sweetens and mellows after cooking.

Grow parsnips in deeply worked, fertile loamy soil in full sun or partial shade or in raised beds if your soil is heavy clay. Like carrots, parsnips will

Deep, loose loamy soil yields straight and full parsnip roots.

become forked and hairy in nitrogen-rich soil, though they do benefit from phosphorous fertilizer.

Sow seeds in early spring to early summer or 90 days before the first frost for a fall crop. Germination usually takes two to three weeks. Buy fresh seed every year to improve chances of good germination. Some standard varieties include 'Lancer' and 'Harris Model'.

Plant seeds 1 inch apart in ½-inch-deep furrows. Fill the furrows with compost or potting soil to prevent a crust from forming. Cover the rows with boards or row covers for 7 to 10 days to maintain constant soil moisture. After removing the cover, water frequently to keep the soil moist until the sprouts appear. Thin seedlings to 6 to 8 inches apart after a month.

Begin harvesting parsnips in late fall, after several frosts. Chilly soil brings out the sweetness in parsnips and improves their texture. You can leave mature roots in the ground all winter and dig them as desired until early spring, before growth resumes. To make digging easier, mulch plants with a 1-foot-deep layer of straw or shredded leaves in early winter. Parsnips are biennial and die early in their second year.

Turnip

- **Site:** Full sun to part shade. Deep, well-drained, fertile, and loose soil without stones and high in organic matter. Ample moisture. Cool.
- **Planting:** Direct-sow 4–6 weeks before last frost. Sow in late summer for fall harvest; in fall for winter harvest in south.
- **Spacing:** ½ inch deep, 2 inches apart, in rows 12 inches apart. Thin to 5 inches.
- **Care:** Mulch to keep soil moist. Avoid excess nitrogen.
- **Harvest:** Pull when roots are about 3 inches in diameter. Leaves are also edible. Days to harvest: 35–75.
- **Pests:** Flea beetles, aphids, and root maggots.

A staple fall crop in the south, turnips (*Brassica rapa*) are a versatile vegetable. Steam the leaves as greens, chop fresh roots into salads, or store mature roots for winter meals.

All varieties offer flavorful leaves to use as cooking greens. For salads, fast-maturing Oriental varieties yield almost as quickly as radishes. Large slower-growing varieties with a smooth texture and full-bodied flavor produce the best roots for storage.

Plant turnips in full sun to partial shade, in soil that is rich, fertile, and high in organic matter. Grow salad turnips and greens in both spring and fall, but turnips for storage are best grown in autumn. Warm temperatures cause bitter flavor.

Turnip seeds germinate fast. Plant them ½ inch deep and 2 inches apart. When plants are 3 inches tall, thin to 5 inches apart. Thinnings make flavorful cooking greens.

Harvest turnip greens by pulling individual leaves, or cut handfuls of leaves 1 inch above the crowns.

Choose 'Gold Ball' turnips (inset) for winter storage, or consider 'Purple Top White Globe' for greens and for eating fresh. Both are heirloom varieties.

Water the plants after harvesting, and they will quickly produce a flush of new leaves. Harvest only a few greens from the plants you are growing for winter storage.

Dig roots when about 3 inches across. Harvest all roots before temperatures drop below 25° F, because a hard freeze can split them and make them woody.

Sweet salad turnips need constant moisture while growing and are best harvested when roots are less than 2 inches in diameter.

SELECTED VARIETIES: 'Hakurei' for sweet salad turnips, 'Shogoin' and 'Tokyo Cross' for tender turnips and greens, and 'Purple Top White Globe' for storage. Heirloom 'Gilfeather' forms a large, sweet root with a green top.

Rutabaga

- **Site:** Same as turnip.
- **Planting:** Direct-seed 4–6 weeks before average last frost. For fall crop, sow seed in late summer in northern regions, in fall in southern regions. Mulch.
- **Spacing:** ½ inch deep, 2 inches apart in rows 18–24 inches apart. Thin to 8 inches.
- **Harvest:** Dig roots as needed when about 4 inches in diameter.
- **Days to harvest:** about 90.
- **Pests:** Clubroot disease, aphids, and flea beetles.

Rutabagas (*Brassica napus*) grow much like turnips, although the leaves are inedible and the roots are larger. Texture is dense and flavor slightly sweet.

For best flavor and texture, keep soil evenly moist. Plants are cold-hardy and can be left in the ground through winter in many areas.

In cold areas, plant rutabagas 90 days before cold weather sets in. Sow seeds 2 inches apart in fertile, well-drained soil with a near-neutral pH. Where winters are mild, plant seeds in early fall after nights have cooled to 50° to 60° F. Thin seedlings to 8 inches apart when they are 4 inches tall.

Aphids can be a problem. Hose off plants to remove them or spray with insecticidal soap.

Wait to harvest rutabaga roots until after several frosts because chilling improves their flavor. Harvest roots only as you need them. In early winter trim the tops of remaining plants and mulch them. This will make them easier to harvest during winter.

SELECTED VARIETIES: Varieties differ mostly in terms of color and disease resistance. 'Marian' resists clubroot disease, and 'Joan' develops yellow-fleshed roots with purple tops.

Cut back tops of rutabagas to within an inch of bulb to ready for storage.

SALAD GREENS

Mesclun

- **Site:** Full sun to part shade. Well-drained, rich soil high in organic matter. Cool, moist weather.
- **Planting:** Direct-sow in rows, bands, or broadcast in patches as soon as soil can be worked in spring. Plant every 2 weeks for continuous harvest. For fall crops, sow in midsummer in northern regions, late summer to fall in southern areas. Grow in cold frames for winter harvest.
- **Spacing:** ¼ inch deep in rows 18–24 inches apart. Thin plants to 10 inches.
- **Care:** Mulch. Suspend shade cloth over plants with stakes or hoops to help crops through summer heat.
- **Harvest:** As needed when leaves are 4–6 inches long. Remove outer leaves or cut at the base.
- **Problems:** Bolting to seed in hot weather.

Mesclun is a mix of greens, not a vegetable. It's a blend of young salad greens, which can be mild, spicy, or bitter depending on the plants you include. It's a good way to get to know salad greens without buying lots of different seed packets.

Mild blends consist mostly of leaf lettuce with small amounts of more flavorful greens, such as endive, arugula, or chervil. Spicy mixtures include mustard greens instead of lettuce.

Sow mesclun by making a ¼-inch-deep trench 2 inches wide and 12 inches long. Scatter seeds ½ inch apart. Cover with ¼ inch of soil. Keep soil moist as seeds germinate.

When leaves are 3 inches long (after about a month), harvest by cutting handfuls of leaves 1 inch above the soil surface. Water and fertilize after harvesting to help plants quickly produce a fresh crop.

Each sowing provides at least three cuttings. To assure a constant supply, sow at least three bands of mesclun each spring, two weeks apart, and more at two week intervals in fall.

Arugula

- **Site:** Same as mesclun. Tolerates dry sites and frost.
- **Planting:** By seed in spring 4–6 weeks before last frost or in late summer for fall crop.
- **Spacing:** ¼ inch deep, 1 inch apart, rows 12 inches apart. Thin to 8 inches apart when plants are 3–4 inches tall.
- **Care:** Benefits from sidedressing of compost or well-rotted manure. Water during drought.
- **Harvest:** Leaves as desired or cut whole plants at ground level.
- **Problems:** May bolt in heat; choose bolt-resistant varieties.

Arugula (*Eruca vesicaria sativa*) is expensive to buy but incredibly easy to grow. Also known as roquette, or rocket, arugula has a rich, full-bodied flavor that is delicious in salads, on sandwiches, or lightly braised.

For best flavor, grow arugula in cool weather and harvest only the youngest leaves. Heat makes older leaves taste sharply bitter. Plant arugula in spring and late summer.

Mesclun isn't a vegetable itself but is a blend of salad greens harvested young.

If you enjoy salads and like to sample unusual flavors, set aside a few square feet of your spring and fall garden for European and Asian salad greens. All are cool-season crops, and some are winter-hardy.

Some are familiar plants formerly known as weeds, such as dandelion and purslane, but now have cultivated varieties that taste better. Keep plantings small as you start out so you can experiment to find personal favorites.

Arugula is peppery, endive and chicory have a distinct bitter edge, and mâche is mild and nutty. Mizuna features a mild flavor, while mustard greens have a hot flavor.

Salad greens require a sunny or partialy shaded, well-drained site and moderately fertile soil. Before planting, mix a balanced fertilizer and compost into the soil. Water regularly for steady plant growth. Remove any flower stalks as they form, and harvest leaves when they are young and tender to enjoy fine salad greens.

For a peppery flavor that's tasty in salads, wraps, or soups, grow arugula.

Sow seeds 1 inch apart in rows or broadcast them in small patches, barely covering them with soil. Water plants regularly.

Begin harvesting leaves 4 to 6 weeks after sowing by pinching off 4-inch-long leaves from the centers of the plants. Or gather by the handful, cutting leaves 2 inches above the ground.

Tiny flea beetles often feed on arugula in late spring, chewing small holes in the leaves. Row covers are the best way to protect plants.

Arugula planted in late summer holds its flavor much longer than plants grown in spring. Sow fall crops 6 weeks before frost. Arugula tolerates light frosts, and plastic tunnels protect plants to 20° F.

Mâche

Mâche (*Valerianella locusta*), also known as lamb's lettuce or corn salad, is mild flavored and extremely cold tolerant. The plants often get lost in mesclun mixtures because they tend to hug the ground.

Mâche is easier to keep track of if planted by itself in early fall. Sow

Few salad greens can match the distinctively nutty flavor of fall-sown corn salad, or mâche.

seeds in a pattern to distinguish seedlings from weeds. Plant seeds ½ inch deep and ½ inch apart. Thin to 2 inches. Most varieties produce glossy, spoon-shaped leaves growing in a circular pattern. 'Vit' is a newer variety with a more upright habit; it's adaptable to cold and heat.

Harvest mâche by pinching off leaf clusters after plants have developed 3-inch rosettes. Cold weather enhances the sweet, nutty flavor, and plants often retain their quality well into fall.

Endive

- **Site: Same as mesclun. Full sun to partial shade.**
- **Planting: Direct-sow 4 weeks before last frost. For fall crop, sow in midsummer in north and late summer to fall in south.**
- **Spacing: ¼ inch deep in rows 18 inches apart. Thin to 12 inches.**
- **Care: Mulch. For milder flavor, blanch leaves by pulling them together; hold with twist ties. Look for self-blanching varieties.**
- **Harvest: Cut young plants off at base. Older plants turn bitter.**
- **Pests and problems: Aphids. Leaves turn bitter in hot weather.**

Endive (*Cichorium endivia*) looks like leaf lettuce and is planted at the same times in spring and fall, though it's more cold tolerant. Its flavor is sharp and almost peppery.

In the north direct-seed endive 4 weeks before the last frost. Thin to 12 inches when leaves are a few inches high. In the south, sow seed in late summer.

Harvest young endive for salad greens, or allow plants to form large, loose heads with white to light green hearts. Sometimes called frisée, mature endive is often blanched for two weeks prior to harvest. To blanch, tie outer leaves into a bundle over the hearts; hold it in place with

string or a rubber band. 'Neos' and 'Galia' are popular varieties.

- **Escarole** is the same species as endive but has wide, scalloped leaves and milder flavor. It's best when it matures in cool weather. Hearts are often lightly braised, which reduces their bitterness and brings out a sweet flavor. 'Batavian Full Heart' is a standard variety.

Asian greens

Asian greens have mild to spicy leaf flavors. Grown similar to mesclun and often found in the mixes, they can be grown individually as well. They're eaten in salads or sautéed. Asian greens feature unusual leaf shapes and colors, making them an edible ornamental.

SELECTED VARIETIES: Mizuna has mild-flavored rosettes of pencil-thin leaves. Tatsoi produces dark, spoon-shaped leaves in a rosette. Shungiku is an edible chrysanthemum featuring tangy leaves and small, yellow flowers. Mustards such as 'Osaka Purple' are larger plants with broad spicy leaves.

"Frisée" refers to the head of mature endive.

Spinacia oleracea
spin-ACH-ee-a o-ler-AY-see-a

Pick a few leaves from spinach plants throughout the growing season.

- Site: Full sun to part shade. Well-drained, fertile soil high in organic matter. Steady moisture.
- Planting: Soak seed overnight. Sow in spring as soon as soil can be worked. Make plantings every 2 weeks until warm weather arrives. Sow again in late summer in the north, fall in the south.
- Spacing: ½ inch deep, 1 inch apart in rows 18 inches apart, or

SPINACH

broadcast seed. Thin to 6 inches.
- Care: Mulch for moisture. Lightly sidedress with nitrogen-based fertilizer to speed growth.
- Harvest: Pick leaves as needed.
- Pests and problems: Mildew, slugs, and leaf miners. May bolt in heat and become bitter.

Fresh spinach leaves turn everyday salads into treats. Cooked, spinach's rich, buttery texture can't be beat.

HOW TO GROW: Spinach can take temperatures as low as 10° to 20° F. A fall planting can survive winter in many areas and yield a second crop the next spring.

Spinach requires more nitrogen than most vegetables. Mix high-nitrogen fertilizer or 2 inches of compost into soil before planting.

Begin harvesting spring-sown spinach when plants are 6 inches tall. If you take two to three leaves per plant, you can harvest from each plant once every 10 days.

Harvest fall-sown spinach the same, but stop picking in early winter. Protect plants with a light mulch of hay or straw or grow them through winter under plastic tunnels. When soil warms in spring, the spinach will produce a heavy crop of sweet, crunchy leaves. Sidedress plants with compost or douse them with fish emulsion.

To control leaf miners, remove and destroy affected leaves. Don't compost these leaves—the insects can return to your garden.

SELECTED VARIETIES: Smooth-leaf types grow best in spring, including 'Space', 'Whale', and 'Olympia'.

Semisavoyed varieties such as 'Tyee' and 'Melody' have slightly crinkled leaves. Savoyed spinach ('Bloomsdale Longstanding') is thick, heavily crinkled, and makes an outstanding fall and winter crop.

Heat-resistant spinach look-alikes such as 'Red Malabar' produce smooth spinachlike leaves on vining plants that thrive in heat.

Ipomoea batatas
ip-po-MEE-a ba-TAH-tas

- Site: Full sun. Well-drained, light-textured soil with 5.5–6.5 pH. Plentiful moisture.
- Planting: By rooted "slips," or by cut sections of tuber with at least one growing point.
- Spacing: 3 feet.
- Care: Mulch. Do not use high-nitrogen fertilizer.
- Harvest: Dig tubers after frost.

For best storage, cure sweet potatoes carefully and thoroughly.

SWEET POTATO

Don't bruise or break tender skins. Cure as detailed below.
- Days to harvest: 90–120.
- Storage: In a cool, dry location.
- Pests: Fusarium wilt, wireworms, and weevils, but less so in northern regions.

Sweet potatoes thrive where warm weather lasts at least three months. Each lovely vine yields four or more tuberous roots.

HOW TO GROW: To grow sweet potatoes in northern gardens, warm the soil with black plastic mulch before planting. Start with rooted stems called slips. Buy certified disease-free slips in late spring or grow your own by forcing them in a good quality potting soil, sand, or vermiculite. Each potato produces a few leafy stems and stringy roots. These roots are the slips. Break off and plant slips when they're 4 to 6 inches long.

After soil warms to 70° F, plant slips diagonally in 4-inch-deep furrows so that only the top three leaves show. Allow 16 inches between plants and 36 inches between rows. Water after planting; keep constantly moist for a week. Plants need an inch of water per week to keep roots from cracking.

Check your crop 80 days after planting; harvest roots when they're 3 inches across. To harvest, loosen soil outside the row, then pull on the vine crown. Brush soil off roots, and cure in the sun for several hours. Let dry at 80° F for 10 days. Gently clean roots again and dry a few more days. Store in a dry, cool place (60° F).

SELECTED VARIETIES: For short summers, grow fast-maturing 'Georgia Jet'. In warm climates, 'Centennial' and 'Beauregarde' yield heavily. 'Porto Rico' and 'Vardaman' have short vines that are ideal for small gardens.

Cucurbita pepo, C. maxima,
C. moschata
kew-KUR-bi-ta PEEP-o,
C. MACKS-i-ma, C. mos-KAY-ta

- **Site:** Full sun. Well-drained, fertile soil high in organic matter. Ample, steady moisture. Warm.
- **Planting:** Direct-seed or transplant. Sow seed indoors in peat pots 3 weeks before setting out. Set out 2 weeks after last frost date. (Old-fashioned "Three Sisters" method of planting vining squashes: Plant squash in every seventh hill of dent, flour, or flint corn. Allow pole beans to climb the corn.)
- **Spacing:** Four to five squash seeds per hill. Six to seven pumpkin seeds per hill. Hills 4 feet apart. Thin to three plants per hill. In rows: bush squashes, 20 inches apart in rows 24 inches apart; vining squashes, 20 inches apart in rows 4 feet apart; pumpkins, 3 feet apart in rows 8 feet apart.
- **Care:** Black plastic or organic mulch. Trellis in small gardens.
- **Harvest:** Pick summer squash young and tender; zucchini, crookneck, and straightneck squashes: when no more than 6 inches long; pattypan squash: while small and pale; winter squash and pumpkins: before first fall frost. Cut off fruit, leaving some stem. Cure in warm, dry place for several days before storing in a cool, dry spot. Days to harvest: 45–120.
- **Pests and problems:** Bacterial wilt, cucumber beetles, squash vine borers, mosaic virus, and mildew. Sensitive to frost.

Squash and pumpkins are closely related members of the cucumber family. They are vigorous, grow quickly, and are very nutritious.

Two groups of vegetables go by the name of squash. Summer squash—including zucchini, Lebanese, pattypan, crookneck, and straightneck—have soft skin. Winter

SQUASH AND PUMPKIN

squash—including acorn, butternut, buttercup, and hubbard—have hard, thick rinds, making them suitable for long-term storage.

Pumpkins and most types of winter squash require plenty of room for their long, wandering vines. Summer squash have a more compact, bushy habit, making them a better fit for small gardens.

Summer squash

Zucchini are phenomenally productive and include numerous hybrids with blackish-green, gray-green, striped, or yellow rinds. Bulbous, light green Lebanese squash are similar to zucchini. Yellow squash have either curved or straight necks, depending on variety. Straightneck hybrids are reliably productive. Pattypan squash are shaped like flattened flowers and add variety to summer gardens. Their colors range from yellow to greenish white to white.

HOW TO GROW: For a head start, start summer squash indoors in containers three weeks before your last frost. Transplant seedlings three weeks later. Or direct-sow seed 1 inch deep, 6 inches apart in fertile soil 2 weeks after your last frost. Thin seedlings to 2 feet apart after they develop at least 2 large leaves.

To keep the harvest interesting, grow several types of summer squash but only a few plants of each. If you intend to save seeds, be aware that summer squash can cross-pollinate one another.

Harvest summer squash when the fruit is young and tender; often with the wilted flower still attached. Squash blossoms are also edible and make colorful additions to many dishes. Promptly remove overripe fruit from the plants. This will encourage the development of new flowers and fruit.

Celebrate the diversity of color and form in summer squash by sowing a few seeds of each variety.

Hand-pollinate squash vines by taking pollen from male flowers to female flowers, using a cotton swab or the male flower part itself to transfer the pollen to the stigma of the female.

SQUASH AND PUMPKIN *(continued)*

Winter squash

Winter squash will store for several weeks, even months, if harvested when its skin is hard and the seeds are fully mature.

Acorn squash requires a little less space than other types of winter squash. Butternuts are highly tolerant of pests, and their flavor often becomes sweeter with storage. Buttercup squash makes terrific pies. Striped 'Delicata' or dumpling squash is ideal for stuffing and baking.

Huge hubbards store for a long time. Other winter squashes include spaghetti, sweet dumpling, kabocha, and turban squash.

HOW TO GROW: Choose a site with full sun and well-drained, fertile soil high in organic matter. Winter squash needs consistent and plentiful moisture.

To grow a low-maintenance planting of winter squash, plan ahead. Work 1 cup of 10-10-10 fertilizer next to each planting hill. Mulch the area with black plastic. Cut holes in the plastic 3 to 4 feet apart and sow three to five seeds in each hole. Two weeks later, thin seedlings to two per hole. You can also set out transplants one to two weeks after the last frost date.

Where summers are cool or insect problems severe, use a row cover until female blossoms appear.

Remove the cover to allow pollination. In small plantings, you can assist pollination by hand-pollinating. In the morning, with a cotton swab, transfer the pollen from an open male flower (it has a thin, straight stem behind the flower) to an open female flower (it has a small fruit behind the flower). After each plant has at least four green fruit, replace the row cover.

Winter squash are ready to harvest when the fruit has a firm rind that is difficult to pierce with a fingernail and plants are looking ragged. Cut fruit from the vine, leaving a stem; wipe it clean with a damp cloth, and store it in a cool, dry place.

SELECTED VARIETIES: Hybrid summer squash are more prolific than open-pollinated varieties so more grows in less space. Many popular varieties such as 'Supersett' and 'Dixie' yellow crookneck, 'Raven' and 'Embassy' green zucchini, 'Butterstick' yellow straightneck, 'Gold Rush' yellow zucchini, 'Magda' Middle Eastern cousa squash, light green 'Starship', and bright yellow 'Sunburst' pattypan are hybrids. There's even a new pear-shaped yellow hybrid summer squash called 'Papaya Pear'.

Kabocha-type buttercup varieties of winter squash, such as 'Hokkori' and 'Sweet Mama', produce heavy, flavorful crops. Butternuts such as 'Nicklow's Delight' are disease resistant. Cooked spaghetti squash flesh resembles pasta.

Delicata or dumpling squash have the sweet potato flavor of butternuts and are the perfect size for cutting in half and baking or stuffing; consider 'Cornell's Bush Delicata'.

'Sweet Meat' is a small, flavorful, hubbard-type squash. 'Table Ace' is a productive acorn type. 'Sweet Dumpling' is a teacup-shaped, ivory-colored squash with a very sweet flesh that is perfect for stuffing.

Harvest winter squash with at least an inch of stem if you intend to store them. Stemless squash spoil quickly. Store at 50° F with about 60 percent humidity.

Pumpkins

Pumpkins are a type of winter squash. They range in size from 3-inch miniatures to giants weighing 1,000 pounds. The best for eating are 5- to 10-pound pie pumpkins.

HOW TO GROW: Plant pumpkins in late spring in cool-summer climates and in early to midsummer in warmer areas. They develop long vines, which benefit from filtered shade. Growing them near sweet corn or along a fence provides ample shade. As vines ramble through the corn or along fences, their huge leaves shade out weeds.

To protect ripening fruit from insects and soil-borne diseases, place a piece of cardboard, folded newspaper, or even an inverted pot between the fruit and bare soil.

To grow giant pumpkins, you'll need at least three plants of a large-fruited variety of *C. maxima*, such as 'Prizewinner' or 'Atlantic Giant'. After the fruit sets, clip off all but one or two of the largest fruits. With regular watering, you should harvest pumpkins weighing at least 50 to several hundred pounds.

Leave pumpkins on the plants until the vines begin to turn yellow and die back. Mature pumpkins are susceptible to chilling injury so protect them from heavy frosts. Store pumpkins like other winter squash.

SELECTED VARIETIES: 'Jack Be Little' is a decorative miniature pumpkin, no more than 3 inches in diameter. Pie varieties are 'Lumina', which is white, and 'Small Sugar'.

For carving and painting, plant 'Connecticut Field', 'Orange Smoothy', or 'Jack-O-Lantern'. For edible seeds, choose either a hull-less or semi-hull-less variety, such as 'Triple Treat'.

'Rouge Vif d'Etampes' is an unusual red-tinted, French heirloom pumpkin, sometimes referred to as the "Cinderella pumpkin."

There's more to squash than zucchini. Gather a harvest of winter squash, and you'll discover everything from familiar pumpkins to exotic Japanese varieties.

PEST WATCH: Squash bugs first appear in early summer and suck the sap from leaves and stems of squash and pumpkin plants. The ⅔-inch-long adults are a mottled brown color with flat backs and orange markings under their wings. They lay glossy brown eggs on leaves in precise groups. Ten days later, small gray nymphs hatch and begin to feed.

Handpick squash bugs as soon as they appear. Thoroughly wetting the plants often makes the adults move to the tops of leaves, where you can easily pick them off. Pyrethrum or another pesticide labeled for use on squash for squash bugs will help with severe infestations.

To harvest ribbon-worthy pumpkins, start with the right variety, such as 'Prizewinner' (shown).

Lycopersicon esculentum | # TOMATO
ly-ko-PER-si-con es-kew-LEN-tum

Most tomato plants require support to help vines hoist fruit above soil to avoid rotting while ripening.

- **Site:** Full sun. Well-drained, fertile soil, slightly acidic, high in organic matter. Consistent moisture prevents blossom end rot.
- **Planting:** Sow seeds indoors 6–8 weeks before transplanting. Plant outside 1–2 weeks after average last frost.
- **Spacing:** Set transplants 2–3 feet apart.
- **Care:** Stake, cage, or trellis indeterminate and semideterminate varieties. Staking is optional for determinates. Pinching off side shoots is necessary only when stake training. Mulch to maintain soil moisture to prevent blossom end rot. Supply consistent moisture when rainfall is less than 1 inch per week.
- **Harvest:** As fruit ripens and is firm and fully colored. Before the first frost, harvest all full-sized green fruit that are nearly mature. Set in a warm location to continue ripening.
- **Days to harvest:** 50–80.
- **Pests and problems:** Tomato hornworms, blossom end rot, early blight, and late blight.

'Celebrity' reliably bears medium-size fruit on disease-resistant plants.

Gardeners are passionate about tomatoes, the most popular vegetable in summer gardens everywhere. Successfully growing them is simple: Choose disease-resistant varieties suited to your climate and do everything you can to help the plants grow steadily and without interruption.

Many of the ways you handle tomatoes are determined by their growth habit, which may be determinate, vigorous determinate, or indeterminate. You'll find this information on the seed packet or plant identification tags, and in seed-catalog descriptions.

Determinate tomatoes: These varieties, sometimes called dwarf varieties, grow into bushy plants that need no support and develop clusters of blossoms and fruit at the stem tips. They mature early and ripen within 1 to 2 weeks, so they are ideal for canning or freezing and for growing in short-season areas. Generally, the fruit ripens over a concentrated period of time, usually three weeks, and then the plants die.

Vigorous determinates: Also called semideterminates, these plants produce a heavy crop all at once, but they do not die afterward. If you prune them back and fertilize them in midsummer after harvest, vigorous determinates produce a light second crop. They are increasingly popular as double-crop tomatoes, especially in warm climates.

Indeterminate tomatoes: These tomatoes produce a summer-long stream of flowers and fruit. The tall, lanky plants require support from stakes, a trellis, or wire cages. Their fruit usually has excellent flavor, and plants remain productive until frost, insects, or diseases kill them.

HOW TO GROW SEEDLINGS: You can buy the most popular tomato varieties as bedding plants. Get them as soon as they arrive in stores, choosing plants that show no signs of flowering or yellowing leaves.

Unless you are ready to plant them within a day or two, transplant the seedlings into 4- or 6-inch pots filled with a good potting soil. Handle them by their leaves and roots and avoid touching their fragile stems. Set plants deep in their new pots because any section of buried stem will grow additional roots. Water well and place the plants under fluorescent lights.

Start unique or unusual varieties from seed about six weeks before your last spring frost date. Tomato seeds germinate best at 75° to 85° F. Grow seedlings under lights for 12 hours each day. Adjust the light every few days to keep it 3 inches above the tops of the plants.

Fertilize seedlings once a week with a half-strength liquid fertilizer. Transplant them to larger pots every three weeks or whenever the plant height is three times the pot diameter. Normal room temperature is fine for tomato seedlings, which may grow too fast if temperatures are above 70° F.

HOW TO GROW TRANSPLANTS: Harden off tomato seedlings for two weeks before transplanting them to the garden. Set plants in the garden after nights are consistently warmer than 50° F and soil is 60° F. In cool climates, cover the soil with red plastic to warm it up. Red plastic

'Brandywine' bears large, ribbed fruit with rich aroma and flavor.

mulch has been shown to increase average tomato yields by 20 percent over black plastic mulch.

Transplant tomatoes on a warm, cloudy day. They need a site with full sun and well-drained soil with a pH between 5.5 and 6.5. Enrich the soil with plenty of organic matter before planting.

Space large indeterminate and vigorous determinate tomatoes at least 24 inches apart. Compact determinates can be grown slightly closer together, but all tomatoes should be spaced far enough apart that air can freely circulate through the foliage when plants are fully grown. Mix compost into each planting hole to improve soil structure, and increase fertility and water-holding capacity.

If garden space is limited, choose tomato varieties suited for pot culture, such as 'Tumbler' or 'Red Currant'.

TOMATO *(continued)*

Special tomato fertilizers have a ratio of 5-6-5 or 3-5-6 and supply a modest amount of quick-release nitrogen along with phosphorous and potassium. Follow package directions when using these products. Most are applied twice a season—once before planting and again after the plants have set their first fruits.

'Sweet Million' lives up to its name, bearing clusters of crack-resistant, cherry-size fruit by the dozen.

Plant seedlings deep enough that soil covers at least 2 inches of the main stem. Deep planting protects the stem from wind damage and encourages development of extensive roots along the length of the buried stem.

Protecting newly transplanted tomatoes from cold wind is as important as fertilizer. Cover transplants with plastic cloches, water-filled frost protectors, or a plastic tunnel. If you plan to use wire cages for support, install them after planting, then wrap the bottom 12 inches of the cages with clear plastic held in place with clothespins. The plastic will buffer strong winds and help keep the seedlings warm.

After the soil warms, remove any cold-protection devices. As plants begin to grow rapidly, mulch to help keep soil constantly moist. Tomatoes need a consistent and plentiful supply of water. In many areas, you can apply an organic mulch after the first fruit have set and the plants have been fertilized. Leave plastic mulch in place all summer.

PRUNING AND STAKING: Because almost every stem of a determinate tomato will produce fruit, do not pinch or prune them off. Keep determinate tomatoes upright by surrounding them with circular wire cages or by placing wood stakes between plants and weaving plastic twine between the stakes and plants in a figure-eight design.

Indeterminate tomatoes are so lush and rangy that you should either prune them and tie them to stakes or support them with wire cages. Prune indeterminate plants according to the weather in your climate. Where summers are hot, you may want to leave the plants unpruned so that leaves shield the fruit from strong sun. In cooler climates, pinch out some of the secondary stems, called suckers,

to open the plants to sunshine and ripen fruit faster.

Use large cages made from concrete reinforcing wire to support indeterminate varieties. Smaller cages will blow over during summer thunderstorms.

HARVEST AND STORAGE: Tomatoes are mature and full flavored when their color fully develops, but you can pick fruit as soon as it shows a hint of color. At this stage, flavor will continue to develop in the fruit even off the vine.

After harvest, keep tomatoes in a warm place until you're ready to eat them. Never chill tomatoes; cool temperatures break down the flavor.

Just before the first fall frost, harvest mature green tomatoes, wrap them loosely in newspaper, and pack them in a box. Kept indoors at room temperature, tomatoes will continue to ripen for several weeks.

SELECTED VARIETIES: Choose an assortment of red varieties for different purposes. 'Celebrity' (vigorous indeterminate), 'Big Beef' (indeterminate), and 'Better Boy' (indeterminate) are disease-resistant hybrids. In the north, look for early-maturing indeterminate varieties, such as 'Early Girl' and 'Early Cascade'. In the south, select heat-resistant cultivars, such as 'Heatwave II'. For containers select the dwarf types 'Container Choice' or 'Windowbox Roma'.

Tomatoes come in colors other than red. Yellow or orange tomatoes such as 'Taxi' (yellow determinate) or 'Husky Gold' (vigorous determinate) offer a change of pace and flavor.

Heirloom varieties have engaging tastes and colors. The red 'Mortgage Lifter' and pink 'Brandywine' are extremely flavorful. 'Cherokee Purple', 'Black Krim', 'White Beauty', and 'Big Rainbow' are heirlooms offering nontraditional colors and flavors. Many heirloom varieties are unusually shaped, have varying disease resistance, and are regionally adapted. For the best performance, select a number of different heirlooms known to grow well in your area.

Paste tomatoes such as 'Roma', 'San Remo', and 'Viva Italia' have solid interiors with little juice. They cook down to a thick sauce. Most plum-shaped paste tomatoes are determinate. For a short-season paste tomato, plant 'Ropreco Paste'.

Cherry and currant tomatoes like 'Sungold' and 'Supersweet 100' have a sweet, fruity flavor. They are so prolific that you need only one or two plants. The heirloom 'Yellow Pear', grown since the late 1800s, prolifically produces pear-shape fruits. They brighten salads and stir-fry meals.

'Matt's Wild Cherry' bears clusters of marble-size tomatoes on vigorous vines. Newer grape-types such as 'Juliet' feature crack-resistant, grape-size sweet fruits,

PEST WATCH: Tomato hornworms, large, colorful green caterpillars with white diagonal stripes on their sides and a fleshy spike or horn on their tails, often appear on tomato plants and sometimes on peppers too. They are the larvae of a large moth that lays tiny green eggs on leaf undersides

Growing up to 4 inches long, hornworms eat so many leaves that they seriously weaken plants. Pick them off as soon as you see them. Despite their ferocious appearance and aggressive attitude, tomato hornworms neither sting nor bite.

Tomatillo

Tomatillo (*Physalis ixocarpa*), a cousin to the tomato, bears green or purple fruits covered with a papery husk. Grow similarly to tomatoes but harvest when husks split and dry. An essential salsa ingredient, tomatillos also contribute to soups, stews, salads, and stir-fry.

Roma tomatoes contain less water than other varieties so are preferred for sauces of all kinds, and canning.

Nothing says summer like a 'Big Boy' tomato. This hybrid favorite yields fruits that weight up to a pound or more. For gardens short on space, plant 'Bush Big Boy'.

WATERMELON

Citrullus lanatus
sit-TRULL-us la-NAY-tus

- **Site:** Full sun. Well-drained, fertile soil high in organic matter. Consistent, plentiful moisture until fruit begins filling out.
- **Planting:** Sow seed indoors in peat pots, 2–3 weeks before setting out in the garden. Transplant 2 weeks after average last frost. In warm regions, direct-sow seed. Plant in hills with three transplants or five to six seeds per hill.
- **Spacing:** Bush types: 3 feet apart each way; vining types: 3 feet apart in rows 8 feet apart. Thin to three plants per hill.
- **Care:** Mulch. Use sturdy trellising for icebox-type melons in small gardens. As fruit develops, support with netting or fabric.
- **Harvest:** When fruits are full size, the surface loses glossy luster, the color on the bottom of the fruit changes to a pale yellow, and tendrils on the stems turn dry and brown.
- **Pests and problems:** Wilt, anthracnose, and cucumber beetles. Sensitive to frost. Needs a long, warm growing season. To ensure ripening in northern gardens, grow faster-maturing small-fruited cultivars such as 'Garden Baby'.

A juicy slice of watermelon is a centuries-old antidote to sweltering summer temperatures. Today, you can beat the heat with more than the classic, red-fleshed thirst quencher. Watermelons now also come in yellow and orange, and there are seedless varieties too.

Watermelons that grow in the typical large oblong shape require a long, hot growing season. Smaller icebox melons, with fruit weighing 10 pounds or less, ripen in as few as 80 days of warm temperatures.

HOW TO GROW: Watermelons need full sun and warm, well-drained, slightly acid soil (pH 6.2 to 6.8) rich in organic matter.

Because watermelon vines can grow 10 to 15 feet long, they require a space at least 8 feet wide and 12 feet long for five small icebox melon plants. It takes a plot twice that size to grow large-fruited watermelons.

PLANTING: To get a head start, plant watermelon seeds indoors about the time of the last spring frost. Sow them in large containers, such as 3-inch peat pots. Thin seedlings to one per pot. Transplant outdoors when 2 to 3 weeks old, disturbing the roots as little as possible.

Seedless watermelons are best started indoors since they can be finicky about germinating. Direct-sow other varieties into the garden. Plant in rows or hills spaced 3 feet apart. Before sowing seeds or transplanting seedlings, incorporate a standard application of a balanced fertilizer into the soil. In cool climates, cover prepared soil with black plastic mulch to warm the soil. Cut holes in the plastic to plant seeds or seedlings.

If direct-sowing after soil is warm, place seeds 1 inch deep and 6 inches apart. If you are using hills, plant four seeds per hill. After the seedlings develop two true leaves, thin to 2 feet apart in rows or two plants per hill.

WEEDS: Watermelons grow rapidly when nights stay above 60° F. Unless you planted the seedlings in black plastic, thoroughly weed and mulch the open ground between plants as soon as the vines begin to run. Weeding among established plants potentially mangles the vines, which in turn causes fruit to ripen unevenly.

WATERING: In dry areas, install soaker hoses or a drip irrigation system in your watermelon patch before the vines run. Young plants need about an inch of water per week. Later, while the fruit is ripening, their need for water doubles. Stop irrigating when the melons are almost ripe, a strategy that may intensify their sweet flavor.

Like cucumbers and squash, watermelons produce both male and

Seedless watermelons, such as 'Deuce of Hearts', offer all the best attributes of summer's juicy, refreshing fruit—but with fewer seeds!

Grow a 'Yellow Doll' watermelon to make your crop the talk of the block. Its sunny-tinted flesh is sweeter than the traditional red fruit.

only 8 to 10 feet. 'Sugar Baby' and 'Yellow Doll', which has yellow flesh, and 'New Queen', which has orange flesh, are good choices.

Intermediate-size melons, weighing between 20 and 30 pounds, usually need 100 days of warm weather to mature. 'Crimson Sweet', along with the heirloom variety 'Moon and Stars', are classics. 'Desert King' features yellow flesh and good drought tolerance.

If you want to grow a massive melon, start with 'Carolina Cross 183'. As with pumpkins, pick off all but one fruit from each vine. Your melon may grow to more than 100 pounds when mature.

Seedless watermelons look like icebox melons on the outside but have very few seeds inside. They produce little pollen, so a few seeds of 'Sugar Baby' or other good pollen producers are included in their seed packets. For this reason, a few melons in a seedless patch will have a normal number of seeds. Some good seedless varieties to grow include 'Seedless Sugar Baby' and 'Triple Crown'.

female flowers, and only the female flowers set fruit. Honeybees and other insects help spread pollen among the flowers. Under sunny, warm conditions, each plant should set two to five fruit.

When the plants have set fruit and are producing only a few flowers near the vine tips, fertilize with a balanced quick-release fertilizer. Or apply a liquid fertilizer through a sprayer to avoid trampling through the vines.

If the season is rainy, carefully place a piece of cardboard or a bed of straw beneath each melon when it is the size of a softball. This will help prevent fruit rot. Other problems you may encounter are anthracnose, a fungal disease, and cucumber beetles, which spread bacterial wilt.

HARVEST AND STORAGE: There are several ways to tell when watermelons are ripe. The surest sign of ripeness of most varieties is the color of the bottom surface. As the melon matures, this ground spot turns from light straw color to richer yellow. Also, check the curly tendril nearest the stem end of the fruit to see if it is dry and brown. Finally, thump the melon soundly with knuckles, and listen for a deep thud. Underripe melons tend to sound high-pitched and tinny, and look powdery or slick on the top.

Leave melons in the garden for a week or so after they ripen or move them into a shady spot outdoors. Unrefrigerated melons will keep for 2 to 3 weeks. Storing them in a cool basement will help hold them a little longer.

SELECTED VARIETIES: If both space and growing season limit your ability to grow watermelons, choose early-maturing varieties with vines that run

Set ripening fruits on a square of carboard to protect them from rot and insects as they ripen.

'Tiger Baby' is a 7 to 10 pound icebox type with pinkish red flesh.

Living with Herbs

IN THIS CHAPTER

Plant Types **72**
Plant Parts **73**
Growing and
Caring for Herbs **74**
Pruning **76**
Propagation **77**

Fill your life with herbs and they will bring beauty and aroma to your yard and bounty to your kitchen. Some can improve your health and appearance, while others fill your home with fragrance. This chapter focuses primarily on culinary herbs, though the entries in the gallery list many other uses for each herb.

Adding herbs to your garden can bring new scents and flavors to both the garden and the kitchen.

More than a thousand plants are considered herbs, so you have lots of candidates for your garden. In the following chapter you'll learn to recognize, grow, and use more than 75 of the most flavorful, beneficial, and fragrant herbs.

What exactly is an herb? More than twelve centuries ago, Emperor Charlemagne, who compelled his citizens to grow herbs, answered this question by saying, "An herb

Borage is an attractive ornamental plant as well as a useful herb.

is the friend of physicians and the praise of cooks."

Not much has changed since then, except that the definition has expanded from medicine and cooking to include plants valued for their household, fragrant, or economic uses. Herbs have played an important part in many civilizations since the earliest times, and they possess a wealth of history and folklore.

Successfully growing and using herbs

Use herbs throughout the home. Besides filling your kitchen cupboards and medicine cabinets, herbs add fragrance and beauty to any room of the house. Use them in wreaths, potpourris, or other aromatic crafts.

It's not difficult to grow and use herbs, but to derive the most pleasure, benefit, and success for your effort, consider the following.

KNOW YOUR HERBS: Minimize both mistakes and confusion by knowing beforehand how each herb grows, the conditions it needs to thrive, and how to use the herb after you harvest it.

Take an herb book with you when you go plant shopping, then keep it handy at home for reference. Label plants in the garden and dried herbs stored in the pantry.

PROVIDE THE RIGHT CONDITIONS: Herbs grow best when light, soil, drainage, and climatic conditions meet each herb's requirements for healthy growth. Many of the general conditions that work best for vegetables are appropriate for herbs too.

PROVIDE THE PROPER CARE: Watering, pruning, pinching,

Fresh salsa brims with flavor when it's created using fresh-from-the-garden vegetables and herbs such as cilantro and mint.

harvesting, and providing winter protection for plants help ensure healthy, vigorous herbs. Many of the same methods used for effective vegetable gardening apply equally well to herbs.

EXPERIMENT IN THE KITCHEN: Don't let culinary herbs intimidate you. If an herb is new to you, nibble on it. Then let your imagination fly with all the possibilities it can bring to your meals. Start with small quantities until you feel sure of yourself. And remember, it's hard to fail with fresh herbs.

FOR HEALTH, USE HERBS WITH CARE: If you intend to use herbs for their health and healing properties, be certain you are using the right herb in the proper manner, and never experiment with any herb if pregnant or nursing. Most herbs are benign, some are potentially dangerous and many may interact with prescription medications in unpredictable ways. Check with your doctor before using medicinal herbs.

When preserving herbs for medicinal use, you can gather, dry, and sometimes grind various parts of the plant, from leaves to roots to petals.

Herbs are also prized for their beauty. Use them dried to create bouquets, wreaths, or swags.

Plant Types

Willows, such as pussywillow, have pain-killing and fever-reducing properties.

Elder forms a veritable herbal pharmacy: Flowers, leaves, bark, and fruit are all used medicinally.

Parsley and sage plants are packed with flavor, rich with medicinal properties, and overflowing with good looks.

When deciding which herbs to grow and how best to use them in the landscape, it's helpful to know something about the many different types of plants and their growth habits.

Trees

Woody plants usually have a single main stem but may have two or three stems. Branches form well above the ground. Leaves may be deciduous or evergreen. Examples of trees that are herbs are willow (*Salix* species) and linden (*Tilia* species).

Shrubs

Woody plants are shorter than trees, with multiple stems and many branches starting near the base of the plant. Leaves may be deciduous or evergreen. Elder (*Sambucus* species) is an herb that grows as a shrub.

Annuals and biennials

Annuals germinate, grow, flower, and die—all in one growing season. Biennials germinate and grow vegetatively the first season, producing only leaves and stems. They go dormant over winter in cold areas, then flower the second growing season before dying. Basil (*Ocimum basilicum*) is an annual herb. Caraway (*Carum carvi*) is a biennial.

Vines

Vines are plants with woody or herbaceous stems that climb supports, either by twining or by means of suction cups or tendrils. Many vines sprawl and must be supported. Honeysuckle (*Lonicera* species) is a vine with herbal uses.

Herbaceous perennials

Plants that usually die back to the ground in winter, then send out new growth in spring, are perennial. Most perennial herbs have soft, herbaceous stems, but some develop woody stems. Sage (*Salvia officinalis*) is an example of a perennial herb.

Other herbs

Many herbs do not fit into the other plant categories listed. These include ferns, mosses, seaweed, horsetail, and some algae. Fungi, which are no longer considered plants, also may serve as herbs. Yeasts are an example of an herbal fungus.

Pinched-off tips on purple and green-leaf basil add distinctive flavor to meals.

Honeysuckle is prized more for its great looks than for its expectorant properties.

Plant Parts

Not all parts of an herb have herbal properties. Be sure to choose the correct part of the plant for the herb in question.

Leaves and stems

Other than a few bacteria, plants are the only organisms that produce their own food. This occurs in the leaves, which are the primary source of the chemicals we seek from herbs. Two plants whose leaves have herbal uses are nasturtium and eucalyptus.

Stems support plants and transport nutrients from roots to leaves and vice versa. Herbaceous stems provide a source of fibers for crafts. Herbal stems include angelica and germander.

Roots

These belowground growths anchor plants in the soil, absorb water and nutrients, and serve as storage organs. They may be thin and fibrous or thick and woody. Other forms include bulbs, corms, and tubers. Rhizomes, runners, and stolons are modified horizontal stems, not roots. One herb that's a root is horseradish.

Flowers

Plants reproduce through flowers. The petals, with their color and scent, attract insects that aid pollination. Calendula, chamomile, and bee balm are flowers used as herbs.

Bark, wood, and resin

Trees and shrubs develop woody stems surrounded by a protective layer of bark. The bark, wood, and sap (or resin) of certain plants have herbal uses. For example, quassia wood produces an insecticide, frankincense is a healing resin, and cinnamon is made from the bark of certain Asian trees in the laurel family.

Seeds, fruits, and nuts

After fertilization, plants form seeds. Each seed contains a store of food and a dormant embryo. Seeds are a major source of the world's food and oil. Some plants, such as dill, produce "naked," or exposed, seed. Others develop seed in a fleshy fruit. A nut is a woody fruit.

Essential oils

The concentrated, aromatic (volatile) oils of plants are the essential oils. Depending on the plant, these oils may come from any plant part. Essential oils perfume, flavor, or heal. Lavender forms an important herbal essential oil.

The dried stems of horsetail help control internal and external bleeding.

The leaves of bay (*Laurus nobilis*) add a pungent seasoning to sauces and soups.

Rose petals yield attar of roses, an oil famous for fragrance, flavor, and medicinal properties.

Dill flowers attract beneficial insects; the seeds and leaves prove flavorful.

Horseradish roots are used to brew a spicy seasoning for foods.

Cinnamon originates from the inner bark of a tree. The spice also has many medicinal uses.

Growing and Caring for Herbs

An herb garden starts with good soil. Till to loosen soil, then add amendments according to soil-test results.

Perennial and annual herbs easily hold their own when tucked into flower beds.

Traditionally, formal herb gardens feature geometric designs defined by paths and planting beds.

Even though many herbs adapt to a range of soils and climates, you can achieve the greatest gardening success by matching the plants you choose to your site's growing conditions. Pay careful attention to an herb's hardiness in your climatic zone, its light and moisture requirements, and your spring and fall frost dates. All these factors influence which herbs you can grow and where and how you can raise them.

Prepare your herb-growing sites as you would a vegetable garden. Do a soil test to assess the need for adding amendments to adjust the pH or supply critical nutrients. Most herbs do best in a slightly acidic to near-neutral pH range of 6 to 7. Dig in generous amounts of organic matter and an appropriate amount of balanced fertilizer (based on soil-test results). Consult with an extension agent or local nursery if you need additional assistance.

Getting started

You can start your herb garden by buying seedlings, but many herbs are easy to start from seed. However, some, such as French tarragon, can be propagated vegetatively only from cuttings or by division.

If you buy plants, make sure they are healthy and not root-bound. Open boxes of mail-ordered plants immediately, water them well, and place the plants in indirect light. Move them to the garden or repot them within the next several days.

To grow your own seedlings, follow the instructions provided for vegetables starting on page 23. Most perennial herbs should be started indoors 10 to 12 weeks before the date of the last spring frost. Start annuals 6 to 8 weeks before the last frost.

The best herbs to sow directly into the garden are

ones that germinate quickly and easily, that you want in quantity, or that do not transplant well. Among them are basil, chervil, cilantro, fennel, and dill. Some herbs are cool-season crops and others prefer summer heat. Check the gallery starting on page 78 or consult seed packets for suggested outdoor planting times.

When planting herbs in the garden, whether direct-seeded or transplanted, follow the recommendations in the gallery to achieve proper plant spacing and thinning.

Garden care

Most herbs are adaptable plants and thrive in a range of moisture conditions. They will appreciate occasional deep watering, just like vegetables. Weeding is important, but make sure you're familiar with the appearance of your herbs, especially perennial species, so you remove only weeds and not herbs, too. Mulch enables soil to retain moisture and can also help lower the number of weeds.

Like garden vegetables, herbs benefit from fertilizer applications. But unlike many vegetables, herbs receiving high levels of nutrients, particularly nitrogen, produce inferior growth with little flavor or fragrance. For that reason, keep your garden soil in the average-to-fertile range. Organic mulch often provides enough nutrients for herbs.

With adequate soil fertility and water, herbs generally have few pest problems. At times, however, they can fall victim to the same pests that are the bane of all gardeners: aphids, whiteflies, caterpillars,

and slugs. For low-impact ways of addressing these problems, see the discussion of Integrated Pest Management on page 26.

Harvesting and preserving herbs

When using herbs fresh, simply cut what you need when you need it. If you are harvesting to preserve herbs, it's important to maximize their essential oils. The timing and method depends on the part of the plant you harvest. See the gallery beginning on page 78 for specific recommendations for each herb. You may need to consult other sources for more information on the best harvest times for certain plant parts and for additional details about drying, freezing, tincturing, and storing herbs.

Living with herbs

As you read on about herbs, keep in mind the ways you want to use them. Because of their beauty and wide range of sizes, shapes, colors, and textures, herbs offer a limitless palette for the landscape. Whether you use them as borders, plant a formal or theme garden, or just scatter them among flowers and vegetables, you'll want to consider the visual and olfactory impact of herbs on your landscape.

Herbs also have a key place in the kitchen, of course. Cooking with herbs is not mysterious or complicated. It's as simple as harvesting a few stems of this and a few leaves of that, then mincing and adding them to the dish being prepared.

There are no hidebound rules about which herb to pair with a particular food.

The best way to acquaint yourself with the possibilities is to taste an herb fresh. If you don't like its flavor alone, then you may not like it in food. If you do like it, think about how it may combine with and complement various foods that you like. Explore ways to use herbs in vinegars, cheeses, syrups, mustards, and beverages. Above all, be adventurous and have fun in your culinary explorations.

You can also employ herbs throughout your home, creating soaps, potpourris, decorative crafts, laundry additives, or handmade paper.

If you choose to use herbs for your health, proceed with caution. The herb gallery provides basic information about the ways that herbs can be used for medicinal and therapeutic purposes. But you need to know what you're doing, so you should do additional research and/or consult credible specialists.

Colorful herbal vinegars are a cinch to make and provide flavorful, thoughtful gifts.

Dry herbs by hanging bundles of stems upside down. Cover loose blooms with paper bags.

Pruning

Pruning shapes herbs and helps them produce plenty of flavorful growth to harvest. The correct pruning times and methods vary from herb to herb. Use the gallery starting on page 78 for specific information.

KEEP CLIPPERS IN SHAPE: Always use a sharp pair of garden scissors or pruners when pruning or harvesting. Dull blades can damage stems, making them more susceptible to disease.

SPRING CLEANUP: In general, prune shrubby perennial herbs with woody stems, such as sage, lemon balm, artemisia, tansy, and rosemary, in the spring, removing dead branches and cutting the rest of the stems back by half. This keeps the plants bushy and well shaped.

SUMMER SHORTCUTS: Trim several inches off stems in midsummer to initiate fresh, tender growth during the latter half of the gardening season. Place these cuts to adjust the plant's overall shape and growth. During the growing season, harvest shoots or leaves as needed.

FLOWER POWER: If you let some culinary herbs flower, such as basil, sage, or mint, leaf flavor changes. Pinch off flowers as long as you want to continue to harvest foliage.

WOODY HERB WISDOM: Avoid trimming woody perennial herbs, such as germander, santolina, and lavender. Their new growth develops on the woody stems that matured during the last growing season. Pruning can keep the plants from growing.

If you're desiring a lush lavender planting, don't trim those plants the first three years of growth. It takes that much time for lavender to establish and mature. Remove only dead plant parts each spring—well after the remainder of the plant has greened up.

PREFROST PRUNING: Do not prune woody perennial herbs later than eight weeks before the average first frost date in fall. If these plants are pruned too late in the season, the new growth won't have enough time to harden before freezing weather arrives.

Potted herbs require frequent pruning. Place cuts to shape the plant and to keep the foliage mass proportionate to the pot size.

Propagation

Multiplying herbs by cuttings, layering, or division is easy and inexpensive. It also affords an opportunity to share favorite plants with friends.

ROOTING CUTTINGS: Rooting cuttings from the stems of woody herbs is a simple way to get many new plants. There are three main types of woody stem cuttings:

■ **Softwood cuttings:** Spring and early-summer cuttings from new growth that has not yet hardened.

■ **Semihardwood cuttings:** Midsummer cuttings from growth that has started to harden at the base.

■ **Hardwood cuttings:** Late-season cuttings made from fully hardened wood.

For all three types, cut 4- to 6-inch-long sturdy pieces of stem, making the cut just below a leaf. Next, pinch off leaves on the lower third of the stem, taking care not to tear the stem. Dust or dip the cut end in a powder or liquid rooting hormone.

With a pencil or chopstick, make a hole in a pot of moistened, sterile potting soil, horticultural vermiculite, or perlite. Insert the stem up to the bottom of the leaves and firm the potting medium around it. Add more cuttings to the pot, placing them 2 inches apart.

Insert a label with the plant name and date planted. Cover the pot with a plastic dome or bag, making sure it doesn't touch the leaves. The dome holds in moisture, keeping cuttings from wilting, but it also can cook plants by retaining heat. Keep the pot out of direct sunlight and open the dome a crack to let heat escape.

Set the pot in a spot with bright, indirect light. Keep the soil moist. Placing the pot on a heating mat speeds rooting.

When cuttings show signs of growth, usually after four to six weeks, remove the dome. If a gentle tug on the cutting yields resistance, the stem is developing roots. How long that takes varies with herb species. At this point, pot the plant and move it outdoors to a location out of direct sunlight for a few days (or weeks) before transplanting it in the garden.

LAYERING: Layering is a good way to propagate low-growing or creeping plants that are difficult to root from cuttings. With layering, rooting occurs while the stem is still attached to the plant.

Bend a shoot to the ground. Scoop out a small hole where the shoot touches the ground, then hold the stem in place with a peg-type clothespin or a hairpin-shaped piece of wire. Mound soil over the pegged stem, gently firming it. Keep the area moist until new growth develops, then cut the newly rooted plant from the main plant. Transplant it immediately.

DIVIDING: Many perennial herbs, such as oregano and lemon balm, send out an ever-widening circle of growth. These new plants crowd the original plant, which then declines.

Dig up an overgrown clump and cut or break it apart. Depending on the plant, an alternative is to dig small plants at the clump edges. Early spring or fall are the best times to divide.

To root stem cuttings, begin with sections 4 to 6 inches long. Remove leaves on the lower stem.

For plants like rosemary, take stem cuttings that contain new wood formed this growing season.

Dip cuttings into rooting hormone, stick them in soil, and cover with plastic.

Separate dug, crowded clumps of perennial herbs with digging forks.

To layer stems, anchor stem sections to the ground using landscape or sod staples.

GALLERY OF
Herbs

This encyclopedia will introduce you to individual herbs. Plants are arranged in alphabetical order by their best-known common name. Each herb's botanical name is also given.

Basic information is given about each herb's folklore, flavor, and medicinal, culinary, or other uses. Be aware that many herbal uses are rooted in folklore and may not have been tested for validity and safety.

Details about the plant's appearance, along with advice on best growing conditions, how to plant, propagate, tend, harvest, and preserve each herb are provided.

You'll also learn whether the herb is an annual, perennial, or woody plant, and its tolerance of winter temperatures. The zones mentioned in the herb descriptions refer to the USDA Climate Zones. A map showing these zones is on page 211.

A gleaning of herbal leaves and edible flowers forms the basis for colorful, fresh-tasting salads.

Aloe vera
AH-low VER-ra

Snap an aloe vera leaf to expose the gel-like sap, which soothes minor burns, dry skin, and insect bites.

ALOE VERA

■ Zones 9–10

Aloe is effective for quick relief of minor burns. It is also used as a soothing element in cosmetics.
Description: A member of the lily family, this perennial grows 12 to 24 inches tall and wide. Sword-shaped, fleshy, pale green, spiny-edged leaves spotted white. Spikes of tubular, 1-inch long, yellow to orange flowers.
Site: Full sun, tolerates partial shade. Average, well-drained soil; pH 7. Space 1 to 2 feet apart. Inside, keep aloe near a sunny window.

Propagation: Starts easily from offshoots, which appear at the base; pull off and replant separately.
Care: Where not hardy, grow in pots outside in summer; take indoors in winter. When moving a plant outdoors, give it several days in the shade to adjust.
Harvest: Pinch off leaf tips as needed. The cut ends heal over; brown residue can later be removed.
For health: Split a leaf and apply the gel directly to minor burns, wounds, dry skin, fungal infections, or insect bites. Add gel to shampoo for dry or itchy scalp or dandruff.

Angelica archangelica (A. officinalis)
an-JELL-i-ka ARK-an-jell-i-ka (A. off-fi-si-NAY-lis)

Angelica thrives in damp meadows and along streambeds.

ANGELICA

■ Zones 4–10

These majestic plants have a licoricelike scent and flavor.
Description: Biennial or short-lived perennial growing 4 to 8 feet. Leaves celerylike to 2 feet long. Big clusters of tiny sweetly scented flowers.
Site: Partial shade. Humus-rich, moist, well-drained soil; pH 6.3.
Planting: Direct-seed in early autumn; requires light to germinate. Self-sows. Thin to 2 feet apart. Refrigerate seed to prolong viability.
Care: To increase the life of the plants, remove flower buds.

Harvest: Leaves or stems before flowering. Ripe seeds in late summer. Year-old roots in autumn. Preserve by drying.
In the kitchen: Seeds in cakes, cookies, or liqueurs. Leaves in salads, soups, or with acidic fruit, such as rhubarb, to reduce sugar needed. Crystallize green stems for decorating pastries. Roots in breads and cakes.
For health: Leaf infusion internally for headache, indigestion, or coughs; externally in baths for sore muscles.
Caution: Do not use medicinally when pregnant.

ANISE

Pimpinella anisum
pim-pi-NELL-a a-NISS-um

■ **All zones (an annual)**

Anise adds a licorice flavor to baked goods, stews, and liqueurs.
Description: Grows to 2 feet tall, 1 to 2 feet wide. Lower leaves rounded to toothed; upper leaves finely divided. Flat clusters of creamy white flowers.
Site: Full sun. Average, well-drained soil; pH 6.0. Space 1 foot apart.
Planting: Direct-sow in late spring.
Care: May need staking.

Harvest: Leaves throughout the growing season. Flowers as they open. Ripe seeds as they turn gray-green. Preserve by drying.
In the kitchen: Whole, crushed, or ground seed in baked goods, apple dishes, pickles, curries, eggs, or soups. Flowers and leaves in fruit salads.
In the home: Seed in potpourri. Leaves or seed in dog pillows.
For health: Chew toasted seed to freshen breath and aid digestion. Seed infusion for colds, indigestion, colic, and to stimulate breast milk.

The blossoms of anise add an airy touch to garden beds and to fresh bouquets.

ANISE HYSSOP

Agastache foeniculum
ah-guh-STACK-ee fe-NICK-yu-lum

■ **Zones 4–10**

Anise hyssop was used as a sweetener and medicine by the Native Americans of the Great Plains. The flavor hints of anise and mint.
Description: Perennial growing to 3 feet tall and 1 foot wide. Oval anise-scented leaves. Blue or white flowers in summer and autumn.
Site: Full sun, tolerates partial shade. Fertile, well-drained soil. Space 1 foot apart. Can be grown in pots.
Propagation: Seed sown indoors in spring. Self-sows. Cuttings in spring

or summer. Division every few years.
Harvest: Leaves as needed. Flowers when three-quarters open. Preserve by drying.
Other: Attracts butterflies and bees. Repels cabbage moth.
In the kitchen: Leaves or flowers with fresh or baked fruit, cakes, cookies, teas, squash, sweet potatoes, carrots, sweet-and-sour pork, chicken, fish, or rice.
In the home: Leaves or flowers in potpourris. Dried flowers in wreaths. Fresh flowers in bouquets.
For health: Leaf infusion for poor appetite, indigestion, nausea, or feverish chills.

Anise hyssop blooms beckon bees and butterflies. As seeds ripen, goldfinches balance on stems to devour them.

ARNICA

Arnica montana
AR-ni-ka mon-TAY-na

■ **Zones 2–8**

Native to the alpine pastures of Europe, arnica has long been a popular remedy for bruises and sprains. Purchase only nursery-propagated plants because arnica is a protected species.
Description: Perennial growing 1 to 2 feet tall and 6 inches wide. Oval, pointed, light green hairy leaves to 5 inches long. Yellow daisylike, 3-inch flowers appear in summer.

The related North American species, *A. chamissonis*, is similar in both appearance and properties.
Site: Full sun. Humus-rich, sandy, well-drained soil; pH 4. Space plants 8 to 12 inches apart.
Propagation: Direct-seed in autumn; germination may take up to two years. Division or cuttings in spring.
Care: Grows best in areas where summers stay cool.
Harvest: Flowers as they become fully open. Preserve by drying.
For health: Flower tincture, oil, or ointment for sprains, bruises,

or muscle pain.
Caution: Do not take arnica internally or apply to broken skin.

Extracts of arnica are common additions to cosmetic products.

ARTEMISIA

Artemisia species
ar-te-MIZ-i-a

■ Zones 4–6

Pungent, usually with silver-gray leaves, artemisias are among the most ancient herbs, used for everything from warding off insects, diseases, and evil to curing baldness and soothing sore feet. Today their use is limited to moth repellents and crafts, but artemisias are favored for the garden.

Several perennial artemisias have ornamental value. Southernwood (*A. abrotanum*); 3 to 5 feet tall; 2 feet wide; upright, branched stems with silver-gray divided leaves (Zone 6). Wormwood (*A. absinthium*); 2 to 4 feet tall and wide; upright with finely divided, gray-green, lemon-scented leaves (Zone 4); 'Silver King' and 'Silver Queen' (cultivars of *A. ludoviciana*); 2 to 3 feet tall and wide; narrow leaves (Zone 5).

Perennial artemisias with an herbal heritage include Roman wormwood (*A. pontica*), feathery silver foliage on plants 2 to 3 feet tall (Zone 5); white mugwort (*A. lactiflora*), deeply cut, green leaves on 5-foot plants, showy white flowers (Zone 5); mugwort (*A. vulgaris*), dark green leaves on red-purple stems to 5 feet tall (Zone 4).

Site: Full sun. Average, well-drained soil; pH 6.6. Space plants 2 to 4 feet apart. Container culture works too.

Propagation: Difficult from seed. Divide in spring or fall every four years. Cuttings in summer.

Care: Trim new growth in spring to shape plants. Dig out wandering roots to curb invasiveness.

Harvest: Leaves as needed. Preserve by drying.

In the home: Dried wormwood or southernwood leaves as moth repellent. Dried branches of any artemisia in wreaths and crafts.

For health: Leaf infusion of southernwood in hair rinses.

Artemisias, like this *A. ludoviciana* 'Silver King', weave a beautiful silvery foliage thread into perennial plantings.

ASTRAGALUS

Astragalus membranaceus
as-TRAG-a-lus mem-bran-AY-see-us

■ Zones 5–9

Also known as huang qi or milk vetch, astragalus roots have been important in Chinese medicine for thousands of years, with uses ranging from treating allergies to a tonic for low energy and poor circulation. Some herbalists credit it with stimulating the immune system and suppressing tumors. Astragalus is also reported to lower blood sugar and pressure. It yields a sweet tonic considered as good as ginseng tonic.

Description: Perennial 12 to 18 inches tall and wide. Leaves divided into 12 to 18 pairs of leaflets. Stalks of yellow pealike flowers.

Site: Full sun. Sandy, well-drained soil; pH 7. Grows well in containers too.

Propagation: Direct-seed in spring or autumn.

Harvest: Four-year-old roots in autumn for use in decoctions, powders, or tinctures. Dry roots for use in herbal treatments.

For health: Root decoction to increase energy and immune resistance, prevent colds, or improve blood circulation.

Caution: Do not take if suffering from skin disorders.

The buttery yellow blooms of astragalus make it an eye-cathing plant in the garden.

BASIL

Ocimum species and cultivars
OS-si-mum

■ **All zones (an annual)**

A culinary herb beloved for its spicy flavor and intoxicating scent, basil is native to Africa, Asia, the Middle East, the Caribbean, and South America. Basil was originally revered for its spiritual powers. Virgil is considered the first writer to mention pesto, which is made from basil.

Ocimum basilicum is the main species for cooking, but basil has numerous varieties in a wide range of leaf sizes, colors, and flavors.

Varieties with a traditional basil flavor, growing about 2 feet tall, with smooth leaves to 3 inches long, include 'Genoa Green Improved', 'Genoa Profumatissima', and the generically labeled 'Sweet Basil'. Similar varieties with leaves up to 6 inches long include 'Napoletano', 'Mammoth', or 'Valentino'.

Varieties growing to a rounded shape 1 foot tall with leaves to 1 inch long include 'Dwarf Bush', 'Dwarf Bush Fine Leaf', 'Bush Green', 'Miniature', 'Dwarf Italian', 'Dwarf Bouquet', 'Green Bouquet', and 'Green Globe'. Taller plants with tiny leaves include *O. americanum* 'Sweet Fine' (3 feet), 'Piccolo' (2 feet), and 'Miniature Puerto Rican' (20 inches).

Varieties of *O. basilicum* with darkly tinted purplish-red leaves include 'Dark Opal', 'Red Rubin', 'Osmin', 'Purple Ruffles', 'Well-Sweep Miniature Purple', 'New Guinea', and 'Purple Thai'.

Of distinctly flavored basils, 'Anise', 'Licorice', 'Thai', 'True Thai', and 'Siam Queen' are variations on anise. Other flavored basils include 'Spice', 'Mexican Spice', 'Cinnamon', 'Karamanos', and 'Puerto Rican'. Basils with a flavor and aroma of citrus include 'Lemon', 'Maenglak Thai', 'Mrs. Burns' Famous Lemon', 'Sweet Dani', and 'Lime'.

O. gratissimum, commonly called East Indian basil, tree basil, or fever plant, grows 4 to 6 feet tall and wide with pungent leaves to 7 inches long. It is mainly used as a medicinal herb, an insect repellent, or as an ornamental. Varieties include 'Clove', 'East Indian', 'Green', and 'West African'.

O. tenuiflorum (previously *O. sanctum*), called holy (or tulsi) basil is sacred to Hindus. Its scent combines mint, camphor, clove, and cinnamon, and it is said to have medicinal uses. A variety called 'Sacred' is quite different, with a citrus and spice flavor.

Site: Full sun. Humus-rich, moist, well-drained soil; pH 6. Space 12 to 18 inches apart. Containers.

Propagation: Seed sown indoors in spring or outdoors a week or two after the average last frost date.

Care: Grows best in areas with hot summers. Remove flowers by cutting one fourth of the stem just above the first set of leaves to encourage branching and more leaves. Smaller-leaved types are easiest for growing indoors in containers.

Harvest: Leaves as needed. Flowers as they open. Preserve by chopping, mixing with oil, and freezing; much of the flavor is lost in drying.

In the kitchen: Leaves in vinegars, pestos, lamb, fish, poultry, beans, pastas, rice, tomato sauces, cheeses, eggs, salads, vegetables, soups, stews, fruit desserts, ice creams, and breads.

In the home: Repels flies and mosquitoes, especially *O. gratissimum* and *O. tenuiflorum*. Add leaves of spice- or lemon-scented varieties to potpourris.

For health: All types as a leaf infusion internally for headaches, indigestion, constipation, fevers, colds, anxiety, or exhaustion; externally in bath to invigorate or in hair rinse for shine. Seed poultice for wounds.

Basil's bright green foliage packs an aromatic punch. The cultivar 'Minette' has tiny leaves on tidy plants perfect for edging beds or growing in pots.

Laurus nobilis
LAW-rus NO-bil-lis

Distinctly aromatic leaves earn bay a place in every kitchen's cupboard. Bay is easy to grow indoors.

BAY

■ Zones 8–10

Bay is an ancient herb from southern Europe, where it was considered sacred to the Greek god Apollo. It was thought to guard against disease. Today the warm, aromatic flavor and scent is considered essential in cooking.

Description: Woody evergreen shrub or tree growing to 50 feet. Leathery, oval dark green leaves. Small, creamy yellow flowers; dark purple berries. 'Angustifolia' has wavy-edged leaves.

Site: Full sun to partial shade. Humus-rich, well-drained soil; pH 6.6. Containers.

Propagation: Seed difficult. Cuttings in autumn, layering in spring, but it takes many months to develop roots.

Care: Where not hardy, grow in pots and bring indoors in winter. Fertilize in spring. Highly susceptible to scale; spray with a horticultural oil or wipe with alcohol. Protect plants from whipping winds.

Harvest: Leaves as needed. Preserve by drying; use a flower press to keep them flat. Dried leaves lose flavor after about a year.

In the kitchen: Leaves in soups, stews, stocks, marinades, tomato sauces, pickles, shellfish boils, beans, grains, or long-cooked meat dishes. Place bay leaves on coals when grilling. Remove leaf from food before serving.

In the home: Wreaths or potpourris. Place leaves in flour, rice, or grains to deter weevils.

For health: Leaf infusion internally for indigestion, poor appetite, or flatulence; externally in bathwater for muscle ache or joint pain; hair rinse for dandruff, skin tonic, or compress for sore joints, sprains, or bruises.

Caution: Never take essential oil or the leaves internally; may also cause contact dermatitis.

Monarda didyma
mo-NAR-da DID-i-ma

Bergamot flowers make an impressive summer display, and are attractive to hummingbirds and goldfinches.

BERGAMOT

■ Zones 4–10

A North American native widely grown as an ornamental; also known as bee balm or Oswego tea. The Oswego Indians drank a tea of the leaves for colds and introduced it to early settlers. Common name is derived from the resemblance of the scent to bergamot oranges.

Description: Perennial growing 3 to 4 feet. Oval, pointed, slightly hairy dark green leaves with a minty citrus scent and flavor. Clusters of tubular, edible scarlet flowers; cultivars available in shades of scarlet, magenta, purple, pink, and white.

Wild monarda *(M. fistulosa)* with white to lavender flowers (Zone 3) and horsemint *(M. punctata)* with purple-spotted yellow flowers (Zone 5) are other perennial types.

Site: Full sun to partial shade. Humus-rich, moist, well-drained soil. Space 2 feet apart. Containers.

Propagation: Variable from seed. Division in spring every three years. Cuttings in early summer.

Care: Control powdery mildew with good air circulation and by cutting plants back to the ground after flowering, or grow resistant varieties, including 'Marshall's Delight', 'Petite Delight', and 'Petite Wonder'.

Harvest: Leaves as needed. Flowers as soon as fully open. Preserve both by drying.

Other: Attracts bumblebees, hummingbirds, and butterflies.

In the kitchen: Flowers or leaves in fruit, salads, teas, flavoring for black tea, wines, lemonade, pork, poultry, sausages, and jellies.

In the home: Leaves or flowers in potpourri. Dried flowers in crafts.

For health: Leaf infusion internally for colds, fevers, indigestion, nausea, flatulence, insomnia, or menstrual pain; externally in baths or in poultices for joint pain.

BLACK COHOSH

Cimicifuga racemosa
sim-mi-si-FYEW-ga ra-see-MO-sa

■ **Zones 3–8**

Originating in the northeastern United States, black cohosh was a Native American remedy for a variety of ills, including "women's problems." It is an outstanding ornamental for shady borders or in a woodland setting.

Description: Long-lived perennial, growing to 6 feet tall and 3 feet wide. Dark green, palmately divided toothed leaves. Bottlebrush spires, to 2 feet, of fragrant white flowers.

Foetid bugbane (*C. foetida*), an Asian species with similar looks and properties, is a traditional Chinese medicine (Zone 4).

Site: Partial shade. Humus-rich, moist, well-drained soil; pH 6. Space 3 feet apart.

Propagation: Direct-seed in autumn. Division in spring or autumn.

Care: Takes several years to become established. Don't allow plants to suffer drought during first two years.

Harvest: Roots in autumn. Preserve by drying.

For health: Root decoction or tincture traditionally used internally for muscle or joint pain, headaches, arthritis, menstrual cramps, coughs, fevers, high blood pressure, and tinnitus. Reduces progesterone levels in women.

Caution: Women who are or could be pregnant or who are nursing should not use this herb.

The towering flower spikes of black cohosh shoot skyward in midsummer.

BORAGE

Borago officinalis
bore-RAY-go off-fi-si-NAY-lis

■ **All zones (an annual)**

Can borage actually make people happy, dispel melancholy, and give courage as believed? Folklore notwithstanding, borage does contain high levels of potassium, which stimulates the adrenal glands. No doubt, too, that the cucumber-flavored leaves and small, starry flowers simply bring pleasure.

Description: Hardy annual growing to 2 feet tall and wide. Hollow, bristly, sprawling stems and bristly oval leaves up to 6 inches long. Flowers, pink maturing to blue, borne freely throughout summer.

Site: Full sun, tolerates partial shade. Humus-rich, moist, well-drained soil; pH 6.6. Space plants 2 feet apart. Thrives in container culture.

Propagation: Direct-seed late spring. Self-sows freely. Does not transplant well.

Care: Remove faded flowers to prolong blooming. Grows best in cool weather.

Harvest: Leaves when young, flowers just as they are fully open. Preserve by drying.

Other: Improves insect or disease resistance in nearby plants. Companion plant to strawberries.

In the kitchen: Flowers in punch, iced drinks, ice cubes, green or fruit salads, vinegars, or diced over sliced tomatoes. Leaves in soups, cooked greens, salads, butters, cheese or yogurt dips, fish, poultry, eggs, teas, punches, sorbets, or vinegars.

In the home: Dried flowers in potpourri blends.

For health: Leaf infusion internally for colds, coughs, fevers, insomnia, or tension. Leaves in face packs for dry skin, in baths, or in a poultice for bruises or irritated skin. Seeds are high in essential fatty acids.

Borage's hairy disposition tends to dispel insects, although its blossoms lure bees by the dozens.

Calendula officinalis
ka-LEN-dew-la off-fi-si-NAY-lis

Whether or not your intentions toward calendula are herbal, give it a place in your garden for its beauty alone.

CALENDULA

■ All zones (an annual)

Commonly called pot marigold, calendula was valued in many ancient civilizations. Bright flowers add color and peppery flavor to food and can be used to make a healing antiseptic for skin.

Description: Annual 8 to 24 inches tall, depending on the variety. Pointed oval leaves to 3 inches long on angular stems. Daisylike flowers 2 to 4 inches across in shades of yellow, gold, apricot, or orange. The best varieties for herbal use are those with large petals, such as 'Pacific Beauty', 'Indian Prince', or 'Sunglow'.

Site: Full sun, tolerates partial shade in hot climates. Average, well-drained soil; pH 6.6. Space 8 to 12 inches apart.

Propagation: Start indoors in spring, or sow outside two weeks before last frost. Self-sows freely.

Care: Grows best in climates with cool summers or in spring and autumn in hotter climates. Deadhead to prolong flowering. Remove mildewed leaves.

Harvest: Young leaves; flowers as they open. Preserve by drying.

In the kitchen: Petals with greens or in salads, soups, stews, sandwiches, cheeses, eggs, butters, grains, rice, dumplings, cakes, cookies, puddings, vinegars, liqueurs, or wines.

In the home: Petals in potpourri.

For health: Petal infusion or tincture internally for indigestion, eczema, or menstrual pain; externally in facial tonic for large pores or acne, mouthwash for infected gums, bathwater to heal and soften skin, hair rinse for oily hair, or compresses for wounds, burns, or stings. Petal oil or ointment for skin rashes, athlete's foot, varicose veins, bruises, or minor cuts or burns.

Caution: Do not take internally during pregnancy.

Carum carvi
KAIR-um KAR-vy

CARAWAY

■ Zones 4–7

Caraway has been a flavoring and medicine for more than 5,000 years. Its herbal folklore properties include keeping both lovers and poultry close to home.

Description: Annual or biennial to 2 feet tall and wide. Finely cut feathery leaves on floppy stems. Flat heads of tiny white flowers. Ridged, ¼-inch-long brown crescent-shaped seeds.

Site: Full sun. Deeply tilled, average, well-drained soil. Space 8 inches apart.

Propagation: Direct-seed in early spring; or in mild winter areas, fall.

Care: Mulch plants in winter.

Harvest: Young leaves as needed. Seed heads as they turn brown; preserve by drying. Roots in autumn after seed harvest.

In the kitchen: Seeds in breads, cakes, cookies, soups, sauces, stews, pork, beef, goose, vegetables, pickled vegetables, sauerkraut, cheeses, eggs, grains, apples, or liqueurs. Young leaves in fruit or green salads, cheeses, or butters. Roots eaten as a vegetable.

For health: Seed eaten raw or in infusion to increase appetite, aid digestion, sweeten breath, relieve flatulence, or ease colic in children; consumed to relieve menstrual cramps or coughs. Chew seeds for fast indigestion relief.

Caution: Do not take essential oil of caraway internally.

Tame caraway's floppy ways with tomato cages or other circular supports.

CATNIP

Nepeta cataria
NEP-e-ta ka-TAY-ri-a

■ Zones 4–10

Catnip's common name is no surprise to anyone who has seen the pleasure cats take in rolling in it. The plant looks great in a perennial border, but site it with care, due to its cat-attracting properties. It is also a seasoning and medicinal herb.

Description: Perennial growing to 3 feet tall and 2 feet wide. Sprawling stems with triangular, toothed 2-inch-long leaves smelling of camphor, thyme, and pennyroyal. Small, tubular white to pink edible flowers whorled around stems.

Site: Full sun to partial shade. Average, well-drained soil; pH 6.6. Good winter drainage is essential or plants may succumb to root rot. Space 12 to 18 inches apart. Grows well in containers.

Propagation: Direct-seed in spring or autumn. Self-sows readily. Division and cuttings in spring.

Care: Protect plants from cats until well established by covering plants with chicken wire. After flowering, cut back to several inches to get more blooms and maintain shape.

Harvest: Leaves when young to eat. Leaves and flowers in full bloom for medicine. Preserve by drying.

Other: Planted near vegetables, catnip is said to deter flea beetles, aphids, and beetles.

In the kitchen: Young leaves in salads or teas. Leaves in stews; rub meat with them before roasting or grilling. Brew a mintish tea with leaves.

In the home: Stuff cloth with dried leaves as toys for cats.

For health: Infusion of leaves internally to relieve colds, flu, insomnia, tension, indigestion, flatulence, or diarrhea; externally to relieve scalp irritations. Poultice of leaves and flowers for bruises. Colic in babies. Catnip lowers fever by increasing perspiration. It also has a sedative effect.

To harvest catnip for herbal use, plant several clumps of it—some for local cats to enjoy and some for you to harvest.

CHAMOMILE

Chamaemelum nobile
kam-ee-MEE-lum NO-bil-ay

■ Zones 4–10

Peter Rabbit's mother wasn't the first to recommend a tea made from chamomile flowers. Chamomile tea was revered by ancient Egyptians for its healing qualities. It's also known as Roman chamomile.

Description: Perennial growing to 8 inches tall and 18 inches wide. Finely cut feathery leaves. Daisylike 1-inch flowers in late summer and autumn. The cultivar 'Flore Pleno' has double flowers.

A similar plant is German chamomile, *Matricaria recutita*, an annual that grows to 24 inches tall and 6 inches wide. Leaves have a lighter scent and less bitter taste, but a slightly higher proportion of the volatile oil that is an anti-inflammatory and analgesic.

Site: Full sun, tolerates partial shade. Sandy, average, well-drained soil; pH 7. Space Roman chamomile 18 inches apart and German chamomile 6 inches apart.

Propagation: Direct-seed in spring or autumn. Divide cultivars in early spring; they do not produce seed.

Harvest: Leaves as needed. Flowers the day they open. Preserve by drying; keep for only one year.

Other: Flower infusion prevents damping-off in seedlings and speeds the composting process.

In the home: Infusion to prolong cut flowers. Flowers in potpourris.

For health: Infusion of flowers used internally for indigestion, nausea, fever, insomnia, hay fever, hyperactivity, or menstrual cramps; externally as a rinse for blonde hair or dandruff; facial tonic, lotion, cream, or steam; hand soak, eye compress, or in bath water. Ointment or oil for wounds, sunburn, eczema, or itchy skin.

Caution: People allergic to ragweed may react to chamomile. May cause dermatitis. Drink tea sparingly, no more than ½ cup daily for no more than two weeks at a time. Do not use chamomile oil during pregnancy.

If you love daisies, add a clump of chamomile to your garden.

CHERVIL

Anthriscus cereifolium
an-THRIS-kus seer-ee-FO-lee-um

■ All zones (an annual)

With its sweet aroma and refreshing flavor, chervil complements a wide range of foods and is essential in French cooking. Grown since ancient Roman times, chervil has long been a spring tonic ingredient because it is rich in vitamin C, beta carotene, iron, and magnesium.

Description: Hardy cool-season annual growing 12–18 inches. Fine-textured fernlike leaves. Clusters of tiny white flowers.

Site: Partial shade. Humus-rich, moist, well-drained soil; pH 6.5. Space 6 inches apart.

Propagation: Direct-seed at two-week intervals from early spring until summer and again late summer

To extend chervil's leaf production season, remove flower stalks as they appear and mulch plants.

to early autumn. Needs light to germinate. Self-sows readily.

Care: Best in cool, moist weather; goes to seed quickly with high temperatures and dry soil. Pinch out flower stalks to prolong growth. For fresh leaves year-round, overwinter in a cold frame or grow indoors.

Harvest: Leaves as needed until flowering. Preserve by freezing.

Other: Is said to repel slugs and keep ants and aphids away from lettuce plants.

In the kitchen: Leaves in salads, vegetables, chicken, fish, eggs, soups, sauces, vinegars, or butters. Add near the end of cooking.

In the home: Leaves or flowers in potpourris.

For health: Leaf infusion taken internally is said to aid digestion and improve liver and kidney functions and circulation; externally in facial cleansers or tonics or in compresses for sore joints, eczema, or wounds.

CHIVES

Allium schoenoprasum
AL-lee-um skee-no-PRAY-zum

■ Zones 3–10

Native to North America, Europe, and Asia, chives were not used in the West until Marco Polo brought them from China. With a delicate onion flavor, chives enhance a number of foods, blending especially well with marjoram and tarragon.

Description: Perennial growing to 12 to 18 inches, forming clumps 12 to 18 inches across. Slender, hollow leaves. Globular 1-inch heads of purplish-pink flowers.

Garlic or Chinese chives *(A. tuberosum)* have flat, solid leaves with a mild garlic flavor and 2-inch heads of white flowers (Zone 3). See growing details in the Gallery of Vegetables, page 47.

In the kitchen: Leaves or flowers in salads, vegetables, poultry, fish, soups, sauces, eggs, cheeses, butters, or vinegars. Add at the end of cooking or use as garnish.

In the home: Dried flowers in wreaths and herbal crafts.

For health: Leaves stimulate appetite and improve digestion.

Other: Leaf infusion as a spray for aphids or mildew. In mixed plantings, helps to repel insects.

Chive blossoms add an oniony, colorful touch to salads and sandwiches.

CILANTRO, CORIANDER, CHINESE PARSLEY

Coriandrum sativum
kor-ee-AN-drum sa-TY-vum

■ **All zones (an annual)**

A very widely used herb: The spicy, citrus-flavored seeds are called coriander; the leaves, called cilantro, have a pungent aroma that is either loved or hated.

Description: Hardy annual growing to 2 feet. Small open clusters of tiny pinkish white flowers. Rounded, ribbed beige seeds. 'Chinese', 'Slow-Bolt', and 'Long Standing' produce longer leaves.

Plants that have leaves with a similar flavor are Vietnamese coriander *(Polygonum odoratum),* a perennial from Southeast Asia, 12 inches with oval, pointed 2-inch leaves, withstands hot weather and grows well indoors (Zone 9). Mexican coriander *(Eryngium foetidum),* evergreen perennial, 18 inches tall and wide (Zone 8).

Site: Full sun to partial shade. Humus-rich, moist, well-drained soil; pH 6.6. Space 6 inches apart. Grows well in containers.

Propagation: Direct-seed after last frost; monthly plantings until late summer. Transplanting may cause plants to bolt.

Harvest: Lower leaves as needed. Seed heads when brown. Roots as the plants die.

In the kitchen: Fresh leaves in salads, salsas, marinades, stir-fries, rice, pastas, or vinegars and with shellfish. Whole or ground seeds in beans, curries, marinades, salad dressings, eggs, cheeses, lamb, sausages, pickles, chutneys, cooked fruits, breads, cakes, cookies, and coffees. Roots as a vegetable.

In the home: Seed in potpourris.

For health: Fresh leaves, seeds, or infusion internally to stimulate appetite or for indigestion, flatulence, or bad breath. Crushed seeds externally in a poultice or infused oil for sore joints or hemorrhoids.

Harvest cilantro's pungent leaves by snipping them at the base or by clipping only the amount you need.

COMFREY

Symphytum officinale
sim FY tum off-fi-si-NAH-lay

■ **Zones 5–9**

Long considered a panacea for many ills, today, comfrey leaves are known to contain alkaloids that cause liver damage and tumors, eliminating its internal use. Externally, it is still important in healing preparations.

Description: Perennial growing 2–4 feet. Hairy, pointed rough-textured leaves to 10 inches long. Spikes of purple to white ½-inch bell-like flowers in late spring. Invasive.

Site: Full sun to partial shade. Humus-rich, moist soil; pH 7. Space plants 3 feet apart.

Propagation: Germination is slow and erratic. Division in fall; cuttings in summer and fall.

Care: Plant where invasiveness is not a problem. If harvesting heavily, fertilize in spring and midsummer.

Harvest: Leaves as needed. Roots in autumn or early spring. Preserve roots by drying.

Other: Use leaves as a potassium-rich mulch around herbs, potatoes, or other plants. Soak leaves in water for a month to make a high-potassium liquid fertilizer. Leaves speed composting. Brew a leaf "tea" to soak compost pile.

For health: Leaf infusion in bath, hair rinses, or lotions and creams to soften skin and renew cells. Leaf or root poultice, compress, or ointment for sore joints, sprains, varicose veins, bunions, minor burns, wounds, bruises, or hemorrhoids.

Caution: Do not take internally.

Comfrey is a beautiful plant for any garden, but site it carefully: It's an invasive plant and will quickly spread.

Tanacetum balsamita
tan-a-SEE-tum ball-sam-EE-ta

Historically, costmary earned a place in every kitchen garden for its medicinal, culinary, and household uses.

COSTMARY
■ Zones 4–9

Costmary was popular during medieval and Elizabethan times for flavoring and preserving beer, strewing on floors, repelling insects, and aiding childbirth. Early American settlers often used a leaf as a bookmark in the family Bible. Fresh leaves are sweet, blending the fragrances of lemon, balsam, and mint; they are leathery when dry.

Description: Perennial ground-hugging plant that reaches 3 feet tall and 2 feet wide when in bloom. Bright green oval leaves to 10 inches long. Clusters of ½-inch daisylike flowers. Plants may need staking. Can be invasive.

Three close relatives of costmary well known for showy blossoms and insecticidal properties are feverfew (*T. parthenium*), painted daisy (*T. coccineum*), and pyrethrum (*Chrysanthemum cinerariifolium*).

Site: Full sun to partial shade. Humus-rich, moist, well-drained soil; pH 6.2. Space 2 feet apart. Plant with rapid spread in mind and do not mulch (runners spread above ground).

Propagation: Divide in spring or autumn. Difficult to grow from seed.

Harvest: Young leaves as needed. Preserve by drying.

In the kitchen: Leaves in green or fruit salads, fruitcakes, lemonade, teas, root vegetables, game dishes, or home-brewed beer.

In the home: Leaves in potpourris or insect repellents. Leaf infusion for a final rinse for linens. The leaf's use as a bookmark led to the common name Bible leaf.

For health: Leaf infusion internally for indigestion or intestinal cramps; externally in baths, as hair rinse, or as facial tonic. Leaf poultice or ointment for insect stings or minor burns.

Primula veris
PRIM-u-la VAIR-is

Cowslip heralds spring's arrival with cheery yellow blooms.

COWSLIP
■ Zones 5–9

Diminutive harbingers of spring, cowslips once grew abundantly in the meadows of Europe and England before the era of modern farming. Much folklore surrounds these plants, including that they are the keys St. Peter dropped from heaven. Legend has it they also preserve beauty in women.

Description: Perennial. Forms a rosette 6 inches across. Crinkled oval leaves. Leafless stems rise to 9 inches, topped by fragrant yellow bells in early spring.

Common primrose (*P. vulgaris*) is sometimes used in garden circles interchangeably with cowslip, but can be dangerous taken internally.

Site: Sun or light shade. Average, well-drained soil; pH 7. Space 6 inches apart.

Propagation: Direct-seed in early autumn. Division in late spring or early autumn.

Harvest: Leaves as needed. Flowers just as they open. Two-year-old roots in spring or autumn.

In the kitchen: Leaves in salads. Flowers in desserts, green or fruit salads, or teas. Flowers also used to make wine.

For health: Flower infusion said to be effective internally for insomnia, tension, allergies, or headaches; externally as facial lotion or ointment for wounds. Root decoction or leaf infusion traditionally used for coughs and colds, as a diuretic, or to slow blood clotting.

Caution: Do not take if pregnant, allergic to aspirin, or taking an anticoagulant drug.

PURPLE CONEFLOWER

Echinacea species
ek-in-AY-see-a

■ Zones 3–10

The roots of purple coneflower were an essential medicine for Native Americans of the prairies and were adopted as a cold and flu remedy by the settlers. Plants have antiviral, antifungal, antibacterial, and antiallergenic properties. They are also believed to stimulate the immune system overall.

Description: Perennial, growing 2–3 feet tall and wide. Pointed oval coarsely toothed leaves 3–8 inches long on bristly stems. Daisylike flowers to 4 inches across, prominent center of tiny purple florets surrounded by drooping magenta or pink petals.

E. angustifolia, E. purpurea, and *E. pallida* have the greatest medicinal potency. *E. purpurea* and its cultivars are widely grown as ornamental plants.

Site: Full sun to partial shade. Humus-rich, moist, well-drained soil; pH 6.5. Space 3 feet apart. Grows well in containers.
Propagation: Seed sown indoors or out in spring. Self-sows. Division in spring or autumn every four years.
Care: Cut off faded flowers. Handpick insect pests such as Japanese beetle.
Harvest: Three-year-old roots after several hard frosts as plant dies back. Replant crown after cutting off the main root.
Other: Attracts butterflies; very hardy; good cut flower.
For health: Root decoction or tincture internally for colds, flu, allergies, or fevers; externally for wounds; as a sore-throat gargle.

Purple coneflower variety 'Magnus' features flowers that attract butterflies in summer and birds in winter.

DILL

Anethum graveolens
a-NE-thum gra-VEE-o-lenz

■ All zones (an annual)

Prescribed 5,000 years ago by Egyptian doctors, mentioned as tax payment in the Bible, and included in magicians' spells and lovers' drinks in the Middle Ages, today dill is most notably appreciated for its tangy flavor.

Description: Annual. Ferny threadlike blue-green leaves. Flat 6-inch clusters of tiny yellow flowers. Flat, oval, light brown seeds. 'Fernleaf' grows to 18 inches and is good for containers.
Site: Full sun. Humus-rich, moist, well-drained soil; pH 6. Space 10 inches apart. Grows well in containers.
Propagation: Direct-seed every three weeks from spring until midsummer for a continuous supply of leaves. Self-sows. Plant in fall in hot climates.

Care: Protect from wind.
Harvest: Leaves as needed; cut off flowers for more foliage. Flowers when fully open. Seeds just as they turn brown. Cut seed heads 2–3 weeks after bloom; hang upside down in paper bags until the seeds dry and drop into the bags. Preserve by freezing or drying.
In the kitchen: Leaves (fresh) or seeds in soups, salads, egg, fish, lamb, pork, poultry, vegetables, vinegars, pickles, sauces, or breads.
In the home: Dried flowers in wreaths and other crafts.
For health: Seeds aid digestion and sweeten breath. Seed infusion internally for indigestion, flatulence, hiccups, stomach cramps, insomnia, colic, coughs, colds, flu, or menstrual cramps; diuretic.

To keep dill producing tasty leaves, clip flower shoots as soon as they form.

Sambucus species
sam-BEW-kus

Birds love elderberry fruit. If you intend to harvest berries, toss netting over plants to protect ripening fruit.

ELDER
■ Zones 3–5

The various species of this imposing shrub have a venerable history in many civilizations. Roots, stems, and leaves release cyanide and should be avoided. Flowers and berries are edible and used in decoctions and infusions to treat colds, burns, bruises, and complexion problems.

American elder *(S. canadensis)* grows to 12 feet with dark purple berries (Zone 3). European elder *(S. nigra)* may reach more than 20 feet with purplish-black berries (Zone 5). European red elder *(S. racemosa)* grows to 12 feet with red berries (Zone 3). All species are deciduous shrubs with leaves composed of five to seven oval, pointed, toothed leaflets and clusters of fragrant, creamy white flowers.

Site: Full sun to part shade. Moist, fertile soil; pH 6.5. Space plants 10 to 20 feet apart.

Propagation: Sow ripe berries outdoors. Semihardwood cuttings in summer. Hardwood cuttings in autumn.

Care: Prune in spring and fall to maintain plant shape and size. Cut back ornamental varieties to just above the ground.

Harvest: Flowers when fully open. Preserve by drying. Berries when shiny and purple or red.

Other: Attracts butterflies.

In the kitchen: Flowers in fritters, sorbets, teas, vinegars, or wines. Berries in pies, jellies, jams, or wines. Do not use raw berries.

In the home: Flowers in bouquets or potpourris.

For health: Flower infusion internally for cold, flu, cough, fever, arthritis, or hay fever; externally in bath, facial tonic, eye compress, or ointment for chapped skin; gargle for sore throat. Berries in syrup for cough or in decoction for sore joints.

Inula helenium
in-YOU-la hell-LEE-nee-um

Brightly flowered elecampane tosses open blooms from midsummer until frost.

ELECAMPANE
■ Zones 5–8

The Roman scholar Pliny reported that the Empress Julia Augusta ate the candied roots of elecamplane "to help digestion, to expel melancholy, and to cause mirth." Recent scientific observation shows that the roots are both antibacterial and antifungal.

Description: Perennial growing 4–6 feet tall and 3 feet across. Oval, pointed, bristly leaves to 2 feet long near the base; upper leaves are smaller. Daisylike yellow flowers to 4 inches across.

Site: Full sun to part shade. Average to rich, moist, clay soil; pH 7. Grow in a moist spot if possible. Shelter from wind. Space plants 3–5 feet apart.

Propagation: Direct-seed in spring. Self-sows. Division in spring or autumn at least every three years to renew the plants.

Care: Remove faded flower heads.

Harvest: Two-year-old roots in autumn after two hard frosts. Flowers when fully open. Preserve by drying.

In the kitchen: Root as a vegetable or a traditional flavoring for sweets.

In the home: Dried flowers in crafts. Petals in potpourri. Dried root as incense (strong smell of violets).

For health: Root decoction internally for various respiratory infections, coughs, or indigestion; externally for acne.

Foeniculum vulgare
fe-NICK-yu-lum vul-GAR-ay

FENNEL

■ Zones 4–9

The perennial herb fennel differs from the annual vegetable fennel (*F. vulgare azoricum;* see page 42) in that it does not form a white swollen base. But it does provide a fine texture in the garden, a softer, nuttier-flavored version of anise in the kitchen, and a gentle remedy for stomachaches. Fennel flowers attractive many beneficial insects.

Description: Perennial growing to 5 feet tall and 18 inches wide. Feathery, threadlike blue-green leaves. Flat 6-inch clusters of tiny edible yellow flowers. Oval, ribbed brown seeds. Varieties 'Bronze' and 'Rubrum' both have edible, bronze-red leaves.

Site: Full sun. Average, moist, well-drained soil; pH 6.5. Space 18 inches apart.

Propagation: Direct-seed in spring.

Care: According to folklore, fennel planted nearby adversely affects the growth of beans, dill (can hybridize with dill to produce unfavorable seedlings), caraway, tomatoes, kohlrabi, coriander, and wormwood.

Harvest: Leaves as needed before flowering. Preserve by freezing. Stems just before flowering. Seeds just as they turn brown.

In the kitchen: Leaves in salads, fish, pork, eggs, beans, rice, butters, vegetables, or vinegars; add near the end of cooking. Stems in salads or soups. Seeds in sausages, duck, grains, rice, eggs, cabbage, beets, sauerkraut, potatoes, breads, or butters.

For health: Leaf or seed infusion taken internally for indigestion, flatulence, or suppressing appetite; externally in facial tonics or steams, gargle for sore throats or mouthwash, or for eye compresses.

Fennel deserves a place in every garden, not just for its ferny texture but for its wonderfully flavorful foliage.

Tanacetum parthenium
tan-u-SEE-tum par-THEE-nih-um

FEVERFEW

■ Zones 4–9

Since ancient Rome, feverfew has been an ingredient in sweets and wines, a medicinal for a wide range of ills, and an insect repellent. Recently it has been asserted that feverfew's bitter leaves can help relieve migraines.

Description: Perennial growing 2–4 feet tall and 18 inches wide. Many-branched plant with yellowish-green, deeply lobed and divided leaves to 3 inches long. Daisylike white flowers 1 inch across from midsummer to early autumn. 'Snowball', 'White Pompon', and 'White Stars' are double-flowered forms. 'Aureum' has golden leaves; it is not as active medicinally.

Site: Full sun to part shade. Average, well-drained soil; pH 6.3. Space 18 inches apart. Invasive; set apart from other plants. Grows well as a container garden plant.

Propagation: Seed sown indoors or outside in spring. Division in spring or autumn. Cuttings in summer.

Harvest: Leaves before flowering. Pick flowers just as they open. Preserve leaves by freezing or flowers by drying.

Other: Repels bees, so do not grow near plants that need bees for pollination, such as vegetables. Resembles chamomile.

In the home: Dried flowers in potpourri or crafts. Leaves in moth-repellent mixtures. Leaf infusion as a disinfectant. Flower heads dried or ground to form a safe insecticide.

For health: Infusion traditionally taken internally for migraine headaches, tension, arthritis, or insomnia. Eat no more than four small leaves daily. Leaf infusion also used for a facial tonic.

Preserve feverfew summer-bright blooms for use in potpourri or dried-flower crafts.

Zingiber officinale
ZIN-ji-ber off-fi-si-NAH-lay

It's possible to grow ginger for harvesting roots in climates with long, warm growing seasons.

GINGER

■ Zones 9–11

Ginger hails from Asia, where its healing properties and flavorful attributes are part of a centuries-old tradition. Combining spice and citrus flavors, ginger roots today flavor foods and beverages around the world and are a favorite medicine.

Description: Tropical perennial growing 2–4 feet. Lance-shaped leaves to 12 inches long and 2 inches wide. Conelike 3-inch spikes of yellow and purple flowers; usually produced only in warm climates with long growing seasons.

Site: Full sun to part shade. Humus-rich, moist, well-drained soil; pH 6.5.

Propagation: Divide rhizomes in early spring; plant horizontally 1 inch deep.

Care: Maintain even soil moisture. Plant typically goes dormant in winter, showing little growth, although stems may remain green.

Harvest: Rhizomes in late autumn, cutting off stalks and removing fibrous roots. Keep some to start next year's plants. Peel, cut into 1-inch cubes, and store in vodka in the refrigerator.

In the kitchen: Fresh rhizome in marinades, stir-fries, drinks, fruit salads, preserves, quick breads, muffins, cakes, cookies, or roast meats; especially wonderful with sweet potatoes, winter squash, carrots, beets, pumpkin, rhubarb, or peaches. Also crystallized as a sweet or used in desserts.

For health: Infusion made from rhizomes for colds, flu, fever, constipation, indigestion, nausea, motion sickness, morning sickness, flatulence, and poor circulation.

Panax species
PA-nacks

Dried roots of ginsing are highly prized for their tonic qualities.

GINSENG

■ Zones 4–7

Ginseng has been valued for its therapeutic benefits for more than 7,000 years. Folklore credits it with everything from providing wisdom, long life, and sexual potency to improving stamina and resistance to disease. It is also believed to battle about 70 other specific conditions. Research suggests it may protect against mental and physical stress, increase physical endurance, and assist in maintaining vitality.

Description: Perennial growing to 18 inches. Young plants have one to two leaves, with up to six leaves after three years, each divided into five toothed leaflets radiating from a central point. Clusters of ½-inch green flowers. Bright red berries, each with two to three white seeds.

American ginseng is *Panax quinquefolius*, and Asian ginseng is *P. pseudoginseng*. Siberian ginseng (*Eleutherococcus senticosus*) is a related, deciduous shrub growing to 10 feet; it has similar properties but is considered to be more stimulating.

Site: Partial shade. Humus-rich, moist, well-drained soil; pH 6. Space 24 inches apart.

Propagation: Seed difficult to germinate; sow ripe seed in autumn in pots left outdoors or in seedbed; a cold period of four months is necessary for germination.

Care: Winter mulch. Good drainage is critical to prevent rot. Requires ample warmth and humidity during the growing season.

Harvest: Five- to seven-year-old roots in autumn. Preserve by drying.

For health: Root decoction or tincture used generally for stress, nervous exhaustion, lack of appetite, or recovery after an illness or injury.

Caution: Do not take ginseng for more than six weeks at a time. Avoid caffeine when taking ginseng; it can result in overstimulation. Do not take when pregnant.

Hydrastis canadensis
hy-DRAS-tis kan-a-DEN-sis

■ Zones 3–7

Goldenseal is a North American medicinal herb prized by the Cherokee and other tribes. They used it externally to repel insects and treat wounds and internally for stomach and liver problems. Astringent and antibacterial properties counter infection and check inflammation.

Description: Perennial growing to 12 inches. Downy 12-inch-wide leaves deeply divided into five to seven finely toothed lobes. Single ½-inch greenish white flowers. Orange-red berries.

Site: Partial to full shade. Humus-rich, moist soil; pH 6.5. Space 8 inches apart.

Propagation: Difficult from seed, germination may take two years;

GOLDENSEAL

direct-seed in autumn. Division in late autumn, when dormant.

Care: Mulch in summer and winter. Protect from wind.

Harvest: Three- or four-year-old roots in autumn. Preserve by drying.

For health: Root decoction internally for stress and anxiety, to reduce heavy menstrual bleeding, and to soothe digestive system; externally as an eyewash; gargle for sore throats and infected gums; douche for yeast infections.

Caution: Has a cumulative effect, so avoid overuse. Avoid if suffering from high blood pressure or if pregnant or nursing.

Goldenseal populations in the wild have been ravaged by collectors. Be sure to purchase nursery-propagated plants.

Humulus lupulus
HEW-mew-lus LUP-yew-lus

■ Zones 3–6

Few herbs are grown on the scale of hops, which are used as a flavoring and preservative in beer. Powerful sedative and antiseptic properties. In the garden, hop vines readily cover trellises and arbors. They can grow 6 to 12 inches a day and as much as 25 feet a year.

Description: Perennial vine growing to 25 feet. Coarse, hairy, 3-inch-long, heart-shaped to lobed leaves with serrated edges. Male and female flowers on separate plants. Many cultivars grown for beer.

Site: Full sun. Like plenty of water. Humus-rich, well-drained soil; pH 6.5. Space 6 feet apart.

Propagation: Start indoors in early spring. Plant cuttings or suckers in early spring.

Care: Vines need ample support and plenty of room to grow.

EUROPEAN HOPS

Harvest: Hops when amber brown and partially dry. Preserve by drying, then refrigerate. Loses effectiveness in six months.

In the kitchen: Hops flavor beer. Young shoots eaten as a vegetable, either raw or steamed like asparagus. Flowers can be used raw in salads.

In the home: Flowers dried in wreaths and arrangements. Vines woven into baskets.

For health: Hop-stuffed pillow or hop infusion for insomnia. Tincture taken internally for stress, anxiety, headaches, indigestion, or menstrual pain.

Caution: Do not take if suffering from depression.

Hops vines leap out of the ground and rocket skyward. Give vines sturdy supports, and they'll hoist themselves heavenward.

Marrubium vulgare
mar-REW-bee-um vul-GAR-ay

HOREHOUND

■ Zones 4–9

Horehound drops or syrups have soothed scratchy throats and coughs with their bittersweet, menthol-like quality since the days of ancient Greece.

Description: Perennial growing 2 to 3 feet. Bushy plants with woolly stems and leaves. Serrated oval leaves to 2 inches long. White to pink-purple flowers in dense whorls.

Site: Full sun. Sandy, well-drained soil; can handle poor dry soil; pH 7. Space 12 to 15 inches apart. Suitable for Container culture.

Propagation: Sow seed indoors or out. Self-sows. Division in spring.

Care: Cut off faded flowers to prevent self-sowing. Seeds easily and can become a nuisance. Trim in spring to keep plants bushy. Diligently remove unwanted seedlings during growing season and especially in early spring.

Harvest: Leaves just before flower buds form. Best leaves at the top third of the plant. Preserve by drying and storing in airtight containers.

Other: Attractive to bees. Thought to discourage flies.

In the kitchen: Leaves and seeds in teas, added to iced tea or lemonade, or flavoring for beer.

In the home: Flowers in dried bouquets and crafts; branches in dried arrangements.

For health: Leaf infusion, syrup, or candy for coughs or sore throats; leaf infusion for bronchitis or coughs.

Remove spent blooms on horehound faithfully to prevent unruly, rapid spread.

Hyssopus officinalis
his-SOAP-us off-fi-si-NAY-lis

HYSSOP

■ Zones 3–11

The minty, bittersweet flavor of hyssop has long played a role in a wide range of foods, including several commercial liqueurs. Hyssop has fine texture and a long bloom period. It also attracts hummingbirds, bees, and butterflies.

Description: Perennial growing to 30 inches tall and 3 feet across. Sprawling stems with semievergreen narrow leaves to 1 inch long. Spikes of ½-inch edible blue flowers from summer to autumn.

Site: Full sun to part shade. Average, well-drained soil; pH 6 to 7. Space 3 feet apart.

Propagation: Seed sown indoors or out. Stem cuttings in late spring or early summer. Plant divisions in spring or autumn.

Care: Remove faded flowers to prolong blooms and encourage bushy growth. Trim in spring and fall to maintain shape.

Harvest: Leaves as needed; best before flowering. Flowers when blooms are three-quarters open. Preserve by drying.

Other: Said to repel flea beetles and lure cabbage moths away from cruciferous vegetables.

In the kitchen: Flowers in salads. Leaves in green or fruit salads, oily fish, game, lamb, poultry, tomatoes, soups, stews, sausages, fruit pies, or dessert syrups. Combine with mint or lemon balm to brew a refreshing tea.

In the home: Flowers or leaves in potpourri. Fresh or dried flowers in bouquets or crafts.

For health: Leaf infusion internally for sore throat, respiratory infection, poor appetite, or indigestion; externally for bath or facial steam. Leaf poultice for wounds or bruises.

Caution: Do not use medicinally when pregnant.

Hyssop leaves and blossoms are edible. Use them in salads for colorful additions, or brew tea with them.

LADY'S MANTLE

Alchemilla mollis
al-ke-MILL-a MOL-lis

■ Zones 4–7

The magical drops of dew that collect in the leaves of lady's mantle were the stuff of alchemists' potions. Its favor today is mainly based on its ornamental beauty.

Description: Perennial growing to 18 inches tall and 24 inches wide. Bushy plants with deeply folded, velvety, rounded 3-inch bright green leaves with scalloped and serrated edges. Open sprays of tiny yellow-green flowers. Plants sold as *A. vulgaris* are usually *A. mollis*. There are more than 200 species.

Site: Full sun or part shade. Humus-rich, moist, well-drained soil; pH 7. Space 2 feet apart. Container culture ok in large containers.

Propagation: Seed sown indoors or out. Self-sows. Plant divisions in spring or autumn.

Care: Remove faded flowers. In hot climates, cut plants back by half in midsummer to stimulate fresh growth for fall.

Harvest: Leaves as needed. Flowers when fully open. Preserve both by drying.

For health: Leaf infusion internally is said to regulate monthly cycle or provide menopause relief. Also said to ease diarrhea. Externally as facial tonic or steam, especially for large pores or acne and for lightening freckles; in cream for dry skin; gargle after tooth extraction. Medicinal compress for inflamed eyes or wounds and inflammation.

Chartreuse blooms blend beautifully with soft green foliage on lady's mantle. Use as an edging plant in borders.

LAVENDER

Lavandula species
la-VAN-dew-la

■ Zones 5–9

Lavender is among the most evocative of all fragrances. A favorite bath additive of both the ancient Greeks and Romans, lavender takes its name from the Latin *lavare,* meaning to wash.

Description: Perennial, growing 18 to 36 inches, depending on cultivar. Bushy to sprawling plants with small, lance-shaped greenish-gray leaves. Spikes of lavender blossoms; also purple, pink, and white forms. Many species and cultivars; grow tender varieties as annuals.

Site: Full sun. Average, well-drained soil; pH 7.1. Space 1 to 3 feet apart. Containers, especially in terra-cotta.

Propagation: Seed sown indoors. Cuttings in spring, summer, or early autumn. Layer in late summer.

Care: Remove faded flowers. Trim in spring to maintain size and shape and to remove dead wood. Do not prune old wood; it will not regrow.

Harvest: Flowers just as they open. Preserve by drying.

In the kitchen: Use fresh or dried flowers sparingly in cakes, cookies, muffins, jellies, black tea, vinegars, fruits, or eggs. Crystallize flowers

In the home: Fresh flowers in bouquets. Dried flowers in wreaths and crafts. Moth repellent.

For health: Flower infusion internally for stress, anxiety, headaches, poor appetite, indigestion, flatulence, fainting, or bad breath; externally for relaxing baths, facial tonics or creams, hair rinses, or cold compresses for headaches. Flower oil massaged on skin for muscle or joint pain, insomnia, stress, inflammation, burns, or cuts (dilute to avoid dermatitis).

Plant lavender for its medicinal uses, but you'll discover you love it for its unbeatable beauty and aroma.

LEMON BALM

Melissa officinalis
me-LIS-sa off-fi-si-NAY-lis

Remove lemon balm stems below flowers when you see blossom buds emerge to encourage bushiness.

■ Zones 4–9

A strong scent of lemon with a touch of mint, lemon balm makes an excellent tea and adds flavor when sprinkled over cooked vegetables or in fruit salads.

Description: Perennial growing to 2 feet tall and wide. Bushy plant with heart-shaped, scallop-edged leaves.

Site: Full sun to part shade. Average, well-drained soil; pH 7. Space 2 feet apart.

Propagation: Seed sown indoors. Self-sows. Cuttings in late spring or early summer. Division in spring or autumn.

Care: Cut back after flowering to prevent self-sowing. Winter mulch. Cut off dead stems in spring as new growth emerges.

Harvest: Leaves as needed. Preserve by drying, but it loses much of its fragrance and therapeutic value.

Other: Attracts bees. Intense scent occurs in poor soils. Tolerates shade and moisture more than most herbs.

In the kitchen: Leaves in teas, lemonade, wines, or liqueurs and in fish, mushrooms, soft cheeses, dips, or fruit salads. Add at the end of cooking.

In the home: Dried in potpourri. Fresh leaves as furniture polish.

For health: Leaf infusion internally for anxiety, mild depression, nervousness, headaches, insomnia, indigestion, or nausea; externally in lotion or ointment for cold sores, cuts, or insect stings.

LEMONGRASS

Cymbopogon species
sim-bo-PO-gon

A clump of lemongrass adds architectural interest, motion, and sound to the garden with its fountain of rustling leaves.

■ Zones 9–11

Lemongrass is an essential element in Southeast Asian cooking, but it can also liven up other foods as well. The leaves brew a wonderfully relaxing tea.

Description: Perennial forming a clump to 5 feet tall and 3 feet wide. Long, slender, arching grassy leaves. Blades are sharp-edged and can cut the skin. Rarely flowers except in the tropics.

Site: Full sun. Humus-rich, moist soil; pH 6.5. Space 2 to 4 feet apart.

Propagation: Division in spring or early summer, cutting back to 4 inches. Can be started from a side shoot planted after frost has passed.

Care: Fertilize monthly during growing season with a balanced water-soluble fertilizer.

Harvest: Leaf base as needed, pulling older, outside stems from the base. Freeze short pieces. Cut leaves as needed. Dry leaves in the dark so they'll hold their color.

In the kitchen: Peeled base of the bulbous stem used in a wide variety of Southeast Asian dishes, as well as in stir-fries, soups, pastas, vegetables, curries, or fish.

In the home: Dried leaves aromatic in potpourri.

For health: Leaf infusion internally for indigestion, stress, flatulence, or fevers; externally as a poultice for muscle pain.

LEMON VERBENA

Aloysia triphylla
a-LOY-see-a tri-FY-la

■ Zones 9–11

A tropical shrub from Chile, lemon verbena has a sharp, intensely lemony fragrance and flavor. The essential oil has been used—and adored—in perfumes since the 18th century.

Description: Deciduous shrub growing to 10 feet tall and 8 feet wide. Slender branches with lance-shaped leaves to 4 inches long and ½ inch wide. Open sprays of tiny white and purple flowers.

Site: Full sun. Average, well-drained soil; pH 7. Space 4 feet apart. Adapted to container culture.

Propagation: Seed sown indoors in spring. Tip cuttings in late spring, late summer, or early autumn.

Care: Bring in container-grown plants before first frost. Plants may drop leaves during winter. In spring prune to maintain shape and size. Fertilize plants in containers during the summer.

Harvest: Leaves as needed. Preserve by drying.

In the kitchen: Leaves in sauces, marinades, salad dressings, teas, drinks, vinegars, fruit desserts, jellies, cakes, or ice creams. Chop tough leaves finely.

In the home: Leaves in potpourri or infused in wax to scent candles.

For health: Leaves in oil for massages, face and hand lotions, and creams. Leaf infusion internally as a sedative tea or for nasal congestion, indigestion, nausea, flatulence, or stomach cramps; externally in bath water for relaxation or in a compress for puffy or irritated eyes.

Caution: Long-term use of large amounts of lemon verbena may cause stomach irritation.

The lance-shaped leaves of lemon verbena can prove somewhat tough to chew. Chop them finely for culinary use.

LICORICE

Glycyrrhiza glabra
gly-kir-RY-za GLAY-bra

■ Zones 7–9

Besides flavoring candy, stout licorice roots are a powerful anti-inflammatory. The Latin name *Glycyrrhiza* comes from *glykys,* meaning sweet, and *rhiza,* root.

Description: Perennial growing to 4 feet tall and 3 feet wide. Large leaves divided into oval leaflets. Spikes of pealike purple-and-white flowers up to ½ inch long.

Gan cao (*G. uralensis* syn. *G. viscida)* has therapeutic qualities similar to licorice and is important in Chinese medicine.

Site: Full sun to part shade. Deep, humus-rich, moist soil; pH 7. Plant 3 feet apart.

Propagation: Grows easily from seed. Division in spring or autumn when dormant.

Care: Grows best with long, hot summers. Invasive; confine with a buried barrier. Winter mulch.

Harvest: Three- to four-year-old roots in early winter. Harvest thoroughly; any piece of root left in the ground will start a new plant. Preserve by drying after peeling bitter bark.

For health: Root decoction or tincture for colds, sore throat, constipation, indigestion, or stomach cramps.

Caution: Large doses may cause headaches, high blood pressure, or water retention. Do not take if anemic or pregnant.

To corral licorice's wandering ways, plant it in a pot with the bottom removed, leaving the pot rim sticking above the soil.

Levisticum officinale
le-VIS-ti-kum off-fi-si-NAH-lay

LOVAGE

■ Zones 3–7

If you like to cook, plant a clump of lovage in your garden. You'll discover an array of uses for it in the kitchen.

Lovage's strong celery-like flavor benefits soups, stews, and roasts; lovage tea settles an upset stomach. Travelers in the Middle Ages laid lovage leaves in their shoes for their deodorizing and antiseptic effects.

Description: Perennial growing to 6 feet tall and 2 feet wide. Glossy deeply divided and toothed leaves on long stems. Flat clusters of tiny yellow-green flowers.

Site: Full sun to part shade. Humus-rich, moist, well-drained soil; pH 6.5. Plant 2 feet apart.

Propagation: Seed sown in late summer or early autumn. Self-sows. Division in spring to early summer every four years.

Care: To encourage bushy growth and continuous leaf production, clip off flowers as they appear.

Harvest: Leaves as needed. Preserve by drying or freezing. Seeds when ripe in late summer (when they first begin to brown). Two- or three-year-old roots just before flowering.

In the kitchen: Leaves or stems in salads, soups, stocks, marinades, stews, cheeses, potato salads, rice, stuffings, tomato sauces, or roasts. Stems or roots cooked as a side dish. Seeds, whole or ground, in pickles, biscuits, cheese spreads, salads, dressings, or sauces.

For health: Leaf infusion or root decoction internally for indigestion, water retention, menstrual pain, urinary tract infections; externally for treating wounds.

Caution: Do not take medicinally when pregnant or if you have kidney problems.

Origanum majorana
or-RIG-a-num ma-jor-RAY-na

SWEET MARJORAM

■ Zones 9–11

If oregano proves too harsh for you, plant sweet marjoram.

Sweet marjoram's spicy-sweet flavor is slightly milder than that of its relative, oregano. It is a primary herb used in preparing Italian food.

Description: Tender perennial treated as an annual, growing to 1 foot tall and 6 inches wide. Velvety oval leaves to 1 inch long. Clustered spikes open into tiny edible pink or white flowers.

Site: Full sun. Average to sandy well-drained soil; pH 7. Plant 8 inches apart.

Propagation: Seed started indoors; slow to germinate. Cuttings or layerings in spring or early summer.

Care: Water sparingly and trim to keep in shape.

Harvest: Leaves as needed or major harvest just before flowering and again before frost. Preserve by drying or freezing.

In the kitchen: Leaves in salads, cheeses, fish, beef, pork, sausages, tomatoes, cabbage-family vegetables, potato soup, or vinegars. Add near the end of cooking.

In the home: Rub fresh leaves on furniture to polish. Dried leaves and flowers in potpourri.

For health: Leaf infusion internally for colds, fevers, coughs, headaches, insomnia, indigestion, menstrual pain, or anxiety; in steam for sinus problems; externally in baths or hair rinse; ointment or compress for sore or stiff joints, muscular pain, or sprains; gargle for sore throat.

Caution: Do not take medicinally during pregnancy.

MARSH MALLOW

Althaea officinalis
al-THEE-a off-fi-si-NAY-lis

■ Zones 3–9

Originally marshmallow candy was made with powdered marsh mallow root, water, and sugar. The mucilage in the leaves, roots, and flowers has soothed since ancient times.

Description: Perennial growing 4 feet tall, 2 feet wide. Velvety gray-green leaves to 3 inches on woolly branching stems. Edible white or pink flowers 1 to 2 inches across.

Site: Full sun. Average, moist to wet soil; pH 7. Plant 2 feet apart.

Propagation: Cuttings in spring; direct sow, fall; divisions, spring or fall.

Care: Cut back by half after bloom.

Harvest: Leaves as needed, before plants bloom. Two-year-old roots in autumn after heavy frost. Dry leaves or roots or make syrup with roots.

In the kitchen: Flowers or young leaves in salads, soups, or stews. In the Middle East, roots are boiled and then fried with onions and butter.

For health: Leaf infusion or root decoction internally for sore throat, indigestion, or insomnia; externally for dry hands, sunburn, or rinse for dry hair; in facial steams, masks, or lotions. Root poultice for warming and healing. Flower poultice for insect bites.

Marsh mallow blooms attract bees and butterflies to the garden.

MEADOWSWEET

Filipendula ulmaria
fill-i-PEN-dew-la ul-MAR-ee-a

■ Zones 3–9

Meadowsweet leaves have a wintergreen fragrance and flowers are almond scented. Contains salicylic acid, an aspirin ingredient.

Description: Perennial growing to 2 feet tall and wide. Dark green deeply veined toothed leaves made of up to five pairs of large leaflets separated by pairs of smaller leaflets. Clusters of small white flowers.

Site: Full sun to part shade. Humus-rich, moist, well-drained soil; pH 7. Space 2 feet apart.

Propagation: Seed sown indoors in spring; divisions in autumn.

Harvest: Leaves as needed before flowering. Flowers as they open. Preserve by drying.

In the home: Dried flowers or leaves in potpourri or in sachets tucked among linens.

For health: Flower infusion used internally for headaches, colds, fever, heartburn, diarrhea, insomnia, or water retention; externally as a facial tonic. Remedy for stomach problems, and hyperacidity.

Caution: Do not use if sensitive to aspirin.

As the name suggests, meadowsweet loves moist meadows where its perfumed blooms glow in the sun.

MILK THISTLE

Silybum marianum
sil-LY-bum mar-ee-AY-num

■ All zones (An annual or biennial)

Milk thistle is an old remedy for liver problems, courtesy of the compound silymarin. Seeds have the highest concentration of it; leaves, flowers, and roots also contain it.

Description: Annual or biennial to 4 feet tall and 2 feet wide. Deeply cut leaves with spiny margins and white veins. Magenta-purple flowers.

Site: Full sun. Average to humus-rich, well-drained soil; pH 6.5. Space 2 feet apart.

Propagation: Direct-seed in spring or autumn. Self-sows.

Care: Remove flowers to prolong attractive appearance.

Harvest: Young leaves as needed. Flowers before they open if eating; after if drying. Roots in autumn. Preserve by drying.

In the kitchen: Flower eaten like artichokes. Young leaves in salads or as cooked greens. Roots boiled.

In the home: Dried flowers in wreaths and crafts.

For health: Seed infusion aids liver function and helps liver renew cells and combat drug or chemical damage. Used as a poison antidote.

Milk thistle leaves boast eye-catching silvery veining.

MINT

■ Zones 5–10

Mint is a widely used flavoring in foods, beverages, chewing gums, candies, and toothpastes. Menthol is the active ingredient in peppermint and Japanese mint. Spearmint and other mints that do not contain menthol are versatile in cooking.

Description: Perennials growing to 2 feet. Oval, pointed 2-inch leaves in pairs on square stems. Spikes of tiny pink or white flowers. Almost all are very easy to grow.

There are more than 600 species and cultivars of mint. Some of the best for cooking include spearmint (*M. spicata*), Austrian mint (*M. ×gracilis*), curly mint (*M. spicata* 'Crispa'), Moroccan mint (*M. spicata* 'Moroccan'), Vietnamese mint (*M. ×gracilis*), 'Bowles Mint' (*M. ×villosa alopecuroides*), red raripila mint (*M. ×smithiana*), and Kentucky Colonel mint (*M. ×cordifolia*).

Flavored mints include apple mint (*M. suaveolens*), pineapple mint (*M. s.* 'Variegata'), ginger mint (*M. ×gracilis* 'Variegata'), chocolate mint (*M. ×piperita* 'Chocolate'), and lemon mint (*M. dulca citreus*).

Mints richest in menthol include field mint (*M. arvensis*), Japanese mint (*M. arvensis* var. *piperascens*), peppermint (*M. ×piperita*), horsemint (*M. longifolia*), orange mint (*M. ×piperita* 'Citrata'), and water mint (*M. aquatica*).

Many mints are low-growing enough to be tried as a groundcover. Corsican mint (*M. requienii*) grows only an inch tall and is considered the least rampant of the mints. Pennyroyal (*M. pulegium*) has a long history as an insect repellent. Do not take pennyroyal internally.

Site: Partial shade, tolerates full sun. Average, moist, well-drained soil; pH 6.5. Plant 2 feet apart.

Propagation: Division in spring or fall; cuttings in spring or summer. Stem cuttings root easily in water, vermiculite, or perlite.

Taste various mints at an herbal nursery. Pineapple mint has a fruity fragrance and flavor.

Care: Grow in large pots above ground or sunk to the rim to restrain invasive roots or sink barriers 12 inches deep on all sides of the plant. Remove flowers to prevent cross-pollination.

Harvest: Pick only the top tender leaves for cooking, best when used fresh. Preserve by drying or freezing.

Other: Bees love mint flowers. Plants can be mowed and will come back vigorously.

In the kitchen: Leaves for potatoes, peas, carrots, fruit salads, meat sauces, jellies, syrups, vinegars, cookies, quick breads, or teas and other drinks. Flowers in desserts, cakes, or fruit salads.

In the home: Fresh leaves in bouquets, baths, sachets, cosmetics and soaps. Dried leaves in potpourris. Pennyroyal may deter ants and fleas.

For health: Leaf infusion used internally for indigestion, colds, flu, hiccups, flatulence, or insomnia; externally for chapped skin, rinse for oily hair, or facial tonic.

Famous for flavoring juleps and chewing gum, spearmint is easy to grow, yielding ample leaves for harvest.

MYRTLE

Myrtus communis
MIR-tus kom-MEW-nis

■ **Zones 9–10**

In ancient Greece myrtle was sacred to Aphrodite, goddess of love and beauty, and brides today still carry it in wedding bouquets to symbolize love and fidelity. Although tender, myrtle grows well in containers and is often trained as a topiary.

Description: Semievergreen shrub growing to 10 feet tall and 7 feet wide. Small, glossy dark leaves with juniper and orange scent. Fragrant white flowers; small purple-black fruit. 'Variegata' has gray-green leaves edged white and is less hardy. 'Flore Pleno' has double flowers. 'Microphylla' and 'Microphylla Variegata' grow to 3 feet tall.

Site: Full sun to part shade. Humus-rich, moist, well-drained soil; pH 7.

Propagation: Seed sown indoors in spring. Cuttings in summer.

Care: Trim plants in spring to shape; also remove dead or damaged wood.

Harvest: Leaves as needed; use fresh or dried. Flowers as they open. Fruit when ripe. Preserve fruit by drying; store whole or ground.

In the kitchen: Leaves with roast pork, lamb, or fowl. Berries can substitute for juniper berries.

In the home: Dried leaves or flowers in potpourri. Leaf infusion for furniture polish.

For health: Leaf infusion considered to be effective internally for urinary infections, vaginal discharge, bronchial congestion, sinusitis, or coughs; externally as an antiseptic wash, facial tonic, or compress for bruises or hemorrhoids; ointment for blemishes; gargle for gum infections. Use berry decoction as a rinse for dark hair.

Myrtle is an ornamental plus to any landscape, but it can be invasive because birds eat the fruit and pass the seeds elsewhere.

OREGANO

Origanum vulgare
or-RIG-a-num vul GAR-ay

■ **Zones 5–9**

The herb that's synonymous with pizza and tomato sauce brings confusion to the garden due to numerous species and cultivars. Oregano is sometimes called wild marjoram. *O. vulgare* often has little flavor; some varieties, however, do provide good flavor.

Description: Perennial growing to 18 inches tall and wide. Upright to lax stems with velvety leaves. Clusters of ¼-inch edible mauve or white flowers.

Flavorful forms include Greek oregano (*O. vulgare hirtum*), Syrian (*O. maru*), Kalitera (*O. 'Kalitera'*), microphylla (*O. microphyllum*), compact (*O. vulgare* 'Compactum'), and Turkestan (*O. tyttanicum*). Pot marjoram (*O. onites*) is also called Greek oregano but is inferior.

Site: Select a site with full sun and average, well-drained soil; pH 6.8. Space plants 18 inches apart.

Propagation: Cuttings in summer. Division in spring or autumn.

Harvest: Leaves as needed. For a large harvest, cut back to 3 inches just before flowering and again in late summer. Preserve leaves by drying or freezing.

In the kitchen: Leaves with salads, cheeses, eggs, tomato sauces, marinated vegetables, roasted and stewed beef, poultry, game, beans, shellfish, soups, vinegars, or pastas. Add toward the end of cooking.

For health: Leaf infusion internally for indigestion, coughs, headaches, or painful menstruation; externally in baths for muscle pain or stiff joints. Flower infusion for seasickness.

Caution: Do not use medicinally during pregnancy.

Golden oregano (*O. vulgare* 'Aureum') does double-duty in the garden, looking and tasting good.

PARSLEY

Petroselinum crispum
pet-ro-se-LY-num KRISS-pum

■ Zones 5–10

Parsley is rich in vitamin C and iron. In cooking, parsley pulls flavors together; the flat-leaf form is especially flavorful.

Description: Biennial, usually grown as an annual. The curly-leaf form grows 8 to 12 inches with finely cut, ruffled deep green leaves on long stems. Several named cultivars. The flat-leaf form grows to 18 to 24 inches with bright green leaves resembling celery. Flat clusters of tiny yellow-green flowers appear during the second year of growth. See the Gallery of Vegetables, page 48.

In the kitchen: Leaves with salads, sandwiches, eggs, vegetables, meats, soups, stews, roasts, sauces, or vinegars. Flat-leaf parsley has a stronger, more pungent taste than curly parsley; use it sparingly so it doesn't overpower other flavors.

For health: Leaf infusion internally for water retention, urinary infections, or indigestion; externally in poultices or compresses for sprains, wounds, or insect bites; in hair rinses, facial tonics, or steams; as a skin lotion. Infusion of leaves and stems is soothing in baths.

Caution: Avoid medicinal use when pregnant because large doses can irritate the kidneys.

Plant curly-leaf parsley for a frilled border edging in the garden.

PINK DIANTHUS

Dianthus species
dy-AN-thus

■ Zones 5–9

With the genus name translating as "divine flower," pink dianthus has been cherished for centuries for its clove scent and delicate flavor.

Description: Evergreen perennial forming a loose, spreading mat 6 to 12 inches tall. Long, narrow blue- to gray-green leaves. Fragrant, edible, single or double, white, pink, bicolored, or red flowers on thin, leafless stems. Numerous cultivars of pinks (*D. plumarius*), cheddar pinks (*D. gratianopolitanus*), and clove pinks (*D. caryophyllus*).

Site: Full sun. Average, well-drained soil; pH 7. Space 1 foot apart.

Propagation: Division in summer after flowering; layering in late summer; cuttings in spring. Variable from seed.

Care: Spider mites may become a problem in long, hot summers; spray with insecticidal soap. Deadheading prolongs blooming. Avoid wet soil to prevent crown rot.

Harvest: Flowers as they open. Preserve by drying.

Other: Attracts butterflies and bees. May self-sow if allowed to seed.

In the kitchen: Remove bitter white heel; then add petals to salads, pies, sandwiches, vinegars, wines, beverages, jellies, or sugar.

In the home: Dried flowers in potpourri blends.

For health: The petals of pinks placed in white wine are said to ease stress or tension.

'Bath's Pink' dianthus stages a long, clove-scented flower show from spring to early summer.

ROSE

Rosa species
ROW-za

No flower has stirred people's passions through the ages like the rose. As an herb, rose petals are valued for their fragrance. The fruit, called hips, are a rich source of vitamin C.

Description: Deciduous shrub growing from less than 2 to more than 20 feet tall. About 200 species and 10,000 cultivars. Leaves composed of oval, pointed, toothed leaflets on woody, thorned stems. Flowers with five to dozens of petals in various colors; borne singly or in clusters throughout the growing season. Hips ripen to red, orange, or yellow.

The species and older varieties have the best herbal properties. Consider the white rose (*R. ×alba;* Zone 5), dog rose (*R. canina;* Zone 3), cabbage rose (*R. ×centifolia;* Zone 6), damask rose (*R. ×damascena;* Zone 5), gallica rose (*R. gallica;* Zone 6), and rugosa rose (*R. rugosa;* Zone 2), plus the cultivars of each. Roses that bear abundant hips include the dog and rugosa roses, eglantine rose (*R. rubiginosa;* Zone 5), and apple rose (*R. villosa;* Zone 5).

Site: Full sun. Humus-rich, moist, well-drained soil; pH 6.7. Space 3 to 5 feet apart.

Propagation: Cuttings in autumn.

Care: On grafted plants, set the graft union 2 to 4 inches below soil level in colder zones; 1 to 2 inches above soil level in warmer climes. Prune to shape and remove dead wood in spring. Spray pests with neem.

Harvest: Flowers as they open. Hips when they ripen after flowering. Preserve by drying.

In the kitchen: Petals (with white heel removed) in salads, teas and other drinks, syrups, sugar, vinegars, fruit pies, cookies, sorbets, or crystallized. Hips in jellies, jams, teas, syrups, or sauces.

In the home: Dried flowers or fruits in wreaths, crafts, or potpourri.

For health: Petal infusion commonly used externally in facial tonics or dry-skin lotions. Oil infusion for massages is said to aid blood circulation and tone capillaries. Hip infusion or syrup for colds or flu.

Rose flowers fade and become hips. If you desire to harvest hips, plant roses known to bear them abundantly.

ROSEMARY

Rosmarinus officinalis
ros-ma-RY-nus off-fi-si-NAY-lis

■ **Zones 8–10**

Indispensable in the kitchen, rosemary is steeped in myth, magic, and medicinal uses. It's the symbol of remembrance, friendship, and love. In colder climates rosemary is often grown in pots and brought indoors for winter.

Description: Woody, evergreen perennial, growing to 3 feet or more tall and wide. Gray-green, resinous needle-shaped leaves. Edible, pale blue ¼-inch flowers along stems. Cultivars with pink, white, or dark blue flowers and forms with trailing growth. The cultivars 'Arp', 'Old Salem', and 'Hill's Hardy' are hardy to Zone 6. 'Blue Boy' is compact and ideal for growing indoors.

Site: Full sun. Average, well-drained soil; pH 7. Space 1 to 3 feet apart. Container culture works too.

Propagation: Seed difficult to germinate. Cuttings in spring or late summer; layering in early summer.

Care: Trim to shape after flowering. For plants in containers that will overwinter indoors, terra-cotta pots seem to improve success.

Harvest: Leaves as needed. Flowers as they open. Preserve both by drying or freezing.

In the kitchen: Leaves with pork, lamb, poultry, game, fish, eggs, cheeses, breads, vegetables, pizza, soups, marinades, beans, vinegars, or beverages. Toss stems on grill to flavor barbecues. Use flowers in salads, sugar, or fruit desserts.

In the home: Dried flowers or leaves in potpourri. Leaf infusion as an antiseptic cleaning solution.

For health: Leaf infusion internally for indigestion, colds, or sinus congestion; externally in baths to stimulate circulation, facial steam, or conditioner for dark hair; antiseptic gargle; ointment for sore muscles and joints, bruises, or wounds.

For blooms in a breathtaking blue, choose 'Benenden Blue' rosemary in containers or planting beds.

Ruta graveolens
ROO-ta gra-VEE-o-lenz

RUE

■ Zones 4–9

Make room for rue in your garden. Its striking appearance easily earns it a spot.

Rue was once thought to cure a wide range of ills and to protect against evil. Now it is mainly grown for its stunning and unique blue foliage. Tiny glands over the entire plant release a volatile oil that has a musky fragrance.

Description: Semievergreen, woody shrub growing to 4 feet. Deeply lobed blue-green leaves to 5 inches long. Loose clusters of ½-inch mustard-yellow flowers in late summer contrast strikingly with the foliage. 'Jackman's Blue' has strongly blue foliage; 'Blue Curl' has curled leaves. 'Variegata' and 'Harlequin' unfurl blue-green leaves variegated with white.

Site: Full sun to part shade. Average, well-drained soil; pH 7. Space 18 inches apart.

Propagation: Seed difficult to germinate. Cuttings in late summer; division in spring; layering in spring or early summer.

Harvest: Leaves before plants bloom. Seedpods as they ripen. Preserve by drying.

In the kitchen: Cautiously try bitter leaves sparingly in salads, sandwiches, cheeses, eggs, or fish. Seed in marinades.

In the home: Dried stems or seedpods in crafts. Dried leaves in insect-repellent mixtures.

Caution: Some people develop a rash much like poison ivy from handling the leaves; wear gloves and long sleeves. Do not use or handle during pregnancy.

Salvia species
SAL-vee-a

COMMON SAGE

■ Zones 4–10

Varieties of common sage 'Icterina' (green, gold) and 'Tricolor' (green, cream, and pink) grace the garden with good taste.

Dried sage dominates food with its flavor. Sage's lemony, camphorlike fragrance and taste are milder and sweeter when used fresh in cooking.

Description: Woody, evergreen perennial growing to 3 feet. Pebbly gray-green 2-inch-long leaves. Spikes of edible ½-inch blue blooms.

There are more than 900 species of sage. The wonderful aromas of the tender perennial fruit sage (*S. dorisiana;* Zone 9) and pineapple sage (*S. elegans;* Zone 9) enhance drinks or desserts. Lyreleaf sage (*S. lyrata;* Zone 6) is a Native American herb for colds and coughs. Red sage (*S. militiorhiza;* Zone 7) is a key Chinese herb for heart or nerve conditions. Clary sage (*S. sclarea;* Zone 4), with a vanilla-balsam aroma, is culinary and medicinal.

Site: Full sun. Average, well-drained soil; pH 6.4. Space 2 feet apart.

Propagation: Seed hard to germinate. Cuttings in late spring or early summer; layering, spring or fall.

Care: Trim to shape after flowering. Replace after five years.

Harvest: Leaves as needed. Flowers as they open. Preserve by drying.

In the kitchen: Leaves with vegetables, breads, pork, poultry, sausage, stuffings, butters, cheeses, jellies, or vinegars.

In the home: Dried leaves in wreaths or insect-repelling sachets. Burn or boil leaves to disinfect a room.

For health: Internally for colds, diarrhea, indigestion, coughs, irregular menstruation, or menopause; externally for bath, facial tonic, facial steam, rinse for gray hair, or gargle. Rub leaves on teeth to whiten.

Caution: Do not take large doses for more than two weeks. Sage contains estrogen; use carefully if pregnant.

Hypericum perforatum
by-PER-i-kum per-for-RAY-tum

ST. JOHNSWORT

The blooms of St. Johnswort pop wide open to reveal a plentiful bouquet of stamens tipped with red.

■ **Zones 4–8**

For centuries, St. Johnswort has been considered a magical plant, one that can repel evil. Best known for treatment of mild depression, it also has antibacterial, antiviral, and astringent qualities.

Description: Perennial to 2 or 3 feet tall and 1 foot wide. Pairs of small leaves with balsam fragrance on upright stems that spread by runners; the transparent oil glands look like holes. Clusters of bright yellow fragrant flowers ¾ inch across with five petals and prominent stamens.

Site: Full sun to part shade. Average well-drained soil; tolerates wide pH range. Space plants 1 foot apart.

Propagation: Seed sown indoors in spring. Self-sows. Division in fall.

Care: Trim back after flowering to prevent self-sowing. To curtail spread by runners, simply clip runners before they take root.

Harvest: Flowers as they open. Preserve by drying.

For health: Flower tincture internally for mild depression, anxiety, tension, insomnia, premenstrual syndrome, menopausal problems, cold sores, chicken pox, or shingles. Flower-infused oil externally for minor burns, wounds, bruises, sprains, stiff or sore muscles or joints, hemorrhoids, or minor insect bites.

Caution: Prolonged use may cause skin sensitivity to sunlight.

Sanguisorba minor
san-gwee-SOR-ba MY-nor

SALAD BURNET

While salad burnet leaves resemble celery, the toothed foliage tastes more like cucumber.

■ **Zones 4–9**

Salad burnet is an easily grown but underutilized herb with evergreen leaves high in vitamin C and a mild cucumber taste. Its roots have been used for over 2,000 years in traditional Chinese medicine.

In the garden, salad burnet is a fragrant, attractive edging for a path, growing best during the cool months of spring and fall. Its mild taste combines well in the kitchen with other herbs, especially basil, chervil, dill, tarragon, thyme, and marjoram.

Description: Evergreen perennial growing to 2 feet tall and 1 foot wide. Mounding rosettes of fernlike stems of 1-inch oval, toothed leaves. Spherical clusters of red flowers.

Site: Full sun to part shade. Average well-drained soil; pH 6.8. Space 1 foot apart. Grows well in a large container.

Propagation: Seed started indoors in spring. Self-sows. Divide established plants in spring.

Care: Remove flower buds to encourage fresh leaf growth.

Harvest: Young, tender leaves as needed before flowers open. Roots can be pulled in autumn.

In the kitchen: Leaves in salads, soups, beverages, cheeses, vinegars, sauces, butters, tomato juice, vegetables, or fish.

For health: Leaf infusion is said to be useful internally for water retention, diarrhea, or hemorrhoids; externally for facial tonic or for minor burns, sores, or sunburn.

SCENTED GERANIUMS

Pelargonium species
pee-lar-GOH-nee-um

■ Zones 9–10

'Chocolate Peppermint' scented geranium smells like minty chocolate candy.

With fragrances of fruits, flowers, spices, and even chocolate, scented geraniums delight the senses. Brought from South Africa in the 17th century, they were favored by Victorian gardeners as much as by the French perfume industry.

Description: Tender perennials growing 1 to 3 feet tall and 1 to 2 feet wide. Velvety to sandpapery leaves, rounded to deeply lobed, green to variegated. Edible pink, deep-rose, or white flowers.

Site: Full sun to part shade. Humus-rich, well-drained soil; pH 6.5.

Propagation: Seed difficult to germinate. Cuttings in spring, summer, or fall.

Care: Trim to shape anytime. Pinch growing tips to promote branching.

Harvest: Leaves as needed; best fragrance just before flowering. Flowers as they open. Preserve leaves and flowers by drying.

In the kitchen: Leaves in jellies, cakes, cookies, other desserts, butters, sauces, syrups, sugar, vinegars, or beverages. Flowers in salads or desserts or crystallized.

In the home: Fresh leaves in nosegays. Dried leaves or flowers in potpourri or sachets.

For health: Leaf infusions used in many external treatments including baths, facial tonics, or facial steams.

SOAPWORT

Saponaria officinalis
sap-o-NAIR-ee-a off-fi-si-NAY-lis

■ Zones 4–10

For practical beauty it's tough to beat pink-flowered soapwort. This herb is easy to use and lovely to behold.

When boiled, the leaves and stems of soapwort yield a soapy liquid that's gentle for washing delicate fabrics, as well as the hair or face. On sultry summer nights the flowers exude the luscious fragrance of cloves and raspberries.

Description: Perennial growing to 2 feet. Oval pointed leaves to 3 inches long on upright stems, spreading by underground runners. Pink 1-inch, fragrant flowers in late summer. Double-flowered forms tend to be less invasive.

Site: Full sun to light shade. Average, well-drained soil; tolerates wide pH range. Space 2 feet apart.

Propagation: Seed sown indoors or outside in spring. Self-sows. Cuttings in early summer. Division in autumn.

Care: Cut back after flowering to encourage a second flowering and to prevent self-sowing. Soapwort can become invasive.

Harvest: Leaves and stems as needed. Preserve by drying.

In the home: Boil leaves and stems in rainwater or distilled water for 30 minutes, and strain for washing delicate fabrics, antiques, or anything that requires an especially mild soap.

For health: Boil leaves and stems as above, and strain for washing hair or face; the liquid is said to control acne, eczema, or other mild skin problems.

Caution: The root is poisonous; do not take internally. Do not grow near fish ponds or other water bodies because the roots can poison fish.

STINGING NETTLE

Urtica dioica
UR-ti-ka dy-OH-i-ka

■ Zones 3–10

This plant with painful, stinging leaves grows throughout most of North America and has a long history as a vitamin- and mineral-rich tonic and medicine.

Description: Perennial to 5 feet tall. Heart-shaped leaves covered with bristly hairs; stems rising from creeping roots. Clusters of green flowers where leaves attach to stems.

Site: Full sun to part shade. Humus-rich, moist, well-drained soil; tolerates wide pH range. Space 2 feet apart.

Propagation: Direct-seed in spring. Division in early spring.

Care: Cut plants back to ground in autumn. Can become invasive.

Harvest: Young leaves in early spring. Roots as needed. Preserve both by drying.

Other: Attracts butterflies, caterpillars, and moths. Soak plants in rainwater for a week, strain liquid, and use as a spray for aphids or a high-nitrogen fertilizer. Leaves speed composting process.

In the kitchen: Young leaves fully cooked in salads, greens, soups, or herbal teas.

For health: Once a popular spring tonic. Leaf infusion internally for hay fever, asthma, heavy menstrual bleeding, anemia, or water retention; externally in bath to improve circulation; in lotion or cream for itching, eczema, or insect bites; or hair rinse for dandruff or hair loss. Root decoction for enlarged prostate, hay fever, or skin conditions.

Caution: Always wear rubber gloves and long sleeves when handling plants. Dock or mullein leaves rubbed over affected skin can relieve the sting of nettles.

Add stinging nettles to your garden with care. It's not a good plant to grow where children play and garden.

SUMMER AND WINTER SAVORY

Satureja species
sat-you-REE-a

■ All zones (an annual)

With a peppery, thymelike taste, savory has enhanced the flavor of food for over 2,000 years. Although the ancient Egyptians incorporated it into love potions, savory's medicinal qualities are more reliably antiseptic and astringent.

Description: Summer savory (*S. hortensis*) is an annual growing to 18 inches tall and 10 inches wide. Narrow, 1-inch-long gray-green leaves. White or pale pink ¼-inch flowers. Flavor is sweeter and more delicate than winter savory.

Winter savory (*S. montana*) is a semievergreen perennial growing to 12 inches tall and 8 inches wide. Narrow 1-inch-long dark green leaves. Spikes of ¼-inch white to lavender flowers. Strong, more piney flavor than summer savory.

Site: Full sun. Average, well-drained soil; pH 6.7. Space plants 10 inches apart.

Propagation: Seed sown indoors in spring; do not cover with soil. Winter savory also propagates readily by cuttings in spring.

Care: Trim plants regularly to encourage new growth. Winter mulch for winter savory.

Harvest: Leaves as needed. Preserve by drying.

In the kitchen: Leaves in beans, lentils, soups, eggs, vegetables, sausages, beef, pork, poultry, fish, teas, butters, vinegars, or jellies.

For health: Leaf infusion internally for indigestion, sore throats, coughs, diarrhea, or flatulence; externally in baths, facial tonics, facial steams, insect bites, or mouthwash.

Caution: Do not use winter or summer savory during pregnancy.

Plant winter savory (above) as a dwarf hedge in an herb garden. Space individual plants 10 inches apart. Summer savory (right) has a milder flavor.

Myrrhis odorata
MIR-ris o-do-RAY-ta

SWEET CICELY

■ Zones 3–8

Among the few herbs that thrive in shade, sweet cicely forms mounds of lovely, lacy foliage. When cooked with tart fruits, less sugar is needed. Leaves, flowers, seeds, and roots are all edible and highly aromatic. Its size makes it a good choice for the back of a border.

Description: Perennial growing to 3 feet tall and 2 feet wide. Finely divided fernlike leaves, velvety on top and whitish underneath, with scent of lovage and flavor of anise. Flat clusters of tiny white flowers open to form a bloom that resembles Queen Anne's lace. Seeds to ¾ inch long with a spicy licorice flavor.

Shade gardeners can cultivate a lovely crop of sweet cicely. Its ferny texture and lacy flowers pair well with hostas.

Site: Partial shade. Rich, moist, well-drained soil; pH 6.5. Space plants 2 feet apart.
Propagation: Direct-seed in autumn. Self-sows readily. Division in spring or early summer.
Care: Needs cold temperatures; does not grow well in hot climates.
Harvest: Leaves as needed. Seeds either green or brown. Dig year-old roots in autumn. Preserve by drying or freezing.
In the kitchen: Leaves in salads, fish, eggs, soups, stews, vinegars, cookies, cakes, or fruit desserts. Flowers in salads or with fruit. Chopped or crushed seeds in fruit dishes, ice creams, or liqueurs. Roots as a vegetable or in soups, stews, or salads.
In the home: Crush seed for furniture polish. Fresh leaves or dried seed heads in bouquets.
For health: Leaf infusion for coughs, anemia, or indigestion.

Tanacetum vulgare
tan-a-SEE-tum vul-GAR-ay

TANSY

■ Zones 3–9

Once thought to grant immortality, or at least good health, tansy is now known to be toxic. It does play an important role in the garden and home for its beauty and insect-repelling qualities.

Description: Perennial growing to 3 feet. Feathery pine-scented leaves on slim stems with vigorously

'Crispum' tansy unfurls feathery fernlike leaves. Stalks topped with bright yellow flowers appear in late summer.

spreading rhizomes. Flat clusters of yellow buttonlike ½-inch flowers blooming freely late summer to autumn. Curly tansy (*T. vulgare* 'Crispum') has crinkled leaves and is more compact and less aromatic.
Site: Full sun to part shade. Average, well-drained soil; pH 6.3. Space 3 feet apart.
Propagation: Seed sown indoors in spring. Division in spring or fall.
Care: Cut back after flowering to maintain shape.
Harvest: Leaves as needed. Flowers as they open. Preserve by drying.
Other: According to folklore, grow near fruit trees to repel insects. Add to compost for its potassium content.
In the home: Dried flowers in crafts. Dried leaves or plants around the house to repel flies, ants, and mice.
Caution: Do not use tansy in any internal medicine or treatment.

Artemisia dracunculus sativa
ar-te-MIZ-ee-a dra-KUN-kew-lus sa-TY-va

■ **Zones 4–9**

Tarragon's flavor—sweet anise with a bite—is essential in French cooking. Except for recipes baked in liquid, add near the end of cooking to prevent bitterness. Blends well with parsley, chervil, garlic, and chives.
Description: Perennial growing to 2 feet tall and 18 inches wide. Upright to sprawling stems with narrow pointed leaves to 3 inches long. Tiny greenish-white flowers. Mexican mint marigold *(Tagetes lucida)* has similar flavor, withstands summer heat, and is a fine substitute.
Site: Full sun to part shade. Rich, well-drained soil. Space 2 feet apart.
Propagation: Sterile, occasionally flowers, but doesn't produce seed. Divide in spring, or take cuttings in spring or summer.

FRENCH TARRAGON

Care: Cut back in fall and mulch. Divide and replant every three years to maintain vigor. Does not grow well in hot, humid areas. If flowers do appear, remove them to keep plants productive.
Harvest: Leaves as needed. Preserve by freezing or drying or in vinegar.
Other: Believed to enhance the growth of many vegetables.
In the kitchen: Is somewhat bitter. Leaves in salads, vinegars, cheeses, sauces, dressings, mayonnaise, soups, grains, rice, eggs, fish, chicken, pork, vegetables, or pickles.
For health: Leaf infusion is rich in vitamins A and C, iodine, and minerals and good as a tonic; stimulates appetite and digestion.

Tarragon holds its own ornamentally in the garden with narrow, medium-green foliage on spreading stems.

Thymus species and cultivars
TY-mus

■ **Zones 4–9**

The thymes consist of hundreds of culinary, medicinal, and landscape staples. Thyme is known as the "blending" herb because it pulls flavors together. Also known for its antiseptic properties.
Description: Perennial, sometimes evergreen, growing from 1 to 12 inches. Oval, pointed ¼-inch-long leaves on wiry stems. Clusters of tiny pink, white, or red flowers. Forms labeled French or English (Zone 4) usually have the best flavor.
Site: Full sun to part shade. Average, well-drained soil; pH 6.3. Space 8 to 12 inches apart.
Propagation: Difficult from seed. Division, cuttings, or layering stems in spring.
Care: Trim in early spring and again after flowering.

THYME

Harvest: Leaves as needed or major harvest just before flowering, cutting plants back to 2 inches. Flowers as they open. Preserve both by drying or freezing.
Other: Companion plant for tomatoes, potatoes, or eggplant.
In the kitchen: Leaves in salads, stocks, soups, stews, stuffings, sauces, vinegars, beef, pork, poultry, seafood, sausages, vegetables, honey, cheeses, eggs, rice, grains, breads, or beans. Flowers in salads or as garnish.
In the home: Fresh leaves or flowers in bouquets. Leaf infusion as household disinfectant. Dried leaves or flowers in potpourri or insect-repelling sachets.
For health: Leaf infusion internally for indigestion, coughs, colds, sore throats, hay fever, insomnia, hangovers, or poor circulation; externally in baths for muscle or joint pain, insect bites or stings, fungal infections, facial tonics or steams, hair rinse for dandruff, mouthwash, or ointment for minor wounds, or sore muscles and joints.
Caution: Do not use medicinally when pregnant or nursing.

Place thyme in the garden along bed edges or rock walls for a creeping mass of flavorful foliage.

TROPICAL HERBS

The staples of the culinary herb world have expanded dramatically in recent years. With increasing interest in Asian, Caribbean, and South American cooking, once-rare tropical herbs now are more available in grocery produce departments and from mail-order, the Internet, and local herb nurseries.

Almost all of these herbs are tender plants that do not withstand freezing. They are best grown in pots, summered outdoors, and then brought indoors during winter. They need bright light and slightly warmer temperatures indoors than temperate-climate herbs.

■ **Cuban oregano** (*Plectranthus amboinicus*) is originally from Southeast Asia but has been widely adopted in the Caribbean and Mexico. Its flavor combines aspects of oregano, thyme, and savory. Plants form spreading mounds 2 to 3 feet wide and tall, with fleshy, velvety oval leaves up to 2 inches long. Hardy to Zone 9, Cuban oregano is best grown in full sun in a sandy, quick-draining potting soil. Pinch back growing tips to keep the plant bushy. Propagate plants from stem cuttings taken in late summer.

■ **Curry leaf** (*Murraya koenigii*) is not to be confused with the fragrant but nonculinary curry plant (*Helichrysum italicum*). Curry leaf is a small evergreen tree native to India, Pakistan, and Sri Lanka. Its fresh leaves are used in curry dishes. Plants grow to 20 feet tall in the tropics, but in containers in temperate climates, it reaches about

A definitively textural plant, Cuban oregano bears sharply pungent leaves.

5 feet. Long, drooping palmlike leaves are composed of narrow 2-inch-long shiny green leaflets. Sprays of white flowers are followed by black berries. Hardy to Zone 9, it grows in full sun to light shade and in standard potting soil. Trim plants to encourage bushy growth. Curry leaf is difficult to grow from seed but can be propagated by cutting off and repotting sucker plants at the base of the mother plant.

■ **Ginger** (*Zingiber officinale*) is a perennial native to tropical Asia with reedlike stems and long, narrow leaves. Its fleshy, sweetly pungent flavored rhizome has been used for culinary and medicinal purposes since earliest times. The related Japanese ginger (*Zingiber mioga*) tastes like bergamot. Both are hardy to Zone 9. For more, see page 92.

■ **Galangal** is the common name for a number of related tropical perennial herbs. Among the most widely used is the greater galangal (*Alpinia galanga*), also known as Thai or Siamese ginger or laos.

Lemongrass performs wonderfully in a temperate garden, forming a tastebud-tempting fountain of foliage that remains upright through winter.

It resembles ginger in appearance and flavor. The fresh rhizome is popular in Indonesian and Malaysian food, where the flowers and young shoots are also eaten.

Two different plants are commonly called lesser galangal. The rhizome of one, *Alpinia officinarum,* has been a medicinal herb as well as a flavoring since ancient times in China. The other lesser galangal (*Kaempferia galanga*), also known as resurrection lily, has fingerlike tubers with yellow-orange interiors. Hardy to Zone 8, the galangals are grown like ginger, but they're not as apt to go dormant, and they take longer to develop rhizomes.

■ **Kaffir lime** (*Citrus hystrix*) is a small, shrubby tree with lemon-scented leaves used for flavoring curries, fish, soups, and other Southeast Asian foods. The rind and juice of the knobby fruit are also used in cooking, and the leaves, fruit, juice, and bark all have medicinal uses. The leaves are unusual: leathery, shiny green, and pointed with a deep indentation in the middle that makes each half look like a separate leaf.

Grow Kaffir lime in pots in standard potting soil and full sun. It is hardy to Zone 10. During winter, let the top half inch of the soil dry before watering. If leaves start to yellow, apply a fertilizer containing iron chelate. Propagate Kaffir lime from cuttings.

■ **Lemongrass** (*Cymbopogon citratus;* also see page 96), native to southern India and Sri Lanka, forms large (up to 2 feet) clumps of grassy lemon-scented leaves. The fleshy base of the plant and its leaves flavor foods, while the leaves make a relaxing tea.

Related plants are the source of citronella oil. Lemongrass is hardy to Zone 9. Grow it in standard potting soil and full sun. Keep soil evenly moist. Propagate plants by division.

■ **Roselle** (*Hibiscus sabdariffa*), also known as Jamaica, Indian, or Guinea sorrel and Florida cranberry, is a woody shrub. Some varieties have lobed rhubarb-flavored leaves.

At the base of pale yellow flowers are vitamin C-rich red calyces (small leaflike structures). Calyces color and flavor herb teas and are made into jams, chutneys, or sauces.

Hardy to Zone 8, roselle grows in standard potting soil and full sun. Propagate it from seeds or cuttings.

■ **Turmeric** (*Curcuma longa*) is a 3-foot perennial native of India with long, broad leaves. For centuries, the pungent rhizomes have flavored foods and served as medicine. The easily recognized bright yellow-orange color of the dried and powdered rhizome is readily identifiable in curry powder and the dye used to color robes of Buddhist monks. Grow turmeric like ginger. Plants are dormant in winter.

Grow a potted roselle plant to harvest your own vitamin C-enriched calyces to add to teas and jams.

The blossom spikes of turmeric resemble ginger flowers because they are in the same plant family. Roots yield vibrant orange and yellow dyes.

Valeriana officinalis
va-leer-i-AH-na off-fi-si-NAY-lis

VALERIAN

■ Zones 4–9

The calming and sleep-inducing effect of valerian has been known since ancient Roman times. A safe, nonaddictive relaxant with no "day after" effects, valerian readily naturalizes in northern states. It's a beautiful garden plant.

Description: Perennial growing to 5 feet tall and 3 feet wide. Toothed fernlike dark green leaves. Tall stems with clusters of small, tubular pinkish-white flowers.

Site: Full sun to part shade. Humus-rich, moist soil; tolerates wide pH range. Space 2 feet apart. Container culture works well.

Valerian adds a stately, majestic presence to any garden with its willowy form and graceful flower stalks.

Propagation: Sow seeds indoors in spring. Self-sows. Division in spring or autumn.

Care: Remove flowers to limit self-sowing. Divide every three years to prevent crowding.

Harvest: Second- or third-year roots in autumn. Preserve by drying.

Other: Boosts growth of nearby vegetables; root decoction sprayed on soil attracts earthworms. Increases mineral content of compost.

In the home: Dried roots or leaves in pillows for cats.

For health: Root decoction or tincture internally for insomnia, stress, anxiety, tension, or tight muscles. Taste can be musty; sweeten tinctures with honey. Externally in baths or on minor injuries or splinters to calm; lotions for acne and skin rashes.

Caution: Don't take in large doses or for more than three weeks at a time.

Viola species
vy-OH-la

VIOLET

■ Zones 4–5

Sweet violet (*V. odorata*) has long enamored herbalists, cooks, gardeners, and romantics. All parts of the sweet violet are edible, it is high in vitamin C; leaves and flowers are medicinal.

Description: Perennial growing to 6 to 12 inches. Often naturalizes. Heart-shaped dark green leaves. Five uneven petals in shades of purple, blue, violet, pink, yellow, or white, singly or in combination.

Site: Prefers part shade. Humus-rich, moist soil; tolerates wide pH range. Space 6 inches apart. Grows well in containers.

Propagation: Seed sown indoors or out in spring. Will self-sow.

If you're digging violets from your lawn as weeds, tuck them in flower beds to harvest them later for herbal uses.

Care: Remove spent blooms to prolong flowering. Grows best in cool weather.

Harvest: Leaves in early spring. Flowers as they open. Preserve by drying.

Other: Susceptible to spider mites as temperatures climb. Clip leaves to soil. As air cools in fall, fertilize plants; new leaves will emerge.

In the kitchen: Flowers in salads, desserts, drinks, syrups, jellies, vinegars, or butters or crystallized. Leaves in salads; infusion in desserts.

In the home: Dried flowers in potpourri. Pressed flowers in crafts.

For health: Leaf or flower infusions or root decoctions of violet internally for coughs, congestion, or chest colds. Leaf or flower infusion of heartsease internally for coughs or bronchitis; externally in bath water, facial tonic, hair rinse, or skin lotion for eczema, dry skin, or itchiness.

Galium odoratum
GAY-lee-um o-do-RAY-tum

■ **Zones 3–9**

When dried, sweet woodruff has a scent combining vanilla and newly mown hay. It is useful for strewing, scenting linen, and stuffing pillows. In the garden, it forms a ground cover that thrives in shade.

Description: Perennial to 12 inches tall. Wiry stems with whorls of narrow pointed 1-inch-long dark green leaves. Starry white blooms.

Site: Shade. Humus-rich, moist, well-drained soil; pH 5.5. Space plants 8 inches apart.

Propagation: Difficult to germinate. Divide in early spring.

Harvest: Leaves as needed. Preserve by drying.

Other: Blooms in late spring at the same time as many azaleas and rhododendrons; a useful companion beneath them in a woodland setting.

SWEET WOODRUFF

In the kitchen: Leaves used to flavor white wine. "May" wine made with sweet woodruff.

In the home: Dried leaves and flowers in potpourri, insect-repelling sachets, or wreaths.

Caution: Do not take internally, other than occasionally in wine; do not ingest if taking blood thinners or anticoagulants because contains closely related compounds.

Sweet woodruff forms a quilt of green with white-petaled knots.

Achillea millefolium
a-kil-LEE-a mil-lee-FOH-lee-um

■ **Zones 3–9**

Fossils found in caves suggest that humans have been associated with yarrow for over 60,000 years. Ancient Chinese cast the I Ching with yarrow stalks, Achilles staunched soldiers' wounds with the leaves, and Native Americans used leaves for injuries and ailments. Except for the Southwest, this herb grows wild over most of the United States.

Description: Perennial growing to 3 feet tall and 2 feet wide. Fine-textured, feathery leaves to 6 inches long and 1 inch wide on stems spreading by rhizomes. Flat-topped clusters of small white flowers.

Ornamental cultivars with yellow, gold, red, pink, or salmon flowers are available, as are smaller forms.

Site: Full sun. Humus-rich, well-drained soil; pH 6. Space 2 feet

YARROW

apart. Grows well in large-sized containers with humus-rich soil.

Propagation: Seed sown indoors or out in spring. Self-sows. Division in spring or fall.

Care: Remove faded flowers to extend blooming.

Harvest: Leaves as needed. Flowers when fully open. Preserve by drying.

Other: Attracts beneficial insects, benefits nearby herbs, and speeds composting process.

In the kitchen: Young leaves in salads, butters, or cheeses.

In the home: Dried flowers in wreaths or crafts.

For health: Leaf infusion or tincture internally for colds, flu, fevers, hay fever, arthritis, indigestion, regulating menstrual cycle, heavy menstrual bleeding or pain, high blood pressure, or improving blood circulation; externally in skin lotions, ointments, or poultices for wounds, chapped skin, rashes, or hemorrhoids; gargle for inflamed gums; rinse for oily hair. Flower infusion for relaxing bath or facial pack, steam, or tonic.

Caution: May cause allergic reaction in rare cases. Do not use medicinally when pregnant.

For a stalwart garden performer, plant clumps of yarrow. Choose cultivars with flower colors that suit your garden.

Fruits, Berries & Nuts

IN THIS CHAPTER

Fruits in the
Landscape **115**

Climate and
Microclimate **116**

A Sample Garden **117**

Dwarf Trees **118**

Planting and Caring
for an Orchard **120**

Soil **122**

Planting **124**

Fertilizing and
Watering **126**

Fruits in
Containers **128**

Pests and
Diseases of Fruits **130**

Pruning and Training
Fruits **140**

Pruning Specific
Fruits **146**

Let your garden do more for you. When you select dwarf varieties and plan carefully, you can grow a wide range of fruits and berries for your family in a small space.

Many gardeners believe that producing a good fruit crop requires the knowledge and skill of the expert orchardist. Extensive maintenance and culture are necessary for maximum commercial fruit production and to some degree, for a top-quality home fruit crop. Yet the home gardener can get by with less-complicated feeding, pruning, and pest management programs and still harvest an acceptable crop, particularly with good advanced planning.

In addition, improved varieties have better fruiting characteristics, disease resistance, and tolerance of special soil and climate conditions. Your success will be determined by your site; variety selection appropriate to your climate; the susceptibility of your crops to frost injury; your soil type; ability to manage diseases, pests, and animal pressure; good cultural practices; and the ability to react and make decisions at the appropriate time. If you learn about your growing conditions, choose the varieties that fit them, start small, and give your plants proper attention and care, you are bound to succeed.

This chapter details the basics of home fruit growing. It covers such elementals as site selection, planting, fertilizing, and pest control. Pruning daunts many first-time fruit growers, so that topic is covered in detail to build your confidence so you can tackle this task with aplomb. If you can't fit a tree or shrub in your yard, you might want to try your hand at fruits in containers. Tips for container growing are included too.

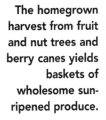

The homegrown harvest from fruit and nut trees and berry canes yields baskets of wholesome sun-ripened produce.

Fruits in the Landscape

Gardeners who grow fruits, berries, and nuts at home will tell you that the fresh-picked taste is more than enough reason to grow them. But fruit plants also easily enhance the landscape—even in a small yard or garden.

Fruit trees are available in a range of sizes that permits using them almost anywhere: sited in the smallest yards and gardens, as borders and hedges, as groundcovers, or even as small shade trees. Modern dwarfing techniques and simplified training methods allow you to grow several fruit trees in the same small garden and still have plenty of space available for vegetables or flowers.

Nut trees are the exception to this trend. In most cases, plenty of space is still necessary for the average nut tree, so they are best situated on large lots.

We describe four techniques for keeping fruit plants compact and productive: pruning, training, container growing, and dwarfing rootstocks. The "Gallery of Temperate Fruits" beginning on page 154, includes many dwarf varieties well suited to home garden fruit production.

The edible landscape

When you landscape with fruit plants, you combine beauty with practicality. Fruit can serve many functions. For example, apple trees make superb shade trees anywhere in the yard if you prune them to a branch high enough to allow walking underneath. A large crabapple tree or a spreading cherry will also provide good shade.

You can use fruit trees you like as a focal point or accent in the yard or garden. The most striking trees in bloom are apples, cherries, quince, crab apples, and some of the showier flowering peach varieties.

Shrub fruits can also play an important role in the landscape, either as individual accents or as hedges or shrub borders. Include blueberries for their vivid fall leaf colors or currants for their beautiful flower clusters and brilliant scarlet fruit.

Genetic dwarf peach trees make splendid blooming hedges, and showy-flowered dwarf or standard peaches can be trained in the same way. Espaliered apple or pear trees can also form attractive hedges or borders.

You can even use fruits as a groundcover. Strawberry plants are effective, especially in smaller areas, but plan to replace them every several years with new plants if you want a heavy fruit crop. The European alpine strawberry ('Alexandria' is one variety) doesn't form runners, so it makes a neat border, groundcover, or container plant in a tightly confined area. The small fruit has an intense "wild" flavor. The alpine plants yield longer than traditional strawberries— for about five years—and propagate themselves freely.

Select dwarf fruit tree varieties, and you will still have plenty of room to grow vegetables.

Standard or full-size fruit trees provide wonderful shade and striking focal points when they bloom.

Climate and Microclimate

To determine which fruit tree varieties will bear well for you, consider your climate.

The fruits discussed in this chapter are temperate-climate fruits. (For information about tropical and subtropical fruits, see page 192.) Temperate climates are characterized by hot summers and cold winters. Most of the United States lies in the Northern Temperate Zone. Within this zone, however, climates vary greatly. Furthermore, they vary not only over large distances, but also within cities, from district to district, and even from place to place within a garden. This is why fruit gardeners must plan their crops in terms of localized microclimates.

Microclimates

Your own garden may have several microclimates. For example, a spot protected from the wind will have a warmer microclimate than will a spot out in the open. If the sheltered spot is backed by a wall that reflects heat, the area will be warmer still.

In a northern garden, such a location might be ideal for helping a tree bear better fruit; in a southern garden, the location might be too hot. Sun, shade, slope, and moisture affect microclimates.

The extreme diversity of North America's climates makes it impossible to provide an exact guide to climatic conditions on a local scale. The information in the individual varietal descriptions will help you choose the plants most likely to do well in your garden.

For more detailed information, check with local nurseries, garden centers, agricultural extension agents, and especially gardening friends, relatives, and neighbors, who can tell you about their own successes and failures. The latter is perhaps your most important source of information, particularly given that depending on your location, your growing season may be several weeks shorter or longer than that of someone located a few miles away within your own county.

Side yards often have warm, south-facing walls, a good location for an espaliered fig.

A Sample Garden

The plan on this page illustrates some of the remarkable space-saving possibilities in gardening with fruits. Notice the orientation of the garden. Fruit trees need sun to set a crop, and the illustrated arrangement shows maximum exposure to the sun as it passes from east to west. If your location does not have sun all day, at least plan to give your fruit plants southern or western exposure.

Air drainage is also important to fruit crops. If it is possible, locate fruit trees on higher ground so that cold air in the spring will drain away from the trees when they are in blossom.

Notice also how this plan makes use of espaliered apple trees and grapevines to provide an attractive border and plenty of fruits and still allow space for many other plants. The raspberries and currants are trained on trellises and oriented approximately north and south. They take up little space and bear heavily. The grapes are planted mainly on the north side of the garden to give them full southern exposure to the sun, which is necessary in order to develop good sugar content in the fruit. Note that there is still room in the center of the garden for dwarf fruit trees, raised beds in which to grow vegetables or flowers, and a plot of annuals.

This plan is based on a real fruit garden situated beside a home in California. It measures only 15×50 feet but contains 17 fruit trees, several grape varieties, cane berries, ornamental plants, and vegetables. The trained plants are key features in the space-saving aspect of this heavily bearing garden.

Similar plans can be adapted for other climatic areas such as the northeast and southwest. Varieties and tree types may change, but the design concepts remain the same.

Despite your eagerness to get as much out of your fruit planting, you may want to begin small, adding plants as you become more comfortable with their care regimen. Most home gardeners begin by planting too many trees and berries and by planting them too closely together. Beginning with just a handful of plants and adding more later as your confidence and experience levels grow will not only save you time and money over the long run, but it will also save you disappointment.

You can achieve the harvest of your dreams no matter how limited your growing area. Creative design and careful planning will earn you amazingly tasteful yields.

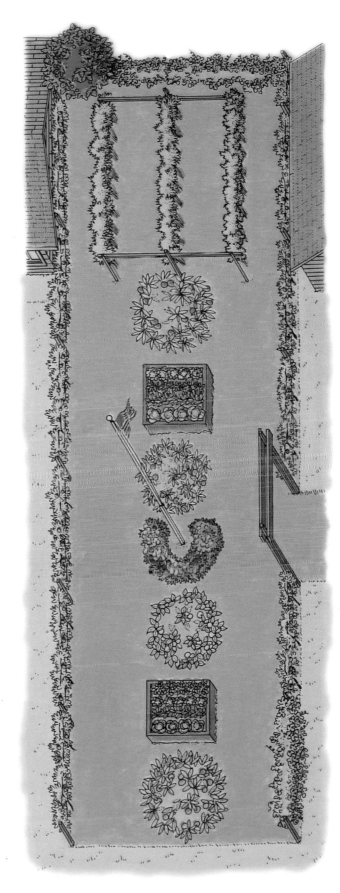

Dwarf Trees

The key to good fruit in the small home garden lies in the effective use of dwarf fruit trees.

A standard-size apple tree can grow from 20 to 40 feet high and spread 30 to 40 feet. Dwarf apple varieties, in contrast, can be held to a height of about 10 feet with a 10-foot spread. Standard apricots, peaches, and plums can grow to 30 feet tall with a spread of 30 feet, and pears to a towering 45 feet with a spread as wide as 30 feet. Most dwarf varieties of these trees can be kept to a height of about 10 feet or even less.

The lilliputian nature of dwarf fruit trees proves tidy enough to fit into whiskey barrels.

Well-known varieties, such as 'Red Delicious' apple, are grafted onto dwarfing rootstocks to yield small trees that bear abundantly.

Genetic dwarf trees

Dwarf trees are produced in nature or through horticultural practices. Natural dwarfs are called genetic dwarfs. Apples, apricots, sweet and sour cherries, peaches, nectarines, and plums all have genetic dwarf varieties.

Among apples, the most common genetic dwarf trees are spur apples, so named because on a given amount of wood they produce more fruiting spurs than ordinary apple trees. Fruit production can have a dwarfing effect because it uses energy that would otherwise go toward tree growth. Heavier crops of spur apples yield slower tree growth. Although spur apple trees grow more slowly, they eventually reach about three-quarters normal size. All genetic dwarfs, however, can be made even smaller by grafting them onto dwarfing rootstocks.

Dwarfing rootstocks

The easiest and most effective way to produce permanent dwarfing is by grafting fruit cultivars (shoots or buds of a desired cultivar) onto dwarfing rootstocks. This method offers many advantages. Grafting is an easy way to produce large numbers of plants in a relatively short time. It ensures true reproduction of a desired variety, which is important because seed does not always breed true. And grafted dwarf trees remain uniformly smaller and tend to bear fruit at a younger age than standard trees, sometimes as early as their second year of growth.

Grafting can provide the tree with other special characteristics too, such as resistance to insects or diseases, more solid anchorage in the ground, and early fruit production. Since the cultivar (variety) is grafted onto the rootstock, you are essentially buying two different plants together—the rootstock that anchors the tree and the cultivar that produces the fruit.

One advantage of growing dwarf trees is easy care. When the distance from roots to treetop is 10 feet or less, sprays for pests and diseases are easier to apply and pruning is less difficult. These advantages increase if you further reduce size by applying various pruning and training techniques.

Grafted dwarf trees are readily available at most nurseries and garden centers. More curious, adventuresome, or enterprising gardeners may want to try their own grafting.

The most extensive research on grafting with growth-limiting rootstocks has been undertaken with apples and has resulted in the development of the numbered 'Malling' rootstocks. Each of these has a different degree of dwarfing effect on the apple variety that is grafted onto it. There is also a dwarfing rootstock for apples called 'Mark' and a recently developed Cornell Geneva Rootstock series that has two rootstocks highly resistant to fireblight: CG.16 and CG.30.

Although soil fertility and culture have an effect on tree growth, the final size of the apple tree depends mainly on the rootstock. It's important to clearly identify the rootstock when purchasing a tree because that dictates final tree size and the space required for it to grow and fruit. Other major fruit trees can also be dwarfed by grafting, but because less research has been done, fewer kinds of

dwarfing rootstocks are known, and these are not always as effective as the ones for apples. For pears, Old Home × Farmingdale rootstocks provide good fireblight resistance. OH×F 333 performs well in the northeast and produces trees that are about 10 to 12 feet tall. Pears grown on OH×F 97 rootstock are nearly as tall as standard trees but produce fruit sooner. Quince also offers a satisfactory rootstock for dwarfing pears, although a dwarfing pear rootstock has been developed.

Apricots, peaches, nectarines, and plums can be dwarfed on 'Nanking' cherry rootstock and cherries on 'St. Lucie' or 'Vladimir' cherry.

Plum trees are commonly propagated on *Prunus* 'St. Julian A' and myrobalan plum *(Prunus cerasifera)* rootstocks. Myrobalan grows in a wide range of soils, including poorly drained sites. Sweet cherries grow well on 'Giessen' rootstocks

By combining dwarf tree size with specific pruning and training methods, you can create a hedge of fruit-bearing trees.

Cordon fruit trees are trained to grow many lateral branches from a single trunk.

Planting and Caring for an Orchard

If you're unable to plant fruit trees at the ideal time for your climate, choose container-grown trees.

Fruit trees depend upon pollination by honeybees or native, solitary bees to set an optimum crop.

The art of growing abundant fruit lies in selecting the right varieties for your region and then growing them with informed skill.

With a few exceptions (certain figs, for example), fruit won't form unless pollen from the male parts of a flower is transferred to the female parts of a flower. Bees are the pollinating insects for most of the fruits in this chapter. The presence of bees around your plants, however, does not necessarily mean you'll get a crop because the pollen they carry must be of the right sort.

Pollination requirements

Some plants are called self-pollinating or self-fertile. This means that their flowers can be fertilized by pollen from flowers either on the same plant or another plant of the same kind. Self-fertile plants will produce fruit even if they are planted far away from any other plant of their kind. Peaches and sour cherries are generally the only tree fruits that are self-fruitful, and even these will produce better when another compatible variety is growing nearby. For optimum production on all other fruits, you'll need at least two cultivars to obtain good fruit set.

Other plants set fruit only when they receive pollen from a plant of a different variety. When a plant's pollen is ineffective on its own flowers, it is called self-sterile. This group includes most apples, apricots, pears, plums, and sweet cherries.

Never assume that because you have a bearing fruit tree, you can plant a new tree of a different variety nearby and be sure of a crop. Plants must bloom at about the same time for successful cross-pollination to occur. For example, an early self-sterile apple won't bear fruit unless the pollinator tree is another early apple flowering at the same time.

Planting for pollination

A fruit plant needs a pollinator close by, 100 feet away or less. The bees that carry the pollen are unlikely to fly back and forth if the distance between the trees is any greater.

If your neighbor has a pollinating variety across the back fence, that's good. If not, do one of the following.
■ Plant two fruit trees fairly close together.
■ Graft a branch of another

variety onto a tree that needs cross pollination.

■ Place a large bouquet of flowers from a pollinating tree in a vase or jar of water and lodge the container in the branches of a second tree.

Choosing good pollenizers for your plants is a very important part of fruit gardening. The gallery beginning on page 154 will tell you which varieties need pollinators and which varieties act as pollenizers. (Pollinators pollinate; pollenizers provide the pollen.)

Pollination depends on many other factors as well. Late spring frost can damage blossoms, and cold or rainy weather during bloom can interrupt pollination.

Native bee populations have been reduced due to pest insects and diseases. Without bees flying and visiting flowers while trees are

in bloom, successful pollination may not happen.

Disease and poor plant nutrition also wreak havoc. Being attentive to all of these factors, as well as providing adequate pollenizers, will help ensure a successful crop.

How fruit plants grow

All plants produce sugar for energy and growth through photosynthesis. You can stimulate this process by planting your fruit trees in a sunny spot and by pruning and training them to maximize leaf exposure to sun.

Maintaining proper soil moisture ensures that leaves expand fully. Keeping leaves free of dust, pests, and disease also prevents barriers to sun absorption. Each piece of growing fruit needs some 30 leaves working for it, not

including the leaves that supply nourishment to roots and branches.

Properly pruned fruit trees have an open shape so that sunlight can penetrate the leaf canopy to reach each leaf.

Planting dwarf fruit trees closely together can help ensure pollination and fruit set.

Soil

It is often said that the year before planting is the most important one for fruit growing. Trees are large, long-lived, and a bit tricky to work around once they are established. Learn what you can about the soil type that you have in the year before planting. Do your soil testing in this important year, and amend your soils accordingly. Once the trees are planted, you have much less leeway for soil improvement.

Soil test kits are available from some local extension services and commercial laboratories. Results provide a recommendation for the crop being grown. This is the best $10 you will spend in your home garden.

Roots depend on the soil for a good supply of air and consistent moisture. The best soils for fruit trees are well drained after a rain or irrigation but do not dry out too quickly.

Some fruits, such as pears, will tolerate but not thrive in heavy soils. Apples and crab apples can withstand short periods of airless soil, but apricots, cherries, currants, figs, plums, and grapes all need fair drainage. Cane berries, strawberries, and peaches require good drainage, and blueberries demand perfect drainage.

Heavy soils are soils that drain slowly and are not recommended for fruit production. You can improve them for fruit trees to some degree by adding plentiful organic matter, and by mounding the soil, so the tree sits on a low mound. However, poorly drained soils are never recommended for planting fruit. This condition is often referred to as "wet feet." Many soil diseases are promoted when fruit trees are grown under wet feet conditions. A general rule of thumb is that the soil is too wet for fruit crops if it is saturated or puddles water for a period of two weeks anytime during the year.

In gardens with extremely heavy soil, you can still plant fruits that prefer porous soils by using containers or raised beds. A raised bed for a

Keep young fruit trees watered well and mulched for their first season and until they are well-established.

Improve clay or sand soils by amending backfill with an organic soil amendment.

standard fruit tree should be 3 feet deep and 6 feet square.

It is also possible to improve the drainage of a wet area by installing a piped drainage system. This involves placing shallow perforated pipes under the ground to drain the water away from a wet area.

Soils that don't hold much water are most easily improved by adding large amounts of organic matter. Most fruit trees can be grown in dry soils, but they should be watered more frequently than trees on better soil. You may need to fertilize at slightly higher rates, but this should still only be done during the spring of the year, never after that point, or trees may become winter injured.

You can supply these needs best if you first examine your soil. To determine what type of soil you have and how to improve it, follow the directions on page 19.

Also assess the soil pH before you plant. It takes time for sulfur or lime to affect pH. Therefore, you need to apply it and work it into the soil well in the year before planting. Determine your soil pH from the soil test you have done on your soil.

Lime raises the soil pH, while sulfur lowers it. Blueberries require a low pH (4.5 to 5.5), while fruit trees and grapes generally grow best at a pH of 6 to 7. Acidifying (lowering the pH) the soil with aluminum sulfate is not recommended because it requires six times more chemical than sulfur does to produce the same effect. In addition, aluminum sulfate applications are costly and can contaminate the soil with excess aluminum—which will appear in your crop.

Planting

After planting, build a water-holding basin over the original root ball and mulch.

Nurseries and garden centers sell plants in three ways: bare root, balled with the root ball wrapped in burlap, or growing in containers.

Most deciduous fruit plants are sold bare-root. The leafless plant is taken from the ground in late fall or winter and shipped to the nursery, where it is held in moist conditions. Bare-root plants are fragile and must be kept cool and moist. Plant them as soon as possible after purchasing them.

Fruit trees are seldom sold balled-and-burlapped, but they are frequently sold in containers made of plastic, pulp, or metal. Balled-and-burlapped plants and container-grown fruit trees should be kept moist and planted promptly. In most of North America, the best planting time is in the spring over a four-week period, starting from the time the buds on native trees are just beginning to show green. Once the days get hot,

success in planting fruit plants decreases rapidly. It is acceptable to plant fruit trees in the fall about the time the foliage on native trees begins to color and air temperatures become cooler.

If you must keep bare-root plants for a time before you can plant them in their final destinations, dig a shallow trench, lay the plants on their sides with the roots in the trench, and cover the roots with moist soil. This is called "heeling in." Keep the soil moist (not soaked). Try to plant within two to three weeks. If the heeled-in plants begin to leaf out and grow, they will be much harder to plant and will be less likely to survive being transplanted.

Planting fruiting trees and shrubs

The best general guide to planting is to dig the planting hole twice the width of the root ball. In heavy clay soil, always plant a little high (1 to 2 inches) above the original soil line on the plant.

The most fragile part of a woody plant is the crown, that section where the roots branch and the soil touches the trunk. The crown must be dry most of the time. Planting high minimizes crown rot by preventing water from puddling near the trunk. If you plant at soil level, the soil in the hole might settle, causing your plants to sink.

Be especially careful when planting grafted dwarf fruit trees. Dwarfing rootstocks may blow over unless they have support. Young fruit trees on dwarf rootstocks typically require staking.

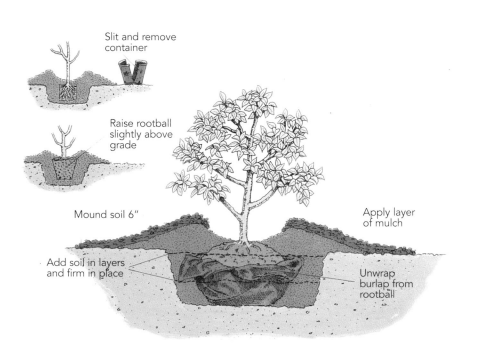

Slit and remove container

Raise rootball slightly above grade

Mound soil 6"

Apply layer of mulch

Add soil in layers and firm in place

Unwrap burlap from rootball

To plant a container-grown fruit tree, slice the side of the pot (above left) and peel it away from the roots. Mound the soil a few inches away from the tree trunk to create a dike to hold water. Natural burlap will decay so can remain around the rootball. But to remove it, tilt the tree to one side and roll the burlap beneath the exposed part of the root ball; then tilt the tree the other way to remove the burlap altogether.

The graft or bud union should be planted 2 to 3 inches above the soil line. If the graft union is buried under the soil, the cultivar that was grafted on top will root, and the benefits of the rootstock will be lost. The bud union shows later as a bulge just above the ground line. Some nurseries place the bud of the fruiting variety high on the rootstock, 6 or 8 inches above the roots. Identify where on the tree the union is so that you position it properly when planting.

Be careful not to bury the bud union in soil or mulch at any time during the life of the tree. Check the bud union frequently for signs of rooting and keep mulches a few inches away from it. Another reason to keep mulch from the base of fruit trees is that mice or voles may use the mulch as cover when chewing on the bark of the tree.

It's usually a good idea to reduce the top of a fruit tree by one-half to one-third of its original size. This puts the top of the tree in balance with the root system because some of the roots were lost when the tree was dug. Choose branches that are healthy, well-positioned around the tree, and have a wide angle from the trunk.

Planting cane berries and grapes

Cane berries and grapes are usually sold bare-root in spring. A line on a bare-root plant indicates the previous soil level; plant these fruits at that same depth. Cut back grape canes to two or three buds. Plant cane berries 4 feet apart; position grapes 6 to 8 feet apart. A trellis may not be

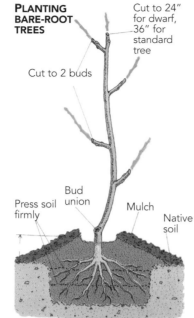

PLANTING BARE-ROOT TREES

Cut to 24" for dwarf, 36" for standard tree

Cut to 2 buds

Press soil firmly

Bud union

Mulch

Native soil

When planting a grafted bare-root fruit tree, position the bud union above the soil. Trim branches by about one-third.

enough to support grapes, but it's optional for cane berries.

Planting blueberries, currants, and gooseberries

These plants are often sold in containers; plant them at the same depth they were grown in the nursery. For currants and gooseberries leave only the three strongest branches, cutting them back to 8 inches. Space plants 3 to 4 feet apart. Space blueberry plants 4 to 6 feet apart.

Planting strawberries

Strawberries are sold either bare-root in early spring or planted in small containers. Bare-root strawberries are typically sold in bundles of 25. Be sure to keep the crown above the soil line and dig a hole large enough to accommodate all the roots.

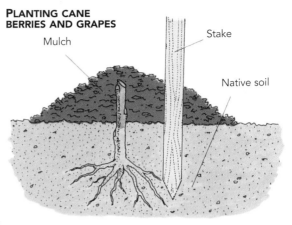

PLANTING CANE BERRIES AND GRAPES

Mulch

Stake

Native soil

Plant a rooted cane berry or grape with two or three buds above the soil. Place a support stake at the same time, then mulch.

Strawberries can be grown in the matted-row or double-row hill systems. In the former, all runners are allowed to grow, forming a mat, giving larger yields the first bearing season. The plants should be spaced 12 inches apart in rows spaced 3 feet apart.

In the double-row hill system, plants are 12 inches apart in rows that are also 12 inches apart. All runners are picked off. Each double row is raised and separated by a 24-inch trough that allows you to walk among the plants. The system lends itself to day-neutral strawberries and those that don't send out many runners. But it's key to note that everbearing strawberries are no longer recommended, having been replaced by the newer day-neutral cultivars.

When planting bare-root strawberry plants, position the crown of the plant slightly above the soil level, like the far-right plant above.

Fertilizing and Watering

Like vegetables and herbs, fruits primarily need nitrogen, phosphorous, potassium, and small quantities of other trace elements. Nitrogen is the element that is most often in short supply, while phosphorous, potassium, and minor nutrients may be naturally available and should be added only based on a soil test. (See page 19 for details on performing a soil test.)

Nitrogen is essential for proper shoot growth, leaf color, and fruiting. Tree fruits (even dwarf tree fruits) should have 6 to 12 inches of new growth per season. If growth is less than that, nitrogen may be needed.

Too much nitrogen, though, can lead to poor fruit set and overvigorous growth. Proper nitrogen levels can enhance fruit set, fruit color, and keep trees a manageable size. Too little nitrogen can reduce tree vigor and fruiting.

For most fruit plantings, apply nitrogen only in spring, with strawberries as an exception. Late applications of nitrogen can cause a late-season flush of growth that delays hardening and increases the risk of winter injury. As a rule, don't fertilize fruit crops after July 4.

Phosphorous is also essential for proper leaf color and growth. Purple leaf color is often a sign of phosphorous deficiency. Always base additions of phosphorous on a soil test because phosphorous doesn't leach out of soils readily and many soils already have adequate amounts.

Potassium is needed for proper shoot elongation, fruit sizing, and leaf coloring. Small fruits and shoots and curled leaves are symptoms of potassium deficiency. Like phosphorous, potassium doesn't move out of soil easily, so make additions only based on soil test results.

Minor nutrients such as zinc and boron may be deficient in specific soil situations, such as alkaline soils. Based on a soil test add these carefully, since plants only need small amounts to grow properly.

Check with your local extension service or local nursery for recommended fertilizer rates for specific fruit and nut trees in your area. Often soils in the same area will have different nutrient compositions, requiring different fertilizing strategies. Fertilizing should be based on the previous year's growth and maturity of the tree.

Fertilizing fruit and nut trees: nonbearing years

Apple, pear, quince, plum, and sour cherry should have about 6 to 18 inches of new growth a year. Peach, nectarine, and sweet cherry should have about 10 to 18 inches a year.

A starting dose of $\frac{1}{10}$ pound of nitrogen for every 1-inch diameter of the tree measured 1 foot above ground is fine for apples and pears. A dose of $\frac{1}{8}$ pound of nitrogen for every 1-inch diameter of the tree measured 1 foot above ground is fine for most other fruits. Be careful not to overfertilize.

Fertilizing fruit and nut trees: bearing years

Apple, pear, quince, plum, and sour cherry should have 6 to 12 inches of new growth a year. Peach, nectarine, and sweet cherry should have 12 to 18 inches a year.

If you have excessive growth and haven't been adding nitrogen fertilizer, check the lawn fertilizer product that you've used. Lawns around fruit trees are often treated with high nitrogen fertilizer that the fruit tree roots also absorb, causing excessive growth. Cut back on your lawn fertilizer if this is the case.

Fertilizing small fruits

Most small fruits such as grapes, raspberries, and blackberries grow fine with annual additions of compost. Check for nutrient deficiency signs—poor fruiting and pale leaf color or shoot growth—and add supplemental fertilizer as needed.

The exception is blueberries. They require an acidic soil and may show deficiency symptoms if the soil pH is too high. First adjust the pH by adding the

Compost adds organic matter as it decays as well as provides small amounts of nutrients.

proper amounts of sulfur based on a pH test. Then check for additional nutrients that need to be added.

Fertilizing with animal manure and compost

Manure and compost improve soil texture, as well as adding nutrients, but they're lower in nitrogen than chemical fertilizers. Compost and manure may also contain salts, which can prove harmful in dry climates. Be especially careful of bird, rabbit, and feed-lot manures. Because manures and compost contain less nitrogen per pound than chemical fertilizers, you can use relatively more. Because they release nitrogen slowly, you can put the whole amount of manure or compost around the tree at one time.

For young trees, begin with a little less than ½ pound of dry bird manure, or about 1 pound of dry cattle manure, and double each year. For mature trees, use 50 to 70 pounds of well-rotted bird or rabbit manure, spreading it under the outer branches in fall. For the same trees, use 100 to 200 pounds of well-rotted cattle manure.

The full effect of composts and manure on the soil nutrition may require three to four years. Observe the growth of the plants for at least two years before adding more compost or manure. Once the nitrogen is added to the soil, it cannot be taken back. It is better to go slowly, adding a little at a time, than to overdo what cannot be undone.

Newly planted trees require ample water.

Drip irrigation is an ideal method for watering young cane berry plants.

Watering

Standard fruit trees need a lot of water. If this isn't supplied by rain, deep irrigation is necessary. Dwarf trees may not need as much water, but they require a constant supply. At planting time, water each layer of soil in the planting hole. Finish by soaking the soil around the newly planted tree.

Do not water again before new growth begins. The roots are not growing actively at this time, and soggy soil will invite root rot. When new growth begins, let the top inch of soil dry and then soak the plant completely. Be sure to water at the top of the planting mound. Your best bet is to water very thoroughly but less often.

Plants that are actively growing generally need 1 inch of water once a week, or about 2 gallons of water per square foot of root spread. (The roots generally spread out somewhat farther than the top canopy of the tree.) A newly planted tree would have a root spread of up to 2 square feet and, therefore, would need 2 to 4 gallons of water a week. Make adjustments for rainfall and soil type. Heavy rainfalls leach nutrients from soil, while clay soils hold nutrients better than sandy soils.

Extend mulch as far as the tree's dripline. Build a series of water dikes to direct irrigation to roots.

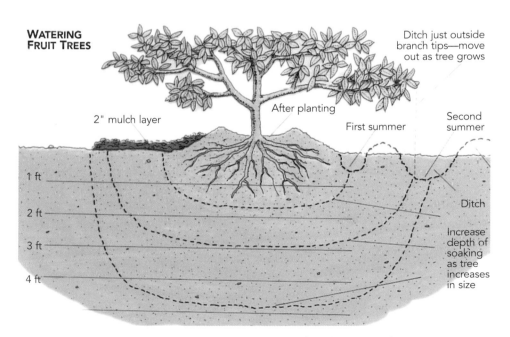

WATERING FRUIT TREES

2" mulch layer

After planting
First summer
Second summer

Ditch just outside branch tips—move out as tree grows

1 ft
2 ft
3 ft
4 ft

Ditch

Increase depth of soaking as tree increases in size

Fruit in Containers

Strawberries adapt well to container culture, bearing heavy crops of sweet, tasty fruit.

Containers make plants mobile. Moving fruit plants to shelter when cold weather comes, or to a shady spot in extreme heat, makes it possible to grow them beyond their normal climate ranges. Relocate plants to find out where they do best and plant varieties not usually recommended for your climate. One caution, however: Plants in containers are not as winter-hardy as those in the ground. You must give them some kind of winter protection in regions where the ground freezes.

Virtually any fruits you like can be planted in containers. Trees, of course, must be dwarfs. Figs, strawberries, blueberries, and currants all make excellent container plants, as do grapes if provided with a trellis or other support.

Choosing containers

Anything is suitable as a container as long as it will hold the plant and a sufficient amount of soil, is nontoxic, and contains drainage holes.

Whatever type of container you choose, it should be just 2 or 3 inches wider than the roots of the plant. The right size container allows roots easy access to water and nutrients without encouraging root growth at the expense of top growth. Let a young tree grow for a season in something about the size of a 5-gallon nursery can and then repot it the following spring in a larger container.

Container soils

Because soil in a container loses moisture easily, it must hold moisture well. It must also have good drainage. Commercial mixes of soil offer several advantages. They are free of disease organisms, insects, and weed seeds; they are lightweight and they can be used right from the bag.

Here is a basic recipe for mixing your own container planting medium:
- 9 cubic feet of fine sand designated as 30-270 (numbers refer to screen sizes the sand will pass through)
- 9 cubic feet of ground bark
- 5 pounds 5-10-10 fertilizer
- 5 pounds ground limestone
- 1 pound iron sulphate

Add compost to make up as much as one-third of the volume if you don't add topsoil. Recent research has shown that some composts will suppress root rot in container-grown plants.

Potting and repotting

Before you pot your fruit plant, make sure your container has drainage holes. Cover the holes with screen or broken pieces of terra-cotta pots. Do not fill the bottom with rocks or coarse gravel. These do not improve drainage; they simply take up space in the container and make it heavy.

For a bare-root plant, place enough tamped-down soil mix in the bottom of the pot so the plant crown is slightly below the container rim when the roots are touching the soil mix. Toss in enough mix to support the plant, tamping lightly and filling with water as you go, and fill the container to about an inch below the rim.

When planting fruits grown in nursery containers, remove the container and scratch the root ball all around with a

To transplant a fruit tree from a nursery pot into your own container, slide it out of the pot. Take a knife and slice off the outer inch of roots; snip any long and pot-encircling roots at the bottom of the root ball.

In the new pot place the plant at the same depth as before.

Use a dowel or stake to remove air pockets around the edges, but don't compress the soil.

Finish by watering deeply, until water runs out of the pot. Cut back top growth by a third.

fork to rough up the roots. Be sure to cut off long roots at the bottom of the root ball. These may have circled the bottom of the pot. Set the plant just as deeply as it was in the nursery container, with at least an inch between the pot rim and the soil level.

Repotting is similar. It is necessary because plants tend to bunch feeder roots at the wall of a container where they dry out and die more easily. When you shave off an inch of root and add fresh soil, the plant will grow healthy young roots in the new reservoir of moisture and nutrients. New top growth will soon follow. After potting or repotting, give the plant a good deep watering.

Feeding fruit plants in containers

If you use a purely synthetic mix, you must be careful about feeding. The added nutrients often wash right through the soil when you water, so you'll have to feed more often.

One good feeding method is to give each plant about half the recommended quantity of complete fertilizer every two or three weeks. If the label recommends 1 tablespoon per gallon of water each month, use ½ tablespoon per gallon instead and feed every two weeks. A liquid fertilizer is easier to measure in exact proportions and is also less likely to burn plant roots.

Another method is using slow- or time-release fertilizers. These pellets release fertilizer with each watering as the plant needs it. Feed from the beginning of the growing season until the end of summer if the plant is to receive winter protection. Stop about mid-July if the plant will stay outdoors through winter. In both cases, ceasing to fertilize gives any new growth ample time to harden off.

Watering fruits in containers

If you check the soil occasionally by digging down an inch or two, you'll soon learn when to water. Water whenever the soil just under the surface begins to dry. The top inch may stay moist for a week in fairly cool weather, but in hot, windy weather you'll need to water more often. Water enough each time so a good amount drains from the bottom of the container. Don't count on rain to do all of your watering. The foliage of plants in containers can act as an umbrella, shedding most of the rainfall.

Vacation watering

When you leave home for a long period, group your containers near a water source and away from afternoon sun. This will help keep them moist and cut the need for water. In addition, grouping them makes it easier for a friend to water, particularly during hot or dry spells.

Leaching

It's important to leach container soil occasionally to remove built-up mineral salts from fertilizers. Brown leaf edges indicate a salt problem. Leach every couple of months by running water through the

soil for several minutes, letting it run out drainage holes, taking the salt buildup with it.

In climates unfriendly to in-ground citrus production, nurture a crop of fruit in containers.

Winter protection

Gardeners in zones with freezing winter temperatures should protect even hardy deciduous plants during the coldest months of the year when they are in containers.

The easiest protection strategy is to move plants into an unheated space. You can also bury the pot in the ground, deep enough that soil covers the rim. Heaping sawdust, leaves, or wood chips around the pot will help protect roots if temperatures don't drop far below freezing.

Cultivate a harvest of peaches from a potted tree that has moved to an unheated space in winter.

Pests and Diseases of Fruit

Sound cultural practices provide the first line of defense against pests and diseases in the home orchard.

When it comes to fruit growing and pests, you may want to give your approach a reality check with respect to the time, money, and energy you're willing to devote to scouting for pests, spraying, and most important, carrying out all the cultural practices that will help you avoid spraying in the first place.

Home gardeners may find it more difficult and expensive to grow high-quality tree fruit than small-fruit plants, such as strawberries, grapes, blueberries, and brambles. One reason is that many different pests and diseases plague tree fruits. Summer rainfall and high humidity favor the growth and spread of disease-causing organisms. Insects are also challenging.

Power spray equipment isn't practical for a small planting, yet getting spray into the canopy of a large fruit tree is a challenge! Dwarf fruit trees offer one solution because pesticides can be applied with hand-operated equipment.

But you'll still need to be on your toes, scouting faithfully for insect presence, noting changes that occur on the leaves and the growing fruits, and keeping track of the weather so you're able to time your sprayings accordingly. Most cooperative extension services have home fruit production guides and websites that provide the specific information home gardeners need to grow fruit crops successfully.

The more energy your plants expend recovering from the effects of pests and diseases, the less fruit they will bear. Here are some tips on giving them a helping hand that will bring ample rewards at harvest time.

As with vegetables, the principles of Integrated Pest Management (IPM) provide the best framework for coping with fruit diseases and pests. Planting resistant varieties is one of the most important practices that assists home fruit growers toward being successful. For example, several apple varieties are available that are resistant to apple scab disease. Growing these varieties eliminates the need to spray fungicides.

Home fruit producers should resist the temptation to grow well-known fruit varieties like 'McIntosh' and 'Gala' apples, which are highly susceptible to numerous disease problems. Disease-resistant apple varieties available to the home fruit grower taste as good but require no disease-prevention sprays. Ask for these at your local nursery or search out your closest source on the Web. You will be rewarded for your extra effort in finding these varieties by growing more blemish-free fruit with less spraying. Although these varieties are disease-free, they will still require insecticide sprays to control insects. However, this will mean making a few well-timed sprays to control insects versus spraying every two weeks to prevent disease buildup on your fruit.

It is also important to nourish your fruit plants well, practice good maintenance, encourage beneficial predators in the local environment, and carefully monitor your crop for signs of trouble. Then use a combination of physical, cultural, and biological controls before turning to chemical agents as a last resort. For more information on IPM, see page 26.

One of the best defenses against pests and disease is a healthy plant. Healthy fruit and nut trees and berry plants resist infection and can overcome insect attacks, but sickly, weak plants easily succumb to these problems. You should also avoid overfertilizing fruit plants. Once a fertilizer (chemical or natural) is added to the soil you can't take it back. You can visually monitor the appropriate vigor of your plants. In general, mature fruiting tree plants should have at least 6 to 12 inches of growth a year. Less than this and they may need a little fertilizer; more than this and they are too vigorous. Both low vigor and high vigor can result in disease problems.

Have a diversity of plantings in your yard to encourage beneficial insects and birds to frequent your fruit plantings. They'll take care of many of the pests before you have to.

Sanitation is another good method of prevention. Be sure to remove all remaining fruits, berries, and nuts at the end of the season and clean up the ground below the plants. This debris can provide a home for overwintering pests; either burn the material or seal it in a bag to be discarded. Your neighbors' trees and shrubs may be the source of some of your trouble, but there is no way to make others keep their plants pest-free.

Be sure to prepare the soil properly by taking soil nutrient tests on a regular basis (every two to three years), and keep your tree, shrub, or vine watered and pruned. Beyond that, you must accept the fact that you may lose some fruit each season: In most cases, there will be more than enough left for a good harvest.

When you use biological (natural insect predators like ladybugs or compost to control soil-disease organisms) and chemical-control measures, read the label carefully and follow all directions exactly.

Fruit pests

The pests listed are among the most common, although you may encounter others. A few are confined to specific regions of the United States.

APHIDS: Soft-bodied insects that damage leaves and fruit by sucking plant sap. A dormant oil spray kills overwintering eggs. Spray foliage with insecticidal soap, horticultural oil, or just a vigorous jet of water to dislodge the aphids. Reduce nitrogen fertilization that causes an abundance of the young, succulent growth that aphids love.

APPLE MAGGOTS: This pest is found primarily east of the Rockies, but it is also becoming a problem in the Pacific Northwest and northern California. Adult flies lay eggs under the skin of the fruit. When the eggs hatch, the larvae tunnel through the flesh. The flies are active from July through harvest. Keep trees clean and remove damaged fruit. Hanging "sticky balls"—red spheres coated with vaseline or latex, which traps the insects—in your trees can let you know when the insects are present, so that effective spray measures can be used. The sticky balls reduce the incidence of maggots, but they are not effective as a complete control measure.

BIRDS: The biggest problem with cherries, blueberries, and other small fruits is that birds can gobble the entire crop. When fruit begins to ripen, cover the whole plant with plastic netting, which is available from nurseries and hardware dealers. Throw the net directly over the plant or build simple wood frames to support netting over dwarfs and bushes. For larger trees, strands of reflective tape, scare-eye balloons, and cotton twine will frighten birds when they try to land and may be sufficient. Plastic owls can also be placed near the fruit crops and moved regularly.

Protect ripening berry crops from foraging birds by covering fruit-laden plants with plastic netting.

Aphids sink their mouthparts into lush new growth, sucking plant juices until growth is deformed.

Apple maggots burrow through ripening fruit. Control adult flies with sprays.

Pests and Diseases of Fruit
(continued)

Once cherry fruit fly larvae burrow into fruit, the only control is to pick and destroy infected cherries.

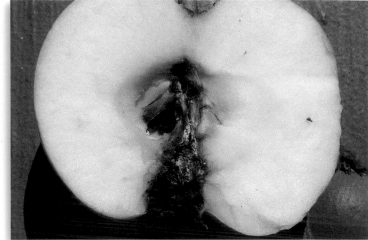

Codling moth larvae damage the inside of apples and pears.

CHERRY FRUIT FLIES: This fruit fly starts as a white larva that burrows through the cherries, leaving a hole. Once inside the fruit, they are difficult to control. Cultivate the soil under cherry trees in fall to expose overwintering larvae and pick and destroy all infested fruits.

CHERRY (PEAR) SLUGS: These small, wet-looking green worms are the larvae of a wasp. They skeletonize leaves, leaving lacy patches. Handpick small infestations or dislodge them with a strong jet of water.

CODLING MOTHS: The major pest of apples and pears, these moths lay eggs in the blossoms and their larvae tunnel in the fruit, leaving holes and droppings (frass). Codling moths are difficult to control with chemicals because sprays need to be precisely timed. By using pheromone traps you can time sprays for best effect. For small plantings, cover individual fruits when they are 1 inch in diameter with special bags to prevent adults from laying eggs.

FLATHEADED BORERS: This western pest is the larva of a beetle. The borer burrows into bark that has been damaged or sunburned. To avoid the pest, prevent trunk damage. Paint or wrap young trunks or those exposed by heavy pruning and be careful not to cut them with tools or machinery. When you find tunnels and droppings, cut away bark and wood, dig out the borers, then paint the wound with tree seal.

Combat cherry (pear) slugs by blasting them off leaves with a spray of the garden hose.

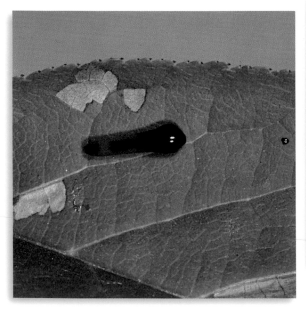

Inadvertent damage to fruit tree trunks by string trimmers or sunscald can open doors to pests like the flatheaded borer.

Grape berry moths feed on fruit stems and developing fruit.

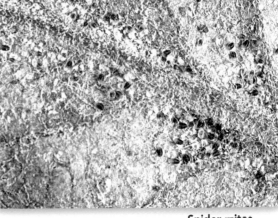

GRAPE BERRY MOTHS: Active in the northeastern part of the country. This insect overwinters on pieces of grape leaves on the ground, so its numbers may be reduced by tilling the leaves into the soil.

LEAF ROLLERS: This moth larva hides in rolled leaves and feeds on both foliage and fruit. Once established it is protected from spray. Infested leaves must be picked off. Leaf rollers can be controlled using *Bacillus thuringiensis*

(Bt, a parasitic bacteria).

MITES: Well-watered, vigorous plants are much less susceptible to spider mite infestations than plants subject to drought, dust, and dirt. Overspraying for other insects may trigger a mite attack because spraying kills the mites' enemies. You'll know mites are present if there is a silvery webbing under the leaves or if the leaves are curled, stippled, or bronzed. Kill overwintering mites with dormant oil spray in winter. In

summer kill spider mites with forceful sprays of insecticidal soap, testing it on a few branches to be sure it doesn't harm the leaves.

ORIENTAL FRUIT MOTHS: The larvae of this pest of peaches, plums, nectarines, and apricots burrow into twigs, which causes the tips to wilt. The most serious damage occurs later in the season when larvae feed on the fruit. Proper sanitation and cleaning up dropped fruits can reduce this pest's numbers.

Spider mites multiply when it's hot and dry. They're tiny and hard to spot; webbing and stippling on leaves usually give them away.

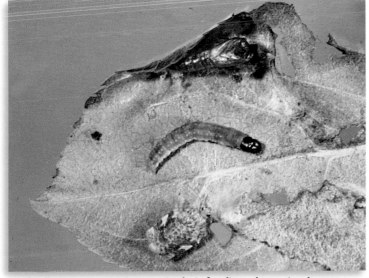

Leaf rollers prove omnivorous in their feeding, devouring leaves and fruit. Parasitic wasps prey upon leaf roller larvae.

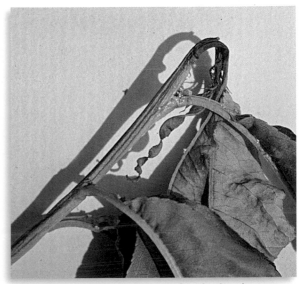

When Oriental fruit moth larvae hatch, they burrow into twigs, causing wilting.

Pests and Diseases of Fruit
(continued)

One type of peach tree borer burrows into twigs, causing wilt and later, defoliation.

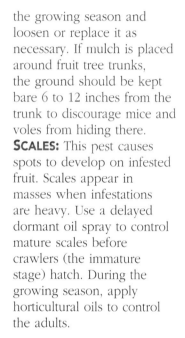

Plum curculios create crescent-shaped scars on fruit.

PEACH TREE BORERS: One type bores into twigs and fruit; another very common borer attacks the trunk at the soil line. If a tree is growing poorly, check for the borer below the soil line. Dig soil away from the trunk and check for tunnels and droppings. Kill the worm by pushing a bit of wire down its tunnel. Check cherry, plum, and nectarine trees for infestations of the same pest.

Trunk borers can also be controlled by maintaining vigorous growth with appropriate water and fertilizer applied as needed.

Trees damaged by lawn mowers, frost cracking, or other borers are more susceptible to infestation by peach tree borer.

PEAR PSYLLA: Related to aphids, the larvae cluster on leaves, suck plant juices, and excrete a sticky, sweet "honeydew" that coats the leaves and fruits. A black, sooty fungus may grow on the honeydew, reducing photosynthesis and weakening the tree. Dormant oil spray, applied just before the buds swell, and a horticultural oil spray applied to adults are effective treatments against pear psylla.

PLUM CURCULIOS: This beetle is a serious problem for apples, peaches, cherries, and other wild and cultivated fruits east of the Rockies. Both adults and larvae damage fruit. Look for the crescent-shaped scars on fruit made by the female when laying eggs. The pests are active for three to four weeks, starting at petal fall. Two timed sprays of phosmet will control this pest.

RODENTS: Mice, voles, and rabbits all eat the bark of young trees, especially when the ground is covered with mulch or snow in winter and better food is unavailable. If enough bark is removed, the tree will die after the first growth surge of spring. Protect the lower trunk in winter or year-round with a cylinder of hardware cloth. Check it occasionally during the growing season and loosen or replace it as necessary. If mulch is placed around fruit tree trunks, the ground should be kept bare 6 to 12 inches from the trunk to discourage mice and voles from hiding there.

SCALES: This pest causes spots to develop on infested fruit. Scales appear in masses when infestations are heavy. Use a delayed dormant oil spray to control mature scales before crawlers (the immature stage) hatch. During the growing season, apply horticultural oils to control the adults.

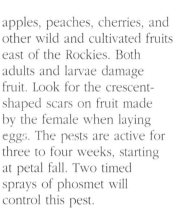

Adult pear psylla are winged; young forms are wingless.

Scale insects cover stems, sucking plant sap.

TENT CATERPILLARS: You probably won't see this pest if you have sprayed early for others. Tent caterpillars build large webs among branches; these webs contain hundreds of hairy caterpillars that emerge to eat leaves. Tent caterpillars can be eradicated by spraying Bt or physically removing the nests with pruners.

Fruit diseases

The following are the most common of the many fruit tree diseases. The best strategy is to choose resistant plants, keep them well fed and watered, and clean up all plant debris. Some require the removal and burning of infected plant parts. Some are controlled with proper sprays (timing is very important).

APPLE AND PEAR SCAB overwinter on apple and pear leaf debris, so be sure to rake up under trees and destroy the material. This fungus infects foliage and fruit. The disease is most severe in wet weather and is less a problem in dry areas. Because multiple sprays will be needed to control this disease, depending on the weather, the safest measure for the home gardener is to grow disease-resistant apple varieties and reduce wetting fruit foliage. Use a fungicide to control this disease. In wetter areas, applications are made every two weeks from budbreak until midsummer.

BACTERIAL LEAF AND FRUIT SPOT primarily attacks cherries, peaches, and plums. This bacterial disease lives through winter in leaf debris, so proper fall cleanup is essential for control. In the east and south of the United

Cut down tent caterpillar nests and bury them or simply dispose of them. Caterpillars can't survive long enough to find their way back to the host plant.

The best defense against apple and pear scab disease is variety selection: Grow scab-resistant cultivars.

States, Japanese plums are difficult to grow due to this problem. The infection, which occurs during rainy periods in the spring, causes brown spots that form in the leaves and develop into widening holes. It may attack fruit spurs and cause fruit drop. It is very difficult to control this disease with materials available to home fruit producers. If you live in a wet area (eastern United States) select varieties resistant to this disease.

Cleanliness wins the war against bacterial leaf and fruit spot, which overwinters in fallen leaf litter. Rake up and destroy all leaves in fall.

Pests and Diseases of Fruit
(continued)

Bacterial canker of cherry causes gumming on infected limbs and deeply sunken, dark areas on infected fruit.

Apples affected by bitter rot have sunken lesions that carry rot all the way to the core of the fruit.

The knobby fungal growths of black knot can girdle and kill affected branches.

BACTERIAL CANKER of cherries causes long, narrow gum-edged patches on the trunk or branches. Branches die as they are girdled by these patches. The disease can also affect apricots, blueberries, peaches, and prune plums. Choose disease-tolerant rootstocks and varieties and avoid planting in poor soils. Prune out infected branches below the canker and destroy them.

BITTER ROT is the most serious fruit rot of apples in the southeast, but this disease also occurs in the mid-Atlantic states and in the northeast. Dark round lesions appear on fruits; irregular brown spots show on leaves. Remove mummified and newly infected fruit. Reduce practices, such as nitrogen fertilization, that increase vegetative growth. Keeping the trees well pruned in the dormant season will open the tree up to faster drying during the growing season, reducing the potential for disease development. A fungicide will control this disease if applied after petal fall until fruit ripens.

BLACK KNOT causes black tarlike swellings on plum and cherry branches. The infection can spread from infected wild cherries and plums to cultivated trees, so plant at least 600 feet from any infected trees. Prune out and destroy infected twigs and branches in the fall and winter, making sure to cut at least 4 inches below visible signs of infection.

BLACK ROT diseases are caused by fungi. There are two major types. One affects apples and is sometimes called frog-eye leaf spot because it causes brown spots surrounded by purple margins on the leaves. It is one of the three fruit rots important on apples in the eastern United States. The rotted area is characterized by concentric, alternating black and brown rings. Control by pruning out diseased branches, removing mummified fruit, and applying an appropriate fungicide.

The other black rot is the most serious disease of grapes in the east. Attacking all young growing parts of the plant, it first appears as soft, round tan spots on the berries. Eventually the berries shrivel to hard, dry mummies resembling raisins. A fungicide is also effective in controlling this disease if applied from bloom until the individual green grapes are pea size or a little larger.

Plants that dry off quickly are less likely to get black rot; so choose a site in the sun with good air circulation and prune the plants annually. Except in unusually wet seasons, muscadine varieties are not attacked by black rot; most table grapes and wine grape varieties are susceptible.

BROWN ROT is serious on all stone fruits, but especially apricots, peaches, and nectarines; it usually prevents the maturation of harvestable fruit. The disease causes blossoms to brown and drop. Brown rot eventually causes fruit rot on the tree. Infected fruit must be removed by hand to prevent reinfection.

To control the blossom-blight phase, spray with a protectant fungicide such as copper when the first pink petals show but before the flowers open. Be certain to remove last year's fallen fruit mummies from the tree or ground prior to bloom. The

When black rot first appears on young grapes, it forms tan spots. Ultimately the grapes shrivel to look like raisins.

Brown rot attacks apple leaves, forming spots that can kill leaves. Cankers also appear on twigs and limbs.

disease spreads from the mummified fruit back to the blossoms.

To control attacks on fruit, spray as the fruit begins to ripen (green fruit is rarely attacked) and repeat if there is a period of wet weather. On peaches and nectarines, the disease may attack twigs and overwinter on them. Pruning out dead twigs and removing overwintering fruit mummies helps to control the disease in the following year.

CEDAR APPLE RUST appears only where the alternate host, certain species of juniper or red cedar, grows near apples. Apple leaves first show orange spots and odd cup-shaped structures; then they turn yellow and fall. To prevent, remove junipers and red cedars or avoid planting them; less effective is to remove the galls that form on cedars. (Galls are brownish and globe shaped and look like part of the tree.)

CROWN GALL is a bacterial disease that occurs in many soils. It attacks young trees, producing soft, corky galls, or swellings, on the crown and roots. The galls often grow until they girdle and stunt the tree's growth.

The best way to avoid this disease problem is to buy from a well-established nursery with a good reputation. Avoid buying young trees that show galls and plant young trees carefully to avoid injury, which makes the plant susceptible to bacteria.

Grapes may develop the disease after cold damage. It is recommended that grapes such as wine grapes that have been grafted to a rootstock be covered with soil to cover the graft union in colder climates over the winter. The soil is removed in the spring before vines leaf out.

The bacteria that cause crown galls (woody tumorlike structures on roots) actually live in many soils.

Yellow-orange spots on apple leaf undersides indicate cedar apple rust. The disease also infects juniper, Eastern red cedar, and hawthorn.

Pests and Diseases of Fruit

(continued)

Waterlogged soil invites crown rot to infect tree branches, trunks, and roots.

When grape clusters first appear, so may downy mildew. Look for white patches on leaf undersides.

The best fireblight control for home gardeners is severe pruning and burning affected plant parts.

CROWN ROT, a fungus, can occur on almost any plant growing in a soil that is frequently or constantly wet. Soil that remains waterlogged for more than two weeks any time during the growing season is too wet for fruit plants. Infected branches redden and foliage yellows or discolors. If bark below the soil line is dead, scrape it away and pull back the soil so air can reach the infection. Avoid crown rot on established trees by planting high and watering away from the trunk.

DOWNY MILDEW may attack grapes in the northeast when the weather is warm and moist from the time the clusters first become visible until just before harvest. Most table and wine grapes are susceptible to this disease. Native American grapes (Concord) are less susceptible. A white cottony growth appears, usually on the oldest leaves, but it can also attack young shoots, tendrils, berries, and clusters. Control by cleaning up dead leaves, where the fungus overwinters, and keeping the leaves of the vines as dry as possible. Do not overfertilize because it stimulates excessive growth. Prune in the dormant season. A fungicide is usually helpful in controlling this disease.

FIREBLIGHT is caused by bacteria and is spread by splashing rain and insects during the bloom period. It shows up in spring as new growth wilts, turns dark, and finally blackens as if burned. Infected brown shoots often take on the "shepherd's hook" appearance. Prune out infected branches well below (12 inches or more) the brown tissue. Sterilize pruning tools between each cut by dipping them in a 10 percent bleach solution or full-strength rubbing alcohol. Severe pruning and burning of infected wood has proven an effective control for the home gardener. Overfertilization will cause this disease to become more severe. Choose resistant fruit varieties.

GUMMOSIS, peach canker, and cytospora canker appear as deposits of gum on branches of stone fruits (peaches, nectarines, apricots, plums, and cherries). It is fairly common and may be caused by mechanical damage, insect damage, or a fungal disease. Peach canker will follow winter injury to the trunk or branches, large pruning cuts, and infections of leaf scars from weak shaded branches on the inside of the tree. Healthy trees will naturally defend large pruning cuts when the tree is actively growing. Prune stone fruit trees only after trees begin to grow in the spring. Prune trees on a regular basis (yearly) so large pruning cuts (greater than 1 inch) are not necessary. Fertilize to maintain the health and vigor of the tree (6 to 12 inches of new shoot growth each year).

Stone fruit trees should not be grown in grass (sod) up to the trunk. Stone fruit trees have shallow roots and do not compete well for water and nutrients with grass. Stone fruit trees will grow poorly in grass and won't be able to defend themselves from disease attack.

If cankers do occur, you can cut the diseased area away with a large pocket knife. Carefully cut straight into the bark, penetrating to the hard wood below the

Gummosis occurs as a result of wounding or making pruning cuts on large-diameter wood.

bark. Cut an outline around the diseased area about 1 inch away from the diseased tissue. With the tip of the knife, remove the diseased area and bark down to the wood inside the outlined area. The keys for this process to be successful are to perform this technique from early spring until midsummer and to obtain a green, healthy edge around the margin of the outlined area. No wound treatment is necessary.

Another disease that often causes gummosis is bacterial canker of cherries, described earlier on page 136.

PEACH LEAF CURL first shows up as a reddening of leaves.

Leaves then turn pale green or yellow, curl, blister, and may have a powdery look. Finally the affected leaves fall off. A second crop of healthy leaves will grow, which will not be affected. Growing a second flush of leaves utilizes critical food reserves in the tree needed to maintain tree health and fruitfulness. Several years of defoliation will weaken the tree to the point that it may not survive the winter. To control leaf curl, spray immediately after leaf drop or just before the buds break with a fixed copper spray or lime sulfur, wetting every twig and branch completely. No spraying is effective once disease symptoms have appeared.

POWDERY MILDEW is a fungus that causes a grayish powdery coating to form over young shoots, leaves, and flower buds, often deforming or killing them. It thrives in still, shady spots. When an infection begins, clip off severely mildewed twigs. Oil, sulfur, and copper sprays can prevent this disease. Also alternative materials such as food-grade mineral oil and baking soda formulations have proven effective in controlling powdery mildew. Check with your local suppliers for availability.

WHITE ROT is an important fruit rot wood disease of apples in the eastern United States. The disease organism overwinters and survives through the growing season in papery orange to brown cankers on branches. Prune out weak and dead branches. Remove pruned branches and wood from the orchard entirely. Promptly destroy them by burning.

Once peach leaf curl appears, it's too late to treat it. In the future, spray during the growing season to prevent recurrence.

Remove twigs and branches that are heavily infested with powdery mildew.

White rot survives winter in cankers on wood. Remove all infected tree parts from the orchard and destroy them.

Pruning and Training Fruit

The pruning toolshed should contain a collection of cutting implements (clockwise, from bottom left): hand pruners, long-handled pruning saw, pruning saw, and loppers.

Properly placed pruning cuts shape a tree canopy so that sunlight can penetrate easily to all branches and so that fruit-bearing branches can handle the weight of fruit.

The goal of pruning and training is to open up the tree canopy so all parts of the tree are exposed to light, the structure of the tree supports the fruit crop, and the tree dries off quickly to reduce foliage and fruit diseases. Pruning encourages healthy growth and larger fruit; training conserves space, develops a strong limb structure, and makes harvesting easier.

Apples, pears, cherries, and plums produce their best fruit on two- to three-year-old wood. Peaches bear their fruit on last year's growth. One of the reasons for pruning each year is to encourage productive fruiting wood—one-year-old wood on peaches, and two- to three-year-old wood on the others.

Unpruned trees lose their productivity quickly because of reduced light levels in the center of the tree and a reduction in the growth of new fruiting wood. Older fruit trees can still bear fruit because annual pruning promotes the right amounts and kinds of growth. After just a bit of practice at pruning and training fruit trees, you'll feel like a pro.

Most training involves manipulating, spreading, and tying or propping branches to create the desired angle at the crotches of the branches. Your goal is to encourage horizontal growth—branches that form a 60-degree angle with the trunk. It's on this growth that much of the fruiting will occur. Vertical branches tend to produce less fruit, and branches with narrow crotch angles are weak and break more easily under the weight of fruit. Narrow crotches can also serve as an entry point for organisms that cause disease and decay. Training during the early years to promote wide branch angles is probably the most important training you'll do in the life of your trees.

Most of us have seen long-neglected apple or pear trees or unpruned tangles of blackberry vines that still bear delicious fruit. Plants will live, grow, and bear fruit without ever being pruned, but experience has shown that good pruning and some training can prevent or remedy many problems that arise in plants.

Pruning is probably the most effective means to head off trouble, improve your plants' performance, and keep them in excellent condition. Training can elevate the craft of raising fruit trees into an art. Trees can be trained to create beautiful, functional, or even whimsical forms.

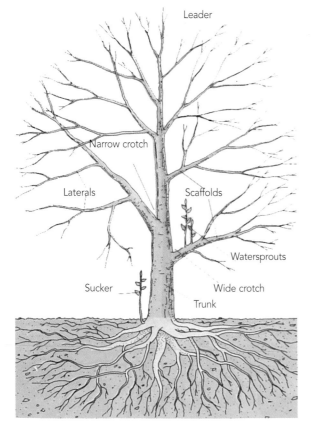

Leader

Narrow crotch

Laterals

Scaffolds

Watersprouts

Sucker

Wide crotch

Trunk

Pruning procedures

Pruning removes part of a plant to benefit the whole. Cutting away any part of a plant directly affects its growth. Depending on how and when it is done, pruning can be used to achieve the following results:

■ Shape a young tree
■ Produce new growth where desired
■ Help control and direct overall growth
■ Correct or repair damage
■ Help control and prevent insects and diseases
■ Rejuvenate or reshape an older plant
■ Bring about earlier blooming and fruiting
■ Increase the production, size, and quality of fruit

These advantages make pruning worthwhile, even if you are inexperienced and, like many, timid about cutting your plants.

Good pruning requires knowledge, foresight, and care. Pruning naturally invigorates a tree, causing more growth. It's often better to make fewer, thoughtful, and occasionally larger cuts than to nip away at the plant with small, tentative, but poorly placed cuts. If you remember that proper pruning is beneficial to plants and then proceed carefully, you'll get good results.

The objective in pruning a fruit tree is to produce abundant good-quality fruit throughout the branches, including the lower and interior ones. An unpruned peach or nectarine tree, for instance, will bear mostly on branch tips, and the leaves that nourish the plant and help sweeten fruit will grow only where they receive enough light for photosynthesis. A pruned peach or nectarine, however, bears fruit along branches, and foliage is balanced over the entire tree.

When to prune

In freezing climates, prune in late winter to spring, just as the buds begin to swell. The exception would be stone fruits, such as peaches and plums. Prune stone fruits at or just after blooming in the northeast to avoid a canker disease. Avoid pruning early in the dormant season, November or December, in such areas. Freezing injury can occur to plants if they are pruned in fall or early winter.

In more moderate climates, you can prune anytime during the dormant period, that is, the period between leaf fall and the beginning of bud swell in the spring.

Getting started

Begin pruning a mature fruit tree by removing all dead wood. Dead branches may harbor disease organisms that will affect leaves, fruit, or even the tree itself, causing early death. Do not leave pruning stubs longer than a quarter inch.

Next remove branches that grow toward the trunk of the tree and downward from horizontal. Branches that grow down often do not fruit well. Then remove branches that cross over each other.

The right tools are crucial. You'll need a good pair of pruning shears, and if you plan to make larger cuts, you'll need other tools, such as those shown opposite, top. The best-quality pruning tools are more expensive but are worth the extra cost: They will last much longer than inexpensive tools.

If you're confused about where to begin, remember that you can't hurt a plant by cutting out dead, diseased, or damaged wood or branches that cross and rub against other wood (which can cause wounds susceptible to infection). Such pruning is good for the tree, opening it to more air and light. Eliminating these problems also provides a clearer view of the tree and of the remaining work to be done.

Snip twigs and branches (left) to reduce the density of the plant canopy (right). This kind of thinning permits more sunlight to reach more leaves.

Use hand pruners to remove thin twigs. If branches are too thick for hand shears, then don't force the cut—you may damage your tool and the branch.

Proper pruning cuts leave no more than a quarter-inch stub where twigs or branches were removed.

Pruning and Training Fruit
(continued)

Familiarize yourself with the parts of a typical fruit tree branch (clockwise, from top left): overall branch, growing bud, lateral buds, bud scar, and fruiting spur.

A well-pruned central-leader tree will have a whorl of branches that are growing from the trunk of the tree like the spokes of a wheel (more or less). The branches should be growing at a 60- to 90-degree angle from the trunk. Whorls of branches should be 8 to 10 inches apart with an open space between each whorl. The number of branch whorls will depend on the tree's size.

There are two basic types of pruning cuts: heading back and thinning cuts. Thinning removes wood and ends growth. All thinning cuts are to the base of the branch or sucker so that no buds are left to sprout new growth.

Heading back removes the main shoot, causing new growth to emerge from lateral buds. Make cuts at an angle.

Heading is the process of shortening a branch, not removing it entirely. Buds on the remaining portion of wood are stimulated to grow when growth above them is removed. A third type of pruning cut is pinching—removing, with your fingers, a bud or branch tip growing in the wrong direction.

Fruit trees vary in their pruning needs. Some need a lot of pruning every year; some need only a little in a lifetime. Others never need pruning unless injured. In general, pruning requirements vary widely among different types of fruit trees. If you want to grow beautiful fruit, you must learn the difference between pruning an apple and a peach tree.

The illustrations on this page will help you recognize the various parts of a plant that you need to know when you begin to prune.

Making a cut

When you cut away part of a plant, a wound is left, which is susceptible to pests and diseases. To avoid trouble, make wounds as small as possible. Annual pruning will also reduce the need, down the line, to prune out large-diameter branches.

The smallest possible wound is made by removing a bud or twig. If a new sprout is growing in toward the center of the tree or the trunk or threatening to tangle with another branch, pinch it off anytime during the growing season to save pruning later. If you see the bud of a sucker near the soil, rub it off.

Always make cuts close to a node. Branches (and leaves) grow only at these nodes, and if you leave too long a stub (over ¼ inch) beyond the node, the stub will die, rot, and perhaps allow disease organisms into the heart of the tree. Be sure to cut at a slight angle so there is no straight "shoulder" left to allow water to collect on the cut surface where diseases or burrowing pests could get started in the wood.

Summer pruning

If a tree grows too vigorously while it is young, fruiting will be delayed several years. Avoid overfertilizing young fruit trees; too much food stimulates too much growth. A general rule of thumb for fertilizing fruit trees is 1 pound of 10-10-10 fertilizer per year of tree age. If trees are growing more than 12 inches per year reduce fertilizer. Overvigorous trees produce many watersprouts— vertical shoots that spoil the shape of the tree and take energy away from fruiting.

Control overly vigorous growth by summer pruning. Just be cautious, though, because too much summer pruning can damage a tree. Experience will teach you how much pruning is necessary. Follow these guidelines for summer pruning. In early summer remove only watersprouts, cutting them off at the base. Also, throughout summer, remove any suckers from below the bud union, cutting to the base.

Spreading branches

Training branches to the proper angle, especially when the trees are young, is perhaps more important than pruning later on. With proper branch training, you can avoid many problems such as branches breaking and insects and disease attacking later in the tree's life.

Ideally branches should be equally positioned around the trunk in a whorl at a 60-degree angle from the trunk. Branches should be positioned so they don't cast shade on other branches below them. If the young branch is in the proper scaffold position but has a narrower angle, use a spreader (piece of wood that forces the angle wider). Keep the spreader in place until the branch naturally begins growing at the desired angle.

Another method is to weigh down a branch by hanging fishing weights or baggies filled with sand from the branch tips. Again, weigh it down so the branch is at the proper angle and remove the weights when the branch can stay at that angle on its own.

Young, newly planted trees typically require very little pruning. The primary goal in training a young tree is to develop a set of branches on the tree that will fruit well and that are strong enough to hold a heavy fruit load without breaking. Branches that are growing horizontal to the ground or are growing slightly upward will be the most fruitful and the strongest.

You can use a spring-type clothespin to spread the branch angle of young limbs. Spreading is best done while the young branches are 6 to 8 inches long and are still green and actively growing. Place the grasping end of the clothespin around the trunk and the pinching part of the clothespin on the young branch, bending the branch to the desired angle. Young branches are very flexible and won't break if handled carefully. After just a few weeks, the branches will remain spread to the larger angle even if the clothespin comes off.

Larger woody branches may also be spread to larger angles, but they require pieces of wood, wire, or weights to hold them in place.

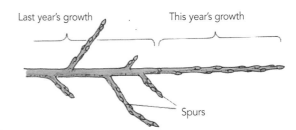

Last year's growth · This year's growth

Spurs

On apricots and Japanese plums, fruits come on spurs at the base of the current season's growth (above). Cut back forking branches (left) to different lengths for a stronger tree.

Training methods

Productive fruit trees should be trained to one of three forms (vase shape, central leader, or modified central leader) starting when the trees are planted. Such pruning and training will keep the tree balanced in form and—more important—balanced in new and young wood. Dwarf trees require less severe pruning because they are smaller.

Left unpruned, a tree will become dense with weak, thin, twiggy growth and overloaded with small, less healthy fruit.

Late winter on a sunny afternoon is the perfect time to prune fruit trees. Use a stepladder to reach higher branches.

GALLERY OF
Temperate Fruit

By choosing fruit varieties adapted to your climate, you'll have harvests of fresh flavor—perfect for eating, for cooking, or for preserving.

IN THIS CHAPTER

Gallery of Temperate
Fruit **154**
Berries **171**
Nuts **182**

The information in this encyclopedia is designed to help you choose the best possible fruits for your garden. In some cases, varieties are known by more than one name, so the most commonly used name is listed first with alternatives in parentheses.

Many fruit varieties have chilling requirements that must be met for fruit to develop properly. The three general categories are determined by the number of hours of exposure to winter temperatures below 45° F.

■ **Low chill:** 300 up to 400 hours below 45° F.
■ **Moderate chill:** 400 up to 700 hours below 45° F.
■ **High chill:** 700 up to 1,000 hours below 45° F.

You may be able to raise the fruit in other parts of the country if special varieties are available for your region or if you use special techniques, such as bringing the plants into a greenhouse for the winter.

Just because a variety is recommended for one area does not mean that it can't do well in others. Local climate,

as well as special treatment from the gardener, can support plants that are not expected to do well in a given region.

If you can't decide on a specific variety, look at some of the two-in-one trees. These are apple, cherry, plum, or other fruit trees that nurseries have grafted different compatible varieties onto one tree. Though these trees are not as prolific bearers as trees dedicated to a single variety, they do give you a sample of a few different types of fruits.

APPLES

Malus species
MAY-lus

More than a thousand apple varieties are available today. Many are sports or accidental mutations of another variety. Others, especially the more recent introductions, are the result of painstaking crossing and selection by apple breeders. Sports may occur at any time, often without apparent reason: Suddenly one branch of a tree is different. Occasionally the odd branch results from mechanical damage, such as pruning; sometimes experimenters purposely change genetic structure with chemicals or radiation. Most sports are worthless, but now and then one turns out to have characteristics that make it worth propagating to create an entirely new strain of apples.

The extensive work on dwarfing rootstocks for apples has produced plant sizes ranging from a 4-foot bush to a 30-foot spreading tree. There are even true, or genetic, dwarfs that stay small on any rootstock. Another dwarfing achievement in the apple world is columnar trees. They produce only one vertical trunk with fruit all along it. No side branches are produced. They're great for container grown culture and growing apples in very tight quarters.

Spur-type apple varieties are sports of standard varieties. They grow more slowly than other plants, and their spurs are packed closer together on the branch. This less vigorous growth means that they are a kind of genetic dwarf, but they are still good-sized trees unless grafted to dwarfing roots. Spur varieties are difficult to train formally. If you buy spur varieties on dwarfing roots, use a training method that doesn't call for any particular form.

Thinning is crucial with apple varieties. If left alone, the trees set too much fruit, and the heavy crop can snap branches. Even more important, many apple varieties tend to bear every other year. If you leave too much fruit, you encourage this alternate bearing. The following year you may find that your tree bears only a handful of apples because the large crop of the previous year has depleted the tree's energy reserves. But the most important reason for thinning is that the quality of the remaining fruit is better after thinning.

The best thinning method for apples is to make a light first thinning by the time the fruit is pea size. After the natural fruit drop in June, thin the remaining fruit to a single apple every 6 inches along the branches. Each spur may have a cluster of fruit. A single fruit is less likely to become diseased, so leave only the largest fruit on each spur.

Thin carefully or you will damage the spurs or even pull them off with the young fruit. If the apples are small one year, thin more heavily the following year. If the fruit set is light but the fruit is large, thin the crop less next season.

Most apples are self infertile, so for a good crop most varieties need a pollenizer. Almost any two kinds that bloom together offer good cross-pollination. The following varieties produce poor pollen and thus cannot pollinate other varieties: 'Jonagold', 'Spigold', 'Mutsu', 'Gravenstein', 'Winesap', 'Stayman', and 'Stayman' sports 'Blaxstayman' and 'Staymared'. If you plant one of

'Northern Spy' apples ripen late in the season. The fruit is tasty enough to eat fresh but is fabulous in applesauce.

these varieties, you will need to plant three different varieties in total to get fruit from all of them. Also, if you plant only a very early and a very late variety, they will not cross-pollinate.

All apples need some cool winter weather, but there is an enormous range in this requirement. Varieties are available for any climate except tropical and low desert regions.

Homegrown apples may not have the picture-perfect looks of their supermarket cousins, but they boast flavor, color, and freshness that can't be beat.

APPLES (continued)

EARLY-SEASON APPLES

■ **'Akane':** Bright red skin; crisp, juicy white flesh; and 'Jonathan'-like flavor. The moderately productive tree is less susceptible to fireblight than the 'Jonathan' parent. 'Akane' is considered to be a "shy bearer" with weak growth, but it tends not to get much scab.

■ **'Jerseymac':** A 'McIntosh' cross that ripens in August. Red fruit is medium firm, juicy, and of good quality. The tree produces a crop every year.

■ **'Liberty':** The medium-sized fruit is sweet and juicy, somewhat coarse grained, and abundant; the skin is almost entirely red. Excellent resistance to rust and scab and high resistance to fireblight and mildew. Flavor is excellent; ripening takes place over a longer period than some varieties.

■ **'Lodi':** The fruit is up to 3 inches in diameter with light green skin, sometimes with a slight orange blush. The flesh is nearly white with a greenish tinge; fine grained, tender, and juicy but sour. Eating quality is only fair, but excellent in sauce and pies. The tree tends to overset fruit and must be thinned.

■ **'Sansa':** Considered by many to be the best all-around early apple. Keeps for up to three weeks, which is unusual for an early apple. Because of its 'Akane' parentage, does show some scab resistance.

■ **'Tydeman Early':** A 'McIntosh' type, similar in shape and ripening four weeks earlier, this apple is almost entirely red from a very early stage. Fruit drops quickly at maturity and should all be picked within a few days for optimum quality and flavor. Eating quality is good and the fruit keeps much longer than most early varieties. Branches are undesirably long and lanky and need regular pruning. For best results, grow on a dwarf or semidwarf rootstock. Hard to thin and does require rigorous thinning each year.

EARLY- TO MID-SEASON APPLES

■ **'Gravenstein':** Fruit is large but not uniform, with skin that's red against light green. The greenish-yellow flesh is moderately fine textured, crisp, firm, and juicy. It is excellent for eating fresh, in sauce, and in pies. The trees are strong, vigorous, upright, and spreading. Widely available along with 'Red Gravenstein'. Tends toward a biennial habit of bearing. Huge tree; must be grown on dwarf rootstock.

'Golden Delicious' apples are renowned for flavor. Home orchardists rave about the tree's easily trained branches.

■ **'Jonamac':** This 'McIntosh'-type dessert apple is of very good eating quality, milder in flavor than the 'McIntosh'. Most underrated for home use, it never misses a year of production. Needs thinning.

■ **'McIntosh':** If you write down the attributes of a great apple—medium to large fruit with sweet, tender, juicy white flesh; very good fresh or in sauce, pies, or cider—you are describing 'McIntosh'. The skin is yellow with a bright red blush. The tree is strong and very vigorous.

■ **'Paulared':** This apple rates high on several counts. Its color is a solid red blush against a bright yellow background. The flesh is white to cream and nonbrowning. Its excellent slightly tart flavor is good both for eating and in sauce and pies. It colors early but should not be picked until nearly mature for best quality. Fruit holds well on the tree and is harvested in two pickings; it has a long storage life. The tree is very attractive—strong and upright with good branch

When you thin an apple crop, leave one apple per spur to reduce disease incidence. Take care when thinning not to damage fruiting spurs.

structure. Branches are upright and difficult to spread. A difficult tree for homeowners because it requires heavy annual thinning.

■ **'Prima':** This juicy red apple offers fair quality, but its main feature is its resistance to scab, mildew, and fireblight.

MID-SEASON APPLES

■ **'Cortland':** According to many apple growers, this is excellent— even better than 'McIntosh'—as a apple for both eating and cooking. The tree bears heavy crops of large red-striped fruit with white flesh that is slow to turn brown when exposed to air. The tree is strong and vigorous with a spreading, drooping growth habit, but it is a "tip bearer," meaning flower buds tend to be on the tips, an important trait to know before doing any pruning.

■ **'Empire':** This cross between 'McIntosh' and 'Delicious' has medium uniform fruit with dark red striped skin and creamy white flesh that is firm, medium textured, crisp, very juicy, and of excellent eating quality. A major fault is that it develops full color long before maturity, tempting the grower to harvest too early. The trees are moderately vigorous and of spreading form. In some areas with extreme cold, 'Empire' will suffer winter injury to blossoms.

■ **'Gala':** This variety earns high marks for quality as a fresh fruit with the advantage of long storage life. The medium-sized fruit is yellow, brightly striped with red, and borne on a large, upright tree. Somewhat challenging for the homeowner because of scab susceptibility.

■ **'Jonathan':** The standard 'Jonathan' is one of the top varieties grown in commercial orchards in the central states. Fruit is medium sized and uniform; the skin is pale red and pale yellow; the flesh is firm, crisp, and juicy. Rich flavor makes it a good choice for eating and all culinary uses. Trees bear heavily.

■ **'Spartan':** A cross between 'McIntosh' and 'Yellow Newtown', the fruit is medium sized, uniform, and symmetrical. It has solid dark red skin and firm, tender, crisp, light yellow juicy flesh. The tree is strong, moderately vigorous, and well-shaped. The crop must be thinned to assure good size and annual bearing.

MID-SEASON TO LATE APPLES

■ **'Golden Delicious':** Highly regarded for eating and cooking. The fruit is medium to large and uniform in size. The skin is greenish yellow with a bright pink blush. The flesh is firm, crisp, juicy, and sweet. The tree is of medium height, moderately vigorous, upright, and round with wide-angled crotches. It bears very young and continues to bear annually if thinned. This is an excellent pollenizer and will set some crop without cross-pollination. One of the best for applesauce and is wonderful to train. Annual bearing.

■ **'Hudson Golden Gem':** A fully russet-hued apple with excellent keeping quality. Bears early, and fruit keeps great.

■ **'Jonagold':** A cross of 'Jonathan' and 'Golden Delicious', this is a beautiful large apple with a lively yellow green background color and bright red blushes. The cream-colored flesh is crisp and juicy and has good flavor. It is good for cooking, is among the very best apples for fresh eating, and stores well. The trees are vigorous and sturdy with wide-angled branches.

■ **'Red Delicious':** The number-one supermarket apple, there is no question about its dessert and fresh-eating quality. The fruit is medium to large with striped to solid red skin. The flesh is moderately firm in texture and very sweet and juicy. Your best choices are the red sports, such as 'Wellspur' or 'Royal Red'. The tree tends to produce full crops every other year unless properly thinned for annual bearing.

For versatility, few apples compare to 'Jonathan' and its cultivars. Use 'Jonagold' (shown) for fresh eating, in pies, for drying, or for sauce.

■ **'Yellow Newtown':** The medium-sized fruit has greenish-yellow skin and crisp, firm flesh. It is good for eating fresh and excellent for sauce and pies. The trees are strong and vigorous in the home orchard.

When most people think of an apple, they imagine a 'Red Delicious', with its classic apple coloring and shape.

APPLES *(continued)*

LATE-SEASON APPLES

■ **'Crispin':** Formerly referred to as 'Mutsu'. A cross of 'Golden Delicious' and the Japanese 'Indo', this cultivar has gained the approval of both growers and consumers. Large, oblong greenish fruit develops some yellow color when mature. The flesh is coarse, firm, and crisp. The flavor is excellent (tarter than 'Golden Delicious') when eaten fresh, and it is good for sauce, pies, and baking. Unlike 'Golden Delicious', it does not shrivel in storage. The tree is vigorous and spreading.

Favored for pies, tarts, and dumplings, 'Granny Smith' apples require a long growing season to ripen fully.

■ **'Fuji':** This variety is later to ripen than 'Granny Smith' and, like that variety, needs a long growing season (at least 200 days). 'Fuji' is one of the best-keeping sweet apples. It's useful for eating fresh and for cooking and baking.

■ **'Goldrush':** Only in the longer growing-season areas should this be raised, but it is excellent, has disease resistance, and will keep through the winter in good storage conditions. Flavor actually improves with storage.

■ **'Granny Smith':** The fruit is medium to large and a glossy bright green. The flesh resembles 'Golden Delicious' but is more tart. It is very good eaten fresh or in desserts, salads, sauce, and pies. The tree is strong, vigorous, upright, and spreading, but it requires a very long growing season. It has recently become the favorite tart apple in grocery stores.

■ **'Idared':** A cross of 'Jonathan' and 'Wagener', this hybrid has an attractive nearly solid red skin with a smooth finish. The large, uniform fruit has white, firm, smooth-textured flesh that is excellent for eating fresh and for cooking. It has a long storage life. The tree is vigorous, upright, and productive. Easy to thin, bears each year, and improves in storage.

■ **'Keepsake':** One of the longest-lasting varieties to grow at home. This variety is well-adapted to cold climates, like those found in the upper plains and mountain states.

■ **'Mutsu':** This is an alternate name for the variety 'Crispin'. (See preceding description of 'Crispin'.)

■ **'Northern Spy':** Trees of this variety are very slow to begin bearing; sometimes 14 years elapse before they produce their first bushel (but they bear much sooner on dwarf rootstock). The fruit is large, with yellow and red stripes, and the flesh is yellowish, firm, and crisp. The quality is excellent fresh and for pies. It also makes good applesauce.

The fruit bruises easily but has a long storage life. Trees are vigorous and bear in alternate years.

■ **'Rome Beauty':** This variety and its sports are the world's best baking apples. Many red sports (such as 'Red Rome') are available in a beautiful, solid medium-dark red. The fruit is large and round, and the flesh is medium in texture, firm, and crisp; it has a long storage life. The tree is moderately vigorous, starts to produce at an early age, and produces heavily. Does produce fruit every year, but should be used only for processing.

■ **'Stayman':** This variety is a very late ripener. Where its fruit can be grown to maturity, it is good for cooking or eating fresh. The fruit is juicy with a moderately tart, rich, winelike flavor. The skin is bright red and has a tendency to crack. The flesh is fine textured, firm, and crisp. The tree is medium sized and moderately vigorous.

NORTHERN-LATITUDE APPLES

In severe-weather areas where some of the favorite apple varieties are subject to winter damage, gardeners may choose one of three hardy varieties developed by the University of Minnesota.

■ **'Honeygold':** Mid-season to late. This apple boasts a 'Golden Delicious' flavor. The fruit is medium to large with golden to yellowish-green skin and yellow flesh that is crisp, smooth, tender, and juicy. It is good for eating fresh and in sauce and pies. The tree is moderately vigorous.

■ **'Red Baron':** Mid-season. This cross of 'Golden Delicious' and 'Red Duchess' has round, medium-sized fruit with cherry-red skin. The flesh is crisp and juicy with a pleasantly tart flavor. It is good eaten fresh and in sauce and pies.

■ **'Regent':** Late-season ripener. This variety is recommended for a long-keeping red winter apple. The fruit is medium sized with bright red skin and crisp juicy creamy white flesh. Rated excellent for either cooking or eating fresh, fruit retains its fine dessert quality late into the winter. The tree is a hardy, vigorous grower.

SOUTHERN-LATITUDE APPLES

■ **'Anna':** Early. This apple flowers and fruits in Florida and southern California. The apple is green with a red blush and fair quality. It is normally harvested in July but sometimes sets another late bloom that produces apples for the fall. Plant an early blooming variety such as 'Dorsett Golden' or 'Ein Shemer' as a pollenizer.

■ **'Beverly Hills':** Early. This is a small- to medium-sized apple, striped or splashed with red over a pale yellow skin. The flesh is tender, juicy, and tart. Overall the apple resembles 'McIntosh'. Use it fresh or in sauce or pies. The tree is suited mainly to cooler coastal areas since heat spoils the fruit. Locally available.

■ **'Dorsett Golden':** Early. This large 'Golden Delicious'-type fruit requires no frost or significant winter chill and performs well in coastal southern California and the hot-summer regions of the Deep South. Use it for eating fresh or for cooking. 'Dorsett Golden' is a good pollenizer for 'Anna' and 'Ein Shemer'.

■ **'Ein Shemer':** Early. Another 'Golden Delicious'-type fruit that is well-adapted to the Deep South, Texas, and southern California. The tree begins bearing at an early age. Makes a good pollenizer for 'Dorsett Golden'.

■ **'Gordon':** Early to mid-season. The crisp flesh is enclosed in red-striped green skin. The bearing period is unusually prolonged— August to October in California. It performs particularly well in coastal southern California. The fruit is good both for eating fresh and for cooking. Self-fruitful.

■ **'Winter Banana':** Mid-season. The large fruit is strikingly beautiful. The skin color is pale and waxy with a spreading pink blush. The flesh is tender with a wonderful bananalike aroma and tangy flavor. Wonderful for making cider. 'Winter Banana' requires a pollenizer such as 'Red Astrachan' in order to set a good crop. Locally available.

■ **'Winter Pearmain':** Mid-season. This large green apple has moderately firm flesh of excellent quality. A favorite dessert apple. It is a consistent producer in southern California.

For a classic, beautiful, and deliciously versatile apple, plant 'Idared'.

It can be difficult to tell when an apple crop is ripe. Check fruit by slicing one open. Seeds should be brown, not pale. Store apples in plastic bags in the refrigerator, separating bruised or overripe fruit for immediate use.

Prunus armeniaca
PROO-nus ar-men-i-AY-ka

APRICOTS

Apricots typically yield best in regions without spring frosts, which can damage the early blooms. In recent years, however, breeders have produced hybrids with hardy Manchurian apricots that will fruit fairly regularly in the northern plains.

Dwarfed apricots on special rootstocks produce fair-sized trees. A full-sized tree fills a 25-square-foot site. Train a tree to branch high, and use it for shade. Trees live from 15 to 30 years, depending on care.

Many apricots are self-fertile, but in colder regions it's best to plant a second variety for pollination to encourage heavy fruit set. Frost may thin much of the young fruit.

Thinning is usually natural, either from frost or from natural drop in early summer. If a tree sets heavily, you'll get larger apricots by thinning to 2 inches between each fruit. For pruning details, see page 146.

Apricots can also be used as stock plants for grafts. Plums do well on apricot roots, and peaches may take, but the union is weak. An apricot tree can bear several different fruits over a long season. Brown rot and bacterial canker are serious pests.

VARIETIES

Check for climate adaptability and pollinating requirements. Be sure to buy hardy trees in colder regions. Apricots need excellent soil drainage.

■ **'Blenheim' ('Royal'):** Best eating, drying, and canning apricot in California. Requires moderate chilling; won't tolerate temperatures over 90° F at harvest time.

■ **'Chinese':** Good choice for coldest regions of the west. Late flowering helps blooms escape late frosts. Bears heavy crops of small, sweet, juicy fruit at an early age.

■ **'Flora Gold':** Genetic dwarf apricot; reaches half the size of a full-sized tree. Small, high-quality fruit best for eating fresh and canning. Heavy crops ripen early. Moderate chill requirement.

■ **'Goldcot':** Late flowering, late bearing, is hardy to -20° F. Good for midwest and east. Medium fruit is tough skinned and flavorful; eat fresh or can. Self-fruitful.

■ **'Harcot':** Cold-hardy variety flowers late but ripens early. Medium fruit is flavorful. Heavy-bearing, compact trees resist brown rot; somewhat resistant to bacterial spot.

■ **'Harogem':** Small fruit blushed bright red over orange; flesh is firm. Fruit ripens mid-season and is especially long lasting when picked. Tree is resistant to perennial canker and brown spot.

■ **'Moorpark':** The standard of excellence among apricots. Large orange fruit. Orange flesh has excellent flavor and perfume. Ripens unevenly, with half the fruit still green when the first half is already ripe. Grows well in all but the most extreme climates.

■ **'Perfection' ('Goldbeck'):** Light orange-yellow fruit is very large. Bright orange flesh of fair quality. Vigorous, hardy tree blooms early; uncertain in late-frost areas. Requires little winter chill so grows in mild-winter areas. It needs a separate pollenizer and sets a light crop. Good for the south and west.

■ **'Rival':** Well adapted to the northwest. Large, heavily blushed fruit is firm, mild flavored, and good for canning. Tree is large, rangy, and blooms early. Pair with 'Perfection' for pollination.

■ **'Royal Rosa':** Good for fresh-off-the-tree eating. Bright yellow fruit has firm, aromatic, sweet flesh with a tart tang. Compact, medium-sized tree bears heavy, early crops.

■ **'Scout':** Flat, medium bronzy fruit with yellow flesh. Used for fresh eating, canning, or jams. Tall tree is vigorous and hardy. Fruit ripens in late July. Good for the midwest.

■ **'Sungold':** Must be planted with 'Moongold' for pollination. Medium fruit with a tender golden skin. Mild sweet flavor makes fruit good fresh or preserved. Tree is upright and vigorous. Fruit ripens somewhat later than 'Moongold'. Good for all zones.

■ **'Tilton':** Bears heavily. Yellow-orange fruit tolerates heat when ripening. Chill requirement is high, but grows well in hot summers.

■ **'Wenatchee':** Large fruit with orange-yellow skin and flesh. Trees last from 15 to 30 years, depending on care. Does well in the Pacific Northwest and the west.

'Moorpark' apricot sets the standard against which all other cultivars are measured. The tree bears well in all but the most extreme climates.

Prunus species.
PROO-nus

CHERRIES

Cherries come in three distinct forms with many cultivars in each category. All cherries require considerable winter chilling, which rules out planting in the mildest coastal and gulf climates, but they're also damaged by early intense cold in fall and by heavy rain during ripening.

Sweet cherries are grown in the coastal valleys of California, near the Great Lakes, and in the northwest. They're tricky for the home gardener, but plant them where summer heat and winter cold aren't too intense.

Sour or pie cherries are good for cooking and canning and the most reliable for home gardens. The trees are more adaptable, withstanding both cold and poor spring weather better than sweet cherries. All sour cherries are self-fertile. There are two types: the amarelle, with clear juice and yellow flesh; and the morello, with red juice and flesh. In coldest climates the amarelle is the commercial cherry.

Duke cherries have sweet cherry shape and color and sour cherry hardiness, flavor, and tartness.

Standard sour cherries and sweet cherries on dwarfing roots both reach 15 to 20 feet. A standard sweet cherry without a dwarfing rootstock is one of the largest fruit trees and can equal a small oak in size. Use such cherries as shade trees.

All sweet cherries, except for 'Stella', need a pollenizer. Plant at least two varieties or use a graft on a single tree. Dwarf pie cherries have lovely flowers, make fine hedges, and bear good crops. Graft larger cherries onto them for a choice of fruit and good pollination.

Birds are the major pests, but cherries also need protection from fruit flies, pear slugs (an insect larva), and bacterial leaf spot. Cherry trees require good soil drainage.

EARLY-SEASON CHERRIES

■ **'Black Tartarian':** Sweet black cherry that is firm when picked but softens quickly. One of the earliest cherries; an excellent pollenizer. Erect, vigorous trees. Use any sweet cherry as a pollenizer. Good for all zones.

■ **'May Duke':** Dark red fruit. Excellent flavor for cooking or preserves. In cold climates use an early sweet cherry for pollination. In mild climates it's self-fertile. Good for the west.

■ **'Northstar':** This genetic dwarf sour morello is excellent for home gardens. Red fruit and flesh; resists cracking. Small, attractive, vigorous, hardy tree resists brown rot. Fruit ripens early but will hang on the tree up to two weeks. All zones.

■ **'Sam':** Sweet black cherry. Fruit is firm, juicy, and resists cracking. Tree is very vigorous, bearing heavy crops. Use 'Bing', 'Lambert', or 'Van' as a pollenizer. Good choice for the north and west.

MID-SEASON CHERRIES

■ **'Bing':** The standard for sweet black cherries. Deep mahogany fruit is firm and very juicy. Subject to cracking and doubling. Spreading tree yields heavy crops. Bacterial leaf spot attacks tree in humid climates. It's popular but difficult to grow. Use 'Sam', 'Van', or 'Black Tartarian' as a pollenizer (not 'Royal Ann' or 'Lambert'). Good for the west.

■ **'Chinook':** Like 'Bing' with large, heart-shaped, sweet fruit with mahogany skin and deep red flesh. Spreading, vigorous tree is a good producer. Slightly hardier than 'Bing'. Use 'Bing', 'Sam', or 'Van' as a pollenizers. Good for the west.

■ **'Corum':** Sweet variety with yellow fruit and thick, firm, sweet, flesh. Moderately resistant to cracking; a good canning cherry. Use 'Royal Ann', 'Sam', or 'Van' as a pollenizer. Recommended pollenizer for 'Royal Ann' in the Pacific northwest. Locally available in the Pacific Northwest. Good for the west.

■ **'Emperor Francis':** Yellow blushed cherry resembling 'Royal Ann' but redder and more crack resistant. Firm sweet flesh. Very productive; hardier than 'Royal Ann'. Use 'Hedelfingen' or 'Rainier' (not 'Royal Ann' or 'Windsor') as pollenizers. Good for the north.

■ **'Garden Bing':** Genetic dwarf reaches only a few feet high in a container; will grow to 8 feet in the ground. Self-pollinating; bears sweet, dark red fruit. Good for the west.

■ **'Hartland':** Bears early; doesn't crack much. Excellent flavor.

■ **'Kansas Sweet' ('Hansen Sweet'):** A fairly sweet pie cherry with firm fleshed red fruit. Eat fresh

The 'Bing' cherry sets the standard for sweet black cherries. The trees typically produce heavy crops.

Sour cherries, also known as pie or Montmorency cherries, are self-fertile trees that produce heavy crops.

CHERRIES *(continued)*

and in pies. Tree and blossoms are hardy in Kansas. It is self-fertile.

■ **'Meteor':** A genetic dwarf (to 10 feet tall) amarelle sour cherry. Bright red fruit with clear yellow flesh is large for a pie cherry. Especially hardy but also does well in mild climates. Ideal home garden tree for all cherry climates. For all zones.

■ **'Montmorency':** Amarelle. Standard sour cherry for commercial and home planting. Large red fruit with firm yellow flesh. Highly crack resistant. Medium to large tree: vigorous and spreading. Various strains have different ripening times and fruit traits. Good for all zones.

■ **'Rainier':** Sweet cherry with a 'Bing' shape but a blushed yellow hue like 'Royal Ann'. Productive and spreading to upright spreading tree. Particularly hardy. Use 'Bing', 'Sam', or 'Van' as a pollenizer. Good for the south and west.

■ **'Royal Ann' ('Napoleon'):** The standard for blushed yellow cherries. Used commercially in candies and maraschino cherries. Firm, juicy fruit. Excellent fresh; good for canning. Very large, extremely productive tree is upright, spreading with age. Use

'Corum', 'Windsor', or 'Hedelfingen' as a pollenizer (not 'Bing' or 'Lambert'). Moderately hardy.

■ **'Schmidt':** Replacing 'Bing' as the major commercial black cherry in the east. Large fruit with thick skin and sweet but astringent wine-red flesh. Large, vigorous tree, upright and spreading. Hardy, but fruit buds fairly tender. Use 'Bing', 'Lambert', or 'Royal Ann' as a pollenizer. Good for the north and south.

■ **'Stella':** First true self-fertile sweet cherry. Large dark fruit is moderately firm. Vigorous hardy tree bears early. Use as a pollenizer for any other sweet cherry. Good for the south and west.

■ **'Utah Giant':** New sweet variety with large dark fruit comparable to 'Bing' and 'Lambert'. Fresh fruit is excellent; retains color, firmness, and flavor canned. Good for the west.

■ **'Van':** Large, dark sweet cherry. Very hardy tree; especially good in borderline areas, because it has a strong tendency to overset and therefore may produce a crop when other cherries fail. Bears from one to three years earlier than 'Bing'. Use 'Bing', 'Lambert', or 'Royal Ann' as a pollenizer. Good for all zones.

LATE-SEASON CHERRIES

■ **'Angela':** Dark cherry similar to 'Lambert' but hardier and late flowering; frost less likely to damage blooms. Fruits more crack resistant than 'Lambert'. Tree easier to manage; productive. Use 'Emperor Francis' or 'Lambert' as pollenizers.

■ **'Black Republican' ('Black Oregon'):** Firm very dark sweet cherry with slightly astringent flesh. Hardy tree tends to overbear heavily and produce small fruit. Use any sweet cherry as a pollenizer.

■ **'English Morello':** Sour cherry, dark red, and crack resistant. Tart firm flesh good for cooking and canning. Drooping branches on a small productive tree. Good for the north.

■ **'Hedelfingen':** Sweet dark fruit with meaty firm flesh. One strain resists cracking, but some trees sold under this name don't. Hardy tree with a spreading, drooping form; bears heavily. Use any sweet cherry listed here as a pollenizer. Good for the north and south.

■ **'Lambert':** Large, dark sweet cherry similar to 'Bing' but ripens later. Tree is more widely adapted than 'Bing' but bears erratically in many eastern areas and is more difficult to train and prune. Strongly upright growth produces weak crotches if left untrained. Use 'Van' or 'Rainier' as a pollenizer (not 'Bing', 'Royal Ann', or 'Emperor Francis'). Good for all zones.

■ **'Late Duke':** Large and light red; ripens in late July. Use for cooking or preserves. In cold climes needs a sour cherry pollenizer. In mild areas is self-fertile. Good for the west.

■ **'Windsor':** The standard late, dark sweet cherry in the east. Fruit isn't as firm as 'Bing' or 'Lambert'. Buds are very hardy; reliably bears a heavy crop. Good for difficult areas where other cherries fail. Use any sweet cherry for a pollenizer except 'Van' and 'Emperor Francis'. Good for the north and south.

'Royal Ann' is a blush yellow cherry.

'Stella' is a self-fertile cultivar.

CRAB APPLES

Malus species
MAY-lus

Fine for jellies or pickled whole fruit, crab apples are decorative fruit trees. Flowers range from red to pink to white; fruits vary widely in size. Cultivars sold for flowers have edible fruit, but plant large-fruited types if your aim is to grow fruit for jelly.

Crab apples range from small 10-foot trees to spreading 25 foot trees. Large-fruited kinds are larger trees. If you have no space but want a crop for jelly, graft a branch to an existing apple tree. All types are self-fertile; graft several kinds that bloom at different times onto one tree to extend the flowering season.

Crab apples get the same diseases as apples; scab is a problem for some. Choose resistant kinds.

VARIETIES

■ **'Barbara Ann':** Dark ½-inch reddish-purple fruit; reddish pulp. Blooms 2-inch, purple-pink, double. Tree to 25 feet tall; reasonably disease resistant.

■ **'Chestnut':** Very large, bronze-red; good flavor; makes deep pink jelly. Very hardy, medium, reasonably disease-resistant tree.

■ **'Dolgo':** Small, oblong juicy red fruit; pick before fully ripened for easy gelling into ruby-red jelly. Vigorous, hardy, productive tree.

■ **'Hyslop':** Medium-sized yellow fruit blushed with red. Use whole for relishes or for pale pink jelly. Hardy tree; single pink flowers.

■ **'Katherine':** Tiny yellow fruit with heavy red blush; makes pink jelly. Small, slow-growing hardy tree to 15 feet tall; flowers/fruits every other year. Some disease resistance.

■ **'Profusion':** Tiny scarlet fruit; good in jellies. Small tree to 15 feet; spreads slightly; open small single flowers; deep red in bud, open purple-red to blue pink. Moderately susceptible to mildew.

■ **'Siberian Crab':** Clear scarlet, medium fruit; jelly or pickle whole. Vase-shaped tree to 15 to 30 feet. Fragrant, 1-inch-wide white flowers.

■ **'Transcendent':** Large yellow fruit; blushed pink on one side. Use for clear jellies or eat fresh. Medium tree somewhat disease resistant.

■ **'Whitney':** Old favorite with very large fruit; ripens yellow with red stripes. Use for fresh eating, jelly, preserves, and apple butter. Hardy, medium-large, disease-resistant tree.

Pink flowers of 'Hyslop' crab apple ripen to yellow fruit blushed with red. It's a favorite for making pale pink jelly.

PEACHES

Prunus persica
PROO-nus PER-si-ka

One of the most popular homegrown fruits, peaches have a major drawback: their susceptibility to pests. If you choose not to spray your peach trees, you will lose some or all of your crop in a bad year. Since peaches are such vigorous growers and producers, you also need to be committed to annual heavy pruning and hand-thinning.

Peaches don't tolerate extreme cold or late frost, so in northern plains states and northern New England, they're purely experimental. The hardiest, such as 'Reliance', may survive and bear in a protected spot, but you can't be sure. Peaches thrive in temperate climates near the Great Lakes, but select a protected sunny spot where cold air can't collect.

Some of the world's greatest peach-growing country is in the west: California alone produces 50 percent of the commercial U.S. crop. Peaches do well in semicoastal areas of the east, South Carolina, Georgia, and dry areas of Washington.

The standard tree on a peach rootstock grows to about 15 feet tall and wide. It could grow larger but is best pruned heavily each year to maintain that size and encourage lots of new growth along branches.

Thin young fruit when they reach thumbnail size. For early-season peaches, leave 6 to 8 inches between fruit; for late-season varieties, leave 4 to 5 inches between fruit.

A few varieties need a pollenizer. Normally trees are self-fertile, but bees help transfer pollen.

The universal peach ailment in the west is leaf curl, which is easily controlled with a copper spray. You

Select a peach with nonbrowning flesh, such as 'Sunhaven', for fresh eating out of hand and in fruit salads.

PEACHES *(continued)*

will also probably encounter the major insect pest, the peach tree borer, gnawing the trunk at ground level. Brown rot attacks fruit but is controllable with sprays. In the east and south, look for varieties resistant to bacterial spot. Brown rot and plum curculio are the chief pests in the north and south.

VERY EARLY PEACHES

■ **'Desert Gold':** Medium fruit; yellow skin blushed red. Firm semifreestone yellow flesh. Fairly vigorous tree needs heavy thinning. Very low chilling requirement: 200 to 300 hours. Good for desert and coastal areas of the west.

■ **'Springtime':** Small fruit; yellow skin with a high blush and abundant short fuzz. Semifreestone white flesh. Good for the west.

■ **'Tejon':** Yellow with a red blush; light fuzz. Semifreestone yellow flesh. Bears very well. Good for the west, particularly southern California.

EARLY PEACHES

■ **'Fairhaven':** Large, bright yellow peach with red cheek and light fuzz. Firm freestone yellow flesh is red at the pit. Fruit freezes well; flowers are showy. Good for the west.

■ **'Flavorcrest':** Large, firm yellow freestone with good flavor; skin is blushed red. Good for California.

■ **'Garnet Beauty':** Early sport of 'Redhaven'. Medium semifreestone fruit hangs on tree until overripe. Firm yellow flesh streaked with red; slightly fibrous. Hardy tree yields heavy crops that achieve good size and color even inside the tree. Susceptible to bacterial leaf spot. Good for the north.

■ **'Golden Jubilee':** Old standby. Medium freestone with skin mottled bright red. Firm, coarse yellow flesh. Hardy tree sets heavy crops but is self-thinning. Good for all zones.

■ **'Redhaven':** One of the finest early peaches. Medium freestone has deep red skin over a yellow ground. Yellow flesh doesn't brown; freezes well. Heavy thinning yields superb

fruit. Spreading, highly productive tree resists bacterial leaf spot. Good for all zones. 'Early Redhaven' nearly identical but two weeks earlier. One of the best for the northeast.

■ **'Redtop':** Large fruit nearly covered with blush and light fuzz. Unusually firm yellow freestone flesh good for canning or freezing. Moderately vigorous tree somewhat susceptible to bacterial leaf spot. Showy blooms. Good for the west.

■ **'Reliance':** Very winter hardy; withstands -20 to -25° F and still produces that year. Large freestone, fruit with dark red skin and yellow ground. Medium-firm bright yellow flesh. Showy flowers. Needs heavy thinning. Good for the north and west.

■ **'Springcrest':** Medium, flavorful yellow freestone. Showy blooms on a productive tree. Good for the west.

■ **'Sunhaven':** Medium to large peach with bright red skin over a golden ground; short, soft fuzz. Firm, fine-textured, nonbrowning yellow flecked with red flesh. Vigorous, consistently productive tree. Good for all zones.

■ **'Ventura':** Low-chill yellow-fleshed freestone. Average vigor and productivity. Flavorful yellow-skinned, red-blushed fruit with firm flesh. Good for Southern California.

■ **'Veteran':** Medium yellow fruit splashed with red; medium fuzz. Soft, nearly yellow freestone flesh. Vigorous, highly productive tree. One of the very best in cool Pacific climates. A favorite in Oregon and western Washington; also good for the north and west.

MID-SEASON PEACHES

■ **'Babcock':** Small to medium fruit; light pink blushed red with little fuzz. Skin peels easily. Tender, juicy, mild white flesh, and red near the pit. Spreading, vigorous tree; thin heavily early in the season to produce large fruit. Good for the west, particularly southern California.

'Redhaven' peach trees bear well, but crops require considerable thinning.

■ **'Early Elberta' (Gleason Strain):** Large freestone with yellow flesh matures 3 to 10 days before 'Elberta' with better flavor. Good for canning and freezing. Hardy, productive tree. Good for the south and west.

■ **'J. H. Hale':** Extra-large freestone; deep crimson skin over a yellow ground; nearly fuzzless. Firm golden flesh. Cross-pollination gives best production. Good for all zones.

■ **'July Elberta' ('Kim Elberta'):** Medium, greenish-yellow fruit blushed and streaked with dull red; very fuzzy. High-quality yellow flesh. Vigorous tree bears heavily but susceptible to bacterial leaf spot. Good for the west, especially in Oregon's Willamette Valley.

■ **'Loring':** Medium freestone; slight fuzz; blushed red over a yellow ground. Firm, medium-textured yellow flesh. Resists bacterial leaf spot. Good for the north and south.

■ **'Suncrest':** Large firm, freestone; red blush and yellow skin. Susceptible to bacterial leaf spot. Grow in the west and other areas free of this disease. Hardy in cold sections of the north.

LATE PEACHES

■ **'Belle of Georgia' ('Georgia Belle'):** Outstanding white peach with red blush over creamy white skin. Firm white flesh has excellent flavor. Fair for freezing; poor for canning. Winter-hardy productive tree is very susceptible to brown rot. Good for the north and south.

■ **'Blake':** Large freestone has slightly fuzzy, red skin. Firm yellow flesh good for freezing; excellent for canning. Susceptible to bacterial canker. Good for north and south.

■ **'Cresthaven':** Medium to large freestone; almost-fuzzless bright red skin over a gold ground. Nonbrowning yellow flesh good for canning and freezing. Hardy tree. Good for the north and south.

■ **'Elberta':** Large freestone; old favorite for mid-season crop. Deep golden skin with red blush. Fruit tends to drop when mature. Tree resistant to brown rot. All zones.

■ **'Fay Elberta':** Most popular all-purpose freestone in California. Equals 'Elberta' for eating fresh,

cooking, and canning, but better for freezing. Ranks below 'Elberta' in adaptability, growing where winters fall to 20° F. Yellow skin blushed with red. Requires heavy thinning for large fruit. Blossoms showy.

■ **'Jefferson':** Especially suited for late spring frosts. Skin bright red over a orange ground. Firm yellow flesh has great flavor. Reliable producer; cans and freezes well. Trees have some resistance to brown rot. Good for the north and south.

■ **'Madison':** Adapted to Virginia's mountain areas. Shows exceptional tolerance to frosts during blossoming season, setting crops while others fail. Medium freestone fruit; bright red skin over a bright orange-yellow ground. Very firm, fine-textured orange-yellow flesh. Tree has average to vigorous growth. Good for the north and south.

■ **'Raritan Rose':** Vigorous winter-hardy tree produces delicious white-fleshed freestone peaches. Skin is red. Unusually attractive. Available in the east and north.

■ **'Redskin':** This popular peach ripens after 'Elberta'. Good red color; handles well. Excellent for freezing, canning, and eating fresh. Widely available in the east and north.

■ **'Rio Oso Gem':** The skin of this large freestone is red over a yellow ground; yellow flesh is firm, fine in texture, and nonbrowning. Good both fresh and for freezing. Large, showy light pink blossoms appear later than most peach flowers. The tree is productive but not vigorous. Good for the south and west.

■ **'Sunhigh':** A very good medium to large freestone. Bright red skin over a yellow ground. Yellow and firm flesh. Good for the north and south, but disease prone.

Prunus persica nucipersica
PROO-nus PER-si-ka NEW-see-per-si-ka

The nectarine is simply a fuzzless peach. Peach trees can produce nectarines as sports, and nectarine trees can produce fuzzy peach sports. The two plants are nearly identical, requiring the same care, although nectarines are more susceptible to brown rot. Southern gardeners may battle brown rot because hot, humid weather favors it. Spray regularly to control it.

EARLY-SEASON NECTARINES

■ **'Earliblaze':** Medium, yellow-fleshed clingstone fruit ripening ahead of 'Redhaven' peach. Red skin. Good for the north and south.

■ **'Independence':** Medium, oval cherry-red fruit. Firm yellow-fleshed freestone. Moderately vigorous tree; showy flowers. Can take warm winters. Good in the south and west.

■ **'Pocahontas':** Medium to large fruit; bright red. Slightly stringy yellow semifreestone flesh. Resists

NECTARINES

frost during the blooming season; also resists brown rot. Good for the north and south.

■ **'Silver Lode':** Red skin; sweet white freestone flesh. Needs little chilling. Good for south and west.

■ **'Sungold':** Medium freestone; red skin, firm yellow flesh. Moderate-chill variety; has some resistance to brown rot. Good for the south.

■ **'Sunred':** Small yellow-fleshed clingstone with red skin. Low chill; adapted to Florida with May ripening.

MID-SEASON NECTARINES

Listed cultivars are vigorous productive trees, unless noted.

■ **'Fantasia':** Large yellow fruit with red blush. Smooth, firm yellow freestone flesh. Moderate chilling. Brown rot and bacterial leaf spot a problem. Good for south and west.

■ **'Flavortop':** Large, mostly red; firm, yellow freestone flesh. Showy flowers. Moderate chill. Susceptible to bacterial leaf spot and brown rot. Good for the south and west.

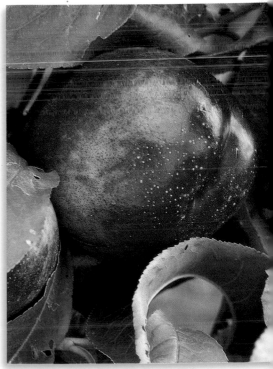

Nectarines offer the juicy flavor and bright flesh of a peach without the fuzzy skin. 'Earliblaze' ripens quickly.

NECTARINES *(continued)*

A genetic dwarf, 'Bonanza' thrives in containers. It grows to 5 or 6 feet.

■ **'Mericrest':** Very winter-hardy yellow-fleshed, red-skinned fruit. Resists bacterial leaf spot and brown rot. Good for the north.

■ **'Nectared 4':** Large yellow fruit with red blush. Semifreestone yellow flesh. Showy flowers. Good for the north and south.

■ **'Nectared 5':** Smooth, large yellow fruit with a blush. Yellow-fleshed semifreestone until fully ripe, then freestone. Good for the south.

■ **'Panamint':** Red skin, yellow-fleshed freestone. Needs little winter chilling. Good for the south and west.

■ **'Pioneer':** Thin-skinned red fruit. Yellow freestone flesh; red near the pit. Rich, distinct flavor. Big, showy blooms. Tree needs little chilling. Good for the west. Locally available.

■ **'Redchief':** Bright red medium fruit. Fairly firm, white freestone flesh. Showy flowers; very resistant to brown rot. Good for the south.

■ **'Redgold':** Hardy, firm freestone; fruit glossy with red skin. Resists brown rot and cracking; susceptible to mildew. Good for the north and south.

LATE NECTARINES

■ **'Cavalier':** Medium orange-yellow fruit with red splashes. Firm, yellow freestone flesh; aromatic; slightly bitter. Resists brown rot. Good for the north and south.

■ **'Fairlane':** Very late ripening. Yellow clingstone. Good in the west.

■ **'Flamekist':** Large fruit; yellow clingstone flesh. Moderate chill. Susceptible to bacterial leaf spot and brown rot. Good for the west.

■ **'Gold Mine':** Old favorite. Large white fruit blushed red. Juicy white freestone flesh has sweet aroma and excellent flavor. Moderate chill. Good for the west.

GENETIC DWARF PEACHES AND NECTARINES

Genetic dwarf peaches and nectarines form dense bushes with long leaves trailing in tiers from the branches. In spring, showy flowers hide branches. Use in the landscape as edible ornmentals. Fruit is normal size, but flavor and texture aren't as good as that from standard size cultivars. Fruit must be thinned.

Grow plants in containers until 5 feet tall. In the ground they grow 6 to 8 feet and spread 6 to 9 feet. Plants require minimal pruning. Dwarf peaches are more susceptible to mites than normal-size trees.

GENETIC DWARF PEACHES

■ **'Bonanza':** Medium yellow-fleshed freestone; red blush. The original genetic dwarf peach for home gardens. Moderate chill. Good for the west and south.

■ **'Compact Redhaven':** Larger than other dwarfs (up to 10 feet). Leaves and growth habit similar to standard trees. Fruit like 'Redhaven' in size, quality, and color. Tolerates cold better than other dwarfs. Good for all zones, especially the north, midwest, and east.

■ **'Empress':** Medium yellow-fleshed clingstone with pink skin; sweet flavor; juicy texture. Moderate chill. Good for the west and south.

■ **'Garden Gold':** Large yellow-fleshed freestone with red skin. Moderate chill. Showy flowers. Good for the west and south.

■ **'Garden Sun':** Large yellow-fleshed freestone; red skin. Moderate chill. Good for the west and south.

■ **'Honey Babe':** Large, firm orange-fleshed freestone with red skin; good flavor and sweetness. Moderate chill; ripens before 'Redhaven'. Good for the west and south; try in the east with protection.

■ **'Southern Flame':** Large yellow freestone; red skin. Good low-chill eating fruit for the west and south.

■ **'Southern Rose':** Large, firm yellow-fleshed freestone with red blush. Good for low-chill areas of the west and south.

■ **'Southern Sweet':** Medium yellow-fleshed freestone; red blush. Good flavor. Moderate chill; matures ahead of 'Redhaven'.

■ **'Sunburst':** Large, firm yellow-fleshed clingstone with a red blush. Juicy good-flavored flesh. High chill. Good for warm areas of the east and south and colder areas of the west.

GENETIC DWARF NECTARINES

■ **'Garden Beauty':** Yellow-fleshed clingstone; red skin. Big double blooms. Low chill. Good for the south and west.

■ **'Garden Delight':** Yellow-fleshed freestone; red skin. Low chill. Good for the south and west.

■ **'Garden King':** Yellow-fleshed clingstone; red skin. Low chill. Good for the south and west.

■ **'Golden Prolific':** Large yellow-fleshed freestone; orange skin. High chill. Good only for high-chill areas in the west; worth trying in the east and north with winter protection.

■ **'Nectarina':** Medium yellow-fleshed freestone with a red blush. Low chill. Good for the south and west.

■ **'Southern Belle':** Large yellow-fleshed freestone with red blush. Low chill. Good for the south and west.

■ **'Sunbonnet':** Large, firm yellow-fleshed clingstone with a red blush. Moderate chill.

Pyrus communis
PIE-rus kom-MEW-nis

PEARS

Pear trees are attractive even in winter, require little pruning after they begin to bear, begin to bear early, and the fruit stores well. Plants take well to formal or informal training so space isn't a problem.

Standard pears spread 25 feet across and grow as tall or taller. A dwarf in natural shape needs a space about 15 feet square, but with pruning and training methods described on page 152, you can grow a pear flat against a fence or wall using very little space.

You don't need to thin fruit, but if a heavy crop sets, remove damaged or undersized pears. Thin a few weeks before harvest, when fruit is the size of a half dollar.

All pears need a pollenizer. Use any other pear. 'Bartlett' is a poor pollenizer for 'Seckel', however, and 'Magness' won't pollinate anything.

The one drawback with pears is fireblight disease. Work around it by choosing resistant varieties. Fireblight is more severe in spring, when splashing rain and insects carry it from tree to tree. Remove any diseased wood (cut well below the infection) and burn it. Other pests are codling moth, mites, pear psylla, and pear slug.

Most fruits are best when picked ripe or nearly so. Pears are the exception. A tree-ripened pear breaks down, turning soft and brown at the core. Harvest pears when they have reached full size but are still green and firm. Store them in a cool, dark place if you intend to

eat them within a few weeks. For longer storage, refrigerate the fruit; remove it from cold storage about a week before you want to use it. Pears ripen faster if they're held with other pears in a poorly ventilated spot. For fast ripening, place several in a sealed plastic container.

EARLY PEARS

■ **'Clapp's Favorite':** Large yellow fruit. Soft, sweet flesh good for eating and canning. Fruit doesn't store long. Very productive tree; highly susceptible to fireblight. Hardy; best in cold late-spring regions. Good in the north and west.

■ **'Moonglow':** Soft, juicy large fruit with mild flavor. For canning or eating fresh. Upright, vigorous tree; heavily spurred; bears when young. Resistant to fireblight. For all zones

■ **'Orient':** Round; firm flesh good for canning. Bears moderately. Resists fireblight. Good for the south

■ **'Red Clapp' ('Starkrimson').** Good quality red-skinned sport of 'Clapp's Favorite'. Susceptible to fireblight. Good for the west and north.

MID-SEASON PEARS

■ **'Bartlett':** Medium to large thin-skinned yellow pear. Sweet, tender flesh fine for eating; good for canning. Tree lacks good form; subject to fireblight. Takes summer heat if provided adequate cold in winter. In cool climates it needs a pollenizer to set fruit well. Good for all zones. Probably the best overall.

■ **'Lincoln':** Large fruit; heavy crops. Extremely hardy; blight resistant.

'Bosc' pears have fragrant flesh that's delicious fresh, canned, or cooked.

Plant pears with use in mind. 'Comice' is delicious fresh, but cans poorly.

Good for the north and south; dependable in the midwest.

■ **'Magness':** Medium oval fruit; perfumed flesh. Vigorous, spreading tree highly resistant to fireblight. Bears small amounts of good-quality fruit. Won't pollinate other pears. Good for the south and west.

■ **'Maxine' ('Starking Delicious').** Large fruit; firm, juicy, sweet white flesh. Somewhat blight resistant. Good for the north and south.

■ **'Parker':** Medium to large; yellow with red blush. Juicy, sweet white flesh. Upright, vigorous, fairly hardy tree. Susceptible to fireblight. Good for the north.

■ **'Sensation Red Bartlett' ('Sensation'):** Juicy, 'Bartlett'-flavored white flesh; yellow skin heavily blushed red. Tree form resembles 'Bartlett' but is smaller; leaves and shoots have reddish tinge. In cool climates it needs a pollenizer. Susceptible to fireblight. Good for the west; difficult to grow in the north.

As a 'Barlett' pear ripens, skin color shifts from green to chartreuse to golden.

PEARS *(continued)*

LATE PEARS

■ **'Anjou':** Large green fruit with a stocky neck. Firm flesh, mild flavor, and not juicy. Stores well; good for eating fresh or canning. Upright, vigorous tree. Susceptible to fireblight. Not recommended for hot-summer areas. Good for the west; challenging for the north.

■ **'Bosc':** Long, narrow; dark russet hue. Firm, crisp flesh with heavy perfume. Use for eating fresh, canning, or cooking. Large tree bears each year. Susceptible to fireblight. Good for the north and west.

■ **'Concord':** Tree structure easier to prune. Bears easily. Stores well.

■ **'Comice':** Large round fruit; tough skin; sweet, aromatic, juicy flesh. Finest eating pear; not good for canning. Large, vigorous tree slow to bear; best grown on dwarfing quince rootstock. Moderately susceptible to fireblight. Sets fruit better with a pollenizer. Specialty of Oregon's Medford region, also in home gardens along the California coast. Good for the west.

■ **'Duchess':** Very large, fine-textured, good-flavored pear. Symmetrical tree bears annually. Good for the north.

■ **'Kieffer':** Large yellow fruit, often gritty. Poor for fresh use but keeps well in storage; excellent for cooking and canning. Nearly immune to fireblight. Needs little winter chill; stands both cold and heat well. Good for most growing areas.

■ **'Mericourt':** White flesh nearly grit free; good fresh or for canning. Vigorous tree; withstands -23° F during full dormancy. Resists leaf spot and fireblight. Good for the south.

■ **'Seckel':** Small yellow-brown fruit; finest aroma and flavor of any home garden pear. Eat fresh or use whole for spiced preserves. Highly productive; very fireblight resistant. Sets fruit best with a pollenizer (any pear but 'Bartlett' or 'Magness'). Good for all zones.

ASIAN PEARS (APPLE PEARS)

Asian pears (*Pyrus pyrifolia*) are true pears, just a different species. The common name "apple pear" derives from the texture: Fruit is crisp like an apple. Some have an apple shape.

Native to Japan and China, these pears were selected for size, shape, flavor, and lack of grittiness. Fruit is eaten firm like an apple and keeps in the refrigerator for four to eight months without getting soft. Trees bloom and ripen like a 'Bartlett' and are pruned like ordinary pear trees. They also espalier well. All varieties are susceptible to fireblight and need cross-pollination with any pear that flowers at the same time.

Asian pears grow well on the West Coast and may grow in the south or east with adequate fireblight protection. Best grown on Asian rootstocks; very dwarf on quince rootstock. Six to seven weeks after bloom, thin fruit to one per spur when fruit is ¾ inch in diameter.

VARIETIES

■ **'Chojuro':** Flat and russet-skinned; strong flavor; very firm. Stores a long time. Bears yearly.

■ **'Hosui':** Golden brown skin on large apple-shaped fruit. Fine-textured, juicy, sweet flesh. Fruit lasts up to six months after picking.

■ **'Kikusui':** Flat yellow pear; very juicy and mild flavored. Pick when skin begins to turn yellow.

■ **'Shenseiki':** Flat yellow pear with good texture and flavor. Earliest-maturing quality Asian pear. Pick when skin is yellow.

■ **'Shinko':** Medium apple-shaped; golden russet; fine textured; rich flavored. Stores for two to three months. Heaviest-bearing Asian pear.

■ **'Twentieth Century' ('Nijisseiki'):** Flat, green pear. Most popular Asian pear in California. Bears in alternate years since it crops very heavily. Thin to one fruit per cluster.

■ **'Ya Li':** Pear shape; fine textured; good flavor. Sets fruit without a pollenizer but yields heavier crop with one. Blooms early; use an early pollenizer ('Tsu Li' or 'Seuri'). Thin for best size and bearing. Extremely low chill. Fruits in warm areas.

Asian pears earn their common name, apple pears, because of their crunchy flesh. Fruit lacks the grittiness of pears and stores for months in the refrigerator without spoiling. Flavor is distinctly delicious. Fruit shape varies from round to pear shape.

PERSIMMONS

Diospyros species
dy-OS-py-ros

The American persimmon, *Diospyros virginiana*, is native from Kansas to Connecticut and southward. It bears small fruit to 2½ inches in diameter.

Oriental persimmon, *Diospyros kaki,* is the large persimmon found in markets. The tree grows well in any well-drained soil, making a fine shade tree. Large, glossy leaves turn a rich gold to orange-red in fall. Orange fruit decorates bare branches until winter. It grows in southern states and on the West Coast.

To store, refrigerate persimmons; use only after they soften. Place fruit in a bag with an apple to hasten ripening. Eat them when softened or use the flesh as you would bananas or applesauce. To store it, mash the soft pulp out of the skin for freezing, discarding the tough skin.

Since persimmon grows slowly, it's easy to espalier. Train one against a flat surface or use a trellis to form a persimmon hedge. It grows well as a single lawn tree, but in late fall the soft fruit does drop and squash.

Some American persimmon trees are male, producing pollen but no fruit, while others are female, producing fruit. Plant both unless you have wild trees near your garden. Improved varieties bear fruit without a separate pollenizer.

Oriental persimmons set fruit without pollination. Pick the large fruit before first frost. Oriental persimmons stand temperatures to about 0° F but need only a short chill period (100 to 200 hours below 45° F) to fruit in southern locations.

In the west the persimmon has no serious pests. In the east a flat-headed borer may attack the trunk, but it can be removed by hand.

VARIETIES

Oriental persimmons are the larger, more commercial type. Choose 'Chocolate', 'Fuyu', 'Tanenashi', or

Persimmon tree foliage stages a breathtaking color show in autumn, complementing ripening fruit.

'Hachiya', the popular commercial variety. 'Meader' is the most common variety of American persimmon. It is hardy, and sets fruit without a pollinator.

PLUMS

Prunus species
PROO-nus

Of all the stone fruits, plums are the most varied. They range from hardy little cherry plums and sand cherries to hybrids with the hardiness of natives, sweet European plums, and sweet or tart Japanese plums.

European plums tend to be small and egg-shaped. The flesh is rather dry and very sweet. Prunes from these plums are the sweetest and easiest to dry. Plants are fairly hardy, but some varieties do well in mild-winter areas. All varieties are self-pollinating, except for those noted.

Japanese plums have relatively large, soft, juicy fruit. The plants are the least hardy of the plums, although selected varieties are grown in milder northern areas. Japanese plums need cross-pollination, except 'Santa Rosa', 'Methley', 'Beauty', and 'Climax', but all plums set fruit better with a pollenizer. Most are very susceptible to bacterial leaf spot in the south and east. Local extension agencies rate resistant varieties; check with your local agent when selecting cultivars.

Plum trees bear for 10 to 15 years or more, and standard plum trees take space. Expect your tree to fill an area 15 to 20 feet wide and long. Bush and cherry plums reach 6 feet or so and spread as wide or wider. A dwarfed European plum on 'Nanking' cherry roots will grow to 10 to 12 feet tall.

All the large-fruit Japanese plums must be thinned five to eight weeks after bloom. Thin fruit to 4 to 6 inches apart. Thin European plum clusters to two or three fruit per spur. Prune young trees as discussed on page 149. Bush varieties need oldest shoots cut off at ground level after about four years of bearing to encourage new growth.

Tree plums don't lend themselves to confinement, so use bush types if space is tight. Grow bush types as shrubby screens or in containers.

Brown rot is a major concern. Bacterial leaf spot is a serious

A very sweet European plum, 'Italian' is favored in Washington and Oregon.

PLUMS *(continued)*

problem for Japanese plums in the south and the east, but it's not a problem on other types of plums. Japanese types do best in the west; European types are best in the east; and bush types grow well in the south, midwest, and north.

EARLY-SEASON PLUMS

■ **'Mariposa':** Large, heart-shaped Japanese. Skin mottled red and yellow; sweet, red freestone flesh. Good for eating fresh and cooking. For pollenizers use 'Late Santa Rosa', 'Santa Rosa', or 'Wickson'. Low chill. Good for mildest winter climates. For better crops pollinate with 'Shiro' or 'Burbank'. Good for the north.

■ **'Santa Rosa':** Large Japanese; deep crimson skin; flesh purplish near the skin; yellow streaked with pink near the pit. Good for dessert or canning. Use any early or mid-season plum for improved pollination. Good for all zones. Good for warmer areas of the west.

EARLY MID-SEASON PLUMS

■ **'Satsuma':** Meaty small to medium Japanese with red juice.

'Shiro' is a yellow Japanese plum that bears heavily in all growing Zones.

Dull, dark red skin; mild red flesh; small pit. For dessert or preserves. Use 'Santa Rosa' or 'Wickson' as a pollenizer. Good for all zones.

■ **'Shiro':** Medium to large Japanese is round; yellow; has good flavor. Use fresh or for cooking. Tree yields heavily. Use 'Early Golden', 'Santa Rosa', or 'Methley' as a pollenizer.

MID-SEASON PLUMS

■ **'Burbank':** Large red Japanese; amber flesh; excellent flavor. Fairly small drooping trees. For canning or dessert. Use 'Early Golden' or 'Santa Rosa' as a pollenizer. Good for all zones.

■ **'Damson':** Old European derived from a different species than other European plums. Smallish blue fruit best for jams, jellies, and preserves. Improved varieties include 'Blue Damson', 'French Damson', and 'Shropshire Damson'. Small self-pollinating trees. A late plum in the north. Good for all zones.

■ **'Green Gage' ('Reine Claude'):** Greenish-yellow European; amber flesh. Use fresh, cooked, or preserved. Medium self-pollinating trees bear lightly. Fruit ripens midsummer; later in the north. Good for all Zones because it has a low-chill requirement and is cold-hardy.

■ **'Queen Ann':** Large freestone purple fruit; golden-orange flesh. Juicy, rich flavor; no tartness at the pit. An esteemed dessert plum. Tree is less vigorous than other Japanese plums. Use 'Santa Rosa' as pollenizer.

■ **'Stanley':** Large, dark blue fruit; firm, richly flavored yellow flesh. Bears heavily every year; self-pollinating. Most widely planted European plum in the east, midwest, and south; hardy into northern Iowa. The standard for the north.

■ **'Yellow Egg':** Golden-yellow European; thick skin; yellow flesh. Round-topped, vigorous, hardy, productive, self-pollinating tree. Good for the north and west.

Like all self-fertilizing plums, 'Victoria' bears more heavily when pollinated.

LATE-SEASON PLUMS

■ **'French Prune':** Small, red to purplish black; very sweet with mild flavor. Main commercial variety in California. Large long-lived tree, often surviving after orchards have become housing developments. Self-pollinating. Good south and west.

■ **'Italian Prune' ('Fellenberg'):** Dark blue European; very sweet; good for dessert, canning, or drying. Major plum for Washington-Oregon area. Good for the south and west.

■ **'President':** Large dark blue, amber flesh; ripens very late, after other plums. Flavor not outstanding; use for winter cooking or canning. Pollinate with another late European plum. Good for the north.

HARDY PLUMS

These were especially selected for the coldest northern climates.

■ **'Superior':** Large, conical red fruit; firm yellow flesh. Excellent fresh. Tree bears very young and prolifically. Pollinate with 'Toka'.

■ **'Toka':** Large, pointed medium red fruit. Firm yellow flesh with a rich, spicy flavor. Spreading medium tree yields heavily but may be short-lived. Pollinate with 'Superior'.

Berries

Berries offer rich rewards for a small investment of time and space. A little sunlight and a pot, for example, are all you need to grow luscious strawberries. Where tree fruits are a large commitment of time and energy, berries require less care overall. In addition, they tend to be expensive to purchase in the store, so growing them at home is doubly rewarding.

The small-fruited plants can return bumper crops with minimal effort on your part, and several of the shrubby or vining plants can also add beauty to your landscape.

Strawberries are without question the easiest plants to work into any available space. On a south-facing apartment terrace you can produce a crop in special containers. The European wild strawberry, or *fraise de bois,* is ideal for this situation because it won't make runners and grows in a clump, so a container planting stays compact.

The cane berries—blackberries and raspberries—take more space, although you can grow a few in large containers. If you train them carefully along a fence or trellis and keep them pruned, they won't take much space and will produce heavy crops of fruit with flavor not available in their store-bought cousins. Even a small number of berries benefits from the use of a V trellis and rewards you with larger numbers of clean fruit.

Blueberries and currants make lovely ornamental shrubs, covered with bloom in spring and with decorative fruit in later seasons. Blueberries require light acid soil and constant moisture with excellent drainage. Currants and gooseberries are the only fruit crops that tolerate partial shade, which makes them a wonderful choice if that's your only available site. They are an interim host to a serious disease of five-needle pines, white pine blister rust,

Homegrown berries prove to be one of the most rewarding fruits to grow, giving high yields with little effort.

so in some areas it is illegal to plant them. Check with your county extension service to determine the legalities in your area. Where they are permitted, nothing takes less care, is more decorative, or gives a tastier crop.

Rubus species
ROO-bus

BLACKBERRIES

Blackberries and raspberries are closely related. A main difference is that when you pick blackberries, the white receptacle stays attached to the berry, but with raspberries it stays attached to the plant, which is why the berries have a hollow center. Blackberries are often larger and more vigorous; some cultivars are less hardy. Blackberries have two distinct forms—erect and trailing. They may be thorny or thornless.

Erect blackberries are hardy stiff-caned plants. The trailing kind, also called dewberries, are tender and grown mainly in the south. Thornless cultivars tend to be more tender and are susceptible to rodent damage. Trailing plants from the Pacific Coast are sold under cultivar names—for example, 'Boysen' and 'Logan'. These will freeze in the east and north without winter protection.

Stiff-caned berries need no support; trailing blackberries require support. Cut canes to the ground

after fruiting, destroying clippings to reduce disease spread. New growth that sprouts during late summer will fruit the following year. Blackberries can be invasive; if ignored, they grow out of control quickly.

Blackberries like a light well drained soil with a high moisture-holding capacity. Do not plant them where tomatoes, potatoes, or eggplants have grown previously since the site may be infected with verticillium wilt, making the berries unable to grow there.

Plant in early spring a month before the last frost. Set plants 4 to 6 feet apart in rows 6 to 9 feet apart. Before planting, clip canes to 6-inch stubs; plant at the depth they grew in the nursery. As soon as new growth begins, cut any stubs that do not sprout and burn them to protect plants from anthracnose, a fungal cane and leaf spot disease found in warm, moist climates.

Use several inches of mulch to keep soil moist, prevent weed

growth, and prevent suckers. Don't fertilize too heavily or you'll get lush plant growth instead of fruit.

Blackberries are subject to many pests and diseases. Buy only certified plants and resistant varieties.

Fruit color shifts from red to black as blackberries ripen.

Berries *(continued)*

BLACKBERRIES *(continued)*

Semitrailing blackberries are easier to pick when canes are trained to a support structure.

ERECT BLACKBERRIES

Erect blackberries aren't suggested for the very coldest northern regions but may succeed if you bundle up canes in straw and burlap for winter.

■ **'Bailey':** Large, medium firm, good-quality berry; productive, reliable bush. Good for the north and parts of the Pacific Northwest.

■ **'Black Satin':** Large dark berries; good for fresh eating or cooking. Vigorous, thornless semierect vines. Heavy crops. Good for the south.

■ **'Brainerd':** Large, high-quality fruit; excellent for processing. Hardy, productive, vigorous plant. Good for the south.

■ **'Brazos':** Large fruit; matures early, bears over a long period. Vigorous disease-resistant plant. Popular in Texas, Arkansas, and Louisiana. Good for the south.

■ **'Cherokee':** Medium-sized berries mid-season; heavy crops. Moderately thorny canes. Good for the south.

■ **'Comanche':** Similar to 'Cherokee', but berries are bigger, better for eating fresh, and ripen two weeks earlier. Good for the south.

■ **'Darrow':** Large, irregular, firm berries. Ripen over a long season, sometimes into fall. Hardy and reliable where cold isn't too intense.

■ **'Ebony King':** Large, sweet, tangy glossy black fruit; ripens early; resists orange rust. Good for the south, north, and Pacific Northwest.

■ **'Eldorado':** Old variety; very hardy and productive. Resembles 'Ebony King'. Immune to orange rust. Good for the south and north.

■ **'Flint':** Large berries in clusters of 8 to 15. Needs moderate winter chill. Highly resistant to leaf spot and anthracnose. Good for the south.

■ **'Humble':** Large, soft berries; comparatively few thorns. Low-chill Texas cultivar. Good for the south.

■ **'Jerseyblack':** Large fruit looks and tastes like 'Eldorado'. Mid-season crop. Semitrailing, vigorous plant; rust resistant. Good for the south.

■ **'Smoothstem':** Soft berries ripen late. Heavy crop in large clusters. Thornless plant is hardy from Maryland southward.

■ **'Thornfree':** Medium tart fruit. Semierect tender canes to 8 feet; up to 30 berries per fruiting twig.

■ **'Williams':** Medium fruit early summer; very good fresh. Semierect thorny bush. Resists most cane and leaf diseases. Good for the south.

TRAILING BLACKBERRIES

All of these berries are tender and need protection from cold.

■ **'Aurora':** Very early, large, firm fruit; excellent flavor. Canes most productive on bottom 5 feet; plant closely together; cut back heavily.

■ **'Boysen' ('Nectar'):** Large aromatic fruit over a long season. Vigorous, thorny plant. Pacific Coast

Some blackberry cultivars, such as Pacific Coast-favorite 'Thornless Logan', ripen to a reddish tint.

cultivar. Good for California (where it may produce two crops) and the south and Pacific Northwest.

■ **'Carolina':** Very large-fruited dewberry; productive. Resists leaf spot diseases. Good for the south.

■ **'Cascade':** Unsurpassed flavor fresh or preserved. Vigorous, tender productive plant. Good in milder parts of the Pacific Northwest.

■ **'Early June':** Large round fruit; excellent flavor; acid enough for jam, jelly and pies. Semithornless; somewhat resistant to anthracnose and leaf spot. Good for the south.

■ **'Flordagrand':** Large, very soft, very early tart fruit. For cooking and preserves. Evergreen canes. Must be planted with 'Oklawaha' for pollination. Good for the south.

■ **'Lucretia':** Very large, long, soft early fruits. Hardy old favorite; vigorous and productive. Needs winter protection in the north.

■ **'Marion':** Medium to large, long quality berries mid-season; excellent flavor. Vigorous very thorny canes up to 20 feet long. Good for the milder parts of the Pacific Northwest.

■ **'Olallie':** Large, firm, high-quality sweet fruit. Thorny productive canes. Low chill. Resists verticillium wilt and mildew. Especially good for southern California.

■ **'Thornless Boysen':** Summer-bearing flavorful, aromatic Pacific Coast berry. Tender plants must be trained. Bury canes for winter in colder climates.

■ **'Thornless Evergreen':** Large, firm, sweet fruit; top commercial berry in Oregon. Vigorous plants produce heavily; very tender.

■ **'Thornless Logan':** Large, reddish, tangy Pacific Coast berry. Good for jam, pies, and a syrup base for drinks. Bury canes in winter in colder climates.

■ **'Young':** Large purplish-black dewberry; excellent flavor. Easy to pick; plant produces a few long canes. Anthracnose a serious threat. Good for the south.

BLUEBERRIES

Vaccinium
vak-SIN-ee-um

Blueberries demand the right climate and soil but take little care if you provide a site suitable to their somewhat exacting conditions. They need a fair amount of winter chill and won't grow well in mild winter climates. Blueberries need a frost-free growing season of 140 days.

Blueberries belong to the heath family and count rhododendrons, mountain laurel, huckleberries, and azaleas among their cousins. If any of these grow naturally near your garden, or if you have prepared an artificial site that suits them, then blueberries will also do well.

Blueberries like soil rich in organic material such as peat—very acidic but extremely well drained. They also need constant moisture, even though they cannot tolerate standing water.

Southern gardeners have a choice of two kinds of blueberries, depending on climate. The highbush blueberry grows commercially in large plantings in southeastern and western North Carolina. The rabbiteye blueberry, or southern highbush blueberry, grows wild along streambeds in Georgia and northern Florida. With proper care it thrives in areas where muscadine grapes succeed.

Protect ripening blueberries from hungry marauding birds with netting.

For both drainage and soil acidification, add large amounts of peat moss or other organic material to the planting site, up to three-quarters by volume for soils that tend to be heavy. Never add manure; it is alkaline.

Purchase two- to three-year-old plants from a reputable nursery. Bare-root blueberries tend to do better than container plants. Do not expose the roots to sun and wind. Dig a planting hole somewhat broader and deeper than the roots of the young plant and spread the roots in the hole. Prune back to 8 inches at planting, or roughly half their original size.

Set highbush blueberry plants about 4 feet apart with about 10 feet between rows. Choose two varieties for cross-pollination. Since the rabbiteye plants grow much larger, plant them 6 to 8 feet apart in rows 10 to 12 feet between rows.

Do not feed plants the first year. In succeeding years use cottonseed meal, ammonium sulfate, or any product suitable for camellias, azaleas, or rhododendrons. Mulch plants heavily with any organic material and renew it regularly to keep it about 3 to 6 inches deep.

BLUEBERRY MAGGOT. Small white maggots attack the berries, one per fruit, and usually cause them to drop, decreasing yield.

FUSICOCCUM CANKER. 'Jersey', 'Earliblue', and 'Bluecrop' are all very susceptible to this disease. It appears as small reddish spots on the canes, often around a leaf scar near the ground. Plant parts above the canker suddenly wilt and die during dry, warm weather. Prune diseased canes as they appear. Uncommon except in colder regions. Plant the resistant cultivar 'Rancocas'. 'Coville', 'Berkeley', 'Blueray', 'Burlington', and 'Rubel' are moderately susceptible.

Successful blueberries hinge on acid soil that's moist but well-drained. Standing water kills bushes.

MUMMYBERRY. This fungal disease causes young shoots and leaves to wilt, turn brown, and die, so infection is similar in appearance to frost damage. As harvest approaches, berries that develop from infected blossoms become cream-colored, shrivel into hard mummies, and drop off. Rake all old berries into the ground before budbreak in spring or cover with 2 inches of composted sawdust mulch to limit the spread. Resistant varieties include 'Burlington', 'Collins', 'Jersey', 'Darrow', 'Rubel', 'Bluetta', and 'Dixi'. 'Earliblue' and 'Blueray' are susceptible.

PHOMOPSIS CANKER. This disease causes new shoots to wilt and die back from the tips toward the crown. If single canes suddenly die while the rest of the plant remains healthy, it is likely phomopsis canker. Maintain plants in a vigorous, healthy condition and take all possible precautions to minimize winter injury and early frost damage. Prune and burn diseased twigs and canes as they appear.

Berries *(continued)*

BLUEBERRIES *(continued)*

EARLY BLUEBERRIES

■ **'Earliblue':** Large, firm light blue berry. Picking scar is small; fruit doesn't shatter easily from the plant. Keeps well; resists cracking. Upright, comparatively hardy plant. One of the best for all zones.

■ **'Ivanhoe':** Large, firm, light blue. Very tender plant. One of the best berries for the south.

■ **'Northland':** Moderately firm fruit; good flavor. Hardy spreading plant reaching 4 feet at maturity. Good for the north and west.

'Coville' blueberries offer some of the largest and latest crops. Plants are well-suited to many growing regions.

■ **'Woodward':** Large, mildly flavored light blue berries; tart until fully ripe. Short spreading plant; early ripening rabbiteye. Best in low-elevation areas of the south.

MID-SEASON BLUEBERRIES

■ **'Berkeley':** Large, firm pale blue berry; stores well; resists cracking. Fairly upright and hardy. Good for all zones, especially the Pacific Northwest.

■ **'Bluecrop':** Large, tart light blue fruit; stores well; good for cooking. Berries stand cold well; good for the shortest growing seasons. Medium-hardy upright plant.

■ **'Blueray':** Very large, firm sweet fruit. Upright spreading plant. For all zones, but especially for Washington.

■ **'Croatan':** Medium fruit ripens quickly in warm weather. Canker resistant. Good for the south; recommended for North Carolina.

■ **'Darrow':** Exceptional flavor for the home gardener.

■ **'Jersey':** Medium, firm berries. Good keepers, resist cracking, and good flavor. Plants productive, erect, vigorous, and easy to prune.

■ **'Northblue':** Large berries; outstanding flavor. Half-highbush type to 2 feet tall, giving it complete snow cover in most winters. Developed to withstand harsh northern winters. Needs a pollenizer such as 'Northsky'.

■ **'Northsky':** Highly flavorful smaller fruit; produced in smaller quantity than 'Northblue', which should be used as a pollenizer. Another blueberry bred for northern winters. Fall foliage deep red.

■ **'Stanley':** Medium, firm berry; good color and flavor. Hardy, vigorous upright bush. Easy pruning because only a few main branches. Good for the north and west.

■ **'Tifblue':** This rabbiteye type is a Southern favorite because of its dependable production of large tasty berries.

Large, flavorful berries of 'Dixi' are a Pacific Northwest favorite.

LATE BLUEBERRIES

■ **'Coville':** Inconsistent variety with large light blue fruit that remains tart until near harvest. The plant is medium hardy. It is good for all zones and widely available.

■ **'Delite':** This is the only rabbiteye variety that develops some sugar in berries early. Medium-large berries are easy to pick and have excellent flavor.

■ **'Dixi':** The fruit is large, aromatic, flavorful, and good fresh. Popular in the northwest.

■ **'Herbert':** Very large, medium blue berries. Flesh is tender; flavor is excellent. Fruit resists cracking; doesn't shatter from the bush. Plants are vigorous and open and spreading in habit.

■ **'Lateblue':** Late-ripening, firm highly flavored light blue berries. They ripen very late but in a relatively short period of time, about one week after 'Coville'.

■ **'Southland':** The firm light blue berries have a waxy bloom, and the skin can tend to be tough late in the season. This is a particularly good plant for the Gulf Coast region.

CURRANTS AND GOOSEBERRIES

Ribes species
RYE-beez

Currants and gooseberries are among the most beautiful of the small fruits. They're easy to care for and productive, so northern gardeners can tuck a few among other shrubs for the flowers, fruit, and fall color. The crop can be used for jellies, pies, or eating fresh for those who like a tart fruit.

Only red and white currants (*Ribes sativum*) and the gooseberries *R. hirtellum* and *R. grossularia* are discussed here. The black currant, *R. nigrum*, was banned in many places because it is an alternate host of white pine blister rust. In the early 1900s, federal and state governments outlawed growing currants and gooseberries to prevent the spread of white pine blister rust. The federal ban was rescinded in 1966, but some northern states still prohibit planting black currants.

Four rust-resistant currant cultivars include 'Consort', 'Crusader', 'Coronet', and 'Titania'. They can be planted where other currants and gooseberries are permitted. Some counties still restrict *Ribes* planting. Do not transport any currant or gooseberry from outside your region.

Fall or winter planting is best since plants leaf out early. In cold climates, plant right after leaves drop; roots will be established before winter. Space plants 4 feet apart. Both do poorly in hot-summer areas but may survive if planted against a north-facing wall. In most areas plant in the open, but be sure soil moisture is constant.

Plants prefer rich, well-drained soils that are also moist. Cool, moist locations on the north side of buildings, with good air drainage, are desirable.

Plants bear full crops their second or third year; fruiting is strongest on spurs of two- and three-year-old canes. Prune lightly annually to remove four-year-old canes by cutting oldest canes at the base. Prune in late winter or early spring.

CURRANT VARIETIES

■ **'Blanka':** Widely available white cultivar. Large mild berries.

■ **'Jumbo':** Large, sweet pale green fruit. Upright vigorous plants.

■ **'Perfection':** Old variety; red fruit in loose clusters. Nice foliage; upright, productive, vigorous plant. Good for Washington and Oregon.

■ **'Primus':** White cultivar that many prefer over 'Blanka'.

■ **'Red Lake':** Medium-to-large light red berries in long easy-to-pick clusters. Slightly spreading plants produced highest yield in Canadian trials; also produce well in California. Good for everywhere currants are allowed.

■ **'Rovada':** Excellent red currant. Large easy-to-pick berries. Reliable, late ripening, and very productive.

■ **'Stephens No. 9':** Large red berries in medium clusters. Plants are spreading and productive. Great Lakes cultivar.

■ **'White Grape':** Widely sold white; surpassed in quality by 'White Imperial', a rare similar cultivar.

■ **'Wilder':** Dark red berries; very tart. Long-lived large, hardy plants. Very old Indiana cultivar.

GOOSEBERRY VARIETIES

■ **'Captivator':** Nearly thornless and mildew-resistant cross of American and European cultivars. Reddish fruit.

Choose currants if you want to tend an edible, ornmental landscape.

■ **'Clark':** Large red fruit. Mildew-free plants. Good Canadian variety.

■ **'Fredonia':** Large dark red fruit. Productive vigorous plants with open growth habit.

■ **'Hinnonmaki Red' and 'Hinnonmaki Yellow':** Red and green fruit, respectively. Medium sized good-quality berries.

■ **'Oregon Champion':** Medium-sized green fruit; bears prolifically. Good for the Pacific Coast and the east.

■ **'Pixwell':** Berries hang away from the plant, making them easy to pick; canes have few thorns. Fresh flavor mediocre. Very hardy variety for central and plains states.

■ **'Poorman':** Red fruit; spiny, spreading plants. Good for Pacific Northwest and central states.

■ **'Welcome':** Wine-red fruit in abundance; sweet-tart flavor.

'White Imperial' currant produces high quality cream-colored fruits.

Gooseberries tend to be tart. They're best in jams and pies.

Vitis species
VY-tis

GRAPES

Three types of grapes are commonly grown: American, European, and French-American hybrids. The American grape entered our history more recently than European vines but has played an important role. Its roots saved European grapes from extinction during the 19th century *Phylloxera vitifoliae* plague, which threatened to destroy European grapes. The remedy was grafting them to American rootstocks. Recently American grapes have created sturdy hybrids that carry European wine grapes far north of their original climate area.

Grapes need full sun, deep soil that's not too wet or dry, and 150 frost-free days. They tolerate a broad range of soil types but prefer deep well-drained loam soil. Grapes send their roots deep where they can and prefer soil rich in organic material. Boost growth by adding organic matter at planting time and mulching roots. Your site needs good air circulation because grapes are subject to disease in stagnant air.

Homegrown seedless grapes will never grow as large as those at the market because commercial growers spray gibberellic acid (a plant hormone) to increase fruit size. But homegrown grapes have more flavor and last longer on the vine because they're less susceptible to rot.

Sometimes grapes never taste sweet, no matter how long you wait. This means that you may have planted the wrong variety for your area or that unseasonably cool weather has failed to sweeten the crop. Switch varieties or replant in a hot spot against a south wall or in a west-facing corner. Always choose cultivars suited to your area.

If vines overproduce and have too many bunches, the grapes will never get sweet. Remedy this in future years by pruning more extremely in the dormant season or by thinning bunches to balance the leaf area with the grape load. The two kinds of grapes are pruned differently (see pages 150–151 for instructions).

Grapes mildew badly, but providing good air circulation and following excellent cultural practices helps avoid the need for fungicides. The classic remedy is copper sulfate.

A number of pests attack grapes and birds love grapes, but you can save the fruit by placing whole bunches in paper bags. Thwart birds with reflective tape, scare-eye balloons, or bird netting.

GRAPES FOR THE NORTHEAST AND MIDWEST

Many of the following grapes also grow well in the Pacific Northwest.

AMERICAN GRAPES

■ **'Buffalo':** Fairly large clusters of reddish-black berries; good for wine or juice. Ripens midseason. Cane prune this vigorous vine. Performs well in the Pacific Northwest.

■ **'Catawba':** Red grape; popular commercial variety good for wine or juice. Requires long season to ripen; does well in southerly areas with the longest growing seasons. Thinning hastens development.

■ **'Concord':** Often the quality standard for judging American grapes. Dark blue slipskin berries; rich in "foxy" flavor. Ripens late.

■ **'Delaware':** Small clusters and berries; good for wine and juice; excellent eating. Major wine grape.

■ **'Edelweiss':** Hardy medium grape; good dessert quality.

■ **'Fredonia':** Top black grape in its season; hardy. Sometimes has difficulty with pollination; allow vines to set heavily.

■ **'Interlaken Seedless':** Small, seedless berries with greenish-white adhering skin. Crisp, sweet flesh. Ripens early. Fairly hardy vine does best with cane pruning. Good substitute for 'Thompson Seedless' in Pacific Northwest.

■ **'New York Muscat':** Reddish-black berries; rich, fruity muscat aroma. Good for wine and juice. Air below 15° F can cause winter injury.

■ **'Niagara':** Most widely planted white grape; more productive than Concord; good for wine and juice. Vigorous and moderately hardy.

■ **'Ontario':** White berries in loose clusters; vigorous, productive, moderately hardy vines prefer heavy soils. Cane pruning is best. Also grown in the Pacific Northwest.

■ **'Schuyler':** Resembles European grapes in flavor; soft and juicy with a tough skin. Hardy and disease resistant. Good for the northwest.

'Interlaken Seedless' resembles 'Thompson Seedless'.

'Baco Noir' is a French-American hybrid grown for wine-making.

'Seneca': Small to medium berries resemble European grapes; tender golden skin; sweet, aromatic flavor. Hardy vine; cane pruning best. Good for the Pacific Northwest.

'Swenson Red': Medium-large red grapes; good flavor; hardy.

FRENCH-AMERICAN HYBRID GRAPES

Spur prune vines. Primarily for wine or juice but also good eaten fresh.

'Aurore' ('Seibel 5279'). Very early soft white grape; pleasant flavor. Dependable crops. Vigorous grower; better in sandy than heavy soils. Good for early ripening.

'Baco 1' ('Baco Noir'): Small clusters; small black grapes; midseason. Vigorous and productive; tends to bud out early; subject to frost injury. Not cold-hardy.

'Cayuga White': White grapes in tight clusters; good dessert quality.

GRAPES FOR THE WEST

Success with grapes in the west starts with choosing the right variety.

TABLE GRAPES

'Cardinal': Large dark red berries; ripen early; firm greenish flesh. Abundant bearer. Use this one to cover an arbor. Spur prune. Performs well in coastal and central valleys.

'Concord': Doesn't like high California heat or coolest northwest summers, but does well elsewhere. Cane prune.

'Emperor': Large red grape; crunchy, firm flesh. Ripens late. Berries store longer than other varieties. Spur prune. Adapted to hottest part of San Joaquin Valley.

'Flame Seedless': Crisp light red table grape; seedless; sweet flavor. Elongated, loose medium clusters ripen early. Spur or cane prune.

'Muscat of Alexandria': Large green berries splotched with amber; loose clusters; musky, rich flavor; best eaten fresh or dried as seeded raisins. Spur prune. Requires high heat of the San Joaquin Valley or inland valleys but not the desert.

'Niabell': Large black berries; good fresh or as juice. Vigorous vines resist powdery mildew; cane prune to long canes. Good for hot interior regions and coastal valleys.

'Niagara': Best in coastal regions. Cane prune.

'Pierce': Hot-summer 'Concord'. Good for central California's warmer regions. Very vigorous. Cane prune.

'Ribier': Large jet-black berries; dessert grape. Fruit softens quickly in storage and loses its mild flavor. Overproductive vines; use short spur pruning and thin flowers. Best in hot interior valleys.

'Thompson Seedless': Top commercial seedless green grape. Long clusters; mild-flavored fruit. Excellent fresh if clusters are thinned; also used for raisins. Grow only in hot climates. Cane prune.

'Tokay': Large, very firm red grapes; little flavor. Good for cooler valley climates. Spur prune.

WINE GRAPES

'Cabernet Sauvignon': European black grape used for red Bordeaux wines of France. Cane prune.

'Chardonnay': White grape used to make French white Burgundy. Vigorous grower; moderate producer. Berry clusters small. Best in cool coastal areas. Cane prune.

'Chenin Blanc': Medium white grapes. Vigorous productive vines. Good for coastal valleys and San Joaquin Valley. Cane prune.

'French Colombard': Productive white grape; high in acid. Adapted to coastal valleys and Central Valley of California. Cane or spur prune.

'Pinot Noir': Small black grape used to make French Burgundy wines. Cane prune.

'Zinfandel': California specialty for red and white wines. Makes drinkable wine in variety of climates.

GRAPES FOR THE SOUTHEAST

Two different American grapes are grown in the southeast: the bunch grape and the muscadine grape. The bunch grape is typified by 'Concord', described above. This type prefers a cool climate, but cultivars are

Adaptable 'Zinfandel' wine grapes grow in nearly any climate.

available for most regions. The muscadine has smaller clusters of berries and likes hot weather.

MUSCADINE GRAPES

Many muscadines are sterile and need a pollenizer. "Perfect" cultivars pollinate themselves and others.

'Hunt': Dull black fruit ripens evenly. Excellent quality; very good for wine and juice. Vigorous productive vine.

'Jumbo': Very large black grape; good quality. Ripens over several weeks; excellent for fresh home use. Disease-resistant vines.

'Scuppernong': Late-ripening juicy sweet grape; aromatic flavor. Color varies from greenish to reddish bronze, depending on sun. Good for eating fresh or for wine.

'Southland': Perfect. Very large purple grape; dull skinned; good flavor; high sugar content. Vigorous productive vines. Good for Gulf Coast states.

'Thomas': Small to medium reddish-black berries; very sweet; excellent for fresh juice.

'Yuga': Reddish-bronze sweet berries; excellent quality; ripens late and irregularly.

Berries
(continued)

Rubus species
ROO-bus

'Heritage' is an everbearing raspberry that thrives in all climates.

Raspberries are the hardiest of the cane berries and perhaps the most worthwhile home-garden crop. Homegrown fruit is cheaper than the market counterparts and can be eaten at peak flavor. Various ripening times and colors make it easy to enjoy a long harvest with a diversity of beautiful fruits.

What makes a raspberry a raspberry is that it pulls free of its receptacle when it's picked, leaving a hollow spot in the fruit. Other bramble fruits, like blackberries, keep the core when picked.

Raspberries come in a variety of colors—red, purple, yellow, and black—and in different plant forms. Red and yellow fruits grow one or two crops on stiff canes; purple and black fruits grow one crop on trailing canes that require trellising.

Summer-bearing (single-crop) raspberries produce fruit on canes that grew the previous year. Two-crop (everbearing) raspberries produce some fruit at the top of current-season canes in fall, then produce a second crop on the rest of the cane the following year.

Raspberries are extremely hardy, so no winter protection is needed except in the very coldest climates. When canes do show winter injury,

RASPBERRIES

prune out injured portions in spring. Raspberries do poorly in much of the south and throughout California and Arizona. They need cold winters and a long, cool spring, and they don't like spring and summer heat.

Raspberries absolutely cannot tolerate poor drainage. In poorly drained soils, they are highly susceptible to phytophthora root rot and often die quickly. Even soils that are poorly drained for short periods in spring may not be suitable.

Raspberries are subject to the same troubles as dewberries but less so in colder climates where raspberries grow best. Any history of verticillium in the soil rules them out entirely, however.

Black raspberries are highly susceptible to viral diseases. Often these viruses may be tolerated and carried by red raspberries. It's often not practical in the home garden, but, ideally, plant black raspberries at least 700 feet from any reds. Always purchase virus-free stock from a known source.

Black and purple raspberry canes arch to the ground and root at the tips to form new plants. If you want more plants, leave a few canes unpruned. In late summer pin the tip to the ground. Dig and separate the new plant in spring. For pruning information, see page 150.

RED AND YELLOW ONE-CROP RASPBERRIES

■ **'Amber':** Yellow berry; excellent dessert fruit. Good for the north.

■ **'Boyne':** Excels where winters are cold and summers no more than warm. Red fruit has strong, sweet-tart flavor. Moderately vigorous plant is subject to anthracnose.

■ **'Canby':** Large, firm midseason berries; good for freezing. Plants are semithornless and do best in light soils in the west and northwest.

■ **'Cuthbert':** Once the leading commercial raspberry; still unexcelled for dessert, canning, or freezing. Difficult to pick, but this is

not a big problem in the home garden. Good for the west.

■ **'Fairview':** Large to fairly large light red berries. Tall, branched, moderately hardy canes. Especially suited to western Washington and generally good for the west.

■ **'Festival':** A nearly thornless summer-bearing red that is very hardy and productive.

■ **'Hilton':** Largest of the reds; excellent quality. Vigorous, hardy, productive plants. Good for the north.

■ **'Killarney':** A beautiful, hardy red raspberry with firm productive fruit.

■ **'Latham':** Early midseason cultivar is the standard eastern red raspberry. Large firm berry; tart flavor. Somewhat resistant to viral diseases.

■ **'Meeker':** Firm, sweet bright red berries. Botrytis resistant, strong plants. Pacific Northwest favorite.

■ **'Pocahontas':** Large, firm red berries; tart flavor. Winter-hardy, productive plant. Good for the south. Recent introduction.

■ **'Prelude':** An early summer-bearing red; very hardy.

■ **'Puyallup':** Late-ripening large berries; somewhat soft. Does best in light soils in the northwest; also generally good for the west.

■ **'Sumner':** Medium to large berry; firm and sweet; intense flavor. Does well in heavy soil; recommended for western Washington or south along the coast to Monterey, California.

■ **'Sunrise':** Firm, fine-textured, early, good quality fruit. Hardy plant; very tolerant of disease. Works well in the south.

■ **'Taylor':** Firm red berries of excellent quality; mid- to late-season. Vigorous, hardy plants are good for the north.

■ **'Willamette':** The berries ripen in midseason and are large, round, firm, and good for freezing or canning. This is a vigorous, widely planted commercial variety. Good for the west.

Yellow raspberries, like 'Fallgold', have an irresistible honey-sweet flavor.

RED AND YELLOW
TWO-CROP RASPBERRIES

■ **'Amity'**: Highly flavored dark red fruit; good fresh or canned. Bicoastal raspberry developed and popular in the northwest; also proving itself in the northeast.

■ **'Autumn Bliss'**: Late-season red with excellent hardiness.

■ **'Cherokee'**: Large, firm berries; winter hardy; productive. Good for the south, particularly Virginia's Piedmont area.

■ **'Durham'**: Very good flavor. Very productive plants, bearing a second crop early. Good for the north.

■ **'Fallgold'**: Tawny gold fruit; very sweet flavor. Not for warm climates.

■ **'Fallred'**: Berries of fair quality. Plants are nearly thornless. First crop appears in spring. Good for the south and north.

■ **'Goldie'**: Yellow raspberry fruiting late in the fall with good productivity and hardiness.

■ **'Heritage'**: Firm medium-sized fruit in July and September. Stiff-caned plants need little support. Mow all canes in late winter to get a single August crop. Good anywhere; the standard for excellence in a fall-bearing (everbearing) red.

■ **'Indian Summer'**: Large fruit. First crop light; fall crop very late but abundant. For all zones.

■ **'Kiwigold'**: Late-season yellow; excellent hardiness and fruit quality.

■ **'September'**: Medium to large berries; good quality. Vigorous hardy plant; best in coldest regions. Good for the north and south.

■ **'Southland'**: Recommended for farther south than any other; large fair-quality fruit.

PURPLE RASPBERRIES

■ **'Amethyst'**: Early berry; high quality. Good for the north.

■ **'Brandywine'**: Vigorous with 10-foot canes; good crops of tart red-purple berries good for jam.

■ **'Clyde'**: Early large, firm dark purple berry; excellent quality. Plant is vigorous. Good for the north.

■ **'Royalty'**: Very vigorous purple-red hybrid; very large sweet fruit; good for eating fresh, cooking, and preserving. Plant is immune to raspberry aphid, which carries a debilitating viral disease.

■ **'Sodus'**: Midseason berry; large, firm, good quality but tart. Plants are productive. Good for the north.

BLACK (BLACKCAP) RASPBERRIES

Gardeners in the south and west should be aware that black raspberries are least able to tolerate mild climates.

■ **'Allen'**: Large berries; vigorous plant. Good for the north.

■ **'Alleghany'**: Hardy and productive; very good fruit firmness.

An easy way to grow 'Heritage' berries is to mow canes in late winter.

Pick 'Royalty' fruit at any color stage. The purple hue, which means a sweet flavor, occurs between the early red tone and the overripe dark color.

■ **'Black Hawk'**: Late variety; large berries; good flavor and yield. Good for the north.

■ **'Bristol'**: Large, firm, glossy berries; good quality. Good for the south and west.

■ **'Cumberland'**: Favored variety has large, firm berries of fine flavor. Vigorous productive plants. Good for the south and north.

■ **'Huron'**: Excellent firm fruit, ripening at the end of the summer season.

■ **'Jewel'**: Good-tasting fruit; productive hardy plants.

■ **'Logan' ('New Logan')**: Plants bear heavy crops of large, glossy good-quality berries. Plants hold up well in drought and also tolerate mosaic virus and other raspberry diseases. Good for both the south and north.

■ **'Manteo'**: Fruit resembles 'Cumberland'. The plant survives farther south than any other black raspberry.

■ **'Munger'**: Medium-sized fruit; good quality. Plants are especially recommended for western Oregon. They are worth trying in western Washington, but they may succumb to disease. Good for the west.

Berries
(continued)

Fragaria species
fra-GAIR-ee-a

STRAWBERRIES

Gardeners can grow three types of strawberries: June bearing, everbearing, and day neutral. Everbearing types bear two crops per season: in summer and fall. Newer varieties are truly everbearing, producing fruit, spring, summer, and fall. These are listed in catalogs as "everbearers" or "day-neutrals" (they fruit regardless of day length).

Strawberries need full sun and soil with excellent drainage and good water-holding capacity. Mound the planting site if you're not sure about drainage. The most critical task the first year is weeding. Strawberries are shallow rooted and need to be watered during dry spells.

Unlike June-bearing strawberries, day-neutral plants flower and produce fruit any time temperatures are between 35° F and 85° F. Instead of a large crop in June and July, you pick fruit from summer to fall, including the planting year.

Always plant to the crown; not too deep, but just so roots are covered and the new leaf bud in the center of each plant sits level with the soil surface. Plants may appear small and scruffy, but dig an adequate hole and ensure that roots have enough space.

The most common planting method is to create two rows on top of a raised bed. Plant strawberries about 9 to 12 inches apart in the rows in the bed. In the matted-row system allow runners to form baby plants for next year's production. Or remove runners and allow mother plants to flower and fruit instead.

Provide winter protection where alternate freezing and thawing of soil may heave plants and break roots. Low temperatures also injure plant crowns. In fall, after soil has frozen to a depth of 1 inch, place straw mulch 3 to 4 inches deep over plants.

In early spring remove the mulch when the centers of a few plants show a yellow-green color. Leave an inch of loose straw, and add some fresh straw between rows for comfort during picking. Berries will often also grow well with a plastic mulch, especially in cooler regions, where the plastic will increase soil temperature and keep the berries off the soil.

In general, plant strawberries in spring. In mild-winter regions, plant them in the fall.

STRAWBERRIES FOR THE SOUTH

- **'Albritton':** Large late berry; excellent fresh and for freezing. Richly flavored in North Carolina.
- **'Blakemore':** Small, firm early berry; high acid and pectin content; excellent for preserves. Vigorous plants; good runner production; high resistance to viral diseases and verticillium wilt.
- **'Cardinal':** Large, firm, and sweet; good for fresh eating and processing. Plants resistant to leaf spot, powdery mildew, and leaf scorch.
- **'Daybreak':** Large; good flavor; preserving quality. Very productive.
- **'Dixieland':** Early, firm, acidic in flavor, and excellent for freezing. Sturdy vigorous plants.
- **'Earlibelle':** Early, large, and firm; good for canning and freezing. Good runner production and resistance to leaf spot and leaf scorch.
- **'Florida Ninety':** Very large; good flavor and quality. Heavy producer of fruit and runners.
- **'Guardian':** Large, midseason, and firm; good dessert quality; freezes well. Vigorous, productive plants resist many diseases.
- **'Headliner':** Midseason; good quality. Vigorous, productive; makes runners freely. Resists leaf spot.
- **'Marlate':** Very large fruit; good fresh and freezes well. Extremely hardy plant; productive, dependable late variety.
- **'Pocahontas':** Good fresh, frozen, or in preserves. Vigorous plants resist leaf scorch. Adapted from southern New England to Norfolk, Virginia.
- **'Redchief':** Medium, firm, glossy surface; extremely productive and resistant to red stele (root rot).
- **'Sunrise':** Firm; very good flavor; flesh too pale for freezing. Vigorous; resists disease.
- **'Surecrop':** Large, round, firm, and good dessert quality. Space plants 6 to 9 inches apart. Resists diseases and drought. For all zones.
- **'Suwannee':** Medium to large, early, and tender; very good quality, fresh or frozen. Poor shipper; excellent for the home garden.
- **'Tennessee Beauty':** Medium, firm, and late; good flavor; good for freezing. Productive of both fruit and runners. Resists leaf spot, leaf scorch, and viral diseases.

'Surecrop' bears reliably and heavily in all growing areas.

STRAWBERRIES FOR THE NORTHEAST AND MIDWEST

■ **'Canoga':** Late and heavy-bearing; large sweet fruit lasts well because of firm flesh and tough skin.

■ **'Catskill':** Large and midseason; good dessert quality; excellent for freezing. Grown over a wide range of soil types from New England and New Jersey to southern Minnesota.

■ **'Cyclone':** Large and flavorful; good for freezing. Hardy; resists foliage diseases; for north central.

■ **'Dunlap':** Medium; doesn't ship well; good for home garden. Hardy plants adapted to a wide range of soil types in northern Illinois, Iowa, Wisconsin, Minnesota, North Dakota, South Dakota, and Nebraska.

■ **'Earliglow':** The best early strawberry available. Excellent flavor; size decreases as season progresses.

■ **'Fletcher':** Medium; excellent flavor; good for freezing. For New York and New England.

■ **'Holiday':** Ripening continues through summer with large fruit. Heavy producer.

■ **'Howard 17' ('Premier'):** Medium good-quality berries. Productive; resistant to diseases. Locally available in the northeast.

■ **'Jewel':** Excellent flavor, large, and productive. Currently one of the most widely grown in the northeast.

■ **'Midland':** Very early; good to excellent fresh; freezes well. Plants do best when grown in the hill system. From southern New England to Virginia; west to Iowa and Kansas.

■ **'Midway':** Large; good dessert quality and for freezing. Susceptible to leaf spot, leaf scorch, and verticillium wilt. Good in Michigan.

■ **'Northeaster':** Large; ripens early. Resistant to red stele; does well in heavier clay soils.

■ **'Redstar':** Late, large, and good dessert quality. Plants resist viral diseases, leaf spot, and leaf scorch. Good for southern New England to Maryland and west to Missouri and Iowa.

■ **'Robinson':** Exceptionally large, picture-perfect berries; vigorous, easy-growing, heavy-bearing plants. Prolonged fruiting period.

■ **'Sparkle':** Fairly soft; good flavor. Productive; midseason.

■ **'Trumpeter':** Medium and soft; very good flavor; late. Hardy and productive. For the upper Mississippi Valley and plains states.

EVERBEARING STRAWBERRIES FOR THE NORTHEAST AND MIDWEST

■ **'Gem':** Yields small, tart glossy red fruit of good dessert quality.

■ **'Geneva':** Large vigorous plants fruit in June and throughout summer and early autumn. The berries are soft and highly flavored.

■ **'Ogallala':** Soft, medium, and tart flavor; good for freezing. Vigorous hardy plants.

■ **'Ozark Beauty':** Everbearing variety for cooler climate zones. Large, sweet, and good flavor. Only mother plants produce in any one season, yielding crops in summer and fall. Runner plants produce the following season.

EVERBEARING STRAWBERRIES FOR ALL REGIONS

■ **'Seascape':** Large fruited.

■ **'Tribute':** Tart; disease resistant.

■ **'Tristar':** Disease resistant. Sweet; highly recommended.

STRAWBERRIES FOR WESTERN WASHINGTON AND OREGON

■ **'Hood':** Large; midseason. Held high in upright clusters; good fresh or in preserves. Resistant to mildew but susceptible to red stele.

■ **'Northwest':** Firm and flavorful; good fresh, in preserves, or for freezing. Late midseason. Large fruit at first, smaller later in season. Very productive, resistant to viral diseases.

■ **'Olympus':** Late midseason; medium to large. Vigorous plants produce few runners. Resists red stele and viral diseases; somewhat susceptible to botrytis infection.

■ **'Puget Beauty':** Highly flavored, excellent fresh, good for freezing and preserves. Large, upright plants with moderate runner production. Resists mildew; somewhat susceptible to red stele.

■ **'Quinault':** Large, soft fruit. Everbearer; moderately early crop; heavier July through September. Plant produces good runners.

■ **'Rainier':** Late midseason; large, firm, and good quality. Vigorous plants; moderate runner production.

STRAWBERRIES FOR CALIFORNIA

■ **'Douglas':** Large, midseason, and firm. Very vigorous; produces early berries when planted in October. Good in southern California.

Day-neutral cultivars, like 'Tristar', bear throughout the growing season.

■ **'Sequoia':** Early; may bear in December. Large; excellent flavor. Harvest frequently for best quality. Vigorous plant; many runners. For central and south Pacific Coast. Plant in October and November.

■ **'Shasta':** Large and midseason; good for freezing or preserves. Fairly vigorous; moderate number of runners. Some resistance to mildew and viral diseases.

EVERBEARING CULTIVARS FOR CALIFORNIA

Everbearers for California are heavy berry producers and don't form many runners. Plant them anytime; they'll produce medium size berries in just 90 days. Consider 'Aptos', 'Brighton', 'Fern', 'Hecker', and 'Selva'.

Nuts

Nut trees—with the exception of the filbert, or hazelnut—grow into very large trees. They make excellent shade trees and are beautiful when grown to full maturity, but they are not suitable for small yards. Like any fruit tree, they are subject to a fair amount of disease and insect attack. Thus, nut trees should be viewed as large shade trees that often reward you with nuts, but not always.

All nut trees need plenty of water because they are large and deep rooted. Where summer rainfall is adequate, little irrigation is needed. In warm, dry climates where summer rainfall is uncommon, nut trees need occasional deep watering. Run the hose at a trickle for 24 hours on each quarter of the root system. That is, water for four days, moving the hose to the next quadrant of the root circumference each day. This may be necessary every two weeks, monthly, or only once during the summer, depending on the weather.

Established nut trees require little care. In dry regions, you may need to water.

A nut harvest brings a mix of wonderful flavors to the table.

The hardy almond tree is a beautiful edible ornamental—with lovely blooms and tasty nuts.

Prunus dulcis
PROO-nus DULL-sis

Almond trees produce best in California and Arizona, where spring frosts and summer rain are rare. The best almond climates are where a late frost isn't likely to damage blossoms, and where summers are long, warm, and dry. In less than ideal climates where untimely frosts pose potential problems, select only late-flowering cultivars. Plant on a

Almonds mature inside a fuzzy peachlike fruit.

ALMONDS

north slope, where cold air drains away. Cool, moist summer regions usually don't provide enough heat for ripening fruit.

A mature almond tree is 20 to 30 feet tall and dome shaped with a spread equal to the height. Newly planted trees bear in about 4 years; the productive lifespan is 50 years. Most cultivars need another almond to pollinate them, although some are self-fertile. If you don't have enough room for two trees, dig an extra-large planting hole and plant two almonds close together. See page 146 for training instructions.

Almonds grow best in deep well-drained soil. They're more drought tolerant than other fruit trees, but drought reduces crop quantity and quality. If summer rainfall is light, water thoroughly whenever soil dries to a depth of 3 to 5 inches.

Shot hole and rhizopus fungus can ruin almonds if rains occur in

spring or summer. Navel orange worms can ruin kernels if almonds aren't harvested promptly or if old nuts are left on the tree where worms can overwinter. Mites may attack foliage. Birds are a big problem: They will flock to a heavily fruiting tree.

VARIETIES

■ **'All-in-One':** Blooms mid- to late season; self-fruitful. Use as pollenizer for 'Nonpareil' and 'Texas'.

■ **'Garden Prince':** Flowers in midseason; self-fruitful. Genetic dwarf; grows 10 to 12 feet tall; can be grown in containers.

■ **'Ne Plus Ultra' ('Neplus'):** Flowers very early; avoid in late-frost regions. Pollinate with 'Nonpareil'.

■ **'Nonpareil':** Standard commercial almond; midseason blooms. Adapted to all almond-growing areas but has bud failure in hottest regions. Pollenizers are 'All-in-One', 'Hall', 'Ne Plus Ultra', or 'Texas'.

Castanea species
kas-TAY-nee-a

CHESTNUTS

Chestnuts for home planting include the European chestnut, the Chinese chestnut, and hybrids between European and Chinese that involve the American species. The Japanese chestnut, *C. crenata*, produces a large nut with quality inferior to that of the others.

Chinese chestnut, *C. mollissima*, will grow in regions that produce good peaches; trees are hardy to 15° F. It's slightly susceptible to chestnut blight, but pruning infected branches usually controls the problem. The mature size is 60 feet high with a spread of 40 feet. Compared to the European chestnut, nuts are smaller, drier, and not as highly flavored.

European chestnut (*C. sativa*) can reach 100 feet tall by 100 feet wide, though 40 to 60 feet in both directions is more typical. Its successful range is the same as for its Chinese counterpart except that blight susceptibility rules it out of eastern gardens. Nuts are larger and more flavorful than those of the Chinese species. These are the chestnuts usually sold in markets.

The best soil is deep, well-drained, not alkaline, and reasonably fertile. Chestnuts grow rapidly, start to bear three to five years after planting, and are long-lived. Young trees grow best with regular watering; mature trees need supplementary watering only where summers are hot and dry. If soil is good, trees usually need no fertilizer. For a nut crop, you need another tree as a pollenizer. See page 142 for pruning and training instructions.

Chestnut burrs split open in early fall, releasing one to three nuts. Gather the harvest daily, and dry nuts for a day or two in the sun. Then store them dry at a cool but not freezing temperature.

VARIETIES
- **'Colossal':** One of a few named hybrids, it is sold in the west. The chestnuts are large, flavorful, and peel easily.
- **'Silver Leaf':** This hybrid is so named because the leaves' undersides turn silver at the time of nut fall. Smaller than 'Colossal' but with similar sweet flavor.

Chinese chestnuts bear spiny pods that open to release the crunchy nuts.

Corylus species
COR-i-lus

FILBERTS (HAZELNUTS)

Filberts and hazelnuts are one and the same. Species hail from Europe, North America, and eastern and western Asia. Nut-producing filberts grow into large suckering shrubs that form thickets. They're usually trained to form trees 15 to 25 feet tall.

Filberts offer seasonal interest. Rounded, ruffled leaves are attractive in their green spring and summer phase; in fall they turn clear to rusty yellow. During winter, long male catkins decorate bare branches.

Filberts start to bear at 4 years and have an average 50-year productive lifespan. Choose filbert species and cultivars based on your climate. Female filbert blossoms appear in mid- to late winter or earliest spring, and will be ruined if temperatures drop below 15° F.

Filberts thrive in deep, well-drained, fertile, slightly acid soil. Plant in full sun for best nut production. With regular summer rainfall, filberts need little watering.

Harvest involves picking nuts from the ground after they've been released from their husks. If you want to beat wildlife to the crop, pick nuts as soon as you can twist them in their husks. Nuts aren't fully colored at that time but are completely ripe and color up after picking. Place nuts in the sun to dry for several days before storing in cool but not freezing temperatures. Heavy crops tend to come in alternate years.

EUROPEAN VARIETIES
European filberts have the largest, most flavorful nuts.
- **'Barcelona':** Standard commercial cultivar, also sold for home planting. 'Royal' and 'DuChilly' are pollenizers.
- **'Butler':** Heavy cropper; pollinates 'Barcelona' or 'Ennis'.
- **'Daviana':** Grown to pollinate 'Barcelona', 'DuChilly', and 'Royal'.
- **'DuChilly':** Flavorful, elongated nut; handpick because nuts don't fall freely from the husk.
- **'Ennis':** Like 'Barcelona' but heavier crop with larger nuts.
- **'Royal':** Ripens three to four weeks ahead of all other cultivars.

Hazelnuts ripen inside husks, which split and drop nuts to the ground below.

Carya illinoinensis
KAH-ree-a ill-i-KNOW-een-en-sis

PECANS

At heights of 70 feet or more, with a spread nearly as great, pecans are imposing shade trees. For best nut production, most pecan varieties need another tree nearby as a pollenizer, so getting a pecan crop requires space and commitment.

One word describes the best pecan climate: hot. A pecan tree needs a long summer with hot days and nights to produce fully ripe nuts. Outside of native pecan territory in the southern and south-central United States, the southwest desert regions (with irrigation) offer congenial conditions. In the upper south and central midwest, choose from among the short-season cultivars listed below.

Pecan cultivars fall into two broad groups. The larger and more widely planted of the two is the group often called "papershell" pecans. They are reliably hardy where winter

Pecans ripen inside thick, fleshy husks. Mature nuts don't fall from trees but must be knocked down with a stick.

temperatures fall no lower than 0° F, and for nut production they need a growing season of 270 to 290 days. The second group includes the northern or hardy pecans, which grow in regions where winter lows range from -10° to 10° F; these varieties ripen where the growing season is as short as 170 to 190 days.

Papershell pecans are divided into two categories based on resistance to pecan scab disease, which prevails where summer weather is hot and humid. Eastern varieties are disease-resistant and will grow throughout papershell territory; susceptible western cultivars are limited to desert and dry southwest areas.

Pecans need deep, well-drained soil that is slightly acid (pH 6 to 7 is best). They will not tolerate saline soils, a limitation in some otherwise acceptable desert regions. Within their native range, pecans get plenty of rainfall during the growing season. In dry-summer regions, or where rainfall is skimpy, give trees a deep soaking at least every 14 days so that nuts will fill out well.

See page 148 for pruning and training instructions.

Trees start to bear 5 to 8 years after planting and have a productive life extending at least 70 years beyond that. Harvest time runs from late summer into fall, depending on the variety. Most nuts do not fall free from the tree but have to be knocked free with a long pole.

Where soil is above pH 7 (neutral), zinc deficiency may show in a condition called pecan rosette, clusters of stunted leaves at branch ends. Contact your county or state agricultural agent for the best corrective measures in your area.

Pecan scab is the most serious disease, especially in humid-summer regions. Proper cultivar selection will lessen the problem, though even eastern papershells are not totally immune. Aphids may appear throughout pecan territory. In the

south and southeast, the season's first generation of an insect known as the pecan nut casebearer may damage new shoots; later the second generation may infest the developing nuts. The pecan weevil is the last pest to appear, attacking nearly mature and mature nuts.

EASTERN PAPERSHELL PECANS
- **'Desirable':** Heavy cropper with brittle wood. Pollinate with 'Stuart', 'Cheyenne', or 'Western Schley'.
- **'Mahan':** Produces a very large nut. Pollenizers are 'Cheyenne' or 'Western Schley'.
- **'Stuart':** Large nuts; tree is partially self-fruitful but bears better crops if pollenized by 'Desirable'.

SOUTHEASTERN PAPERSHELL PECANS
- **'Cherokee':** Medium size nut. Pollenizers are 'Mohawk' or 'Wichita'.
- **'Cheyenne':** Medium nut; pollinate with 'Mohawk', 'Sioux', or 'Wichita'.
- **'Kiowa':** Large nut. Pollenizers are 'Cherokee' or 'Cheyenne'.
- **'Mohawk':** Very large nuts; tree is partially self-fruitful but produces better if pollenized by 'Cheyenne' or 'Western Schley'.
- **'Sioux':** Smaller-than-average tree. Pollenizers are 'Cheyenne' or 'Western Schley'.

WESTERN PAPERSHELL PECANS
- **'Western Schley' ('Western'):** Heavy cropper; elongated nuts. Wide soil adaptability; less affected by zinc deficiency. Pollenizers are 'Cheyenne', 'Mohawk', or 'Wichita'.
- **'Wichita':** Highly flavored medium-sized nuts. Weak crotches and brittle wood leave it vulnerable to wind damage; blooms sensitive to late frosts. Pollenizers are 'Cherokee', 'Cheyenne', or 'Western Schley'.

NORTHERN (HARDY) VARIETIES
- **'Major':** Standard pecan in northern gardens. Medium to small nut cracks easily. It needs pollen from a late pollen-shedding cultivar such as 'Colby' or 'Greenriver'.

WALNUTS

Juglans species
JUG-lanz

Most familiar in the marketplace and certainly most important to the home gardener is the so-called English or Persian walnut *(Juglans regia)*, which hails from southeastern Europe and southwestern Asia. The nuts are large, flavorful, and enclosed in relatively thin shells.

The black walnut *(J. nigra)* from the eastern United States is famous for its fine-tasting nut encased in a shell of rocklike hardness. Another eastern tree with a similar reputation is the butternut *(J. cinerea)*. The western states have one important native, *J. hindsii*, the California black walnut; it is valued more as a rootstock on which to graft English walnut cultivars than for its nuts.

English walnuts are fast-growing, heavy-textured trees. The limb structure is thick and sturdy, and mature height may reach 60 feet with a spread to match. These walnuts grow over quite a climatic range, but the key to a successful crop is proper cultivar selection.

Where winter lows are normally -20° to -30° F, plant only those designated as Carpathian walnuts. These are frequently seedling-grown trees (rather than individual varieties), the original stock of which stems from the Carpathian Mountains of Eastern Europe. If late spring frosts are common in your area, choose cultivars that leaf out and shed their pollen late. And if your winters are fairly mild, select one of the cultivars that needs little winter chill. Where summers are hot and humid, the pecan will be a better nut tree to plant because it is not nearly as disease prone as the walnut under those conditions.

Some walnut varieties are self-fruitful, and some need pollenizers, an important distinction if you have room for only one tree. If you are allergy prone, take note that walnut pollen is a well-known allergen.

English walnuts are prized for their tasty fruits. The cultivar 'Eureka' matures late in the growing season.

When planting walnuts, remember that their pollen can be an allergen for many allergy sufferers.

Good soil for English walnuts is fairly deep and definitely well-drained. The trees need regular deep watering for production of top-quality nuts (trees are actually somewhat drought tolerant), but cannot tolerate moist soil continually at the trunk base. Countless old orchard trees have succumbed to crown rot when the orchard has been converted to a subdivision and the trees subjected to lawn watering.

If a walnut and lawn or garden must coexist, it's better to have the tree at the garden margin where routine watering won't reach the trunk. The best watering method for walnuts is basin irrigation beneath the tree's canopy. Form an inner earth ring about a foot out from the trunk to keep water from pooling near the trunk during waterings.

Black walnuts have a thick husk that is difficult to remove and causes very dark stains. These trees also inhibit the growth of various plant species beneath their canopy and in their root zones many feet beyond the spread of the branches.

GROWING AND CARING FOR
Subtropical Fruits

IN THIS CHAPTER

Gallery of Subtropical
Fruits **192**

Subtropical fruits may be grown in a variety of climates when given proper care. The horticultural requirements for each plant are described in the "Adaptation" section of each encyclopedia entry.

It's possible to tend a crop of oranges in virtually any part of the country. In cold regions, beat winter's chill by growing fruit in containers.

Cold tolerance

Each plant has a low-temperature limit. Consult the USDA Plant Hardiness Zone Map on page 211 as a guide to whether a plant will be hardy where you live.

Flowers and fruit of subtropical plants are almost always less hardy than foliage and will usually be damaged if temperatures stay below freezing for very long. But soil insulates roots against cold, so even if the top of a plant is killed, new shoots may sprout the following spring. However, if the plant was grafted, the shoots that do appear likely won't produce the fruit desired.

To encourage hardiness, avoid fertilizing from mid- to late summer. Beyond that are many ways to protect plants from the cold, as shown in the illustrations on page 24.

Heat requirements

Insufficient warmth is another limiting factor to growing subtropical fruits. The usual result is that fruit will not ripen properly. Without enough heat, bananas just hang on the plant without ripening. Citrus won't sweeten. Passionfruit flowers will not set fruit.

Some fruits are also damaged by too much heat. Several plants will not set fruit in the heat of the desert southwest. Many fruits are ruined by sunburn in very hot, arid climates.

Rainfall and humidity

Abundant rainfall and high humidity ease watering chores but also promote fungal and bacterial diseases. On the other hand, lack of humidity may dry out flowers and

Star fruit, *Averrhoa carambola*, earns its name because slices of the fruit are shaped like a five-pointed star. Older trees can withstand temperatures as low as the mid-20s, but younger trees suffer damage in 32° F weather.

Cherimoya trees grow in such a way that they form a natural espalier, but they won't grow in containers.

prevent self-pollination. It is crucial to carefully monitor your subtropical fruits' needs for moisture and then irrigate accordingly.

Sunlight

Almost all subtropical plants must be grown in full sun. Sunlight supplies the energy for manufacturing the sugars that make fruit sweet and delicious. In desert areas, however, many plants benefit from partial shade during the hottest part of the day.

To prevent sunburn, especially on recently pruned plants, paint exposed branches and the trunk with water-based white paint (diluted with water 1:1) or with commercially available tree paints.

Chilling requirements

Several subtropical fruits, including kiwi and figs, require exposure to a certain number of hours of temperatures between 32° and 45° F in winter. This number of hours is known as a plant's chilling requirement.

Insufficient chilling causes slow leaf-out, irregular bloom, and an overall decline in vigor and yields. To achieve maximum chilling, place plants in low spots or areas adjacent to a wall at the bottom of a slope where cool air collects.

Some fruit species have "low-chill" varieties that have been developed for growth in mild winter climates. They need fewer hours of chilling to bear a good crop of fruit.

Soil salts

Most subtropical plants are sensitive to salts. Salty soils are most commonly found in areas with low annual rainfall and alkaline soil, such as portions of the desert southwest. These salts may originate in irrigation water or fertilizer residues. If you suspect that high salt levels are damaging your plants, leach the soil by watering very deeply every third or fourth irrigation. If your soil is both salty and poorly drained, consider growing your subtropical plants in raised beds or containers.

Growing and Caring for Subtropical Fruits
(continued)

Surinam cherry (*Eugenia uniflora*) bears fruit in three weeks from flowering. Mature plants are drought-tolerant and hardy to 22° F.

Climate regions

Subtropical fruits can be grown in four general climate areas: tropical, semitropical, subtropical, and temperate.

Tropical climates

Consistency is a major feature of tropical climates. These regions have no distinct seasons, with abundant rainfall, high humidity, and warm temperatures throughout the year. Many of the fruit described here are native to tropical climates and therefore prefer those consistent conditons.

Semitropical climates

Southern Florida has a typical semitropical climate, and conditions along the Gulf Coast are similar. Humidity and annual rainfall are high, but there are recognizable seasons. Summers are hot, and winters are generally warm with occasional cold spells. During some winters, cold Arctic air flows in, often devastating tender plants.

Subtropical climates

These areas are dramatically different from semitropical regions. Humidity may be very low in inland areas. Rainfall is often concentrated in the winter months and may amount to less than 10 inches a year.

Subtropical climates are generally found in the low-elevation regions of California and Arizona, although with great variation. Southern California and inland desert areas are hot and dry with relatively warm winters. Farther north, winters are colder, rainier, and frosts are common. Frost-free areas exist near the coast, but they are generally cool throughout the year. Inland valleys can be quite warm in summer.

Temperate climates

Temperate climates are found throughout most of the United States. They have well-defined seasons, but their lengths and extremes differ according to latitude and local geographical features. To grow subtropical plants successfully in these climates, you will need to move them to a protected area in the winter.

Passionfruit vine requires a sturdy support.

Microclimates

As described in the previous chapter, localized conditions create distinct microclimates. Modifying the microclimate in your garden can help your subtropical plants thrive.

Sunlight and heat

Take advantage of the ways that solar energy is absorbed and reflected to suit the needs of your subtropicals. It may be desirable or undesirable, depending on where you live, the season, and the plants' requirements. Generally, plant on the southern or western side of your home for maximum heat.

Loose organic mulches store less heat than gravel. Light-colored surfaces reflect more than dark ones, and dark surfaces absorb more heat that can be released later. Planting next to a light-colored wall maximizes the heat a plant receives during the day. Conversely, a plant next to a dark-colored wall stays warmer at night.

Frost protection

To protect subtropicals from the cold, many gardeners plant in containers and move their fruit trees indoors during the winter. Others construct plastic covers to trap heat radiating from the soil.

Most important is recognizing cold spots in the garden and selecting the warmest possible planting site. For example, avoid low spots, where cold air settles. Planting sensitive species next to a south-facing wall or underneath a roof overhang can provide additional protection during cold snaps.

Raising subtropical plants in temperate zones means bringing plants indoors in winter for protection. Place fruit trees in unheated rooms and water sparingly (only when soil is dry) throughout winter. The cold air of an unheated room can meet the plant's chilling requirement.

Once that requirement is met, plants may break bud—while winter is still raging outdoors. Don't panic. Water plants more as growth commences. When night temperatures warm, move plants outside, acclimating them gradually.

Propagating subtropical fruits

There are four primary methods of propagating plants: germinating seed, grafting and budding, rooting cuttings, and air layering. The success of each method varies among species and even among different varieties of the same species.

Savor the luxurious scent of spring in a semitropical clime when you raise orange trees. Waxy blooms exude a rich perfume; fresh fruit is wonderful.

Growing and Caring for Subtropical Fruits
(continued)

You can multiply your tropical fruit trees by raising young starts from cuttings, grafting, or layering.

The most common lemon in Florida and in grocery stores is 'Lisbon'. It adapts well to container culture, especially the dwarf form. They bloom sporadically throughout the year, and fruit matures through winter into early spring, when it's ready to pick.

Growing plants from seed

Most subtropical fruits can be propagated from seed. Because fruit quality and other characteristics are variable in seed-grown plants, however, other propagation methods are often more desirable and prove more advantageous.

Grafting and budding

Budding and grafting involve fusing a piece of stem or a single bud of a selected variety (scion) with a rootstock. The cambium areas (a thin layer of growing tissue beneath the bark) of the scion and the rootstock must be in contact. Formation of a callus at the union between the scion and the rootstock means that the bud or graft is "taking."

Deciduous plants are grafted while dormant. Evergreen plants are usually grafted in spring. High humidity and warm temperatures tend to favor successful grafting.

Budding is probably the easiest grafting method. It can be done whenever the bark is slipping (separating easily from the cambium), usually in the spring. See the illustration, opposite, for details.

Rooting cuttings

Cuttings are short pieces of stem that are removed from a plant and stimulated to form roots. A cutting taken from new growth at the tip of a branch is a softwood cutting; one taken from six- to eight-week-old growth is a semihardwood cutting;

and a section taken from the oldest growth of the current or past season is a hardwood cutting. Subtropical fruits differ in which type of cutting is most effective, so it's important to take cuttings at the right time and from the right place.

Air layering

In this method, a shoot is partially severed from the parent plant and forced to grow roots by being covered with moist sphagnum moss and wrapped in plastic. After the shoot roots into the sphagnum moss, it is completely removed from the parent and planted.

Subtropical fruits in containers

Growing subtropical fruits in containers gives you control over growing conditions. Especially if you live in a cold climate, containers allow you to enjoy subtropical fruits that would not survive outdoors through the winter.

The general requirements for container type, soil mixture, watering, and fertilizing are the same as for growing other types of fruits in containers.

Three other rules are advisable for growing subtropicals in containers: Make smooth transitions between the outdoors and the indoors; maintain high humidity around the plants indoors; and adjust watering, feeding, and lighting care to indoor conditions.

The subtropical plants that are best adapted to container growing include banana, dwarf citrus, feijoa, fig, guava, loquat, and passionfruit.

ROOTING SOFTWOOD AND SEMIHARDWOOD CUTTINGS

1. Remove leaves from bottom 3 inches of cutting.

2. Slice a strip of bark from each side of base.

3. Dip end of cutting in rooting hormone and plant in rooting medium.

4. Cover with plastic to maintain humidity.

WHIP-GRAFTING

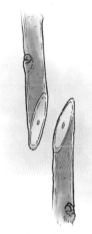

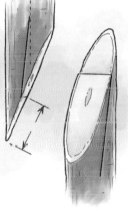

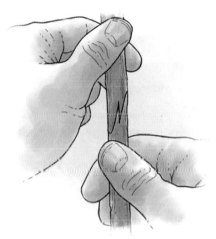

1. Cut scion and stock at same angle.

2. Make slits in cut ends, starting a third of the way from point and angling toward center.

3. Join so they lock with cambium layers in contact. Tape together to hold pieces in place.

T-BUDDING AND SHIELD BUDDING

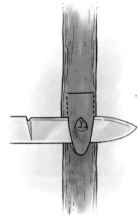

1. Remove bud by cutting from ½ inch below bud to a cut ¾ inch above bud.

2. Make a T-shaped cut in stock and separate flaps.

3. Insert the bud into cut until the top is even with top of "T" and wrap with tape.

4. Cut stock above bud after 6 to 8 weeks when the bud has sprouted.

GALLERY OF
Subtropical Fruits

Subtropical fruits lend themselves to fresh eating but also to all sorts of desserts and preserves.

The following encyclopedia describes a variety of subtropical fruit, some familiar, some uncommon. Most are damaged by temperatures near zero, and best regions are listed. In marginal areas, choose hardy varieties and plant them in areas protected from cold.

The individual entries describe the plant's growth habit and ornamental quality and provide information on adaptation, pollination, propagation, site selection, care, and harvesting and storing the fruit.

As with other fruits, unless a plant breeds true from seed, selected varieties should always be your first choice to assure you will get superior fruit quality or a specific growing adaptation.

Like other fruits, subtropical fruits are either self-fruitful or self-unfruitful. In the absence of natural pollinators, some fruit must be hand pollinated. For more information on pollination, see page 120.

AVOCADO

- **Growth habit:** Evergreen tree, 20–60 feet high, 25–35 feet wide. Moderate growth rate.
- **Adaptation:** Hardiness varies according to variety. Specific varieties recommended for Florida, California, Hawaii.
- **Harvest season:** Variable.
- **Begins bearing:** Grafted plants; 2–3 years; seedlings; 8–12 years.
- **Recommended varieties:** California: 'Anaheim' (A), 'Fuerte' (B), 'Hass' (A), 'Jim' (B), 'Mexicola' (A), 'Nabal' (B), 'Pinkerton' (A), 'Reed' (A), 'Zutano' (B). Florida: 'Booth 7', 'Brogdin', 'Choquette', 'Gainesville', 'Hall', 'Lula', 'Mexicola', 'Monroe', 'Pollock', 'Simmonds', 'Tonnage', 'Waldin'. Hawaii: 'Beardslee', 'Case', 'Chang', 'Frowe', 'Greengold', 'Hayes', 'Kahaluu', 'Masami', 'Murashige', 'Nishikawa', 'Ohata', 'Sharwil'. Dwarf varieties: 'Gwen' (A), 'Little Cado' (B), 'Whitsell', 'Yamagata' (B).
(Letters in parentheses indicate pollination habit. In California, combine A and B types for maximum yields.)

Avocados are large trees that provide an abundant harvest of rich, buttery fruit. Mexican and Guatemalan avocados and their hybrids are best adapted to California and the southeast. West Indian varieties do best in south Florida and Hawaii. Mexican varieties are hardier and the fruit has smoother, thinner, shiny green or black skin. Guatemalan avocados require frost-free climates and bear blackish-green fruit with a thick, bumpy rind. West Indian varieties are the most frost sensitive and have thin, smooth greenish-yellow skin.

Avocado trees can become quite large under ideal growing conditions, living 20 or more years. Mature foliage is deep green and leathery. New growth is coppery red. Mexican-variety leaves smell like anise; flowers are borne in clusters.

ADAPTATION

Avocados are widely grown in the mild-winter areas of Florida, California, and Hawaii. Some hardier varieties can grow in cooler parts of northern and inland California and along the Gulf Coast.

POLLINATION

Most avocados are self-fruitful, though they are classified as having two types of flowers. In California combining varieties with different flower types can increase yields. But a single tree will produce enough fruit for most families.

PROPAGATION

Avocado seeds usually germinate, but a seedling won't bear fruit for years, and the quality will likely be inferior. Use seedlings as rootstocks for grafting your own tree. Seedlings are ready to graft when they reach ¼ to ⅜ inch in diameter. In spring obtain budwood from dormant terminal growth that's starting to swell. Remove leaves to keep the wood from drying out.

SITE SELECTION AND PLANTING

Plant avocados in full sun in deep, well-drained soil with a pH 5.5 to 6.5. The tree will need room to spread. Plant in spring, setting the crown slightly higher than it was in the nursery pot to allow for settling.

CARE

Watering: Too much water is as dangerous as not enough. Feeder roots concentrate in the top 15 inches of soil. Let this zone dry before watering mature trees. In dry climates, water deeply every two to four weeks; young trees require more. Organic mulch, 3 to 6 inches deep and kept 12 inches away from the trunk, helps keep feeder roots cool.

Fertilizing: Apply small amounts of a complete fertilizer spring through summer. In cold climates do not fertilize after late summer to allow the trees to become cold hardy.

Pruning: Avocados require little pruning. Shape when young; faithfully remove dead branches.

Pests and diseases: Avocado root rot is a major disease in California. Select disease-free certified plants; avoid planting where avocados once grew. The disease is transported by equipment, tools, and shoes from infected soils. In the humid southeast, fungus diseases such as scab, anthracnose, and powdery mildew are common.

HARVEST AND STORAGE

Knowing when to pick an avocado can be tricky. 'Fuerte' requires 8 to 10 months to ripen, but 'Hass' needs 13 to 14 months. Some varieties can be stored on the tree for 9 to 20 weeks; others have only 6 to 8 weeks of peak flavor. Avocados should be picked when mature but still hard and ripened off the tree.

Dark varieties turn from green to black when mature. Green varieties develop a yellowish tinge. When ripe the fruit feels soft under gentle pressure. A dark brown paper-thin seed coat signifies a mature fruit.

The secret to raising avocado crops is twofold: having good soil drainage and knowing when to pick the fruit.

Hybrids of *Musa acuminata* and
M. balbisiana

*MEW-sa a-kew-mi-NA-ta and
MEW-sa ball-bih-zee-AY-na*

- **Growth habit:** Fast-growing, herbaceous perennial 5–25 feet high, huge leaves. Spreads by underground rhizomes.
- **Adaptation:** Freezing temperatures kill foliage; rhizomes are hardy to 22° F. Requires ample fertilizer, water, heat. Dwarf varieties available.
- **Harvest season:** 4–8 months after flowering.
- **Begins bearing:** 12–18 months after planting.
- **Recommended varieties:** Some varieties are bred for specific climates; many are known by different regional names. Top dwarf variety recommendations for home gardeners in North America: 'Apple', 'Chinese', 'Dwarf Brazilian', 'Gold Finger', 'Ice Cream', 'Largo', 'Rajapuri', 'Valery', 'Walha', and 'Williams'.

Bananas are herbaceous perennials arising from underground rhizomes. The fleshy stalks sheathed with

Banana trees are shallowly rooted plants. Provide wind protection to prevent toppling.

BANANA

huge, broad leaves can rise 5 to 25 feet in as little as six months. Each stalk produces one huge flower cluster, which develops fruit, then dies. New stalks then grow from the rhizome. Fruit size and flavor vary, but most home garden varieties are 4 to 8 inches long and very sweet.

ADAPTATION
Bananas grow best with uniform warmth, requiring 10 to 15 months of frost-free conditions to produce a flower stalk. Fruit takes 4 to 8 months to mature. All but the hardiest varieties stop growing when the temperature drops below 53° F.

Freezing temperatures will kill a banana to the ground, however, the underground rhizome will usually survive to 22° F.

In most areas bananas require wind protection because they are susceptible to being blown over.

POLLINATION
Bananas develop without pollination. The plant produces a long flower stalk with rows of female flowers called "hands." The fruit, or "fingers," begin to develop at the base of the stalk, eventually curving upward. Once bananas appear, you can cut off the bottom male bloom, or "tail."

SITE SELECTION AND PLANTING
Bananas are usually sold as semidormant rhizomes. Plant rhizomes close to the surface of rich, well-drained soil with pH between 5.5 and 6.5 in full sun.

CARE
Watering: Regular deep watering is absolutely necessary during warm weather. Do not let plants dry out, but don't overwater, which can cause root rot. Use an organic mulch to conserve moisture and protect the shallow roots.

Fertilizing: Bananas are heavy feeders. Apply balanced fertilizer once a month, keeping it away from the trunk.

Pruning: Only one primary stem on each rhizome should be allowed to

Bananas require 4 to 8 months to ripen. Remove the stalk from the plant when the first fruits turn yellow.

fruit; remove other shoots. Once the main stalk is six to eight months old, let one sucker develop as a replacement growing and fruiting stalk for the following season.

When the fruit is harvested, cut the fruiting stalk back to 30 inches above the ground. Remove the stub several weeks later. Dispose of cut stems to prevent disease.

Pests and diseases: Bananas have few troublesome pests or diseases outside tropical countries.

HARVEST AND STORAGE
Bananas carried on the plant through the winter will mature quickly in warmer weather. In cooler areas covering fruit clusters with plastic can help hasten maturity.

Bananas must be ripened off the plant, or the fruit may split. But bananas acquire most of their nutrients and sugars in the month prior to maturity, so don't pick too early. When hands at the top of the stalk begin to turn yellow, cut the entire stalk.

A mature stalk of bananas can be stored at 55° F for 1 to 2 weeks; do not refrigerate.

Annona cherimola
a-NO-na chair-a-MO-la

- **Growth habit:** Briefly deciduous tree or large shrub 15–25 feet high by 15–20 feet wide.
- **Adaptation:** Hardy to 29° F. Best adapted to the cooler, dry-summer climates characteristic of southern California.
- **Harvest season:** February through April.
- **Begins bearing:** 2–5 years after planting.
- **Recommended varieties:** 'Bays', 'Booth', 'Chaffey', 'Deliciosa', 'El Bumpo', 'Honeyhart', 'Mariella', 'McPherson', 'Ott', 'Pierce', 'Sabor', 'Spain', 'Villa Park', and 'White'.

Cherimoyas have an unusual appearance—something like an artichoke crossed with a pineapple—and a delightful flavor: hints of pineapple, banana, and papaya, wrapped up in a custardy texture. They are best served chilled, cut in half, and eaten with a spoon.

The cherimoya is also an attractive tree, with leaves that are dull green on top and velvety green on the bottom. It can be pruned as a spreading multitrunked tree 15 to 20 feet high or as an erect tree growing 25 feet high.

ADAPTATION

Cherimoyas grow best in areas with moderately warm summers and low relative humidity where winter temperatures drop below 45° F but not below freezing. Winters should provide some chilling (between 50 and 100 hours) but be relatively frost-free. Southern California provides the best growing conditions in the United States. In the tropical lowlands of Florida and Hawaii, the atemoya is a better choice.

POLLINATION

Hand pollination is necessary to ensure fruit production in the United States, because the insect pollinator of the cherimoya is not found here.

CHERIMOYA

The plants flower over a long period in midsummer, so pollination every couple of days during bloom can extend the harvest over the course of several months.

SITE SELECTION AND PLANTING

Cherimoyas prefer full sun and deep well-drained soil with a pH between 6 and 7.

CARE

Watering: Cherimoyas need plenty of moisture while they are growing actively but should not be watered when dormant.

Fertilizing: Fertilize cherimoyas regularly. Apply about 2 ounces of a balanced fertilizer to young trees each month during the growing season until midsummer. Increase applications by an ounce each year until trees begin to bear fruit.

Pruning: Cherimoyas have rather brittle wood. Prune during the dormant period to develop strong branches that can support the heavy fruit. Also, prune to encourage new growth and fruiting near the center of the tree.

Pests and diseases: Cherimoyas have few troublesome problems under good growing conditions.

HARVEST AND STORAGE

Cherimoyas develop a pale green to yellow color as they reach maturity. Pick when firm and allow to soften at room temperature. Ripe fruit will deteriorate quickly but can be frozen and eaten like ice cream.

CHERIMOYA RELATIVES

Relatives of the cherimoya also produce delicious fruit.

The sweetsop, or sugar apple, *Annona squamosa*, is similar to the cherimoya but better adapted to Florida. It is not hardy below 29° F.

The atemoya is a hybrid of the cherimoya and the sweetsop. It is most widely planted in Florida.

The soursop (*Annona muricata*) is a smaller, less-hardy tree than the sweetsop. It will usually be damaged if temperatures drop below 30° F.

Enjoy cherimoya fresh off the tree, or freeze it for later, eating it like ice cream.

Citus or Fortunella
SIT-rus or *for-tew-NEL-la*

- **Growth habit:** Varies by species and variety. Most are evergreen shrubs or trees from 8 to more than 20 feet tall.
- **Adaptation:** Primary areas are California valleys, California and Arizona low deserts, Texas and the Gulf Coast, and Florida.
- **Harvest season:** Mainly late October through April, depending on variety and growing area. Some varieties ripen later.
- **Begins bearing:** 3–4 years for grafted trees; full production in 7–8 years for standard trees.

Citrus plants are among the most rewarding for home gardeners. Fragrant and attractive ornamentals, they offer great diversity. Mature plants range in size from small

CITRUS

shrubs to large trees. Foliage shape and texture and fruit size, color, and flavor are tremendously variable.

ADAPTATION

Climate variations affect citrus drastically. The lowest temperature at which growth occurs is 55° F; the highest is approximately 100° F. Optimum temperature for orange growth is between 70° and 90° F. Citrus hardiness differs according to species and sometimes variety. Gardeners in marginal citrus areas select early-maturing varieties, which usually ripen before the first frost.

Citrus also have specific heat requirements. All grapefruit varieties require long, hot growing seasons to reach peak quality and sweetness. Lemons probably have the lowest heat requirement and can be grown in California's cool coastal areas.

Citrus varieties are recommended according to the following areas.

California valleys: Southern California is a traditional citrus area. Northern California has frost-free areas, but along the coast summers are too cool for many varieties; more are adapted to the inland areas.

California and Arizona deserts: These low-elevation areas have extremely hot summers, warm winters, strong sunlight, and gusty winds. Varieties with high heat requirements are best here.

Texas and the Gulf Coast: Usually hot and humid with some rainfall year-round; western Texas is drier and warmer. Cold Arctic air is common in winter, so select hardy early types that ripen before winter.

Florida: This hot, humid region has many frost-free areas, although occasionally a freeze will devastate citrus throughout the state. Rainfall is spread throughout the year.

CLIMATIC EFFECTS

Climate influences citrus in the following ways.

Bloom: Trees flower earliest in hot, humid areas and latest in cool, semiarid coastal areas.

Maturity: Fruit grown in a hot area ripens before fruit of the same variety grown in a cooler area.

Fruit size: Fruit is usually largest in hot, humid climates, becoming progressively smaller in hot, arid climates and cool, arid climates.

Peel characteristics: Peels are thin and smooth in hot, humid Florida and Texas. In the arid west they are thicker with a rougher texture.

Color development: In tropical areas citrus remain green when ripe. The most intense color develops in arid climates of the west, where low temperatures prevail for several weeks before harvest.

Juice content: Citrus fruits are juiciest when grown in hot, humid climates and less juicy in regions that are hot and arid or cool and humid.

Flavor: Fruit grown in arid climates with a cold period before maturity has more acid and a better balance between sugars and acids than those grown in humid climates. Fruit from arid areas usually has richer flavor.

Tree habit: Trees grow fastest in hot, humid climates and slowest in cooler areas. Trees in colder climates are usually more compact.

POLLINATION

Most citrus are self-fruitful, but some produce more fruit when pollenized by another variety. Others develop more seeds when pollinated.

Citrus fruit shape (*above*) runs the gamut from tidy spherical orbs to ovals and fountains of finger-like projections. Fruit size can be marble-like or hefty and huge, as large as a softball.

PROPAGATION

Most citrus are propagated by budding the desired variety to a specific rootstock. These trees are reliably true to type, come into production sooner, and benefit from desirable rootstock effects, such as disease resistance, cold tolerance, dwarfing, better fruit quality, or early maturity.

SITE SELECTION AND PLANTING

Citrus trees are usually sold in containers but are sometimes balled and burlapped. Trees purchased by mail may be shipped bare-root. Ideal planting time is early spring, after frost danger has passed. Soil pH should be between 6 and 7.

All citrus prefer full sun, but in desert climates, shade during the hottest part of the day prevents sunburned fruit. In cool climates plant in the warmest possible microclimate.

CARE

Watering: Citrus trees need adequate soil moisture for healthy growth and good fruit production. Plant in well-drained soil; water regularly during dry periods.

Fertilizing: Citrus trees need regular fertilization. The number of applications depends on the region; consult an extension agent or nursery for recommendations. Foliar sprays can help overcome soil micronutrient deficiencies.

Pruning: Citrus trees don't require pruning and are usually allowed to develop on their own. Prune to control size, remove deadwood, and keep centers open.

Pests and diseases: Vigorously growing trees have few problems, but they may occasionally become infested with mites, scale, thrips, or whiteflies. Trees in poorly drained soils often succumb to diseases and cankers of the roots or trunk.

HARVEST AND STORAGE

The only sure way to determine maturity is to taste the fruit. Many fruits have fully colored rinds months before they can be eaten.

Lemons, limes, and other acid citrus are an exception. They can be picked whenever they reach acceptable size and juice content.

Once mature, most citrus fruits can be left on the tree several weeks. Most can be stored in the refrigerator for two to three weeks.

TYPES OF CITRUS

Citron: Citrons (*Citrus medica*) are large, thick-skinned fruit resembling lemons. Trees are scraggly and very frost sensitive, sometimes grown as a novelty or for ceremonies associated with the Jewish holiday *Sukkot*. 'Etrog' is the most common variety, but the fingered citron, or 'Buddha's Hand', is grown as an ornamental for its unusual shape. Only a citron's thick rind is used—candied, for flavoring, and in marmalades.

Grapefruit and hybrids: Grapefruit trees are large with big leaves. The fruit needs a long, hot growing season to reach peak quality. Because fruits can hang on trees for long periods without deteriorating, they can attain good flavor in cooler areas. Pink and white grapefruit have the same flavor, but seedy fruits have richer flavor and separate into segments more easily than seedless kinds. 'Oroblanco' and 'Melogold' are sweet hybrids between grapefruit and pummelo that need less heat to ripen.

Kumquats and their hybrids: Kumquats are hardy species of *Fortunella*. Trees can get large on vigorous rootstocks but are usually small and compact—ideal for pots. Because they're hardy (to 18° F), kumquats have been hybridized with other citrus, such as oranges (orangequats) and limes (limequats).

Kumquats are usually preserved and used whole as garnishes or made into marmalade. They're tasty eaten fresh. Kumquat hybrids range in sweetness; orangequat is the sweetest; limequat is very tart.

Lemon: Lemon trees can reach over 20 feet high. They respond well to pruning; cut them regularly to keep

A limequat bears fruits that are tart like limes on kumquat-hardy trees.

fruit easy to reach. Lemons are best adapted to western states, where fruits remain small and trees are less likely to be infected with disease. In hot, humid climates limes are preferred. In coastal California, lemons bear several crops a year. In warmer areas, fruit is picked from fall through winter.

The 'Meyer' lemon isn't a true lemon but a popular substitute. The tree is compact, hardier than regular lemons, and bears for years in pots. 'Improved Meyer' is a virus-free form that has replaced the original clone.

Lime: Limes can be divided into two groups: the small-fruited 'Mexican', West Indian, or Key lime and the large-fruited Persian or 'Tahiti' lime. The 'Mexican' lime is the most important commercial variety and is referred to as the bartender's lime. The deep green fruit is borne on small, thorny, frost sensitive trees. Persian limes are a few degrees hardier and more compact. Fruits are lighter green with a good lime flavor. 'Bearss' is the common variety.

Lemon trees grow fast and tall. Prune often to keep fruit within picking reach.

'Mexican' lime is known as bartender's lime.

In hot climates easy-to-peel tangelos yield lots of juicy fruit.

'Ruby' blood orange often develops a red blush on its rind.

'Valencia' oranges are grown worldwide for juice and eating.

Blood oranges produce a refreshing red juice.

'Chinotto' or 'Myrtle-leaf' is a type of sour orange

The sweetest of the mandarin varieties are the namesake.

Eat honey tangerines fresh for explosive flavor.

In California, lemons bear several crops per year.

Grafted kumquats thrive in containers, yielding tasty fruit.

A 'Temple' orange is actually a tangor, a mandarin orange.

The thick rind of citron is used in marmalade.

'Satsuma' mandarin is one of the hardiest citrus grown.

West Indian limes are highly aromatic, preferred for marmalades and the famous Key lime pie. Juicy Persian limes are suited for making limeade and marinades. If sliced very thin, they can be eaten, rind and all.
Mandarins and their hybrids:
These are often called kid-glove or loose-skin oranges because they're

Blood oranges serve up a berrylike juice that plainly reflects the name.

so easy to peel. Foliage is hardier than that of an orange, but fruit isn't. Flavor varies from sweet to spicy.

Choose mandarin varieties carefully, and you can harvest from November to April or May. Fruit won't hold on the tree as well as oranges. Some mandarin varieties set more fruit if pollinated by another variety planted nearby.

■ **Tangelos:** Tangelos are hybrids of mandarins with grapefruits or pummelos. Fruits vary tremendously in color and size, and flavors are all distinctive, aromatic, and rich. Most are best adapted to hot climates.

■ **Tangors:** Tangors are hybrids between mandarins and oranges, with the flavor varying between orange and mandarin. Trees are about as hardy as oranges and are slightly smaller. Tangors are best adapted to Florida.

Although varieties differ, the sweetest of the mandarin group

are the mandarins themselves. Mandarins, tangelos, and tangors are best when heavy and full of juice.

Orange: Oranges can be sour or sweet. Sweet oranges are divided into three types: blood oranges, common oranges, and navel oranges.

■ **Blood orange:** Under certain climate conditions, blood oranges develop pink or red flesh, juice, and rind. They have a distinctive, berrylike flavor. Some varieties have smaller, more-compact trees than most sweet oranges.

■ **Common orange:** Common oranges are divided into two groups: those best adapted to the southwest and those best adapted to the southeast. 'Valencia', the most widely grown variety, is an exception; it's widely planted throughout the commercial citrus areas of the world. Common oranges are usually used to make fresh juice. Trees are generally about the same size as navels.

■ **Navel orange:** Navel oranges have an undeveloped secondary fruit opposite the stem end. As this fruit enlarges, it forms the small hole or navel. 'Washington' is the most widely planted; 'Cara Cara' has pink flesh. All navel oranges are best adapted to intermediate climates of California. Standard navel oranges reach 16 to 20 feet high; sports are smaller and slower growing.

Sour orange: Sour oranges are very bitter; they are used to make marmalades and liqueurs. Trees are often planted as ornamentals for their clean foliage, bright fruit, and fragrant flowers.

Pummelo: Larger than grapefruit, pummelos are more popular in Asia. Varieties offer white or pink flesh that's firmer, sweeter, and less acidic and juicy than grapefruit. Eat them peeled and segmented with membranes removed. Trees grow 15 to 18 feet high and wide.

RECOMMENDED CITRUS VARIETIES

FL = FLORIDA; GC = GULF COAST; DS = DESERTS; CA = CALIFORNIA

NAVEL ORANGE: 'Cara Cara' (FL, GC, DS, CA), 'Lane Late' (CA), 'Robertson' (DS, CA), 'Washington' (FL, GC, CA, DS)

COMMON ORANGE: 'Diller' (FL, GC), 'Hamlin' (FL, GC, DS), 'Marrs' (FL, GC, DS), 'Parson Brown' (FL, GC, DS), 'Pineapple' (FL, GC, DS), 'Shamouti' (DS, CA), 'Trovita' (DS, CA), 'Valencia' (FL, GC, DS, CA)

BLOOD ORANGE: 'Moro' (FL, GC, DS, CA), 'Sanguinelli' (FL, GC, DS, CA), 'Tarocco' (DS, CA)

SOUR ORANGE: 'Chinotto' (FL, GC, DS, CA), 'Seville' (FL, GC, DS, CA)

MANDARIN ORANGE: 'Ambersweet' (FL, CA, GC), 'Calamondin' (FL, GC, DS, CA), 'Changsha' (GC), 'Clementine' (FL, GC, CA), 'Dancy' (FL, GC, CA, DS), 'Encore' (FL, GC, DS, CA), 'Fairchild' (GC, DS, CA), 'Honey' (FL, GC, DS, CA), 'Kara' (CA), 'Kinnow' (DS, CA), 'Page' (FL, GC, DS, CA), 'Pixie' (CA), 'Satsuma' (FL, GC, CA)

LEMON: 'Eureka' (DS, CA), 'Improved Meyer' (FL, GC, DS, CA), 'Lisbon' (DS, CA), 'Ponderosa' (FL, GC, DS, CA)

LIME: 'Bearss' (FL, GC, DS, CA), 'Mexican' (FL, GC, DS, CA), 'Rangpur' (FL, GC, DS, CA)

GRAPEFRUIT: 'Duncan' (FL, GC), 'Flame' (FL, GC), 'Marsh' (FL, GC, DS, CA), 'Melogold' (DS, CA), 'Oroblanco' (DS, CA), 'Redblush' (FL, GC, DS, CA), 'Rio Red' (FL, DS, GC, CA), 'Star Ruby' (FL, DS, CA)

KUMQUAT: 'Nagami' (FL, GC, DS, CA), 'Meiwa' (FL, GC, DS, CA)

LIMEQUAT: 'Eustis' (FL, GC, DS, CA), 'Tavares' (FL, GC, DS, CA)

ORANGEQUAT: 'Nippon' (FL, GC, DS, CA)

PUMMELO: 'Chandler' (FL, GC, DS, CA)

TANGELO: 'Minneola' (FL, GC, DS, CA), 'Orlando' (FL, GC, DS)

TANGOR: 'Temple' (FL, DS), 'Murcott' (FL, CA)

Feijoa sellowiana
fay-YO-a sell-oh-ee-AY-na

- **Growth habit:** Slow-growing evergreen shrub that can reach 15 feet high and 15 feet wide.
- **Adaptation:** Prefers cool winters and moderate summers but generally adapted to areas where temperatures stay above 15° F.
- **Harvest season:** September through November.
- **Begins bearing:** Grafted or cutting-grown plants require 2–3 years; seedlings, which have unpredictable fruit quality, take 4–6 years.
- **Recommended varieties:** 'Apollo', 'Choiceana', 'Coolidge', 'Edenvale Improved Coolidge', 'Edenvale Late', 'Edenvale Supreme', 'Gemini', 'Magnifica', 'Mammoth', 'Nazemetz Pineapple Gem', 'Superba', 'Trask', 'Triumph'.

Feijoa earns its keep by virtue of its striking flowers, which open in spring. The petals are edible and fruity.

FEIJOA, PINEAPPLE GUAVA

The feijoa is an attractive shrub that bears delicious fruit with an unusual and refreshing pineapple-mint flavor. The leaves are soft green on top and silvery underneath. In late spring the shrub is covered with inch-wide white flowers with scarlet stamens.

The fruit is best when fresh, simply cut in half and eaten with a spoon. The seeds are very small and edible, and the flower petals are a refreshing addition to spring salads. The feijoa is high in both acid and pectin and makes excellent jellies and preserves.

ADAPTATION

Feijoas are widely adapted to areas of the west and southeast where winter temperatures do not fall below 15° F. The best fruit is produced in areas with moderate summers and cool winters. A small amount of winter chilling (between 100 and 200 hours) ensures abundant bloom.

Even though the plants are relatively hardy, frosts can be damaging. Spring frost damage is most likely in mild-winter areas, where the plants are not completely hardened off and respond to warm spells by blooming early.

PROPAGATION

The seeds of the feijoa germinate easily, but seedlings grow slowly and rarely produce quality fruit. Success with cuttings differs among varieties. Grafting methods and layering are sometimes successful.

SITE SELECTION AND PLANTING

Feijoa fruit quality declines if the temperature regularly exceeds 100° F. When the ripe fruits fall to the ground (a sign of peak quality), they spoil rapidly at high temperatures. To protect the fruit, choose a planting site away from hot, reflected sun. In desert areas, plant feijoas where they will receive partial shade during the hottest part of the day.

Feijoas will grow in a wide variety of soils, but they prefer well-drained soil with pH between 5.5 and 7.0.

Discerning when feijoa fruit is ripe for picking and eating is easy: It drops from the tree.

CARE

Watering: Feijoa can survive considerable drought, but lack of water will cause fruit drop. For quality harvests, water deeply on a regular basis and mulch around the plants to protect the shallow roots.

Fertilizing: Feijoa plants grow slowly and require only light applications of a complete fertilizer, if anything.

Pruning: Pruning is not required to keep plants productive, but light pruning in the summer after the fruit is harvested will encourage new growth and increase yields the following year. When grown as a hedge, the feijoa responds well to heavy pruning or shearing, but this does reduce flower and fruit production.

Pests and diseases: Feijoas rarely have any serious problems.

HARVEST AND STORAGE

The best way to tell when feijoa fruit are fully ripe is to let them fall from the tree. To keep the fruit clean and unbruised, place a tarp or large cloth under the tree to catch them as they fall. Gather them daily once they begin to drop. Feijoas can also be picked when firm and mature. Allow them to ripen at room temperature.

FIG

- **Growth habit:** Deciduous tree. Can reach 60 feet but usually grows 15–30 feet high. Wide spreading. Can be maintained at almost any size with pruning.
- **Adaptation:** Hardy to 12°–15° F if fully dormant. Best fruit quality in hot, dry climates. Chilling requirement less than 300 hours.
- **Harvest season:** Often two crops: one in late spring, another in fall.
- **Begins bearing:** Early, often first year after planting.
- **Recommended varieties:** 'Adriatic', 'Alma', 'Black Mission', 'Blanche', 'Brown Turkey', 'Celeste', 'Conadria', 'Everbearing', 'Genoa', 'Kadota', 'King', 'LSU Everbearing', 'LSU Gold' 'LSU Purple', 'Magnolia', 'Osborne Prolific', 'Panachee', 'Pasquale', 'Verte'.

Fig trees have muscular, twisting silvery-gray branches that spread wider than they grow tall. Leaves are large (4 to 10 inches long) and bright green. The fig is called a fruit, but it's really a cluster of fleshy outside-in flowers. Each flower can develop into a seed if pollinated.

Figs are easy to grow and productive with or without heavy pruning. Even if the plant freezes to the ground in winter, it can spring back and bear fruit the next summer. Figs also grow well in pots.

There are four types of fig: common, Caprifig, Smyrna, and San Pedro. Only the common fig sets two crops of fruit without pollination. The first, or breba, crop is borne in spring on last season's growth. The second, or main, crop is borne in fall on new growth. In cold climates spring frosts may destroy the breba crop.

Caprifigs and Smyrna figs are uncommon because pollination requires a wasp not found in North America. San Pedro figs produce a breba crop without pollination and will grow where summers are cool.

ADAPTATION

Figs are best adapted to areas with long, hot summers. Some varieties require less heat to ripen fruit and can be grown in cooler climates with short summers given careful site selection and good mulching.

Because of low chill requirements, figs may break dormancy during warm spells in winter or early spring, only to be damaged when cold weather returns. Figs adapt well to hot, dry desert climates, surviving periods of drought. But fruit quality is better with regular irrigation.

In the southeast, the dried fruit beetle is a pest, so grow varieties that have a closed eye. The eye is the small hole in the plump end of a fig through which the flowers are pollinated. If the dried fruit beetle gets in, the fruit is ruined.

PROPAGATION

Figs are easily propagated from dormant hardwood cuttings. Select fully mature one-year-old shoots, ⅜ to ⅝ inch in diameter, 8 to 12 inches long. Bury them upright in soil, leaving one node exposed. By spring the ends of cuttings should have white callus growth. Transplanted or left in place, new plants should be established by summer's end.

SITE SELECTION AND PLANTING

Choose a planting site with full sun and well-drained soil. Figs tolerate a variety of soils except salty or alkaline. In areas with short, cool summers, espalier trees against a light-colored south-facing wall.

CARE

Established fig trees survive with minimum watering, fertilizing, and pruning. For a top-quality harvest, however, a little of each is advisable.

Watering: Water young fig trees regularly until fully established. In dry climates water mature trees

Fresh figs must ripen on the tree; they won't ripen after picking.

deeply every week or two. Southern gardeners need to water only in dry spells. Mulch the soil around trees.

Fertilizing: As a general rule, fertilize fig trees if branches grow less than a foot during the previous year. Consult a nursery or extension agent for recommendations.

Pruning: Prune young trees to establish a framework. After that, prune occasionally to remove deadwood and to keep trees from becoming overgrown. Thin to keep inner branches productive.

Mature fig trees can be espaliered or pruned heavily for size control without sacrificing the main crop if pruned when dormant. Dormant-season pruning removes flower buds and reduces the breba crop, thereby increasing the main crop.

Pests and diseases: Aside from fruit flies, which infest fruit with open eyes in the southeast, figs have very few diseases or pests.

HARVEST AND STORAGE

Figs must ripen on the tree before they're picked. They won't ripen if picked when immature. A ripe fruit is slightly soft and starting to bend at the neck. Fresh figs don't keep well; store in the refrigerator for only two to three days. Store dried figs for six to eight months. The milky sap of fig trees irritates the skin of some people. Wear a long-sleeved shirt and gloves while harvesting.

GUAVA

Psidium species
SID-i-um

- **Growth habit:** Evergreen shrubs to small trees, 10–25 feet high.
- **Adaptation:** Various.
- **Harvest Season:** Spring to fall; some ripen year-round.
- **Begins bearing:** 2–3 years.
- **Recommended varieties:** Tropical varieties: 'Detwiler', 'Hawaiian Pear', 'Hong Kong Pink', 'Indonesian Seedless', 'Lucknow 49', 'Mexican Cream', 'Red Indian', 'Ruby', 'Supreme', 'Turnbull', 'White Indian'. Juice varieties: 'Beaumont', 'Ka Hua Kula', 'Waiakea'.

Many homeowners raise strawberry guava for its ornamental qualities as well as its tasty fruit. Strawberry guava trees are hardy to slightly below freezing.

There are two types of guavas: the tropical guava (*Psidium guajava*) and the strawberry, or Cattley, guava (*Psidium cattleianum*). Both types are attractive evergreen plants with shedding bark and fragrant flowers, but they differ in size, fruit quality, and adaptation.

Varieties of tropical guava differ quite a bit in flavor, but most have a musky aroma. They are borne on large shrubs or small trees that can reach 20 to 25 feet high.

Strawberry guavas rarely exceed 10 to 15 feet high and come in red and yellow-fruited varieties. Favored as ornamentals, their glossy deep green leaves frame brightly colored fruit and sweetly fragrant white flowers.

Guavas have a high vitamin content and can be eaten fresh or juiced. They are rich in pectin and used in jellies and preserves.

ADAPTATION

The tropical guava is best adapted to the warm, humid climates of Florida and Hawaii; it can be grown in coastal southern California. It is sensitive to frost. The strawberry guava is a hardier plant, able to withstand temperatures as low as 24° F. Plants are adapted to California and southern Texas but do poorly in hot desert or interior areas.

POLLINATION

Guavas are primarily self-fruitful, although some strains produce more fruit when cross-pollinated with another variety. They bloom throughout the year in mild-winter areas but most heavily at the onset of warm spring. Because flowers are produced on the current season's growth, pruning can help to stimulate flowering.

SITE SELECTION AND PLANTING

Both types of guava prefer full sun and well-drained soil with pH between 5 and 7.

CARE

Guavas are one of the easiest tropical plants to grow.

Watering: Guavas are most productive with regular deep watering. The strawberry guava can withstand brief periods of drought.

Fertilizing: Tropical guavas are fast growers and heavy feeders and benefit from regular fertilizing. Apply monthly, just prior to heavy pruning. Strawberry guavas are less vigorous and get by with about half as much nitrogen. Both types may require chelated micronutrient foliar sprays when grown in containers or areas with alkaline or deficient soils.

Pruning: Guavas respond well to pruning and can be used as informal hedges or screens.

Pests and diseases: Foliage diseases, such as anthracnose, can be a problem in humid climates. Root rot nematodes will reduce plant vigor. Guava whitefly, guava moth, and Caribbean fruit fly can be major problems in southern Florida. Contact your cooperative extension service for control measures.

HARVEST AND STORAGE

In warmer regions guavas will ripen all year. The color and aroma change at ripening.

For the best flavor, allow fruit to ripen on the plant, though it can be picked green (but mature) and ripened off the tree by letting it sit at room temperature.

Strawberry guava fruits earn their keep primarily in jellies and preserves.

KIWIFRUIT, YANG-TAO, CHINESE GOOSEBERRY

Actinidia chinensis
ak-ti-NID-i-a chi-NEN-sis

- **Growth habit:** Vigorous deciduous vine; requires trellis.
- **Adaptation:** Hardy to 10° F. Most varieties require 400–800 hours of chilling, but low-chill selections are available. Blooms susceptible to damage from spring frosts. New growth brittle and easily broken in strong winds. Not adapted to Florida.
- **Harvest season:** October and November.
- **Begins bearing:** 3–4 years for grafted and cutting-grown plants; 6–7 years for seedlings.
- **Varieties:** Male (as pollenizer): 'Chico Male'. Female: 'Abbott', 'Allison', 'Bruno', 'Chico Hayward', 'Hayward', 'Monty', 'Saanichton', 'Vincent'.

Kiwi vines are adaptable to many climates, and close relatives with similar fruit are hardy into the coldest northern regions. In addition to producing delicious fruit, vines have attractive foliage and flowers.

Kiwifruit are borne on fast-growing deciduous vines that need heavy annual pruning to keep them productive and within bounds. A healthy vine may cover an area 10 to 15 feet wide, 18 to 24 feet long, and 9 to 12 feet high. Vines can be trained over an arbor to cast shade, tied to a trellis, or allowed to sprawl over a fence or pergola. The fruit will hang from the vine in clusters throughout the summer.

ADAPTATION

Grow kiwi vines where temperatures don't drop below 10° F. Flowers are susceptible to spring frost damage, and the fruit, which requires at least 240 frost-free days to become sweet, can be damaged by hard frosts in fall. Protect vines from strong winds. Kiwis aren't recommended for Florida or the desert southwest.

Most varieties have chilling requirements between 400 and 800 hours, but low-chill varieties, such as 'Vincent', can be grown in mild areas with fewer than 100 chilling hours.

POLLINATION

Kiwi vines are male or female; you need one of each for fruit. A pair of vines usually supplies enough fruit for home gardeners. Select male and female plants with the same chilling requirements so they flower together. Insects do the pollinating. Don't prune the male vine until after canes have flowered and fruit has set on the female vine.

PROPAGATION

Propagate kiwi vines from dormant hardwood cuttings or semihardwood cuttings. Many nurseries also graft selected varieties onto seedling rootstocks. Either technique is fine in mild-winter areas, but in cold climates cutting-grown plants are superior because if the top of the plant is killed by frost it can resprout from roots and still be true to type.

SITE SELECTION AND PLANTING

Kiwis grow in full sun or partial shade in rich, well-drained, mildly acidic soil. Install a trellis or other support at planting time. Separate male and female vines by 12 to 15 feet to prevent intertwining.

CARE

Watering: Water vines deeply and frequently, keeping soil moist until harvest. Cut back as fall approaches to encourage dormancy. In drier areas, mulch to prevent leaf drop.

Fertilizing: Young vines are sensitive to overfertilization, but otherwise kiwis need substantial fertilization. Spread fertilizer evenly under the canopy after midsummer.

Pruning: Unless pruned and trained carefully, kiwi vines become a fruitless jungle. The two basic methods are the fruiting lateral method and the spur method. Both techniques require a strong support that lasts: Kiwi vines can remain productive for more than 40 years.

Fuzzy kiwifruits dangle in clusters from woody vines.

- **In the fruiting lateral method,** train vines on a five-wire trellis supported 6 feet above the ground by posts topped with T-shaped arms. Fruiting canes develop from permanent arms (called cordons) trained along trellis wires.
- **Use the spur method** where space is limited. Short fruiting spurs originate from the main trunk or permanent cordons. The canes that grow from these spurs each season are tied to a fence, wall, or trellis.

Let young vines grow with little pruning for one to two years after planting. During the training period, direct the plant's energy into a strong trunk and arms; or spurs. After that, prune female vines during the dormant season and occasionally in summer to remove excess growth. Remove about half the growth on male vines after blooming.

HARVEST AND STORAGE

Pick kiwifruit when it's hard; ripen it off the vine. A color change (from greenish brown to brown) is a sign of maturity. You can store unbruised mature fruit in the refrigerator for up to six months.

LITCHI, LEECHEE, LYCHEE

Litchi chinensis
LEE-chee chi-NEN-sis

- Growth habit: Slow-growing evergreen tree or large shrub to more than 30 feet high and wide.
- Adaptation: Hot, humid summers and cool winters required for fruit production. Trees are hardy to about 25° F.
- Harvest season: June through August in Florida and Hawaii, 3–4 months later in California.
- Begins bearing: 3–5 years.
- Recommended varieties: 'Brewster', 'Groff', 'Kaimana', 'Kwai Mi' (same as 'Mauritius'), 'Sweet Cliff'.

Litchi trees have eye-catching sprays of yellowish-white flowers in the spring, followed by large clusters of bright red fruit dangling among shiny dark green leaves. They occasionally grow to 40 feet high, but not often.

The fruit are encased in a brittle, warty shell that contains a sweet gelatinous delicacy. The Chinese have savored the flavor of litchi for more than 2,000 years.

ADAPTATION

Warm, humid summers are best for flowering and fruit development. Most varieties need between 100 and 200 hours of chilling. Cool winters with low rainfall are ideal. Trees become more hardy as they age.

Litchis are best adapted to parts of Hawaii and Florida, but they can also grow successfully in frost-free coastal areas of California.

PROPAGATION

Air layering is the most common method of propagation because grafting is difficult and seedlings do not reliably produce quality fruit. Grow young plants in containers for one or two seasons before planting into the landscape. This allows the root system to develop, which increases the likelihood of successful transplanting.

POLLINATION

Most often, litchi trees are self-fruitful. In very rare cases trees may produce only male flowers and do not set fruit.

The sweet prize of the litchi fruit hides inside a brittle, warty exterior.

SITE SELECTION AND PLANTING

Plant litchis in full sun and rich well-drained soil with pH between 5.5 and 7.5 (plants grow better at the low end of this range). Apply a thick layer of organic mulch.

CARE

Watering: Litchis require very moist soil, but they won't tolerate standing water. Irrigate trees regularly during active growth. Leach even slightly salty soil regularly.

Fertilizing: Young trees grow slowly and should receive only light applications of a complete fertilizer, if anything. Mature trees are heavier feeders; fertilize them regularly from spring to late summer. Use fertilizers formulated for acid-loving plants such as rhododendrons and azaleas.

Pruning: Prune young trees to establish a strong structure for easy harvest. After that, remove crossing or damaged branches and prune to control overall size.

Pests and diseases: Mites, scale, and aphids occasionally infest litchis. Birds are often attracted to litchis, so cover plants with protective netting if this is a problem.

HARVEST AND STORAGE

Fruit must be allowed to ripen fully on the tree. Each variety has a characteristic color change as it ripens. To harvest, snip off the entire fruit cluster.

Litchis can be stored for up to five weeks in the refrigerator. They can also be frozen or dried.

Litchi trees have a form and texture that's pleasing in the landscape. Mature trees thrive in consistently moist soil that's slightly acidic.

Eriobotrya japonica
e-ree-o-BOH-tri-a ja-PON-i-ka

- Growth habit: Large evergreen shrub or tree to 25 feet high and 30 feet wide.
- Adaptation: Foliage is hardy to 20° F, mature trees to 12° F. Fruit and flowers can be damaged by hard frost. Widely grown in the west and southeast.
- Harvest season: January to May in southeast; March to June in the west.
- Begins bearing: 3–4 years.
- Recommended varieties: 'Champagne', 'Gold Nugget', 'MacBeth'.

Loquats are easy-to-grow plants with boldly textured foliage. Small white, fragrant flowers appear at the ends of branches in fall or early winter. The small orange-yellow fruit grows in clusters. Each fruit contains three to five large seeds surrounded by sweet tangy aromatic flesh. Loquats are often grown as ornamentals. Use mature trees to shade a patio.

LOQUAT, JAPANESE MEDLAR

ADAPTATION

Loquats produce the best fruit in areas with mild winters and mild summers. Although the tree is quite hardy, temperatures below freezing usually damage flowers and fruit. Prolonged heat can inhibit flowering.

White-fleshed varieties are better adapted to cool coastal areas, while yellow-fleshed varieties need more warmth to produce sweet fruit.

PROPAGATION

Loquats to be grown for fruit production are usually propagated by budding or grafting. Nurseries sell seedling-grown plants for use as ornamentals, but these trees seldom produce quality fruit.

SITE SELECTION AND PLANTING

Loquats thrive in full sun but also do well in part shade. They adapt to almost any well-drained soil and have good salt tolerance.

CARE

Watering: Loquat trees are drought-tolerant, but they do produce higher-quality fruit when given regular deep watering.

Fertilizing: Loquats benefit from regular light applications of fertilizer, but too much nitrogen will reduce flowering. Fertilize two or three times from spring to early summer.

Pruning: Loquats do fine with a minimum of pruning, but they also respond well to severe pruning and can be trained as an espalier.

Pests and diseases: In California, loquats have few problems. In Florida, the Caribbean fruit fly is a serious pest.

Fireblight may occur with heavy rains or high humidity. To control it, remove the scorched-looking branches. Sterilize shears between cuts by dipping them in bleach or rubbing alcohol. Burn the infected prunings or seal them in a plastic bag before disposal. Anthracnose may also infect loquat trees.

HARVEST AND STORAGE

Loquats should ripen fully before they are harvested. Each variety develops a distinctive color and begins to soften when ripe. Ripe fruit may be stored in the refrigerator for one to two weeks.

Loquat trees are extremely ornamental with white flowers that mature into colorful egg-shaped fruit. Leaves are large (10 to 12 inches long), bright green on top, white underneath.

Macadamia species
mac-a-DAME-ee-a

- **Growth habit:** Evergreen trees 30–40 feet high and wide.
- **Adaptation:** Mature trees can survive to 24° F, but young trees can be killed by light frost. Consistent high heat reduces overall yield.
- **Harvest season:** Late fall to spring.
- **Begins bearing:** Grafted varieties in 4–6 years; seedling trees in 8–12 years.
- **Recommended varieties:** Varieties for Hawaii are all selections of *M. integrifolia*: 'Hinde', 'Ikaika', 'Kakea', 'Kau', 'Keaau', 'Keauhou', 'Makai', 'Mauka', 'Pahala', 'Purvis'. Varieties for California are selections of *M. tetraphylla* or hybrids: 'Beaumont', 'Burdick', 'Cate', 'Cooper', 'Elimbah', 'Fenton', 'Vista'.

Two species of macadamia produce edible nuts. The smooth-shelled macadamia, *Macadamia integrifolia*, is the species grown commercially in Hawaii and marketed as the macadamia nut. Nuts develop from

When macadamia nuts are ripe, they fall to the ground. Place a tarp beneath trees and shake branches to harvest.

MACADAMIA, QUEENSLAND NUT, AUSTRALIAN NUT

creamy white flowers borne in clusters 6 to 12 inches long. Trees have shiny, deep green leaves 5 to 10 inches long, arranged in whorls of three.

Macadamia tetraphylla, or rough-shelled macadamia, is usually grown as a rootstock for the smooth-skinned macadamia; the quality of the kernel is more variable. Well-suited to the home garden, it has pink flowers borne in clusters up to 15 inches long and deep green leaves 8 to 20 inches long arranged in whorls of four.

ADAPTATION

Macadamias are ideally suited to a mild frost-free climate with abundant rainfall distributed evenly throughout the year, such as that found in parts of Hawaii. Both species will grow well in coastal California and southern Florida. Consult an extension agent about varieties best for your area.

Mature trees are fairly hardy, tolerating air temperatures as low as 24° F, but flowers are usually killed at 28° F. Light frosts (less than 33° F but above 28° F) can kill young trees.

Wind can damage the brittle branches, particularly when they're laden with a heavy crop.

PROPAGATION

Macadamias are easily grown from seed, but seedlings may take 8 to 12 years to bear a crop, and the quality of the nuts is unpredictable.

Grafting is the most common method to produce nursery trees. Macadamia trees for bearing are also propagated from softwood cuttings or by air layering.

SITE SELECTION AND PLANTING

Full sun is best, but in windy or hot climates provide protection and partial shade. Deep, rich soil with pH 5.5 to 6.5 is ideal.

CARE

Watering: Macadamias can withstand periods of drought,

Macadamia flowers dangle in panicles nearly 12 inches long. Leaves unfurl to stately lengths as well.

but harvests will be small and low quality. Water regularly and deeply during dry periods.

Fertilizing: Macadamias grow slowly and do not require significant fertilization. Micronutrient deficiencies are common in some areas but can be corrected with chelated supplements.

Pruning: Prune young trees to encourage strong branching. Mature trees need little pruning.

Pests and diseases: Occasionally thrips or mites may be troublesome. Anthracnose may infect leaves and nuts in humid climates.

HARVEST AND STORAGE

Mature macadamias will fall to the ground from late fall to spring. Place a tarp under the tree and shake the branches gently to dislodge the nuts. Gather nuts as soon as possible and remove the husks immediately.

Nuts should be air-dried. They can be stored for six to eight months in a cool, dry place. When dry, remove the shells with a nutcracker.

Dry roast smooth-shelled macadamia nuts at 300° F for 18 to 20 minutes. Roast rough-shelled macadamias at 275° F for 12 to 15 minutes. After roasting, salt and store nuts in airtight jars.

Mangifera indica
man-JIF-fer-ra IN-di-ka

- **Growth habit:** Evergreen tree reaching 50 feet, usually spreading to 30 feet.
- **Adaptation:** Best adapted to frost-free climates of Florida, Hawaii, and southern California.
- **Harvest season:** May to July in Florida and Hawaii; fall to winter in California.
- **Begins bearing:** Grafted trees in 2–3 years; seedlings, 4–5 years.
- **Recommended varieties:** Florida: 'Adams', 'Carrie', 'Cogshall', 'Earlygold', 'Florigon', 'Glen', 'Irwin', 'Keitt', 'Kent', 'Mallika', 'Osteen', 'Palmer', 'Parvin', 'Ruby', 'Saigon', 'Sensation', 'Tommy Atkins', 'Van Dyke'. Hawaii: 'Ah Ping', 'Edwards', 'Fairchild', 'Georgiana', 'Gouveia', 'Joe Welch', 'Julie Ono', 'Pairi', 'Smith', 'Zill'. California: 'Aloha', 'Edgehill', 'Kenny', 'Manila', 'Pina', 'Reliable', 'Surprise', 'T-1', 'Thomson', 'Villasenor 20222' (same as 'Winters').

Mangoes vary in size, shape, and color. When ripe, the flesh has the texture of a peach. The flavor also resembles a peach but with distinctive tropical overtones.

Mango trees make handsome shade trees. The leaves are long, narrow, and deep green. Fragrant yellow to red flowers come in sprays; only a few will set fruit.

There are two types of mangoes. Indian mangoes have brightly colored fruit, are susceptible to anthracnose, and produce seeds that don't grow true to type. Indo-Chinese mangoes don't develop brightly colored fruit, trees are resistant to anthracnose, and seeds yield plants identical to the parent.

Most mangoes bear heavily in alternate years. To minimize this, thin the fruit and fertilize more in a heavy-crop year.

MANGO

ADAPTATION
Mangoes need a frost-free climate, though mature trees can withstand short periods as low as 25° F. Trees need warm, dry weather to set fruit.

POLLINATION
Mangoes are self-fruitful, but fruit set depends on low humidity, warm temperatures, and active pollinating insects. Wet, humid weather favors anthracnose and poor fruit set. Insect activity is reduced below 55° F.

Mango fruit colors vary by variety.

PROPAGATION
Indo-Chinese mangoes are grown from seed. Remove the husk and plant the seed with the hump at soil level. Transplant seedlings carefully, making sure not to sever the taproot. For best results, plant grafted or budded trees.

SITE SELECTION AND PLANTING
Mangoes prefer full sun and well-drained soil with pH between 5.5 and 7.5. Take care not to damage the taproot.

CARE
Watering: Mangoes need consistent moisture to produce quality fruit.
Fertilizing: Mangoes require regular fertilization to promote healthy new growth and flower production. Chelated micronutrients, especially iron, are often necessary.
Pruning: Healthy trees require little pruning, although pruning to stimulate new growth promotes uniform annual bearing. Removing some flower clusters during a heavy bloom year may alleviate alternate

Cool weather and high humidity will inhibit good fruit set in mangoes.

bearing. Pruning to control size in late winter or early spring won't inhibit fruiting.

Pests and diseases: Anthracnose, powdery mildew, and scab can be serious problems in Florida and Hawaii. Consult a coopoerative extension office for preventive tactics. Mexican, Mediterranean, and Oriental fruit flies may be serious pests in Hawaii and the southeast.

HARVEST AND STORAGE
Mangoes mature 100 to 150 days after flowering. The fruit takes less time to ripen and has the best flavor if allowed to ripen on the tree. Ripe fruit turns the characteristic color of the variety and softens to the touch.

Mature well-colored fruit can be picked firm and ripened at room temperature or stored for 20 to 25 days in the refrigerator.

A mango tree laden with fruit beautifies the landscape.

Carica species.
KAIR-i-kuh

- Growth habit: Upright perennial herb 6–20 feet high.
- Adaptation: Frost-free climates of California, Florida, and Hawaii. Needs warm weather year-round.
- Harvest season: 3–4 months after pollination in warm climates, twice as long in cool climates.
- Begins bearing: Within a year of planting.

The papaya is an herb that grows to a height of 6 to 20 feet. Its deeply lobed dark green leaves can reach 2 feet wide.

There are Hawaiian (*Carica papaya*), Mexican (*Carica pubescens*), and babaco (*Carica pentagona*) papayas. Hawaiian types weigh about a pound and have a yellow skin when ripe. Mexican papayas are much larger, weighing

PAPAYA

up to 10 pounds. The flavor is less intense but still delicious. Babacos are long, seedless fruit with melon-flavored flesh. They need warm winters and part shade in areas with hot summers. Babacos are ideal for growing in containers.

Papayas grow quickly and begin producing fruit within a year of germination. Because fruit quality declines as plants age, plan to replace papaya plants every three to four years.

ADAPTATION

For vigorous growth and fruit production, papayas must have year-round warmth. They will be damaged by either light frost or cold, wet soil. Cool temperatures will alter fruit flavor.

POLLINATION

Plants may produce only female flowers, only male flowers, or both. Both types must be present to produce fruit, so always put at least three or four plants in a group to ensure pollination.

PROPAGATION

Most papayas are grown from seed. Extract seeds from ripe fruit, wash them to remove the gelatinous covering, and plant them at once in warm (80° F) potting mix. They will germinate in 10 to 15 days. Plant in large containers so seedlings will have to be transplanted only once into the ground.

SITE SELECTION AND PLANTING

The planting site should have maximum heat and sun. Papayas require well-drained soil; the smallest amount of excess moisture can kill them. Many gardeners install drain tiles in the base of planting beds or plant on beds of perlite.

Plant carefully without breaking the root ball. Set plants a little high to allow for settling. Keep mulch away from the trunk.

CARE

Watering: Watering is the most critical aspect of raising papayas. Plants should be kept on the dry side to avoid onset of root rot, but they also need enough water to support their large leaves.

Fertilizing: Papayas require regular fertilizing. Feed monthly and then adjust the rate according to the plants' response.

Pruning: Papayas do not need to be pruned. But to ensure cross-pollination and high-quality fruit, plant three or four trees and replace them every four years.

Pests and diseases: Fruit flies can ruin fruit in Hawaii and Florida. Consult local extension agents for control measures. Thrips, mites, and whiteflies are potential problems in some areas, as are powdery mildew, anthracnose, and various viruses.

HARVEST AND STORAGE

Harvest papayas when most of the skin is yellow-green. Fully mature fruit will have edible (spicy) dark brown to black seeds completely filling the internal cavity. Mature fruit can be refrigerated for about three weeks without spoiling.

Papayas require a warm climate all year and well-drained soil to yield a good crop.

Passiflora species
pass-i-FLOW-ra

- **Growth habit:** Vigorous climbing evergreen vine. Can grow 15–20 feet per year. Must have strong support. Generally short-lived (5–7 years).
- **Adaptation:** Frost-free climate but not high heat.
- **Harvest season:** 60–80 days after bloom.
- **Begins bearing:** 2–3 years from seed.
- **Passionfruit species:** *Passiflora alata*, fragrant granadilla; *P. coccinea*, red granadilla; *P. edulis*, purple granadilla; *P. edulis flavicarpa*, yellow passionfruit; *P. incarnata*, maypop; *P. laurifolia*, yellow granadilla; *P. ligularis*, sweet granadilla; *P. maliformis*, sweet calabash; *P. mollissima*, banana passionfruit; *P. quadrangularis*, giant granadilla.

The passionfruit is a member of a large family of vining plants, many of which are grown as ornamentals for their beautiful flowers and delicate leaves. Several species and varieties produce edible fruit; the most common is the purple granadilla, *Passiflora edulis*.

ADAPTATION

Passionfruit grows best in frost-free climates, although the vines may survive short periods at temperatures below freezing. Roots often may resprout if the vine is killed. Passionfruit does not grow well in intense heat.

PROPAGATION

Fresh seeds from superior fruit usually produce vines with good fruit. Seeds germinate in 10 to 20 days; do not expose to light during germination.

The more resistant yellow passionfruit is usually used as a rootstock for grafting. Semihardwood cuttings will root easily under mist.

PASSIONFRUIT, GRANADILLA

SITE SELECTION AND PLANTING

Excellent drainage is absolutely necessary. Vines are shallow rooted and benefit from thick organic mulch. Plant in full sun except in very hot areas. Plant vines next to a chain-link fence or install a strong trellis for support.

CARE

Watering: Plants need consistent moisture or harvest and fruit quality will be reduced.

Fertilizing: *Passiflora* vines require regular applications of balanced fertilizer. Too much nitrogen, however, results in vigorous foliage growth at the expense of flowers.

Pruning: Pruning is necessary to keep the vines within bounds and make harvesting easy. In warm climates, prune immediately after harvest. In cooler areas prune in early spring.

Fruiting occurs on the current season's growth, so regular pruning is the key to keeping plants productive. Remove all weak growth and cut back excess growth by at least one-third. Left unpruned, passionfruit vines will grow out of control. In very hot climates, allow a thick canopy of foliage to grow around the fruit to prevent sunburn.

Pests and diseases: Snails can be a serious problem in California. Passionfruit vines are susceptible to nematodes and viruses as well as diseases that thrive in cool soils, such as fusarium.

HARVEST AND STORAGE

Fruit will quickly turn from green to deep purple when ripe and then fall to the ground. They can either be picked when they change color or gathered from the ground.

To store, wash and dry passionfruit gently and place them in plastic bags. They should last two to three weeks at 50° F. Both the fruit and the juice freeze well.

The wonderfully exotic passionfruit flower blooms beckon pollinators (and admirers) without fail. When fruit is ripe, it drops to the ground.

Casimiroa edulis
ka-see-mi-ROH-a ED-you-lis

- **Growth habit:** Fast-growing evergreen tree 25–50 feet high, 25–30 feet wide. Partially deciduous in some areas.
- **Adaptation:** Best adapted to relatively frost-free climates, but mature trees will withstand brief periods as low as 24° F.
- **Harvest season:** August through November in California. May to June in Florida.
- **Begins bearing:** Grafted plants in 3–4 years; seedlings require 5–8 years.
- **Recommended varieties:** 'Bravo', 'Chapman', 'Chestnut', 'Cuccio', 'Dade', 'Denzler', 'Ecke', 'Lemon Gold', 'Louise', 'McDill', 'Michele', 'Pike', 'Suebelle', 'Sunrise', 'Vernon', 'Vista'.

WHITE SAPOTE, MEXICAN APPLE, ZAPOTE BLANCO

The white sapote is a distinctive large tree with glossy bright green, hand-shaped leaves. It produces an abundance of round yellow fruit that has smooth flesh and a flavor reminiscent of peach or banana. Sapotes are best eaten fresh with a spoon, but the pulp can be mashed and made into a sauce with lime or lemon juice. Sapotes are also delicious in baked goods.

ADAPTATION

Blooming occurs in late winter and frosts may destroy flowers and young fruit. Young trees can be damaged at 30° F. White sapotes do poorly in high summer heat or high humidity. They are well adapted to southern and central Florida and southern California.

PROPAGATION

Fresh seed will usually germinate in three to four weeks in warm soil. When the rootstock is ⅜ inch in diameter, it can be grafted or budded. Spring offers the best time for grafting outdoors, but it can be done any time of year in a greenhouse.

SITE SELECTION AND PLANTING

White sapote prefers a well-drained soil with pH between 5.5 and 7.5, but the trees will grow successfully in any well-drained soil if they are not overwatered.

Before planting, consider the mess made by unpicked fruit: Raking fallen fruit is a chore.

CARE

Watering: White sapote trees are drought-tolerant but produce better fruit with regular deep watering, which is also necessary to keep greedy roots where they belong— deep. Shallow watering can encourage surface roots that will break pavement or ruin lawns. Mulch under the tree.

Fertilizing: Sapotes require regular fertilizing to maintain healthy growth. When trees carry a heavy crop, apply extra nitrogen to help offset alternate bearing.

Pruning: Young trees tend to grow vertically without much branching. After planting, pinch out the terminal bud to encourage branching. As the tree matures, prune to encourage compact growth and control size.

Pests and diseases: White sapote has few pest or disease problems.

HARVEST AND STORAGE

White sapotes should be picked when hard and allowed to ripen at room temperature. It is difficult to tell when they are fully ripe. Fruit will soften if picked too soon, but the flavor will be astringent. Mature fruit can be stored briefly, but mashed pulp can be frozen from 8 to 12 months.

Most varieties ripen over a period of several weeks. 'Suebelle' needs more time, up to 6 months, an advantage if you cannot use a lot of fruit all at once.

The fruit of a white sapote boasts flavors of a peach and a banana. Eat it fresh or mash it for a delicious sauce.

The finger-like leaflets of white sapote emerge with a reddish purple color, and later turn glossy green.

USDA Plant Hardiness Zone Map

This map of climate zones helps you select plants for your garden that will survive a typical winter in your region. The United States Department of Agriculture (USDA) developed the map, basing the zones on the lowest recorded temperatures across North America. Zone 1 is the coldest area and Zone 11 is the warmest.

Plants are classified by the coldest temperature and zone they can endure. For example, plants hardy to Zone 6 survive where winter temperatures drop to –10° F. Those hardy to Zone 8 die long before it's that cold. These plants may grow in colder regions but must be replaced each year. Plants rated for a range of hardiness zones can usually survive winter in the coldest region as well as tolerate the summer heat of the warmest one.

To find your hardiness zone, note the approximate location of your community on the map, then match the color band marking that area to the key.

HAWAII

AUSTRALIA

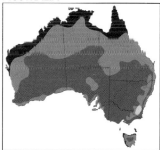

UNITED KINGDOM

Range of Average Annual Minimum Temperatures for Each Zone

Zone 1: Below -50° F (below -45.6° C)
Zone 2: -50 to -40° F (-45.5 to -40° C)
Zone 3: -40 to -30° F (-39.9 to -34.5° C)
Zone 4: -30 to -20° F (-34.4 to -28.9° C)
Zone 5: -20 to -10° F (-28.8 to -23.4° C)
Zone 6: -10 to 0° F (-23.3 to -17.8° C)
Zone 7: 0 to 10° F (-17.7 to -12.3° C)
Zone 8: 10 to 20° F (-12.2 to -6.7° C)
Zone 9: 20 to 30° F (-6.6 to -1.2° C)
Zone 10: 30 to 40° F (-1.1 to 4.4° C)
Zone 11: Above 40° F (above 4.5° C)

Frost Maps

SPRING FROST DATES

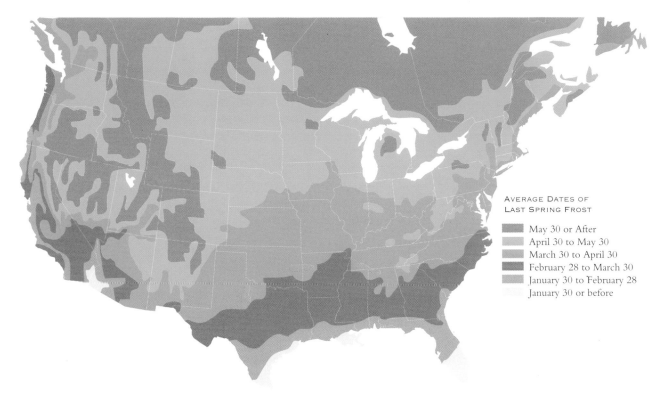

AVERAGE DATES OF
LAST SPRING FROST

May 30 or After
April 30 to May 30
March 30 to April 30
February 28 to March 30
January 30 to February 28
January 30 or before

AUTUMN FROST DATES

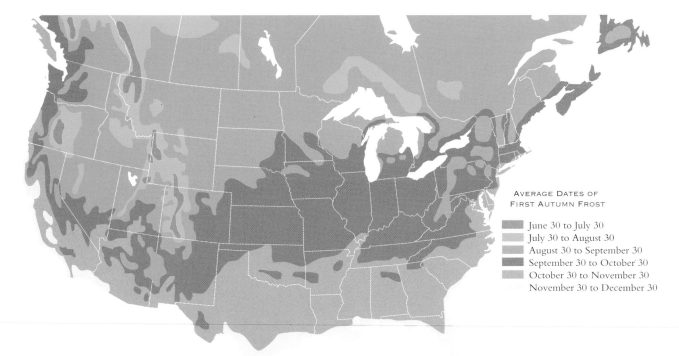

AVERAGE DATES OF
FIRST AUTUMN FROST

June 30 to July 30
July 30 to August 30
August 30 to September 30
September 30 to October 30
October 30 to November 30
November 30 to December 30

Resources

Extension Services

The Cooperative Extension Service is an agency of the U.S. Department of Agriculture located at each state's land-grant university. They offer a variety of horticultural programs, publications, garden problem solving, and soil-testing services. Look in telephone directories for the location of local offices, usually in the government listings or under the university's name followed by "Cooperative Extension."

COOPERATIVE EXTENSION ON THE WEB

Colorado State University
www.ext.colostate.edu/links
  /linkexte.html
Links to many national and state extension web sites.

University of Florida Extension
  Service
http://edis.ifas.ufl.edu/pdffiles
  /CN/CN00800.pdf
Includes lists of tropical fruit nurseries organized by fruits they sell

Ohio State University
http://plantfacts.osu.edu/web
Search a database of online publications from universities, extension services, and other government organizations. It is one of quickest routes to non-commercial gardening information.

Web gardening forums

Join discussion groups on fruits, herbs, vegetables, and many other garden topics.
http://forums.gardenweb.com
  /forums

Food gardening organizations

Seed Savers Exchange
3076 N. Winn Rd.
Decorah, IA 52101
319/382-5990
www.seedsavers.org
Dedicated to preserving heirloom vegetables, flowers, and fruits. Annual $30 membership brings publications and access to rare varieties.

California Rare Fruit Growers
The Fullerton Arboretum,
California State University,
Fullerton, CA 92634
www.crfg.org/index.html
Valuable resource on all aspects of growing subtropical and tropical fruits. Annual $25 membership brings 6 issues of *Fruit Gardener* magazine.

Herb Society of America
9019 Kirtland Chardon Rd.
Kirkland, OH 44094
www.herbsociety.org
Dedicated to the enjoyment of herbs. For the $60 membership receive annual Herbarist, discounts, and access to seeds and plants.

North American Nut Growers
  Association
www.northernnutgrowers.org
Resources for anyone growing nut trees such as walnut or chestnut; also information about paw paw and persimmon. For annual $20 membership receive quarterly newsletter and year-end publication.

North American Fruit
  Explorers
Rt. 1 Box 94
Chapin, IL 62628
www.nafex.org
Devoted to the discovery, cultivation and appreciation of superior varieties of fruits and nuts. The 40-year-old organization publishes the quarterly, *Pomona*. Membership costs $10 annually.

Mail-order nurseries

Start with Cyndi's Catalog of Garden Catalogs where over 2000 mail-order catalogs are listed and evaluated.
www.qnet.com/~johnsonj

VEGETABLES AND HERBS

Abundant Life Seed
  Foundation
P.O. Box 772
Port Townsend, WA 98368
360/385-5660
www.abundantlifeseed.org

Bountiful Gardens
18001 Shafer Ranch Rd.
Willits, CA 95490-9626
707/459-6410
www.bountifulgardens.org

Burgess Seed & Plant Co.
905 Four Seasons Rd.
Bloomington, IL 61701
309/663-9551
www.cometobuy.com/burgess

Comstock, Ferre & Co.
263 Main St.
Wethersfield, CT 06109
800/733-3773
www.comstockferre.com

Resources

(continued)

D. Landreth Seed Co.
P.O. Box 6398
Baltimore, MD 21230
800/654-2407
www.landrethseeds.com
Catalog: $2

DeGiorgi Seeds & Goods
6011 N St.
Omaha, NE 68117
800/858-2580
www.degiorgiseed.com

Earl May Seed & Nursery
Shenandoah, IA 51603
800/831-4193
www.earlmay.com.

Evergreen Y.H. Enterprises
P.O. Box 17538
Anaheim, CA 92817
714/637-5769
www.evergreenseeds.com

Farmer Seed & Nursery Co.
818 NW. 4th St.
Fairibault, MN 55021
507/334-1623

Ferry-Morse Seed Co.
P.O. Box 1620
Fulton, KY 42041
800/283-6400
www.ferry-morse.com

Harris Seeds
P.O. Box 24966
Rochester, NY 14692-0966
800/514-4441
www.harrisseeds.com

High Altitude Seeds
P.O. Box 4619
Ketchum, ID 83340
208/788-4363
www.seedstrust.com
Catalog $3

Irish Eyes—Garden City Seeds
P.O. Box 307
Thorp, WA 98946
509/964-7000
www.irish-eyes.com

J.L. Hudson, Seedsman
Star Route 2, Box 337
La Honda, CA 94020
www.jlhudsonseeds.net

Johnny's Selected Seeds
184 Foss Hill Rd.
Albion, ME 04910-9731
207/437-4301
www.johnnyseeds.com.

J.W. Jung Seed Co.
335 S. High St.
Randolph, WI 53957-0001
800/297-3123
www.jungseed.com.

Native Seeds/SEARCH
526 N. 4th Ave.
Tucson, AZ 85705-8450
520/622-5561
www.nativeseeds.org

Nichols Garden Nursery
1190 N. Pacific Hwy.
Albany, OR 97321-4598
541/928-9280
www.nicholsgardennursery.com

Ornamental Edibles
3272 Fleur de Lis Ct.
San Jose, CA 95132
408/929-7333
www.ornamentaledibles.com

Otis S. Twilley Seed Co., Inc.
121 Gary Rd.
Hodges, SC 29653
800/622-7333
www.twilleyseed.com

Papa Geno's Herb Farm
11125 S. 14th St.
Roca, NE 68430
402/423-5051
www.papagenos.com

Park Seed Co.
1 Parkton Ave.
Greenwood, SC 29649
800/213-0076
www.parkseed.com

Pinetree Garden Seeds
P.O. Box 300
New Gloucester, ME 04260
207/926-3400
www.superseeds.com

Redwood City Seed Co.
P.O. Box 361
Redwood City, CA 94064
650/325-7333
www.ecoseeds.com

Renee's Garden
888/880-7228
www.reneesgarden.com

R.H. Shumway's
P.O. Box 1
Graniteville, SC 29829-0001
803/663-9771
www.rhshumway.com

Ronniger's Seed Potatoes
Moyie Springs, ID 83845
208/267-7938
Catalog $2

Sand Mountain Herbs
321 County Road 18
Fyffe, AL 35971
256/528-2861
www.sandmountainherbs.com

Sandy Mush Herb Nursery
Rt. 2, Surrett Cove Rd.
Leicester, NC
704/683-2014
www.brwm.org/sandymush
   herbs
Catalog $4

Seeds Blüm
Idaho City Stage
Boise, ID 83706
208/343-2202
Catalog $3

Seeds of Change
P.O. Box 15700
Santa Fe, NM 87506
888/762-7333
www.seedsofchange.com

Seeds West Garden Seeds
317 14th St. NW
Albuquerque, NM 87104
505/843-9713
www.seedswestgardenseeds
.com
Catalog: $2

Shepherd's Garden Seeds
30 Irene St.
Torrington, CT 06790-6658
860/482-3638
www.shepherdseeds.com

Stokes Seeds Inc.
P.O. Box 548
Buffalo, NY 14240-0548
800/396-9238
www.stokeseeds.com

Territorial Seed Co.
P.O. Box 157
Cottage Grove, OR 97424
541/942-9547
www.territorial-seed.com

The Cook's Garden
P.O. Box 5010
Hodges, SC 29653-5010
800/457-9703
www.cooksgarden.com

The Pepper Gal
P.O. Box 23006
Ft. Lauderdale, FL 33307
954/537-5540
www.peppergal.com

Thompson & Morgan, Inc.
P.O. Box 1308
Jackson, NJ 08527-0308
800/274-7333
www.thompson-morgan.com

Tomato Growers Supply Co.
P.O. Box 2237
Ft. Myers, FL 33902
888/478-7333
www.tomatogrowers.com

Vesey's Seeds Ltd.
P.O. Box 9000
Calais, ME 04619-6102
800/363-7333
www.veseys.com

Vermont Bean Seed Co.
Garden Lane
Fair Haven, VT 05743
803/663-0217
www.vermontbean.com

W. Atlee Burpee & Co.
300 Park Ave.
Warminster, PA 18991
800/888-1447
www.burpee.com

FRUITS, NUTS, AND BERRIES

Adams County Nursery, Inc.
26 Nursery Rd.
P.O. Box 108
Aspers, PA 17304
717-677-8105
www.acnursery.com

Aesthetic Gardens
P.O. Box 1362
Boring, OR 97009
503/663-6672 fax
www.agardens.com

Ames' Orchard and Nursery
18292 Wildlife Rd.
Fayetteville, AR 72701
501/443-0282

Ahrens Strawberry Nursery
RR1
Huntingburg, Indiana 47642
812/683-3055

W. F. Allen, Co.
Box 1577
Salisbury, Maryland 21801

Bergenson Nursery
Rt. 1, Box 84
Fertile, MN 56540
218/945-6988

Blossomberry Nursery
Route 2
Clarksville, AR 72830
501/754-6489

Brittingham Plant Farms
P.O. Box 2538
Salisbury, MD 21801
301/749-5153

Burnt Ridge Nursery &
  Orchards
432 Burnt Ridge Rd.
Onalaska, WA 98570
360/985-2873
landru.myhome.net/burntridge

Columbia Basin Nursery
P.O. Box 458
Quincy, WA 98848
800-333-8589
www.cbnllc.com

Edible Landscaping
P.O. Box 77
Afton, VA 22920
804/361-9134
www.eat-it.com

England's Orchard and
  Nursery
316 S.R. 2004
McKee, KY 40447-9616
877/965-2228
www.nuttrees.net

Fedco Trees
P.O. Box 520
Waterville, ME 04903-0520
207/873-7333

Foster Nursery Co., Inc.
69 Orchard St.
Fredonia, NY 14063

Four Winds Nursery
www.FourWindsGrowers.com
Mail-order dwarf citrus

Garden of Delights
14560 SW 14th St.
Davie, Florida 33325-4217
800/741-3103
www.gardenofdelights.com

Greenmantle Nursery
3010 Ettersburg Rd.
Garberville, CA 95542
707/986-7504

Hartmann's Plantation Inc.
P.O. Box E
Grand Junction, MI 49056
616/253-4281
www.hartmannsplantcompany
.com

Resources

(continued)

Henry Leuthardt Nurseries
Montauk Hwy., Box 666
East Moriches, NY 11940
516/878-1387
www.henryleuthardtnurseries.
com

Indiana Berry & Plant Co.
5218 West 500
South Huntingburg, IN
47542-9724
800/295-2226
berryinfo@inberry.com
www.inberry.com

Ison's Nursery & Vineyards
Route 1, Box 191
Brooks, GA 30205
800/733-0324
www.isons.com

Johnson Nursery
5273 Hwy. 52E
Ellijay, GA 30540
888/276-3187
www.johnsonnursery.com

Just Fruits Nursery
30 St. Frances St.
Crawfordville, FL 32327
850/926-5644

Kelly Nurseries
P.O. Box 800
Dansville, NY 14437
800/325-4180
www.kellynurseries.com

Lawson's Nursery
2730 Yellow Creek Rd.
Ball Ground, GA 30107
770/893-2141

Logee's Greenhouses
55 North St.
Danielson, CT 06239
888/330-8038
www.logees.com

Mellingers, Inc.
2310PP W. South Range Rd.
North Lima, OH 44452
330/549-9861
www.mellingers.com

Miller Nurseries
5060 W. Lake Rd.
Canandaigua, NY 14424-8904
800/836-9630
www.millernurseries.com

New York State Fruit Testing
Cooperative Association,
Inc.
P.O. Box 462
Geneva, NY 14456
315/787-2205
$10 refundable membership
fee

Nolin River Nut Tree Nursery
797 Port Wooden Rd.
Upton, KY 42784
270/369-8551
www.nolinnursery.com

Nourse Farms Inc.
41 River Rd.
South Deerfield, MA 01373
413/665-2658
www.noursefarms.com

One Green World
P.O. Box 1080
Molalla, OR 97038
503/651-3005
www.onegreenworld.com

Oregon Exotics Rare Fruit
Nursery
1065 Messinger Rd.
Grants Pass, OR 97527
541/846-7578
www.exoticfruit.com
Catalog $4

Pacific Tree Farms
4301 Lynwood Dr.
Chula Vista, CA 91910
619/422-2400
www.kyburg.com/ptf/index.
html

Paradise Nursery
6385 Blackwater Rd.
Virginia Beach, VA 23457-1040
757/421-0201
www.paradisenursery.com

Raintree Nursery
391 Butts Rd.
Morton, WA 98356
360/496-6400
www.raintreenursery.com

Saint Lawrence Nurseries
RD 2
Potsdam, NY 13676
315/265-6739
www.sln.potsdam.ny.us

Southmeadow Fruit Gardens
P.O. Box 211
Baroda, MI 49101
269/422-2411
www.southmeadowfruit
gardens.com

Spring Hill Nurseries
110 W. Elm St.
Tipp City, OH 45371
513/354-1509
www.springhillnursery.com

Stark Brothers Nurseries &
Orchards
P.O. Box 10
Louisiana, MO 63353
800/325-4180
www.starkbros.com

The Banana Tree, Inc.
715 Northampton St.
Easton, PA 18042
610/253-9589
www.banana-tree.com

Van Well Nursery
2821 Grant Rd.
Wenatchee, WA 98807
800/572-1553
www.vanwell.net

Index

Plants are listed under their common names. Page numbers in **bold type** indicate Gallery or Encyclopedia descriptions and generally include a photograph. Page numbers in *italic type* indicate additional photographs and illustrations.

A

Air circulation/drainage, 17, 117
Algae, herbal properties, 72
Almond, 146, **182**
Aloe vera, **78**
Aluminum sulfate, 123
Angelica, 73, **78**
Animal pests. *See* Birds; Rodents
Anise, **79**
Anise hyssop, **79**
Annual plants, herbal, 72
Aphids, 75, 131, *131*, 184
Apiaceae (carrot family), 8
Apple, **155–159**
  branching structure, *146*
  diseases, 130, 135, 136, 137
  dwarf, 118–119, 155
  espaliered, 117, 119, **152**
  fertilizing, 126
  flowers, 115
  in hedgerows, 153, **153**
  insect pests, **131**, **135**, 136
  pollination requirements, 120
  pruning, 140, 142, 144, 145
  as shade trees, 115
  soil requirements, 122
Apple, Mexican. *See* White sapote
Apple maggots, **131**
Apple scab, 163
Apricot, **160**
  diseases, 136–137
  dwarf, 118, 119
  in hedgerows, 153
  insect pests, 133
  pollination requirements, 120
  pruning, 146–148
  soil requirements, 122
Arbors, training grapes on, 151
Arizona, citrus adaptation, 196
Arnica, **79**
Artemisia, **80**
Artichoke, 23, 26, **29**
Arugula, 16, 23, 27, **58–59**
Asian greens, **59**

Asparagus, 8, 23, **29**
Asteraceae (sunflower family), 8
Astragalus (huang qi, milk vetch), **80**
Atemoya, 195
Atremoya, 195
Australian nut. *See* Macadamia nut
Avocado, **193**
Avocado root rot, 193

B

Bacterial canker, **136**
Bacterial leaf and fruit spots, 135, *135*, 161
Balled-and-burlapped plants, 124
Banana, **194**
Bare-root plants, 124, 128
Bark, herbal properties, 73
Basil, 26, **72**, **81**
Bay, *73*, **82**
Bean, 8, 16, 26, **30–31**
Bees as pollinators, *120*, 121
Beet, 8, 23, **32**
Beetles
  Colorado potato, 53, 54
  Mexican bean, 31
  spotted cucumber, 45
  striped cucumber, 41
Bergamot (beebalm, Oswego tea), 73, **82**
Berries, **171**
  in containers, 128–129
  fertilizing, 126–127
  garden design role, 115
  planting, 125, *125*
  pruning, 150, *150*
  sanitation, 130–131
  soil requirements, 122–123
  training, 117, 152
  watering, *127*
  See also specific types of berries
Biennial plants, herbal, 72
Birds
  to control insects, 130
  as pests, 131, *131*, 161, *173*, 176, 182
Bitter rot, 136, *136*
Blackberry, 126, 149, *149*, 150, *150*, **171–172**
Black cohosh, 83
Black knot, 136, *136*
Black rot (frog-eye leaf spot), 136, *137*
Blueberry, **171**, **173–174**

diseases, 136, 173
fertilizing, 126–127
garden design role, 115
pH requirements, 123, 126–127
planting, 125
pruning, 150
soil drainage, 122
Blueberry maggot, 173
Borage, *70*, **83**
Borers
  flatheaded, 132, *132*
  peach tree, 134, *134*
Boron, for fruit trees, 126
Brambles, pruning, 150
Branch collar, *142*
Branch whorls, 142
Brassicaceae (mustard family), 8
Broccoli, 8, 23, 27, **33**
Brown rot, 136–137, *137*, 165
Brussels sprouts, 8, 27, **33**
Budding, 190
Bud types, *142*
Bud unions, 124–125, *125*

C

Cabbage, **34**
  Chinese, 8, 29, **40**
  cold hardiness, 27
  plant family, 8
  planting times, 26–27
  seed-sowing time, 23
Calendula (pot marigold), 73, **84**
California, citrus adaptation, 196, 199
Cane pruning, 150–151
Cankers
  bacterial, 136, *136*
  fusicoccum, 173
  peach or cytospora, 138–139, *139*
  phomopsis, 173
Cantaloupe, 8, 26, **44**
Caraway, 72, **84**
Carrot, 16, 23, 27, *27*, **36**
Carrot family (*Apiaceae*), 8
Caterpillars, 75, 135, *135*
Catnip, **85**
Cauliflower, 8, 27, **34**
Cedar apple rust, 137, *137*
Celeriac (celery root), **37**
Celery, 10, 23, **37**
Central-leader pruning, 144, *144*, *145*
Chamomile, 73, **85**

Chard, 8, 16, 23, 27, **38**
Chenopodiaceae (goosefoot family), 8
Cherimoya, *187*, **195**
Cherry, **161–162**
    diseases, 135, 136, 138–139
    dwarf, 118, 119
    fertilizing, 126
    flowers, 115
    insect pests, 132, *132*, 134
    pollination requirements, 120
    pruning, 140, 147, *147*
    soil requirements, 122
Cherry, Surinam, *188*
Cherry (pear) slug, 132, *132*, 161
Chervil, **86**
Chestnut, 147, **183**
Chicory, plant family, 8
Chilling requirements
    for subtropical fruits, 187
    for temperate fruits, 154
Chinese gooseberry. *See* Kiwi fruit
Chives, 8, 47, **86**
Cilantro (coriander), **87**
Cinnamon, 73, *73*
Citron, 197, *198*
Citrus, *129*, *192*, **196–199**
    See also specific types of citrus
Climate
    for herbs, 74
    plant disease role, 130
    Plant Hardiness Zones, 211, *211*
    as plant selection criteria, 8
    for subtropical fruits, 186–189, 196
    for temperate fruits, 116, 154
Cloches, 24, *24*
Cold frames, 24, *24*
Cold weather damage
    frost protection, 129, 189
    fruit trees, container-grown, 128
    fruits, subtropical, 186, 189,
        190–191
    herbs, woody perennial, 76
    pollination interruption, 121
    vegetables, cool-season, 27
Cole crops, 8, **33–35**
    See also specific cole crops
Collard, 8, 16, **35**
Comfrey, **87**
Compost, 18, 21, *21*, 127
Coneflower, purple *(Echinacea)*, **89**

Container gardens
    about, 16
    fertilizing, 129
    fruits, subtropical, 190
    fruits and berries, temperate, *118*,
        128–129, *128*, *129*
    watering, 129
Container-grown plants
    planting, *120*, 128–129
    vegetable seeds, 23, *23*
Coriander. *See* Cilantro
Corn, 8, *25*, 26, *28*, **39–40**
Corn earworm, 40
Corn salad (mâche), 27, **59**
Costmary, **88**
Cover crops, 19, *19*
Cowslip, **88**
Crab apple, 115, 122, 147, **163**
Crop rotation, 28
Crown, defined, 124
Crown gall, 137, *137*
Crown rot, 138, *138*
Cucumber, 8, 16, 26, **41**
Cucurbitaceae (gourd family), 8
Currant, 117, 122, 125, 150, **171**, **175**
Curry leaf, **110**

D
Damping off diseases, 23
Dianthus, pink, **102**
Dill, 75, **89**
Diseases, plant
    air circulation and, 15
    IPM to control, 26
    pruning role, 141, 142
    of related vegetables, 9
    sanitation to control, 27
    soil drainage and, 15, 122
    soilborne, 16
    *See also specific crops; specific
        diseases*
Double-row hill planting systems,
    125
Downy mildew, 138, *138*, 176
Drainage trenches, 15, 123

E
Echinacea (purple coneflower), **89**
Eggplant, 8, 16, 23, 26, **42**
Elder, 74, *74*, **90**
Elecampane, **90**
Endive (frisée), 8, **59**

Espaliers, 115, *116*, 117, *119*, 152
Essential oils, herbal properties, 73
Eucalyptus, 73

F
Fabacae (legume family), 8
Fall gardens, 27
Feijoa (pineapple guava), 190, **200**
Fennel, 27, **42**, **91**
Ferns, herbal properties, 72
Fertilizers
    applying, 21
    for fruits, nuts, and berries, 123,
        126–127, *128*, 129–130, 143,
        152
    for herb gardens, 74–75
    for indoor seedlings, 23
    manure and compost, 127
    organic, 20–21
    slow-release, 129
    synthetic, 20
    See also Nutrients; *specific crops*
Feverfew, 88, **91**
Fig, 122, 147, **201**
Filbert (hazelnut), 147, **183**
Fireblight, 138, *138*, 167, 205
Florida, citrus adaptation, 196, 199
Florida cranberry. *See* Roselle
Flowers
    of fruit trees, 115
    herbal properties, 73, 76
Foetid bugbane, 83
Fortunella. See Citrus
Frankincense, 73
French-style vegetable gardens, 12
Frisée (endive), 8, **59**
Frog-eye leaf spot (black rot),
    136, *137*
Frost pockets, 15
Fruit flies, 132, *132*, 161, 208
Fruiting spurs, *146*
Fruits, subtropical
    climate considerations, 186–189,
        192
    in containers, 190–191
    encyclopedia, **192–210**
    propagating, 189–191
    soil salts, 187
    See also specific fruits
Fruits, temperate
    branches, *142*, *146*
    climate considerations, 116, 154

in containers, 128–129, *128, 129*
diseases, 135–139
dwarf, 115, *115*, 118–119, *121*,
124, 130
encyclopedia, **154–170**
espaliered, 115, *116, 119*,
152, *152*
fertilizing, 123, 126–127, *126*,
129, 130
garden design role, 115, *115*, 117
in hedgerows, *152*, 153, *153*
how they grow, 121
insect pests, 130, 131–135
planting, *120–125*, 124–125,
128–129, *128*, 131
pollination requirements, 120–121
pruning, *121*, 140–145
in raised beds, 122–123
sanitation, 130–131
site selection, 116, 117
soil requirements, 122–123
thinning, 145
training, *119*, 143
2-in-1 trees, 154
varietal selection, 116
watering, 127, *127*
See also specific fruits
Fungi, as herbs, 72
Fusicoccum canker, 173

G

Galangal (Thai or Siamese ginger;
resurrection lily), **110–111**
Gan cao, 97
Garden cleanup
for fruits, nuts, berries, 130–131
for herbs, 76
for vegetables, 27, 28
Garden design
fruits and berries, 115, *115*, 117
nuts, 115, 182
planning, 7, *7*
pollination considerations,
120–121, *121*
vegetables, 12, 16, *20*, 28
Garlic, 8, 29, **49**
Geranium, scented, **106**
Germander, 75
Ginger, 92, **110**
Ginger, Thai or Siamese. *See*
Galangal
Ginseng, **92**

Goldenseal, **93**
Gooseberry, 125, 150, **171**, **175**
Gooseberry, Chinese.
See Kiwi fruit
Goosefoot family (*Chenopodiaceae*), 8
Gourd family (*Cucurbitaceae*), 8
Grafting
bud union, 124–125, *125*
dwarfing rootstocks, 118–119, *118*
subtropical fruits, 190
2-in-1 trees, 154
Granadilla (passionfruit), *188*,
191, **209**
Grape, **176–177**
diseases, 136, 137, 138
fertilizing, 126
planting, 125, *125*
pruning, 150–151, *150, 151*
soil requirements, 122
training, 117, 151, *151*, 152
Grapefruit, **197**, **199**
Grass family (*Poaceae*), 8
Groundcovers, berries as, 115
Guava, pineapple. *See* Feijoa
Guava, tropical or strawberry, **202**
Gulf Coast, citrus adaptation,
196, 199
Gummosis, 138–139, *139*

H

Hardening off, 23, *23*
Hardpan (soil compaction), 15, 17
Hazelnut. *See* Filbert
Heading back cuts, 142, *142*
Heat requirements for subtropical
fruits, 186, 189
Hedges, fruits and berries as, 115,
152, 153, *153*
Heeling in, 124
Herbal vinegars, 75
Herbs
benefits, 70–71
buying plants, 74
defined, 70–71
encyclopedia, **78–113**
formal gardens, 74
harvesting, 75
pest problems, 75
pH preferences, 74
plant part properties, 73
plant types, 72
planting, 74–75

preserving, *71, 75, 75*
propagating, 77
pruning, 76
tropical, **110–111**
using and growing tips, 71, 74–75
in vegetable gardens, *6*
See also specific herbs
Hoes, for weed control, 11
Honeysuckle, 72, *72*
Hops, **93**
Horehound, **94**
Horseradish, 73, *73*
Horsetail, 72, *73*
Huang qi. *See* Astragalus
Hyssop, **94**

I

Insecticides. *See* Pesticides
Insect pests
IPM to control, 26
of related vegetables, 9
row covers to control, 11, *26*
sanitation to control, 27
of seedlings, 23
*See also specific crops; specific
insects*
Insects, beneficial, 26, 73, *120* 121,
130, 131
Interplanting, 8–9, *9*, 12
IPM (Integrated Pest Management)
for fruit trees, 130
for vegetables, 26
Iron, deficiency symptoms, 21

J

Japanese medlar or Japanese plum.
See Loquat
Jerusalem artichoke, **56**
June drop, 145

K

Kale, 8, 27, **35**
Kiwi fruit (yang-tao, Chinese
gooseberry), **203**
Kniffen pruning system, 151
Kohlrabi, 8, 23, 27, **35**
Kumquat, **197**, *198*, **199**

L

Lady's mantle, **95**
Lavender, 73, 76, **95**
Layering, 77, *77*, 188

Leaching container soils, 129
Leaf rollers, 133, *133*
Leaves, herbal properties, 73
Leek, 8, **47**
Legume family *(Fabacae)*, 8
Lemon, *191*, **196–197**, *198*, **199**
Lemon balm, **96**
Lemon verbena, **97**
Lemongrass, **96**, **111**
Lettuce, 8, 16, 23, 27, *27*, **43**
   See also Salad greens
Licorice, **97**
Liliaceae (lily family), 8
Lime, 197–198, *199*
Lime (calcium carbonate), 21, 123
Lime, Kaffir, **111**
Limequat, *197*, 199
Linden, 72
Litchi (leechee, lychee), **204**
Loquat (Japanese medlar, Japanese
   plum), **205**
Lovage, **98**

M
Macadamia nut (Queensland or
   Australian nut), **206**
Mâche (corn salad), 27, **59**
Mango, **207**
Manure, 18–19, 127
Manure tea, 21
Marjoram
   pot, 101
   sweet, **98**
Marsh mallow, **99**
Matted-row hill planting systems, 125
Meadowsweet, **99**
Melons, 8, **44–45**
Mesclun, 23, 27, **58**
Mexican apple. *See* White sapote
Mexican mint marigold, 109
Microclimates
   frost pockets, 15
   for fruit trees, 116
   intermittent shade, 14, 15, 16
   for subtropical fruits, 189
Micronutrients, 20
Milk thistle, **99**
Milk vetch. *See* Astragalus
Mint, **100**
Mites, 133, *133*, 182
Mizuna, 61
Mosses, herbal properties, 72

Moths
   codling, 132, *132*
   grape berry, 133, *133*
   oriental fruit, 133, *133*
Mowers, for weed control, 11
Mugwort, 80
Mulch
   about, 9–11, *9*, 189
   for fruit trees, *127*
   for herbs, 75
   for pathways, *9*
   for vegetables, 26, *53*, 68
Mummyberry, 173
Mustard, 23, 27, **59**
Mustard family *(Brassicaceae)*, 8
Myrtle, **101**

N
Nasturtium, 73
Navel orange worms, 182
Nectarine, **165–166**
   diseases, 136–137, 138–139
   dwarf, 118, 119
   fertilizing, 126
   insect pests, 133, 134
   pruning, 144
   training, 152, 153
Nightshade family *(Solanaceae)*, 8
Nitrogen
   aphids and, 131
   deficiency symptoms, 21
   for fruit trees, 126
   for herbs, 75
   role of, 20, 126
Northern Temperate Zone, 116
Nutrients
   deficiency symptoms, 21, 126
   micronutrients, 20, 126
   pH and, 20, 126
   uptake by related vegetables, 9
   See also specific nutrients
Nuts
   encyclopedia, **182–185**
   fertilizing, 126–127
   garden design role, 115, 182
   herbal properties, 73
   pests and diseases, 130
   sanitation, 130–131
   soil requirements, 122–123
   watering, 127
   See also specific types of nuts

O
Okra, 26, **46**
Onion, 8, 16, 23, **46–47**
Orange, *186*, *198*, **196–199**
Orange, mandarin, *198–199*
Orangequat, **199**
Oregano, **101**
Oregano, Cuban, **110**
Organic matter
   about, 17, 18
   for fruit trees, 123
   for herb gardens, 74
Oswego tea. *See* Bergamot

P
Painted daisy, 88
Papaya, **208**
Parsley, 23, 27, **48**, 72, **102**
Parsnip, 23, **56**
Passionfruit (granadilla), *188*, **209**
Pea, 8, 23, **49**, **50**
Peach, **163–165**
   in containers, *129*
   diseases, 135, 136–137, 138–139
   dwarf, 118, 119
   fertilizing, 126
   flowers, 115
   insect pests, 133, 134
   pollination requirements, 120
   pruning, 140, 144, 148
   soil requirements, 122
   training, 152, 153
Peach leaf curl, 139, *139*, 163
Peanut, 8, 26, **48**
Pear, **167–168**
   diseases, 135
   dwarf, 119
   espaliered, 115, 152, *152*
   fertilizing, 126
   in hedgerows, 153, *153*
   insect pests, 132, *132*, 134
   pollination requirements, 120
   pruning, 140, 144, *145*, 148
   soil requirements, 122
Pear (cherry) slug, 132, *132*, 161
Pear psylla, 134, *134*
Peat pots, 23, *23*
Pecan, 148, **184**
Pecan nut casebearer, 184
Pecan scab, 184
Pecan weevil, 184
Peppers, 8, 16, 23, 26, **51–52**

Perennials
    herbaceous herbs, 72
    woody, pruning, 76
Persimmon, 148–149, **169**
Pesticides
    herbal, 73
    insecticides for fruit trees, 130
    killing pollinators, 26
    residue in mulch, *9*
    safety, 28
    in soil amendments, 18
    when to use, 26
pH of soil
    about, 20
    for blueberry, 123, 126–127
    for fruit trees, 123, 126
    for herbs, 74
    for vegetables, 28
Phomopsis canker, 173
Phosphorous, 20, 21, 126
Photosynthesis, 121
Phylloxera vitifoliae, 176
Pinching buds, 142
Pineapple guava. *See* Feijoa
Pinks. *See* Dianthus, pink
Plant families, vegetables, 8, *9*
Plant growth, about, 121
Plant Hardiness Zones, USDA,
        209, *209*
Planting
    fruits and berries, *120–125*,
        124–125, 128–129, *128*
    herbs, **74–75**
    seasonal considerations, 22
    vegetables, fall, 27
    vegetables, spring, 23, 25
    vegetables, summer, 22, 26
    watering at time of, *122*, 127
Plum, **169–170**
    diseases, 135, 136, 138–139
    dwarf, 118, 119
    fertilizing, 126
    in hedgerows, 153
    insect pests, 133, 134
    pollination requirements, 120
    pruning, 140, 149
    soil requirements, 122
Plum, Japanese. *See* Loquat
Plum curculio, 134, *134*
Poaceae (grass family), 8

Pollination
    attracting and protecting
        pollinators, 26
    of fruit trees, 120–121, *120*, *121*
    role of, 26
    row covers and, 11, *27*
    See also specific crops
Pomegranate, pruning, 149
Potagers (French-style gardens), 12
Potassium, 20, 21, 126
Potato, 8, 23, **53–54**
Potato, sweet, **60**
Pot marigold. *See* Calendula
Powdery mildew, 139, *139*
Primrose, common, 88
Propagation
    budding, 190
    dividing, 77, *77*
    grafting, 118–119, *118*, 124–125,
        125, 154, 190
    layering, 77, *77*, 190
    root cuttings, 77, *77*
    subtropical fruits, 189–190
    See also Seed starting; *specific*
        crops
Pruning
    herbs, 77
    tools for, 76, *140*, 141
Pruning fruit trees
    functions, 140, 141, 143, *146*
    methods, *121*, *140–146*, 141–145,
        153
    at planting time, 125
    in summer, 143
    timing, 141
    See also Espaliers; *specific crops*
Pummelo, **199**
Pumpkin, 8, 26, **63**
Pyrethrum, 88

Q
Quassia, 73
Queensland nut. *See* Macadamia nut
Quince, 115, 119, 126, 149

R
Radish, 8, 23, 27, **55**
Raised beds, *12–15*, 15–16, 122–123
Raspberry, **171**, **178–179**
    espaliered, 117
    fertilizing, 126

    pruning, 149–150, *149–150*
    watering, *127*
Resins, herbal properties, 73
Resistant plant varieties, 130, 135
Resources, 213
Resurrection lily. *See* Galangal
Rhizobium bacteria, 49, *49*
Rhizopus fungus, 182
Rhubarb, 23, **55**
Rodents, as fruit tree pests, 134
Root crops, 17, **56–57**
    See also specific root crops
Root cuttings, herb plants, 77, *77*
Roots, herbal properties, 73
Rootstocks, dwarfing, 118–119,
        118, 124
Rose, *73*, **103**
Roselle (Jamaica, Indian, or Guinea
        sorrel; Florida cranberry), **111**
Rosemary, **103**
Row covers, 11, 24, *26*, *27*, 28
Rue, **104**
Rutabaga, 8, **57**

S
Sage, 72, *72*, **104**
St. John's wort, **105**
Salad burnet, **105**
Salad greens, 16, **58–59**
Salts in soil, 187
Savory, summer and winter, **107**
Scab, apple and pear, 130, 135, *135*
Scale insects, 134, *134*
Scallion, 27, 47
Seaweed, herbal properties, 72
Seeds, herbal properties, 73
Seed starting
    direct sowing, 25, 26, 27, 74–75
    germination, *28*
    herbs, 74
    indoors, 23
    season-stretching devices, 24
    seed viability, 25
    for spring gardens, 23
    subtropical fruits, 190
    for summer gardens, 28
Self-fertile and self-sterile crops,
        26, 120
Semitropical climates, 188
Shade
    crops tolerant of, 14, 15, 16

fruit trees for, 115
sun and shade patterns, 14, 15, 16
Shallot, 8, 47
Shot hole fungus, 182
Shrubs
fruiting, 115
as herbs, 72, 73
See also specific shrubs
Shungiku, **59**
Site selection
for fruit trees, 116, 117
for herbs, 74
for vegetables, 12, 14–16
Soapwort, **106**
Soil amendments, 18–19
Soil compaction (hardpan), 15, 17
Soil drainage
for containers, 16
correcting problems, 15
crown rot and, 138, *138*
for fruit trees and berries, 122
as site selection criterion, 15
Soil erosion, 17
Soil preparation, 25, 74, *74*, 131, 152
Soils
clay, 10, 17, *17*, 19
for container-grown plants, 16, 128
for fruit trees, 122–123
heavy, defined, 122
for herbs, 74
layers, 17
leaching, 129
loam, 17, *17*, 19
pH of, 20, 28, 74, 123, 126–127
for raised beds, 15
role of, 17
salt content, 187
sandy, 10, 17, *17*, 19, 21
for seed starting, 23
silt, 17
Soil testing
for fruit trees, 122
nutrients, 131
pH, 20, 74, 123, 126
for raised beds, 16
role of, 19
texture, 19
topsoil characteristics, 17
Solanaceae (nightshade family), 8
Solarization, soil, 11
Sorrel, Jamaica, Indian, or Guinea.
    See Roselle

Soursop, 193
Southernwood, 80
Spinach, 8, 16, 23, 27, **60**
Spur pruning, 150, *150*
Spurs, fruiting, *142*
Square foot gardens, 12
Squash, 8, 16, 26, **61–62**
Squash bugs, 63
Star fruit, *187*
Stems, herbal properties, 73
Sticky balls, for insect control,
    131
Stinging nettle, **107**
Strawberry, 115, 122, 125, *125*, **171**,
    180–181
Subsoil, 17
Subtropical climates, 188
Sugar apple (sweetsop), 195
Sulfur, 21, 123
Sunflower family (*Asteraceae*), 8
Sunlight
for seed starting, 23
for subtropical fruits, 187, 189
sun and shade patterns, 14, 15, 16
Sunscald, borers and, 132, *132*
Sweet cicely, **108**
Sweet potato, **60**
Sweetsop (sugar apple), 195

T

Tangelo, **199**
Tangerine, *198*
Tangor, *198*, **199**
Tansy, **108**
Tarragon, **109**
Tatsoi, **59**
Temperate climates, 116, 186
Texas, citrus adaptation, 196
Thinning
direct-seeded plants, 25
fruits, 145
seedlings, indoor, 23, *23*
Thinning cuts, 142, *142*
Thyme, **109**
Tillers, rotary, 11
Tomatillo, **67**
Tomato, 9, 16, 23, *25*, 26, **64–67**
Tomato hornworm, 67
Tools
digging, *17*
pruning, 76

spray equipment, 130
weeding, 11
Topsoil, 17
Training
espaliers, 115, *116*, 117, *119*, 152
fruit trees, 143
functions, 140
grapes, 151
See also Pruning
Transplanting
hardening off, 23, *23*
hot-weather protection, 26
techniques, 25
See also Planting; *specific crops*
Trees
as herbs, 72, 73
See also Fruits, subtropical; Fruits,
    temperate
Tropical climates, 188
Trunk damage, borers and, 132, *132*,
    134
Tunnels, plastic, 24
Turmeric, **111**
Turnip, 8, 27, **57**

V

Valerian, **112**
Vegetables and vegetable gardens
benefits, *6*
buying plants, 25
in containers, 16
cool-season, 22, 27
fall planting, 27
flowers in, 12
French-style, 12
gallery, **29–69**
growing seasons, 8
herbs in, *6*
interplanting, 8–9, *9*, 12
pH preferences, 28
planning, 7–8, *7*, 12, *20*
raised beds, *12–15*, 15–16
season-stretching devices, 24
seed sowing, 8, 23
shade-tolerant, 16
site selection, 12, 14–16
size considerations, 8, *12–13*
spacing, 28
spring planting, 23, 25
square foot gardens, 12
summer planting, 26
walkways, *9*, 16

warm-season, 22
wide row systems, *11*, 12
See also specific vegetables
Vines, herbal, 72
Violet (Johnny-jump-ups), **112**

W

Walkways, *9*, 16
Walnut, 149, **185**
Watering
drip irrigation, 10, *10*, 26
fruits, subtropical, 186–187
fruits, temperate, *122*, 127, *129*,
129, 152
guidelines, 10
herbs, 75
leaching, 129
nut trees, 182
seedlings, indoor, 23
soaker hoses, *10*, *127*
soil texture role, 10, *17*
vegetables, summer, 26
while on vacation, 129
See also specific crops
Watermelon, 8, 26, **68–69**
See also Melons
Watersprouts, 143, *146*
Weed control, 11, 16, 75
Whiteflies, 75

White pine blister rust, 171, 175
White rot, 139, *139*
White sapote (Mexican apple, zapote
blanco), **210**
Wide row gardens, *11*, 12
Willow, 72, *72*
Wind protection, 116
Wood, herbal properties, 73
Woodruff, sweet, **113**
Wormwood, 80

Y

Yang-tao. *See* Kiwi fruit
Yarrow, **113**

Z

Zapote blanco. *See* White sapote
Zinc, for fruit trees, 126

METRIC CONVERSIONS

U.S. Units to Metric Equivalents			Metric Units to U.S. Equivalents		
To Convert From	**Multiply By**	**To Get**	**To Convert From**	**Multiply By**	**To Get**
Inches	25.4	Millimeters	Millimeters	0.0394	Inches
Inches	2.54	Centimeters	Centimeters	0.3937	Inches
Feet	30.48	Centimeters	Centimeters	0.0328	Feet
Feet	0.3048	Meters	Meters	3.2808	Feet
Yards	0.9144	Meters	Meters	1.0936	Yards
Square inches	6.4516	Square centimeters	Square centimeters	0.1550	Square inches
Square feet	0.0929	Square meters	Square meters	10.764	Square feet
Square yards	0.8361	Square meters	Square meters	1.1960	Square yards
Acres	0.4047	Hectares	Hectares	2.4711	Acres
Cubic inches	16.387	Cubic centimeters	Cubic centimeters	0.0610	Cubic inches
Cubic feet	0.0283	Cubic meters	Cubic meters	35.315	Cubic feet
Cubic feet	28.316	Liters	Liters	0.0353	Cubic feet
Cubic yards	0.7646	Cubic meters	Cubic meters	1.308	Cubic yards
Cubic yards	764.55	Liters	Liters	0.0013	Cubic yards

To convert from degrees Fahrenheit (F) to degrees Celsius (C), first subtract 32, then multiply by ⅝.

To convert from degrees Celsius to degrees Fahrenheit, multiply by ⅗, then add 32.

Ortho Complete Guide to Vegetables, Fruits & Herbs
Editor: Denny Schrock
Contributing Technical Consultants: B. Rosie Lerner,
   Michael D. Smith
Senior Associate Design Director: Tom Wegner
Assistant Editor: Harijs Priekulis
Copy Chief: Terri Fredrickson
Copy and Production Editor: Victoria Forlini
Photographers: Marty Baldwin, Scott Little, Jay Wilde
Editorial Operations Manager: Karen Schirm
Managers, Book Production: Pam Kvitne,
   Marjorie J. Schenkelberg, Rick von Holdt, Mark Weaver
Contributing Copy Editor: Sharon McHaney
Contributing Proofreaders: Sara Henderson, Mindy Kralicek,
   Jeanée LeDoux, Ellie Sweeney
Contributing Map Illustrator: Jana Fothergill
Contributing Prop/Photo Stylist: Susan Strelecki
Additional Contributor: Rosemary Kautzky
Indexer: Ellen Davenport
Editorial and Design Assistants: Kathleen Stevens,
   Karen McFadden

**Additional Editorial Contributions from
   Art Rep Services**
Director: Chip Nadeau
Designer: lk Design
Illustrator: Shawn Wallace

Bittersweet Lane Publishing
Publishing Director: Michael MacCaskey
Associate Editors: Alan Berolzheimer, Julie Martens
Editorial Art Director: Michele Newkirk
Technical Consultants: Marcia Eames-Sheavly,
   Charlie Nardozzi, Jim Travis, Lance Walheim

Meredith® Books
Editor in Chief: Linda Raglan Cunningham
Design Director: Matt Strelecki
Executive Editor, Gardening and Home Improvement:
   Benjamin W. Allen
Executive Editor, Gardening: Michael McKinley

Publisher: James D. Blume
Executive Director, Marketing: Jeffrey Myers
Executive Director, New Business Development:
   Todd M. Davis
Executive Director, Sales: Ken Zagor
Director, Operations: George A. Susral
Director, Production: Douglas M. Johnston
Business Director: Jim Leonard

Vice President and General Manager: Douglas J. Guendel

Meredith Publishing Group
President, Publishing Group: Stephen M. Lacy
Vice President-Publishing Director: Bob Mate

Meredith Corporation
Chairman and Chief Executive Officer: William T. Kerr

In Memoriam: E.T. Meredith III (1933–2003)

Note to the Readers: Due to differing conditions, tools,
and individual skills, Meredith Corporation assumes no
responsibility for any damages, injuries suffered, or losses
incurred as a result of following the information published
in this book. Before beginning any project, review the
instructions carefully, and if any doubts or questions remain,
consult local experts or authorities. Because codes and
regulations vary greatly, you always should check with
authorities to ensure that your project complies with all
applicable local codes and regulations. Always read and
observe all of the safety precautions provided by
manufacturers of any tools, equipment, or supplies,
and follow all accepted safety procedures.

Photographers
   (Photographers credited may retain copyright ©
   to the listed photographs.)
L = Left, R = Right, C = Center, B = Bottom, T = Top

William D. Adams: 69BR, 148; **Liz Ball/Positive Images:**
28BL, 94T; **Cathy Wilkinson Barash:** 27TR;
Gay Bumgarner/Positive Images: 182BR; **Brian
Carter/Garden Picture Library:** 151; **David Cavagnaro:**
cover, 11, 14, 18, 21T, 21C, 23BC, 24T, 25, 26TC, 26TR,
28TR, 29B, 30C, 30B, 32T, 35T, 36B, 37T, 38, 40, 42T, 47L,
50BR, 52T, 55C, 56B, 60, 61B, 64R, 68, 69T, 78T, 78B, 86T,
87T, 90T, 96B, 97T, 99T, 105B, 112B; **Walter Chandoha:**
67T, 72TR, 72BL, 154, 178; **Candace Cochrane/Positive
Images:** 23B; **Alan & Linda Detrick:** 23T, 23TC, 26B, 49B,
51B, 72BR, 82B, 91B, 102B, 129T; **Derek Fell:** 9BR, 19, 24B,
29T, 31, 32B, 34BL, 41R, 45, 46, 48B, 52BL, 54, 55T, 56T,
57TLi, 57B, 58T, 59L, 62, 63, 65T, 67B, 73BL, 79C, 88T, 92,
96T, 107B, 121B, 171T, 181, 182TR, 184, 187R, 188T, 193,
200T, 204, 206B, 207C, 210L; **John Glover:** 6R, 27TL, 35B,
43TL, 102T, 153, 170T, 187L, 200B; **Jerry Harpur:** 73CR,
82T; **Marcus Harpur:** 90B; **Neil Holmes/Garden Picture
Library:** 209; **Saxon Holt:** 15, 16T, 21B, 43TR, 58B, 64L,
78C, 79T, 89B, 93T; **Jerry Howard/Positive Images:** 84B,
115B, 143, 175BR; **Jacqui Hurst/Garden Picture Library:**
190B; **Bill Johnson:** 111T, 111B; **Gene Joyner:** 202T;
Rosemary Kautzky: spine, 2; **Dwight Kuhn:** 28TL, 28TC,
120R; **Lamontagne/Garden Picture Library:** 119B;
Andrew Lawson: 8, 87B, 104T, 160; **Lee Lockwood/
Positive Images:** 53B, 83T; **Janet Loughrey:** 28BR, 53T,
72TC, 105T, 106B; **Charles Mann:** 85T; **Clive Nichols:** 9T &
22 (Design:Rupert Golby.Chelsea), 65B, 89T (Piet Oudolf),
101D; **John Parker/Positive Images:** 79B; **Jerry Pavia:** 4B,
20, 29C, 34L, 50TR, 59R, 70B, 80, 85B, 94B, 98T, 99C, 101T,
107C, 110T, 113B, 188B, 206T; **Ben Phillips/Positive
Images:** 34R, 81, 83B, 100L, 104B, 106T; **Diane A.
Pratt/Positive Images:** 61T, 121T; **Ann Reilly/Positive
Images:** 50C; **Howard Rice/Garden Picture Library:** 33B,
49C, 103B, 108T, 189; **Richard Shiell:** 109T; **Pam
Spaulding/Positive Images:** 99B; **Friedrich Strauss/
Garden Picture Library:** 205; **Michael S. Thompson:** 4T,
6L, 9BL, 10BC, 17, 25i, 27B, 30T, 33T, 36T, 37B, 39, 41L,
43B, 44T, 48T, 50BL, 51T, 52BR, 55B, 66, 69BL, 71T, 84T,
88B, 97B, 100R, 107T, 108B, 109B, 112T, 120L, 127L, 129B,
146, 162R, 170B, 183B, 194T, 201; **Michel Viard/Garden
Picture Library:** 202B, 203; **Juliette Wade/Garden Picture
Library:** 98B; **Lee Anne White/Positive Images:** 73TR;
Justyn Willsmore: 72TL, 95T

All of us at Meredith® Books are dedicated to providing you
with the information and ideas you need to enhance your
home and garden. We welcome your comments and
suggestions about this book. Write to us at:
   Meredith Corporation
   Meredith Gardening Books
   1716 Locust St.
   Des Moines, IA 50309–3023

If you would like to purchase any of our gardening, home
improvement, cooking, crafts, or home decorating and
design books, check wherever quality books are sold.
Or visit us at: meredithbooks.com

If you would like more information on other Ortho
products, call 800/225-2883 or visit us at: www.ortho.com